W9-BTP-371

Bangkok

"All you've got to do is decide to go
and the hardest part is over.

So go!"

TONY WHEELER, COFOUNDER – LONELY PLANET

Austin Bush,
Tim Bewer, Anita Isalska, Andy Symington

Contents

Plan Your Trip   4

Explore Bangkok   54

Understand Bangkok   205

Survival Guide   235

Bangkok Maps   263

(left) **Kŏhn dance-drama p223** Based on the Thai epic, *Ramakian.*

(above) **Street food p31** Bangkok is famous for it's outdoor food stalls.

(right) **Garuda at Wat Phra Kaew p64** *Garuda* are sacred birds who guard the temple.

Northern
Bangkok
p156

Thewet
& Dusit
p90

Banglamphu
p77

Ko Ratanakosin
& Thonburi
p58

Chinatown
p98

Siam Square,
Pratunam,
Phloen Chit &
Ratchathewi
p108

Sukhumvit
p142

Riverside,
Silom & Lumphini
p125

Welcome to Bangkok

Same same, but different. This Thailish T-shirt philosophy sums up Bangkok, a city where the familiar and the exotic collide like the flavours on a plate of pàt tai.

Contrasts

It's the contradictions that provide the City of Angels with its rich, multifaceted personality. Here, climate-controlled megamalls sit side by side with 200-year-old village homes; gold-spired temples share space with neon-lit strips of sleaze; slow-moving traffic is bypassed by long-tail boats plying the royal river; Buddhist monks dressed in robes shop for the latest smartphones; and streets lined with food carts are overlooked by restaurants perched on top of skyscrapers. And as Bangkok races towards the future, these contrasts will never stop supplying the city with its unique and ever-changing strain of Thai-ness.

Full-on Food

Until you've eaten on a Bangkok street, noodles mingling with your sweat amid a cloud of exhaust fumes, you haven't actually eaten Thai food. It can be an intense mix: the base flavours – spicy, sour, sweet and salty – aren't exactly meat and potatoes. But for adventurous foodies who don't need white tablecloths, there's probably no better dining destination in the world. And with immigration bringing every regional Thai and international cuisine to the capital, it's also a truly diverse experience. And perhaps best of all, Bangkok has got to be one of the best-value dining destinations in the world.

Fun Folks

The language barrier can seem huge, but it's never prevented anybody from getting along with the Thai people. The capital's cultural underpinnings are evident in virtually all facets of everyday life, and most enjoyably through its residents' sense of fun (known in Thai as *sà·nùk*). In Bangkok, anything worth doing should have an element of *sà·nùk*. Ordering food, changing money and haggling at markets will usually involve a sense of playfulness – a dash of flirtation, perhaps – and a smile. It's a language that doesn't require words, and one that's easy to learn.

Urban Exploration

With so much of its daily life conducted on the street, there are few cities in the world that reward exploration as handsomely as Bangkok does. Cap off an extended boat trip with a visit to a hidden market. A stroll off Banglamphu's beaten track can lead to a conversation with a monk. Get lost in the tiny lanes of Chinatown and stumble upon a Chinese opera performance. Or after dark, let the BTS (Skytrain) escort you to Sukhumvit, where the local nightlife scene reveals a cosmopolitan and dynamic city.

BOONCHIPPA / SHUTTERSTOCK ©

Why I Love Bangkok

By Austin Bush, Writer

Admittedly, there are some things – the hot weather, the traffic, the political instability – that make Bangkok a less-than-ideal city. But there's so much more that makes it amazing. I love the food. What other city has such a full-flavoured, no-holds-barred, insatiable, fanatical approach to eating? I love old Bangkok – districts such as Banglamphu and Chinatown still carry the grit, charm and character of the city that used to be. And I'd be lying if I didn't also say that I love new Bangkok; don't we all have a soft spot for megamalls and air-con?

For more about our writers, see p288.

Top: Classical *lá·kon gâa bon* shrine dancers (p41)

Bangkok's
Top 10

Banglamphu (p77)

1 Easily Bangkok's most charming neighbourhood, Banglamphu is the city's former aristocratic enclave, once filled with minor royalty and riverside mansions. Today, the old quarter is dominated by antique shophouses, backpackers seeking R&R on famous Th Khao San (pictured), civil servants shuffling between offices and lunch spots, and bohemian artists and students. Vendor carts and classic restaurants also make a patchwork quilt of Banglamphu, offering ample options for a roving stomach, and the area is also home to some of the city's best live music.

👁 *Banglamphu*

Open-Air Dining (p26)

2 Bangkok's reputation as a polluted city belies its forte as an outdoor-dining capital. Despite the modern conveniences of air-conditioning and contemporary cafes, some of the most memorable meals in the city (not coincidentally called the 'Big Mango') are had at the open-air markets and food stalls. Forget about three square meals, in Bangkok locals snack throughout the day, packing away at least four meals before sunset. It would be rude not to join them.

🍴 *Eating*

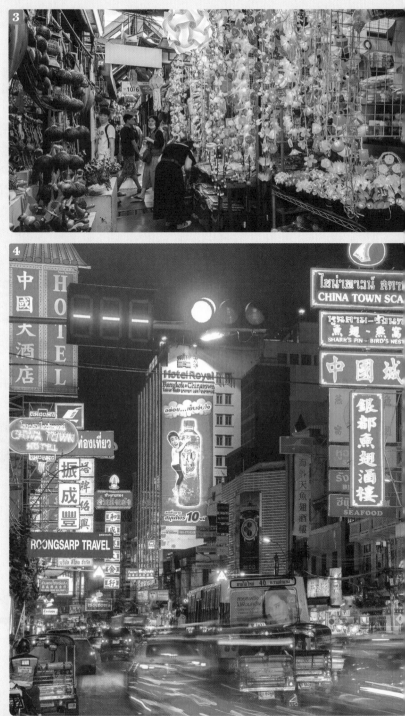

Chatuchak Weekend Market *(p158)*

3 In a city obsessed with commerce, Chatuchak Weekend Market takes the prize as Bangkok's biggest and baddest market. Silks, sneakers, fighting cocks and fighting fish, fluffy puppies and souvenirs for the insatiable *fa·ràng* (Westerner) – if it can be sold in Thailand, you'll find it here. From every day to clubby, clothes dominate much of the market, but this being Thailand, food and drink also have a strong – and refreshing – presence, making Chatuchak as much about eating as it is about shopping.

⊙ *Northern Bangkok*

Chinatown *(p98)*

4 Forgive us for suggesting that Bangkok's Chinatown is something of an Asian El Dorado. The neighbourhood's main artery, Th Yaowarat (pictured), is crowded with gold shops – sealed glassfront buildings that look more like Chinese altars than downtown jewellers. Likewise, the Buddha statue at Wat Traimit has more gold than you've likely ever seen in one place. And the pencil-thin lanes that branch off Talat Mai are decked with goldleaf-coated goods. Throw in the blazing neon signs and smoky, open-air kitchens and you have an urban explorer's fantasy.

⊙ *Chinatown*

Jim Thompson's House *(p110)*

5 Jim Thompson, the late American entrepreneur, used his traditional Thai-style home as a repository for ageing Thai traditions and artwork. Thompson mysteriously disappeared in 1967 and today his former home is a museum – one that every visitor secretly wishes to live in for a day or more. Why? The rooms are adorned with his exquisite art collection and personal possessions, including rare Chinese porcelain pieces and Burmese, Cambodian and Thai artefacts, and the garden is a miniature jungle of tropical plants and lotus ponds.

⊙ *Siam Square, Pratunam, Phloen Chit & Ratchathewi*

Shopping *(p43)*

6 Even avowed anticonsumerists fold in Bangkok. One minute they're touting the virtues of a life without material possessions, the next they're admiring the fake Rolex watches and mapping out the route to MBK Center. Bangkok's malls, however, are just a warm-up for the markets, the cardio workout of shopping. In this city, footpaths are for additional retail space, not for pedestrians. In addition to Chatuchak Weekend Market – one of the world's largest markets – Bangkok is an established destination for bespoke tailoring and has its own emerging fashion scene.

BELOW: SIAM DISCOVERY (P121)

🛍 *Shopping*

Mae Nam Chao Phraya *(p132)*

7 Mae Nam Chao Phraya (the Chao Phraya River) is always teeming with activity: hulking freighter boats trail behind dedicated tugs, river-crossing ferries skip across the wake, and children practice cannonballs into the muddy water. You can witness this from the shore (ideally from Ko Ratanakosin or Thonburi), from a chartered long-tail boat or while on the deck of a river taxi. Regardless of your vantage point, as the blinding sun slips below the horizon in serene streaks of reds and golds of an evening, sooty Bangkok suddenly looks beautiful.

🍴 *Ko Ratanakosin & Thonburi*

Songkran *(p22)*

8 If the idea of a multiday, no-holds-barred, water-based war appeals to you, make a point of being in Bangkok during April. With origins in an ancient religious practice of Buddha images being 'bathed', in recent decades the celebration of the Thai lunar New Year has evolved into a citywide water fight. Foreigners, especially well-dressed ones, are obvious targets and the majority of the mayhem occurs on Th Silom and Th Khao San. In addition to water-throwing, festivities include open-air concerts and visits to Buddhist temples.

❅ *Month by Month*

Thai Cookery Schools *(p50)*

9 Why let a plump tummy be the only sign of your culinary visit to Thailand? Instead, spice up your life – and your future dinner-party menus – by learning to create the kingdom's zesty dishes in your own kitchen. Cooking schools in Bangkok range from formal affairs for amateur chefs to home cooking for the recipe-phobic. Everyone always has a grand time – visiting a wet market, fumbling with ingredients, tasting the fruits of their labour and trotting home with new cooking techniques.

RIGHT: AMITA THAI COOKING CLASS (P75)

⚡ Sports & Activities

Wat Pho *(p60)*

10 The grounds of Wat Pho claim a 16th-century birthday, predating Bangkok itself. In addition to being the country's biggest temple, Wat Pho is home to a school of traditional Thai medicine, where on-site massage pavilions facilitate that elusive convergence of sightseeing and relaxation. Still not impressed? Let us not forget Wat Pho's primary Buddha, a reclining figure that nearly dwarfs its sizeable shelter. Symbolic of Buddha's death and passage into nirvana, the image measures 46m and is gilded with gold leaf, making it truly larger than life.

◉ Ko Ratanakosin & Thonburi

What's New

Sri Trat

Hands down the most interesting Thai restaurant to have opened in Bangkok in the last year or so, Sri Trat specialises in the hard-to-find dishes of Trat and Chanthaburi. (p145)

Tints of Blue

Whereas most of Th Sukhumvit's hotels err towards the large and corporate, Tints of Blue boasts a charmingly leafy location, pocketbook-friendly rates and an authentically homey feel. (p201)

Siam Discovery

A recent renovation has transformed one of Bangkok's oldest malls into one of its most chic. In particular, the architecturally stunning new Siam Discovery is a great stop for both domestic fashion and unique souvenirs. (p121)

The Commons

Who said food halls have to be budget-oriented and characterless? The Commons, a hip new assemblage of eats with cuisine options ranging from Isan (northeastern Thai) to Mexican, proves us all wrong. (p148)

Ku Bar

Concealed at the edge of a hood known primarily for raucous streetside beer joints is Ku Bar, quite possibly the city's most sophisticated and underground-feeling venue for cocktails. (p84)

Tonkin-Annam

Less than a year in and this tiny new *hôrng tăa·ou* (shophouse) restaurant is already serving some of the tastiest Vietnamese food in Bangkok; don't miss Tonkin-Annam's tart, peppery banana blossom salad. (p74)

Bangkok CityCity Gallery

A small yet broad-minded art space, in its short life the new Bangkok CityCity Gallery has hosted a range of exhibitions and performances. (p128)

Fou de Joie

Fou de Joie, a retro-themed French restaurant/barbecue joint/cocktail bar, is a charming addition to the growing number of bars and restaurants that have made Chinatown Bangkok's hippest hood. (p105)

Jaroenthong Muay Thai Gym

Jaroenthong is a sparkling new Thai boxing gym steps from Th Khao San; rookies are encouraged. (p87)

kokotel

A lively new hotel, kokotel proves that family-friendly doesn't have to mean boring or unfashionable. (p199)

Saneh Jaan

Enjoy the formality of hotel dining but don't want blandness? Saneh Jaan features full-flavoured Thai dishes in a charmingly old-school-feeling setting. (p116)

Hazel's Ice Cream Parlor and Fine Drinks

Dessert or cocktails? There's no need to compromise at Hazel's, a new ice-cream-parlor-slash-bar, housed in a former print shop and complete with a vintage printing press, in Bangkok's old town. (p97)

For more recommendations and reviews, see **lonelyplanet. com/thailand/bangkok**

Need to Know

For more information, see Survival Guide (p235)

Currency
Thai baht (B)

Language
Thai

Visas
Thailand is a huge tourist destination and entering Bangkok is generally very straightforward.

Money
Most places deal only with cash. Some foreign credit cards are accepted in high-end hotels, restaurants and shops.

Mobile Phones
GSM and 4G networks available through inexpensive SIM cards.

Time
Bangkok (GMT/UTC plus seven hours)

Tourist Information
Tourism Authority of Thailand (TAT; ☏02 134 0040, nationwide 1672; www.tourismthailand. org; 2nd fl, btwn Gates 2 & 5, Suvarnabhumi International Airport; ◷24hr)

Bangkok Information Center (☏02 225 7612-4; www. bangkoktourist.com; 17/1 Th Phra Athit; ◷8am-7pm Mon-Fri, 9am-5pm Sat & Sun; ⛴Phra Athit/ Banglamphu Pier)

Daily Costs

Budget:
Less than 1500B
➡ Dorm bed/basic guesthouse room: 150–800B

➡ Street-stall meals: 150–300B

➡ One or two of the big-hitter sights: 500–600B

➡ Getting around on public transport: 20–100B

Midrange:
1500–4000B
➡ Flashpacker guesthouse or midrange hotel room: 800–1500B

➡ Street and restaurant meals: 500–1000B

➡ Most, if not all, of the big sights: 500–1000B

➡ Getting around with public transport and occasional taxis: 100–300B

Top end:
More than 4000B
➡ Boutique hotel room: 4000B

➡ Fine dining: 1500–3000B

➡ Private tours from: 1000B

➡ Getting around in taxis: 300–800B

Advance Planning

Three months before Book a room at a smaller boutique hotel, especially if visiting during December/January.

One month before Make reservations at the critically acclaimed nahm (p133) restaurant; if you plan to stay in Thailand longer than 30 days, apply for a visa at the Thai embassy or consulate in your home country.

One week before Book lessons at a Thai cooking school.

Useful Websites

Lonely Planet (www.lonely planet.com/thailand/bangkok) Destination information, hotel bookings, traveller forum and more.

BK (www.bk.asia-city.com) Online version of Bangkok's best listings magazine.

Bangkok 101 (www.bangkok 101.com) Tourist-friendly listings mag.

Bangkok Post (www.bangkok post.com) English-language daily.

@RichardBarrow Informative Thailand-based blogger.

WHEN TO GO

Late December to early January is Bangkok's coolest time and its peak tourist season. Go in November or February for (relatively) fewer people.

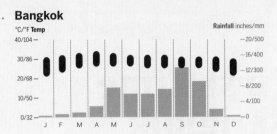

Bangkok

Arriving in Bangkok

Suvarnabhumi International Airport The Airport Rail Link runs from Phaya Thai station to Suvarnabhumi (45B, 30 minutes, 6am to midnight). A bus line runs from Suvarnabhumi to Th Khao San (60B, 6am to 8pm). Meter taxis run 24 hours and cost approximately 200B to 300B plus a 50B airport surcharge.

Don Mueang International Airport There are four bus lines from Bangkok's de facto budget airport (50B, frequent from 7.30am to 11.30pm). Meter taxis from Don Mueang also charge a 50B airport surcharge and trips to town start at approximately 200B.

Hualamphong Train Station Bangkok's central train station is connected to the rest of the city via the MRT (16B to 42B, frequent from 6am to midnight).

For much more on **arrival** see p236

Getting Around

➡ **BTS** The elevated Skytrain runs from 6am to midnight. Tickets 16B to 44B.

➡ **MRT** The Metro runs from 6am to midnight. Tickets 16B to 42B.

➡ **Taxi** Outside rush hours, Bangkok taxis are a great bargain. Flag fall 35B.

➡ **Chao Phraya Express Boat** Runs 6am to 8pm, charging 10B to 40B.

➡ **Klorng boat** Bangkok's canal boats run from 5.30am to 8pm most days. Tickets 9B to 19B.

➡ **Bus** Cheap but a slow and confusing way to get around Bangkok. Tickets 5B to 30B.

For much more on **getting around** see p238 ➡

Sleeping

Travellers are spoilt for accommodation options in Bangkok, with the added benefit that much of what's available is excellent value. If you're on a budget, dorm beds can be had for a little as 150B, while cheap rooms start at about 500B. There's a wide choice of midrange hotels and an astonishing number of top-end places. Be sure to book ahead if you're arriving during peak tourist season (from approximately November to March) and are keen on the smaller, boutique-type hotel.

Websites

➡ **Agoda** (www.agoda.com/city/bangkok-th.html) Asia-based hotel booking site that offers a lowest-price guarantee.

➡ **Lonely Planet** (www.lonelyplanet.com/thailand/bangkok/hotels) Find reviews and make bookings.

➡ **Travelfish** (www.travelfish.org/country/thailand) Independent reviews with lots of reader feedback.

For much more on **sleeping** see p189

First Time Bangkok

For more information, see Survival Guide (p235)

Checklist

➡ Ensure your passport is valid for at least six months past your arrival date

➡ Confirm your airline's baggage restrictions

➡ For visits longer than 30 days, apply for a tourist visa at a Thai embassy or consulate in your home country

➡ Inform your bank and/or debit-/credit-card company that you'll be travelling

➡ Arrange for appropriate travel insurance

What to Pack

➡ Thai language phrasebook

➡ Thailand electrical adaptor

➡ GSM mobile phone and charger

➡ A small day pack

➡ Long trousers/long skirt/long-sleeved shirt (for visiting religious sights)

➡ Lightweight clothes

➡ Hat and sunglasses

➡ Comfortable sandals

➡ Sunscreen (available but expensive in Bangkok)

➡ Earplugs

Top Tips for Your Trip

➡ Eat at the market or the street stalls for true Thai flavour.

➡ Learn a few Thai phrases and always smile.

➡ Don't try to cover too much ground in a day; Bangkok's heat and traffic will ensure that doing so is more of an ordeal than a holiday.

➡ Simply ignore any taxi driver who refuses to use the meter.

➡ The BTS (Skytrain) and the MRT (metro) are the fastest and most convenient ways to get around 'new' Bangkok; the Chao Phraya Express Boat is a slow but steady way to get to the older parts of town.

What to Wear

Light, loose-fitting clothes are generally the most comfortable in Bangkok's tropical, urban heat. Shorts are usually acceptable and comfortable, but when you visit temples, wear clothes that cover you to your elbows and knees (both men and women). Likewise, sandals are cool and easily removed at temples, but bring at least one non-shorts-and-sandals outfit if you plan on clubbing, fine dining or visiting any of the city's nicer rooftop bars.

Be Forewarned

Bangkok is generally a safe city, but there are a few things to be aware of:

➡ In recent years, Bangkok has been the site of political protests that have occasionally turned violent; check your embassy's advisory travel warnings before leaving.

➡ Criticising the Thai monarchy in any way is a very serious social faux pas that carries potentially incriminating repercussions; don't do it.

➡ Avoid the common scams: one-day gem sales, suspiciously low transport prices, dodgy tailors.

➡ Bangkok's streets are extremely dangerous and its drivers rarely yield to pedestrians. Look in both directions before crossing any street (or footpath) and yield to anything with more metal than you.

➡ Most of Bangkok's street-food vendors close shop on Monday.

➡ Bangkok's rainy season is from May to October, when daily downpours – and occasional flooding – are the norm.

Money

Most places in Bangkok continue to deal in cash only. Fortunately, ATMs are ubiquitous and can be relied on for the bulk of your spending cash. However Thai ATMs charge a 200B foreign-transaction fee on top of whatever currency conversion and out-of-network fees your home bank charges. Most ATMs allow a maximum of 20,000B in withdrawals per day.

Credit and debit cards are accepted at some shops, hotels and restaurants. The most commonly accepted cards are Visa and MasterCard. American Express is typically only accepted at high-end hotels and restaurants.

TANG YAN SONG / SHUTTERSTOCK ©

Outdoor dining in Chinatown (p102)

Bargaining

Thais respect a good haggler. Always let the vendor make the first offer, then ask 'Can you lower the price?'. This usually results in a discount. Now it's your turn to make a counter-offer. Always start low, but don't bargain unless you're serious about buying. If you're buying several of an item, you have much more leverage to request and receive a lower price. It helps to keep negotiations relaxed and friendly.

Tipping

Tipping is not generally expected in Thailand, though it is appreciated. The exception is loose change from a large restaurant bill. At many hotel restaurants or other upmarket eateries, a 10% service charge will be added to your bill.

Etiquette

Bangkokians are generally very understanding and hospitable, but there are some important taboos and social conventions to be aware of.

➡ **Monarchy** Never make any disparaging remarks about any member of Thailand's royal family. Treat objects depicting the king (such as money) with respect.

➡ **Temples** Wear clothing that covers you to your knees and elbows. Remove your shoes when you enter a temple building. Sit with your feet tucked behind you to avoid pointing the bottom of your feet at Buddha images. Women should never touch a monk or a monk's belongings; step out of a monk's way on footpaths and don't sit next to a monk on public transport.

➡ **Save Face** Never get into an argument with a Thai. It is better to smile through any social friction.

Language

Don't know a lick of Thai? Don't worry: Bangkok is well stocked with English speakers. Street-stall vendors, shop owners and taxi drivers generally speak enough English to conduct a basic transaction. If there is a communication problem, though, Thais will find someone to sort things out. Thais are patient with (and honoured by) attempts to speak their language; with just a few phrases, you'll be rewarded with big grins and heaps of praise.

Top Itineraries

Day One

Ko Ratanakosin & Thonburi (p58)

 Get up as early as you can and take the Chao Phraya Express Boat north to Chang Pier to explore one of Ko Ratanakosin's museums, such as the **Museum of Siam**, as well as one of its must-see temples, like **Wat Pho**.

> ✖ **Lunch** Plunge headfirst into Bangkok-style street food at Pa Aew (p74).

Riverside, Silom & Lumphini (p125)

☼ Refresh with a spa treatment at **Health Land** or soothe those overworked legs with a traditional Thai massage at **Ruen-Nuad Massage Studio**. After freshening up, get a new perspective on Bangkok with a sunset rooftop cocktail at **Moon Bar**.

> ✖ **Dinner** nahm (p133) serves what is arguably the best Thai food in Bangkok,

Riverside, Silom & Lumphini (p125)

☾ If you've still got it in you, head over to **DJ Station**, **Telephone Pub** or any of the other bars and clubs in Bangkok's small but lively gaybourhood. For a night that doesn't end until the sun comes up, bang on the door at **Wong's Place**.

Day Two

Siam Square, Pratunam, Phloen Chit & Ratchathewi (p108)

 Take the BTS (Skytrain) to National Stadium and start your day with a visit to the popular and worthwhile museum that is **Jim Thompson House**. Follow this by exploring the nearby canalside neighbourhood of **Baan Khrua** or by paying your respects at the **Erawan Shrine**.

> ✖ **Lunch** MBK Food Island (p115) is a tasty introduction to Thai food.

Siam Square, Pratunam, Phloen Chit & Ratchathewi (p108)

☼ Walk, or let the BTS escort you, through Bangkok's ultramodern commercial district, stopping off at linked shopping centres, including **MBK Center**, **Siam Discovery**, **Siam Paragon** and **Siam Square**. Make time for a sweet snack at **Gourmet Paradise** or an air-conditioned afternoon cuppa at the **Erawan Tea Room**.

> ✖ **Dinner** Dip into refined Thai dishes in a likewise setting at Saneh Jaan (p116).

Northern Bangkok (p156)

☾ If it's Tuesday, Friday or Saturday, consider catching a Thai-boxing match at **Lumpinee Boxing Stadium**, or if it's Friday or Saturday, make a point of schlepping over to eastern Bangkok's RCA/Royal City Ave to check out the clubs such as **Route 66** or **Onyx**.

Erawan Shrine (p112)

Day Three

Ko Ratanakosin & Thonburi (p58)

 Take the Chao Phraya Express Boat to Chang Pier and set off on a **long-tail boat tour** of Thonburi's canals. Alternatively, combine canals and the culinary arts with a visit to **Amita Thai Cooking Class**.

> ✖ **Lunch** Take advantage of the air-con and spicy Thai dishes at Err (p74).

Banglamphu (p77)

Spend the afternoon shopping at the **Th Khao San Market** and visiting the surrounding sights, such as the **Golden Mount** and **Wat Suthat**. Or, if you've got energy to spare, book an afternoon or nighttime bike tour of the area with an outfit such as **Velo Thailand** or **Grasshopper Adventures**.

> ✖ **Dinner** Take a temporary break from Thai food at Jidori Cuisine Ken (p147).

Sukhumvit (p142)

End the night with a Thai-themed cocktail at a cosy local, such as **WTF** or **Badmotel**, or a craft beer at **Hair of the Dog**. If it's still too early for you to turn in, extend the night with a visit to a club like **Glow** or **Beam**.

Day Four

Northern Bangkok (p156)

 If it's a weekend, take the BTS north for a half day of shopping at the **Chatuchak Weekend Market**. Otherwise, consider a half-day excursion outside the city to the provincial-feeling **Nonthaburi Market**, the artificial island of **Ko Kret** or the re-created ruins at **Ancient City**.

> ✖ **Lunch** Chatuchak Weekend Market (p158) has cheap and tasty food stalls.

Chinatown (p98)

Recover from the market in the relative cool of the late afternoon before taking the MRT (metro) to Chinatown to visit the home of the Golden Buddha, **Wat Traimit**, and the Chinese-style **Wat Mangkon Kamalawat**. Consider popping over to **Phahurat** to sample that neighbourhood's South Asian feel or, if you're there after dark, the nocturnal flower market at **Pak Khlong Talat**.

> ✖ **Dinner** Follow our walking tour (p102) of Chinatown's best street eats.

Banglamphu (p77)

 Make the brief taxi ride to Banglamphu and begin the evening with drinks at **Madame Musur**, followed by a rowdy live-music show at **Brick Bar** or dancing at the **Club**. If bedtime is irrelevant, head for the rooftop lounge, dance floor and late closing times of the **Bank**.

If You Like...

Urban Exploration

Talat Noi Blaze your own path in this web-like riverside neighbourhood. (p101)

Sampeng Lane Explore the narrow lanes that spread from this market alley in the heart of Bangkok's Chinatown. (p103)

Amulet Market One of Bangkok's most bizarre markets is also a great destination for aimless wandering. (p70)

Baan Khrua Dive into this dense, canalside hood that put Thai silk on the map. (p113)

Church of Santa Cruz Get lost in the winding, elevated lanes surrounding this Thonburi church. (p101)

Eating Like a Local

Likhit Kai Yang Where locals fuel up before the big *moo·ay tai* (Thai boxing; also spelt *muay Thai*) match. (p96)

Krua Apsorn Lauded restaurant serving Bangkok-style flavours. (p83)

Nai Mong Hoi Thod You can't say you've been to Bangkok if you haven't eaten streetside in Chinatown. (p104)

MBK Food Island Do the local thing and forget about ambience and focus on the food at this mall-based food court. (p115)

Pa Aew An open-air curry stall that excels in the flavours of Bangkok and Central Thailand. (p74)

Exploring *klorng* (canals) via long-tail boat (p76)

Muslim Restaurant Step back in time at this classic Bangkok eatery. (p129)

Hipster Haunts

Commons The Thai food court made chic. (p148)

Teens of Thailand Chinatown is now cool; have a gin-based drink at this speakeasy-ish bar to celebrate. (p105)

Siam Discovery A lengthy renovation has made one of the city's oldest malls its edgiest. (p121)

Beam Bangkok's dance club of the moment. (p150)

Chang Chui This alleged art market combines everything from an abandoned airplane to an insect-themed restaurant. (p161)

Studio Lam Bangkok circa 1972 is the new cool at this music-themed bar. (p149)

Architecture

Jim Thompson House Beautiful former home that brings together Thailand's past and present. (p110)

Ban Kamthieng A perfectly preserved northern-style Thai home – right in the middle of modern Bangkok. (p144)

Dusit Palace Park A confoundingly beautiful blend of Thai and European building styles. (p92)

Ancient City See models of Thailand's most famous structures without having to leave the greater Bangkok area. (p25)

Temples

Wat Phra Kaew The grandaddy of Thai temples – not to mention the home of a certain Emerald Buddha. (p64)

Wat Pho If you haven't seen the ginormous reclining Buddha here, you can't claim to have seen Bangkok. (p60)

Wat Suthat One of Thailand's biggest Buddhas and equally impressive floor-to-ceiling temple murals. (p80)

Wat Arun Predating Bangkok, this temple makes the best of a unique riverside location. (p69)

Wat Mangkon Kamalawat The epitome of the hectic, smoky, noisy Chinese-style Buddhist temple. (p101)

Sri Mariamman Temple Bangkok's main Hindu temple practically leaps from the street, taking all comers. (p128)

Boats

Chao Phraya Express Boat The slow but steady (and scenic) way to get around Bangkok. (p238)

Long-tail boat tour of Thonburi canals Race through the narrow, wooden-house-lined canals of Thonburi, James Bond–style. (p76)

Chaophraya Cruise Dinner on the deck of a cruise ship is an admittedly cheesy, yet obligatory Bangkok experience. (p132)

Royal Barges National Museum A riverside museum that's home to some of the most ornate boats in the world. (p72)

Museums

National Museum An occasionally dusty but wholly worthwhile survey of Thai history. (p71)

For more top Bangkok spots, see the following:

➡ Eating (p26)

➡ Drinking & Nightlife (p35)

➡ Entertainment (p39)

➡ Shopping (p43)

➡ Sports & Activities (p48)

PLAN YOUR TRIP IF YOU LIKE...

Museum of Siam A lively summary of the Thai people and their culture. (p70)

Bangkokian Museum A preserved house that's a time warp back to the Bangkok of the early-to-middle 20th century. (p127)

Siriraj Medical Museum Not for the faint of heart: a queasy look at the more graphic side of death. (p70)

Free Stuff

Ban Baat Learn the traditional way to produce *bàht,* the distinctive bowls in which monks receive morning food donations. (p79)

Bangkokian Museum By donation only. (p127)

Golden Mount & Wat Saket A small fee if you want to climb to the summit. (p82)

Lumphini Park Escape the crowds and traffic. (p129)

Pak Khlong Talat Flower Market Wander this sprawling market. (p101)

Amulet Market Check out the remarkable amulets for sale. (p70)

Chatuchak Weekend Market There's not much you can't buy here, but it's free to browse. (p158)

Month by Month

January

The weather is still quite cool; if you're OK with relatively high tourist numbers, January is one of the most pleasant months.

✨ Chinese New Year

Some time between late January and late February, Bangkok's large Thai–Chinese population celebrates the lunar new year (*drùd jeen* in Thai) with a week full of house cleaning, lion dances and fireworks.

February

With fairly comfortable (although increasingly warm) temperatures and few tourists, plus a unique religious holiday, February is a great time to visit.

☆ Kite-Flying Season

During the windy season, from the middle of February to early April, colourful kites battle it out over the skies of Sanam Luang and Lumphini Park.

✨ Makha Bucha

Makha Bucha, held on the full moon of the third lunar month (late February to early March), commemorates the Buddha preaching to 1250 monks who came to hear him 'without prior summons'. It ends with a candlelit walk around the main chapel at every wát.

April

This is the height of the hot season, so it should come as no surprise that the Thais have devised a festival that revolves around splashing water on each other.

✨ Songkran

Songkran is the Thai New Year, and although it has origins in a religious practice of 'bathing' Buddha images, today's celebrations resemble a city-wide waterfight. The most intense battles are fought on Th Silom and Th Khao San.

May

May marks the start of the rainy season, and some of the festivals during these months have origins in this significant occasion.

✨ Royal Ploughing Ceremony

To kick off the official rice-planting season in early May, the king presides over this ancient Brahman ritual held at Sanam Luang. Sacred white oxen plough the earth and priests declare a good or bad year for farmers.

✨ Visakha Bucha

Visakha Bucha, on the full moon of the sixth lunar month (May or June), is considered the date of the Buddha's birth, enlightenment and *parinibbana* (passing away).

☆ Wai Kru Muay Thai Ceremony

A celebration of Thailand's unofficial national sport of *moo·ay tai* (Thai boxing), held at Wat Mahathat in Ayuthaya. The one-day event includes demonstrations and a competition; call Ayuthaya's Tourism Authority of Thailand (TAT) office for dates and schedule of events.

July

The rainy season is well under way. The most significant event is a Buddhist holiday ushering in the rains.

✿ Asanha Bucha & Khao Phansa

Held on the full moon of the eighth lunar month (July or August), Asanha Bucha commemorates the Buddha's first postenlightenment sermon. The following day (Khao Phansa), young men traditionally enter the monkhood and monks sequester themselves in a monastery for three months.

September

September is the wettest month in and around Bangkok, and tourist numbers are correspondingly low. Foodies should coordinate their visit with the annual vegetarian festival.

✰ International Festival of Dance & Music

An extravaganza of arts and culture sponsored by the Thailand Cultural Centre and held at venues across the city.

✰ Thailand International Swan Boat Races

In late September, more than 20 international teams race traditional Thai-style long boats in various classes (the largest has 55 paddlers) along Mae Nam Chao Phraya in Ayuthaya.

✖ Vegetarian Festival

During the first nine days of the ninth lunar month (September or October), this Chinese-Buddhist festival (*têt·sà·gahn gin jair*) sees streetside vendors serving meatless meals to help cleanse the body. Most of the action is in Chinatown: look for yellow banners and white clothes.

October

Bangkok is wet, so festivals are few on the ground. Low tourist numbers mean that it's a great time to come if you want the city to yourself.

✿ Bangkok Pride

Reinstated after nearly a decade, this six-day festival is organised by city businesses and organisations for Bangkok's gay, lesbian, bisexual and transgender community; set for May but occasionally held in October/November.

November

The rain's (mostly) stopped, the weather's (relatively) cool, the crowds are low and the festivals are plentiful: November is one of the best months to visit.

✿ Loi Krathong

On the night of the full moon of the 12th lunar month, *grà·tong* (boats made of a section of banana trunk) are floated on Mae Nam Chao Phraya. The ceremony is both an offering to the water spirits and a symbolic cleansing of bad luck.

◉ Wat Saket Fair

The grandest of Bangkok's temple fairs (*ngahn wát*) is held at Wat Saket and the Golden Mount around Loi Krathong. The temple grounds turn into a colourful, noisy fair selling flowers, incense, bells, saffron cloth and tonnes of Thai food.

December

The coolest month of means tourist numbers are at their peak, but this is arguably the pleasantest month.

✰ Concert in the Park

Free concerts from the Bangkok Symphony Orchestra (www.bangkoksymphony.org) are performed on Sunday evenings (from 5.30pm to 7.30pm) between late November and mid-February at Lumphini Park.

✿ King Bhumibol's Birthday & Father's Day

Celebrating former King Bhumibol's birthday (5 December), the city is festooned with lights and portraits of the king. In the afternoon, Sanam Luang is packed for fireworks that segues appropriately into a noisy concert with popular Thai musicians.

✰ Phra Nakhon Si Ayutthaya World Heritage Fair

A series of cultural performances and evening sound-and-light shows among the ruins of the World Heritage site in the former Thai capital, Ayutthaya; held in mid-December.

With Kids

There aren't a whole lot of attractions in Bangkok meant to appeal specifically to the little ones, but there's no lack of locals willing to provide attention. This means kids are welcome almost anywhere and you'll rarely experience the sort of eye-rolling annoyance often seen in the West.

Dream World (p161)

Parks & Playgrounds

Lumphini Park

Central Bangkok's biggest park (p129) is a trusty ally in the cool hours of the morning and afternoon for kite flying (in season – February to April), swan-boat rentals and fish feeding, as well as stretching of the legs and lungs. Nearby, kids can view lethal snakes becoming reluctant altruists at the antivenin-producing Queen Saovabha Memorial Institute (p129), aka the Snake Farm.

Animals

In addition to the animals, Dusit Zoo (p94) has shady grounds, plus a lake in the centre with paddle boats for hire and a small children's playground.

It's not exactly a zoo, but kids can join the novice monks and Thai children at Thewet Pier as they throw food (bought on the pier) to thousands of flapping fish.

Play Centres & Amusement Parks

For kid-specific play centres, consider **Funarium** (Map p282; ☏02 665 6555; www.funarium. co.th; 111/1 Soi 26, Th Sukhumvit; 110-330B; ⊗9am-6pm Mon-Thu, to 7pm Fri-Sun; ⚑; ⓈPhrom Phong exit 1 & taxi), central Bangkok's largest, or the impressive **KidZania** (Map p274; ☏02 683 1888; www.bangkok.kidzania.com/en; 5th fl, Siam Paragon, 991/1 Rama I; adult 425-500B, child 425-1000B; ⊗10am-5pm Mon-Fri, 10.30am-8pm Sat & Sun; ⓈSiam exits 3 & 5). Alternatively, Siam Park City (p161) or Dream World (p161) are both vast amusement parks north of the city.

Kid Friendly Museums

Children's Discovery Museum

Recently renovated kid-themed museum (p161), with interactive displays ranging in topic from construction to culture.

Museum of Siam

Although not specifically targeted towards children, the Museum of Siam (p70) has lots of interactive exhibits that will appeal.

Madame Tussauds

Siam Discovery has a branch of this famous **wax museum** (Map p274; www.madametus sauds.com/Bangkok/en; 4th fl, Siam Discovery, cnr Rama I & Th Phayathai; adult/child 990/790B; ⊗10am-9pm; ⓈSiam exit 1).

Ancient City (Muang Boran)

Outside of town, this open-air **museum** (เมืองโบราณ, Muang Boran; www.ancientcitygroup.net/ancientsiam/en; 296/1 Th Sukhumvit, Samut Prakan; adult/child 600/350B; ⏲9am-7pm; [S]Bearing exit 1) re-creates Thailand's most famous monuments. They're linked by bicycle paths and were built for being climbed on.

Rainy Day Fun

If you're visiting during the rainy season (approximately from June to October), the brief-but-daily downpours will inevitably complicate things, so you'll need a few indoor options in your back pocket.

Megamalls

MBK Center (p121) and Siam Paragon (p121) both have bowling alleys to keep the older ones occupied. The latter also has an IMAX theatre and Sea Life Ocean World (p122), a basement-level aquarium. For those particularly hot days, CentralWorld (p123) has an ice rink. All of these malls and most others in Bangkok have amusement centres with video games, small rides and playgrounds (they're often located near the food courts). Gateway Ekamai (p147) has an arcade and a branch of **Stanley MiniVenture** (Map p282; www.stanleyminiventure.com; 2nd fl, Gateway Ekamai, 982/22 Th Sukhumvit; adult/child 500/400B; ⏲10am-8pm), a model-train-like miniature town.

Bangkok Doll Factory & Museum

This somewhat hard-to-find **museum** (พิพิธภัณฑ์ตุ๊กตาบางกอกดอลล์; Map p271; ☎02 245 3008; www.bangkokdolls.com; 85 Soi Ratchataphan/Mo Leng; admission free; ⏲8.30am-5pm Tue-Sat; [S]Phaya Thai exit 3 & taxi) [FREE] houses a colourful selection of traditional Thai dolls, both new and antique.

Practicalities

Many hotels offer family deals, adjoining rooms and (in midrange and top-end hotels) cots, so enquire specifically. Car seats, on the other hand, are almost impossible to find. Taxi drivers generally won't temper their speed because you're travelling with a child, so if need be don't hesitate to tell them to *cháh cháh* (slow down).

NEED TO KNOW

Bambi (www.bambiweb.org) A useful resource for parents in Bangkok.

Bangkok.com (www.bangkok.com/kids) This website lists a dizzying array of things to do with kids.

Thorn Tree Kids To Go forum (www.lonelyplanet.com/thorntree/forums/kids-to-go) Questions and answers from other travellers with children on Lonely Planet's community forum.

For moving by foot, slings are often more useful than prams, as Bangkok footpaths are infamously uneven.

Infants

Nappies (diapers), international brands of milk formula and other infant requirements are widely available. For something more specific you'll find the Central Chidlom (p123) as well stocked as anywhere on earth (there's an entire floor devoted to kids). In general, Thai women don't breastfeed in public, though in department stores they'll often find a changing room.

Eating

Dining with children in Thailand, particularly with infants, is a liberating experience, as Thai people are so fond of kids. Take it for granted that your babies will be fawned over, played with – and even carried around – by restaurant waitstaff. Consider this a much-deserved break, not to mention a bit of free cultural exposure.

For the widest choice of food, child-friendly surroundings and noise levels that will drown out even the loudest child, you may find the food courts of Bangkok's many megamalls to be the most comfortable family dining options. High-chairs are rare outside expensive restaurants.

Because much of Thai food is so spicy, there is an entire art devoted to ordering 'safe' dishes for children, and the vast majority of Thai kitchens are more than willing to oblige. Many a child in Thailand has grown up on a diet of little more than *gaang jèut,* a bland, Chinese-influenced soup containing ground pork, soft tofu and a handful of noodles, or variations on *kôw pàt,* fried rice. Other mild options include *kôw man gài,* Hainanese chicken rice, and *jóhk,* rice gruel.

Street food stall

 # Eating

Nowhere else is the Thai reverence for food more evident than in Bangkok. To the outsider, the life of a Bangkokian appears to be a string of meals and snacks punctuated by the odd stab at work, not the other way around. If you can adjust your mental clock to this schedule, your visit will be a delicious one indeed.

Thai-style curry

NEED TO KNOW

Price Ranges

The following price ranges indicate how much you should expect to pay for a main dish in Bangkok.

$ less than 150B
$$ 150B to 350B
$$$ more than 350B

Opening Hours

Restaurants serving Thai food are generally open from 10am to 8pm or 9pm. Foreign-cuisine restaurants tend to keep only lunch and dinner hours (ie 11am to 2pm and 6pm to 10pm).

Bangkok has passed a citywide ordinance banning street vendors from setting up shop on Mondays.

Reservations

If you have a lot of friends in tow or will be dining at a formal restaurant (including hotel restaurants), reservations are recommended. Bookings are also recommended for Sunday brunches and dinner cruises. Otherwise, you shouldn't have a problem scoring a table at the vast majority of restaurants in Bangkok.

Tipping

You shouldn't be surprised to learn that tipping is not obligatory in Thailand. Some people leave roughly 10% at any sit-down restaurant where someone fills their glass every time they take a sip; others don't. Most upmarket restaurants will apply a 10% service charge to the bill.

Other Resources

Keep up with the ever-changing food scene in Bangkok by following the Restaurants section of BK (www.bk.asia-city.com) or Bangkok 101 (www.bangkok101.com).

The Flavours of Bangkok

The people of central Thailand are fond of sweet, savoury, herbal flavours, and many dishes include freshwater fish, pork, coconut milk and palm sugar – common ingredients in the central Thai plains. Because of the region's proximity to the Gulf of Thailand, central Thai eateries, particularly those in Bangkok, also serve a wide variety of seafood.

ROYAL CUISINE

Another significant influence on the city's kitchens has come from the Bangkok-based royal court, which has been producing sophisticated and refined takes on central Thai dishes for nearly 300 years. Although originally only available within the palace walls, so-called 'royal' Thai dishes such as *máh hór* (a small dish combining mandarin, orange or pineapple and a sweet/savoury/peppery topping that includes pork, chicken, peanuts, sugar, peppercorns and coriander root) can be found in a few restaurants across the city.

CHINESE CUISINE

Immigrants from southern China have been influencing Thai cuisine for centuries and it was most likely Chinese labourers and vendors who introduced the wok and several varieties of noodle dishes to Thailand. They have also influenced Bangkok's cuisine in other ways; for example, beef is not widely eaten in Bangkok due to a Chinese-Buddhist teaching that forbids eating 'large' animals. Perhaps the most common Thai-Chinese dish in Bangkok is *bà·mèe,* wheat-and-egg noodles typically served with slices of barbecued pork.

MUSLIM CUISINE

Muslims are thought to have first visited Thailand during the late 14th century. Along with the Quran, they brought with them a meat- and dried-spice-based cuisine from their homelands in India and the Middle East. Nearly 700 years later, the impact of this culinary commerce can still be felt in Bangkok. While some Islamic-influenced

Food Spotter's Guide

Spanning four distinct regions, influences from China to the Middle East, a multitude of ingredients and a reputation for spice, Thai food can be more than a bit overwhelming. So to point you in the direction of the good stuff, we've put together a shortlist of the country's must-eat dishes.

1. Đôm yam
The 'sour Thai soup' moniker featured on many menus is a feeble description of this mouth-puckeringly tart and intensely spicy herbal broth.

2. Pàt tai
Thin rice noodles fried with egg, tofu and shrimp, and seasoned with fish sauce, tamarind and dried chilli, have emerged as the poster child for Thai food.

3. Gaang kĕe·o wăhn
Known outside of Thailand as green curry, this intersection of a piquant, herbal spice paste and rich coconut milk is single-handedly emblematic of Thai cuisine's unique flavours and ingredients.

4. Yam
This family of Thai 'salads' combines meat or seafood with a tart and spicy dressing and fresh herbs.

5. Lâhp
Minced meat seasoned with roasted rice powder, lime, fish sauce and fresh herbs is a one-dish crash course in the rustic flavours of Thailand's northeast.

6. Bà·mèe
Although Chinese in origin, these wheat-and-egg noodles, typically served with roast pork and/or crab, have become a Thai hawker-stall staple.

7. Kôw mòk
The Thai version of biryani couples golden rice and tender chicken with a sweet and sour dip and a savoury broth.

8. Sôm·đam
'Papaya salad' hardly does justice to this tear-inducingly spicy dish of strips of crunchy unripe papaya pounded in a mortar and pestle with tomato, long beans, chilli, lime and fish sauce.

9. Kôw soy
Even outside of its home in Thailand's north, there's a cult following for this soup that combines flat egg-and-wheat noodles in a rich, spice-laden, coconut-milk-based broth.

10. Pàt pàk bûng fai daang
Crunchy green vegetables, flash-fried with heaps of chilli and garlic, is Thai comfort food.

NENEULTIMATE / SHUTTERSTOCK ©

3

NARIN NONTHAMAND / SHUTTERSTOCK ©

CHOOKDEE ROMKAEW / SHUTTERSTOCK ©

5

PAUL BRIGHTON / SHUTTERSTOCK ©

MOXUMBIC / SHUTTERSTOCK ©

10

CBENJASUWAN / SHUTTERSTOCK ©

PIYATO / SHUTTERSTOCK ©

dishes such as *roh·đee* (a fried bread similar to the Indian *paratha*) have changed little, if at all, others such as *gaang mát·sà·màn* (sometimes known as 'Muslim curry') are a unique blend of Thai and Indian/Middle Eastern cooking styles and ingredients.

Where to Eat

During the last couple of decades, Thai food has become internationally famous and Bangkok is, not surprisingly, the best place in the world to eat it. From roadside stalls to restaurants with Michelin stars in their eyes, the whole spectrum of Thai food is available here. And more recent immigration to the city has resulted in a contemporary dining scene where options range from Korean to French, touching on just about everything in between.

MARKETS & STALLS

Open-air markets and food stalls are among the most popular dining spots for Thais, although in recent years the authorities have begun banning them from some parts of town. In the mornings, stalls selling coffee and Chinese-style doughnuts appear along busy commuter corridors. At lunchtime, diners might grab a plastic chair at

yet another stall for a simple stir-fry or pick up a foam box of noodles to scoff down at the office. In Bangkok's suburbs, night markets often spring up in the middle of town with a cluster of food vendors, metal tables and chairs, and some shopping as an after-dinner mint.

SHOPHOUSES

One of the most common types of restaurant in Bangkok – and, if you ask us, the most delicious – is the open-fronted *hôrng tăa·ou* (shophouse) restaurant. The cooks at these places have most likely been serving the same dish, or a limited repertoire of dishes, for several decades and really know what they're doing. The food may cost slightly more than on the street, but the setting is usually more comfortable and hygienic, not to mention the fact that you're eating a piece of history. While such restaurants rarely have English-language menus, you can usually point to a picture or dish.

FOOD COURTS

At home, eating in a mall is generally a last resort. In Bangkok, it's a destination. The city's shopping-centre-based food courts bring together famous vendors and

Street food stall on Th Khao San (p88)

THE END OF STREET FOOD?

It was akin to announcing that Rome's coliseum was going to be razed. In mid-2017, media outlets reported that food stalls and vendors were slated to be banned from the streets of Bangkok.

Locals and visitors were shocked and appalled. The Tourism Authority of Thailand (TAT) rushed into repair mode. Even Thailand's Ministry of Foreign Affairs felt obligated to release a statement. Within days the Bangkok Metropolitan Authority (BMA), the organisation which released the statement and the entity responsible for overseeing street vendors, backpedalled, claiming that it was misquoted and that it was simply planning to enforce already existing laws and regulations.

Yet in the months leading up to the debacle (Streetgate?), the BMA had cleared street vendors from some areas of the city, most notably along Soi 55, Th Sukhumvit (the street colloquially known as Thong Lo) and Th Suan Phlu, in efforts to clean up and unclog the city's footpaths and streets.

What does this mean for the rest of Bangkok's estimated 20,000 street vendors? As with many things in Thailand, the answer is unclear. At press time, the BMA had deployed a team of officers to enforce rules and regulations in Banglamphu and Chinatown, but remained vague about its plans to deal with street food in other parts of the city. For now, the situation appears to be at a stalemate, but other factors, including private development, have already done away with some of Bangkok's most famous curbside eats and it seems likely that in the future the city's streets may be cleaner and clearer, if a lot less delicious.

restaurants from across town in a setting that's clean, convenient and provides English-language menus.

RESTAURANTS

There are plenty of *ráhn ah·hǎhn* (restaurants) in Bangkok. Lunchtime is the right time to point and eat at the *ráhn kôw gaang* (rice and curry shops), which sell a selection of pre-made dishes. The more generic *ráhn ah·hǎhn đahm sàng* (made-to-order restaurants) can often be recognised by a display of raw ingredients – Chinese kale, tomatoes, chopped pork, fresh or dried fish, noodles, eggplant, spring onions – and offer a standard repertoire of Thai and Chinese–Thai dishes. As the name implies, the cooks will attempt to prepare any dish you can name – a potentially difficult operation if you can't speak Thai.

FINE DINING

Bangkok is home to dozens of upscale restaurants. For the most part, those serving Thai cuisine have adjusted their recipes to suit foreign palates – for more authentic food you're much better off eating at the cheaper shophouse-style restaurants. On the other hand, upscale and hotel restaurants are probably the best places in Bangkok for authentic Western-style food. If these are outside your price range, you'll be happy to know that there's also a huge spread of midrange foreign restaurants in today's Bangkok, many of them quite good.

INTERNATIONAL CHAINS

For impromptu drinking and snacking, Bangkok also has an overabundance of modern cafes – including branches of several international chains. Most serve passable takes on Western-style coffee drinks, cakes and sweets.

Cooking Courses

Bangkok has a number of great cooking courses that are geared towards visitors wanting to re-create Thai cuisine at home. Some of our favourites:

➡ **Amita Thai Cooking Class** (p75)

➡ **Bangkok Bold Cooking Studio** (p87)

➡ **Silom Thai Cooking School** (p141)

Food Markets

If you take pleasure in seeing food in its raw form, Bangkok is home to dozens of traditional-style wet markets, ranging from the grungy to the flashy; they can also be a good place to eat. Some of our favourite Bangkok (and around) markets:

➡ **Or Tor Kor Market** (p161)

➡ **Nonthaburi Market** (p161)

➡ **Talat Mai** (p101)

THAI NOODLES 101

In Thailand, noodles are ubiquitous, cheap and tasty. But they're also extremely varied and somewhat complicated to order. So with this in mind, we've provided a crash course.

The Dishes

Some Thai noodle dishes can be ordered *hâang*, meaning 'dry', in which the noodles are served with just enough broth to keep them moist.

Bà·mèe These eponymous Chinese-style wheat-and-egg noodles are typically served with barbecued pork slices, a handful of greens and, if you like, wontons.

Gŏo·ay jáp Rice noodles and pork offal served in a fragrant, peppery broth; a dish popular among the Thai-Chinese.

Gŏo·ay đĕe·o kaang A Thai–Muslim dish of rice noodles served with a curry broth, often including garnishes such as tofu, hard-boiled egg and peanuts.

Gŏo·ay đĕe·o lôok chín This dish combines rice noodles in a generally clear broth with pork- or fish-based (or less commonly, beef or chicken) balls; one of the most common types of noodles across the country. When ordering *gŏo·ay đĕe·o,* the cook will ask which type of noodle you would like – *sên lék* (thin noodles) to *sên yài* (wide noodles).

Gŏo·ay đĕe·o reu·a Known as boat noodles because they were previously served from the canals of central Thailand, these intense pork- or beef-based bowls are among the most full-flavoured of noodle dishes.

Kà·nŏm jeen This dish, named after its noodle, combines thin rice threads and a typically mild, curry-like broth, served with a self-selection of fresh and pickled vegetables and herbs. *Kà·nŏm jeen* varies immensely from region to region, and also tends to be one of the cheapest noodle dishes in the country.

Kôw soy Associated with northern Thailand, this dish combines wheat-and-egg noodles and a fragrant, rich, curry-based broth.

Yen đah foh A crimson broth with meatballs, cubes of boiled blood, and crispy greens, this dish is probably the most intimidating but popular noodle dish in Bangkok.

The Noodles

You'll find four main kinds of noodle in Thailand. When ordering, it's generally necessary to specify which noodle you want. It's also possible to order some types of noodle dishes minus the noodles, with a bowl of rice instead; this is called *gao lǎo*.

Bà·mèe Made from wheat flour and egg, this noodle is yellowish in colour and sold only in fresh bundles.

Kà·nŏm jeen This noodle is produced by pushing a rice-based dough through a sieve into boiling water, much the way some types of Italian pasta are made.

Sên gŏo·ay đĕe·o The most common type of noodle in Thailand is made from rice flour mixed with water to form a paste, which is steamed to form wide, flat sheets, then sliced into various widths.

Wún·sên An almost clear noodle made from mung-bean starch and water, this noodle features occasionally in noodle soups, but is usually the central ingredient in *yam wún sên,* a hot and tangy salad made with lime juice, *prík kêe nŏo* (tiny chillies), shrimp, ground pork and seasoning.

The Seasoning

Thai noodle dishes are often served slightly underseasoned. The idea is to season your own bowl, typically using some or all of four condiments: *prík nám sôm* (sliced mild chillies in vinegar), *nám plah* (fish sauce), *prík pòn* (dried red chilli, flaked or ground to a near powder) and *nám·đahn* (plain white sugar). These condiments offer three ways to make the soup hotter – hot and sour, hot and salty, and just plain hot – and one to make it sweet.

The typical eater will add a teaspoonful of each one of these to the noodle soup, except for the sugar, which in sweet-tooth Bangkok usually rates a full tablespoon. Until you're used to these strong seasonings, we recommend adding them a small bit at a time, tasting the soup along the way to make sure you don't go overboard.

Eating by Neighbourhood

→ **Banglamphu** (p82) Classic old-school Bangkok-style eateries.

→ **Thewet & Dusit** (p96) Breezy, riverfront dining.

→ **Chinatown** (p104) Thai-Chinese street eats.

→ **Siam Square, Pratunam, Phloen Chit & Ratchathewi** (p115) Mall-based food courts and domestic and international franchises.

→ **Riverside, Silom & Lumphini** (p129) The full spectrum of Thai food, from cut-rate lunchtime food courts to decadent hotel restaurants.

→ **Sukhumvit** (p145) This seemingly never-ending street has an outpost of just about every global cuisine.

→ **Northern Bangkok** (p162) Head to the burbs for vibrant markets and restaurants serving regional Thai cuisine.

PLAN YOUR TRIP EATING

Thai-style seafood and noodles

Lonely Planet's Top Choices

nahm (p133) Upscale Thai that's worth every baht.

Eat Me (p132) The best of contemporary, eclectic dining.

Krua Apsorn (p83) Full-flavoured central Thai fare in a homey setting.

Jay Fai (p83) Decades-old shophouse serving flash-fried masterpieces.

MBK Food Island (p115) Cheap, cheerful and tasty: Bangkok's best food court.

Soul Food Mahanakorn (p145) Flavour-forward Thai in a foreigner-friendly atmosphere.

Best by Budget

$

Nai Mong Hoi Thod (p104) Long-standing hole-in-the-wall serving delicious fried oysters and mussels.

Thip Samai (p82) The city's most legendary venue for *pàt tai*.

Nuer Koo (p115) Sublime beef noodles at this, the street stall in a mall.

$$

Likhit Kai Yang (p96) Generations of Thai boxing fans can't be wrong about this temple to northeastern Thai cuisine.

Kai Thort Jay Kee (p133) Decadent fried chicken with a dedicated fan base.

Err (p74) Sophisticated Thai-style bites and booze.

$$$

Little Beast (p148) Flavourful, fun, American-influenced fine dining.

Ginzado (p147) Flawless Korean barbecue.

Bo.lan (p148) Thai taken upscale.

Best Bangkok-style Food

Khun Yah Cuisine (p104) Travel back to the flavours of Bangkok's past.

Toy (p116) Go-to place for the city's famous 'boat noodles'.

Pa Aew (p74) Simple street stall touting Bangkok's sophisticated tastes.

Klang Soi Restaurant (p145) Old-school Bangkok flavours in air-conditioned comfort.

Best Old-school Thai Dining

Muslim Restaurant (p129) Classic eatery with more than seven decades under its belt.

Baan Pueng Chom (p163) Thai-style 'garden' restaurant – a dying breed.

Karim Roti-Mataba (p82) Epitome of the Bangkok shophouse restaurant.

Ming Lee (p74) Ancient Thai dishes in a likewise dining room.

Best Regional Thai Cuisine

Sri Trat (p145) New eatery serving the dishes of Thailand's eastern seaboard.

Dao Tai (p74) The best of a knot of simple restaurants specialising in southern Thai cuisine.

Khua Kling Pak Sod (p163) Full-flavoured southern Thai dishes in a semiformal setting.

Jay So (p131) Unfettered northeastern Thai served in a streetside shack.

Prai Raya (p146) The flavours of Phuket – in Bangkok.

Best Street Stalls

Nay Hong (p104) A delicious introduction to Chinatown-style street eats – if you can find it.

Thanon Phadungdao Seafood Stalls (p105) These stalls are so 'street' you risk getting bumped by a car.

Foontalop (p160) Open-air dining in the middle of Chatuchak Weekend Market.

Nay Lék Ûan (p104) Arguably one of the city's most famous stalls.

Best Dessert

Puritan (p163) Excellent cakes in a whimsical setting.

Old Siam Plaza (p104) A candy-land of traditional Thai sweets.

Hazel's Ice Cream Parlor and Fine Drinks (p97) 'Adult' ice creams.

Gourmet Paradise (p116) Mall food court with an emphasis on the sweet stuff.

Best Foreign Cuisine Restaurants

Jidori Cuisine Ken (p147) Chicken skewers grilled over coals with a precision that could only be Japanese.

Appia (p147) Italian that manages to feel both homestyle and decadent.

Tonkin-Annam (p74) Casual, full-flavoured Vietnamese.

Moon Bar (p135)

Drinking & Nightlife

Shame on you if you think Bangkok's only nightlife options include the word 'go-go'. As in any big international city, the drinking and partying scene in Bangkok ranges from trashy to classy and touches on just about everything in between.

NEED TO KNOW

Opening Hours

Officially, Bangkok's bars and clubs close by midnight, a rule that's been enforced recently. A complicated zoning system sees venues in designated 'entertainment areas', including RCA/Royal City Ave, Th Silom and parts of Th Sukhumvit, open until 1am or 2am, but even these 'later' licences are subject to police whimsy.

Dress Code

Most rooftop bars enforce a dress code – no shorts or sandals. This is also the case with many of Bangkok's dance clubs.

ID

The drinking age in Thailand is 20, although it's only usually dance clubs that ask for ID.

Resources

To keep crowds interested, clubs host weekly theme parties and visiting DJs. To find out what's on, check out Dudesweet (www.dudesweet.org) and Paradise Bangkok (www.facebook.com/paradisebangkok), organisers of hugely popular monthly parties, or local listings such as BK (www.bk.asia-city.com), Bangkok 101 (www.bangkok101.com), the *Bangkok Post's* Friday supplement, *Guru,* or Siam2nite (www.siam2nite.com).

Smoking

Smoking has been outlawed at all indoor (and some quasi-outdoor) entertainment places since 2008.

The Scene

Bangkok is a party animal – even when on a tight leash. Way back in 2001, the Thaksin administration started enforcing closing times and curtailing other excesses that had previously made the city's nightlife famous. Since his 2006 ousting, the laws have been increasingly circumvented or inconsistently enforced. Post the 2014 coup, there are indications that Bangkok is seeing something of a return to the 2001-era strictly enforced operating hours and zoning laws.

BARS

Bangkok's watering holes cover the spectrum from English-style pubs where you can comfortably sit with a pint and the paper to chic dens where the fair and beautiful go to be seen, not imbibe. Perhaps most famously, Bangkok is also one of the few big cities in the world where nobody seems to mind if you slap a bar on top of a skyscraper (it's worth noting that most rooftop bars enforce a dress code – no shorts or sandals). But many visitors associate Bangkok with the kind of bars that don't have an address – found just about everywhere in the city. Think streetside seating, plastic chairs, car exhaust and tasty dishes absent-mindedly nibbled between toasts.

Bangkok bars don't have cover charges, but they do generally enforce closing time at midnight – sometimes earlier if they suspect trouble from the cops.

DANCE CLUBS

Bangkok's club scene is a fickle beast, and venues that were pulling in thousands a night just last year might be a vague memory this year. Clubs here also tend to heave on certain nights – Fridays and Saturdays, during a visit from a foreign DJ, or for a night dedicated to the music flavour of the month – then hibernate every other night.

What used to be a rotating cast of hot spots has slowed to a few standards on the sois off Th Sukhumvit, Th Silom, Th Ratchadaphisek and RCA/Royal City Ave – the city's designated 'entertainment zones' – which qualify for the 2am closing time (at the time of research, some of the bigger places were stretching this to 3am). Most joints don't begin filling up until midnight. Cover charges can run as high as 600B and usually include a drink or two. At the bigger places you'll need ID to prove you're legal (20 years old); they'll card even the grey-haired.

If you find 2am too early to call it a night, don't worry – Thais have found curiously creative methods of flouting closing times. Speakeasies have sprung up all over the city, so follow the crowds – few people will actually be heading home. Some places just remove the tables and let people drink on the floor (somehow this is an exemption), while other places serve beer in teapots.

THAI PILSNER PRIMER

We relish the look of horror on the faces of Bangkok newbies when the waitress casually plunks several cubes of ice into their pilsners. Before you rule this supposed blasphemy out completely, there are a few reasons why we and the Thais actually prefer our beer on the rocks. Thai beer does not possess the most sophisticated bouquet in the world and is best drunk as cold as possible. The weather in Thailand is often extremely hot, so it makes sense to maintain your beer at maximum chill. And lastly, domestic brews are generally quite high in alcohol and the ice helps to dilute this, preventing dehydration and one of those infamous Beer Chang hangovers the next day. Taking these theories to the extreme, some places serve *bee·a wún*, 'jelly beer', beer that has been semifrozen until it reaches a deliciously slushy and refreshing consistency.

Drinks

Bangkok is justifiably renowned for its food and nightlife, but markedly less so for its beverages. Yet drinks are the glue that fuse these elements, and without them, that cabaret show would be markedly less entertaining.

BEER

People in Bangkok generally drink a lot – and a lot of the time, that means beer. Yet until recently, there was very little variety in the domestic beer scene.

Advertised with such slogans as *'þrà·têht row, bee·a row'* (our land, our beer), the Singha label is considered the quintessential Thai beer by *fa·ràng* (Westerners) and locals alike. Pronounced *sǐng* and boasting 6% alcohol, this pilsner claims about half the domestic market. Singha's biggest rival, Beer Chang, pumps the alcohol content up to 7%. Boon Rawd (the maker of Singha) responded with its own cheaper brand, Leo. Sporting a black-and-red leopard label, Leo costs only slightly more than Beer Chang but is similarly high in alcohol. Other Thai-brewed beers, all at the lower end of the price spectrum, include Cheers and Beer Thai. Also popular are foreign brands brewed under license in Thailand such as Asahi, Heineken, Kirin and San Miguel. A small trickle of domestic microbrews was appearing at the time of research, an indication that more variation in Thai beer brands is likely in the coming years.

Conversely, the selection of imported microbrews is astounding, with bottled and draught beers and ciders from across the world available in Bangkok. The city is now home to several pubs that specialise in imported beers, so if you're missing your local brew, it's entirely possible that you may be able to find it in Bangkok.

RICE WHISKY, WHISKY & RUM

Thai rice whisky has a sharp, sweet taste – not unlike rum – with an alcohol content of 35%. The most famous brand for many years was Mekong (pronounced *mâa kŏng*), but today there are domestic brands meant to appeal to the can't-afford-Johnnie-Walker-yet set, including Blue Eagle, 100 Pipers and Spey Royal, each with a 40% alcohol content. Also popular is Sang Som, a domestic rum. In Thailand, booze typically comes in 750mL bottles called *glom*, or in 375mL flask-shaped bottles called *baan*.

Thais normally buy whisky by the bottle and drink it with ice, plenty of soda water and a splash of Coke. If you don't finish your bottle, simply tell your waiter, who will write your name and the date on the bottle and keep it for your next visit.

Drinking & Nightlife by Neighbourhood

➡ **Ko Ratanakosin & Thonburi** (p75) Romantic riverside sipping.

➡ **Banglamphu** (p84) Rowdy Th Khao San is one of the city's best areas for a night out.

➡ **Siam Square, Pratunam, Phloen Chit & Ratchathewi** (p118) Bangkok's most central zone is home to a scant handful of bars.

➡ **Riverside, Silom & Lumphini** (p134) Bangkok's gaybourhood has fun bars and dance clubs open to all comers.

➡ **Sukhumvit** (p149) This long street is home to Bangkok's most sophisticated bars and clubs.

➡ **Northern Bangkok** (p164) Suburban RCA/ Royal City Ave is the city's best clubbing strip; good live-music venues dot other regions.

Lonely Planet's Top Choices

WTF (p149) A sophisticated yet friendly local boozer.

Q&A Bar (p149) Creative cocktails in a slick setting.

Moon Bar (p135) Casual ambience and stunning views make this our favourite of Bangkok's original rooftop bars.

DJ Station (p136) One of the most legendary gay dance clubs in Bangkok – if not Asia.

Smalls (p134) An eclectic interior and fun events make this one of our favorite bars in town.

Beam (p150) Bangkok's It Club – for the moment, at least.

Best Bars for Chilling Out

Hippie de Bar (p85) Kick back with locals at this retro Th Khao San spot.

Walden (p150) Known for its Japanese-style 'highballs' and US craft beers.

Black Amber Social Club (p151) A whisky bar caught in a time warp.

Telephone Pub (p136) Streetside people-watching at its best.

Viva & Aviv (p134) Think casual riverside relaxing.

Best Bars for Cocktails

Sugar Ray (p150) Some of Bangkok's wackiest – and tastiest – cocktails.

Vesper (p134) One of the best places in town to sip the standards.

J. Boroski Mixology (p150) Leave it to the creative barkeeps

here to concoct your drink on the spot.

Ku Bar (p84) Edgy cocktails in an even edgier locale.

Tep Bar (p105) Cocktails with unique Thai touches.

Best Bars with Food

Tuba (p149) Full-flavoured bar snacks that span from Isan (northeastern Thailand) to Italy.

Mikkeller (p149) Craft beers and clever bites.

Madame Musur (p85) Singha almost tastes good when coupled with the northern-Thai-style dishes here.

Badmotel (p150) Quirky twists on Thai and international dishes.

Hair of the Dog (p118) Couple your draught cider with a hearty plate of poutine (chips and gravy).

Best Bars with Views

Roof (p75) Incomparable views of the river and Wat Arun.

A R Sutton & Co Engineers Siam (p149) One of the most unique interiors of any bar in Bangkok.

Long Table (p152) Boasting a bird's-eye view of one of the city's busiest intersections.

Above 11 (p151) Rise above it all at this lofty Th Sukhumvit bar.

Best Dance Clubs

Studio Lam (p149) The themed DJ nights here are some of the best fun in town.

Route 66 (p163) Join the throngs at this long-standing megaclub.

Glow (p150) *The* destination in town for EDM snobs.

Sing Sing Theater (p151) Tiny dance floor, big fun.

The Club (p85) Dance with a virtual UN of partiers at this Th Khao San–based disco.

Demo (p151) Where the Thais go to shake.

Best Late-Night Bars & Clubs

Wong's Place (p137) Open from midnight until the last punter crawls out.

The Bank (p85) Puff on *shisha* or dance into the wee hours on Th Khao San.

Narz (p152) With three vast zones to keep clubbers raving till dawn.

Levels (p151) When most Soi 11 bars begin to close, this club heats up.

Mixx (p119) Basement-level late-night disco.

Scratch Dog (p152) For when closing times trump quality music.

Best Rooftop Bars

Sky Bar (p135) Quite possibly the city's most famous rooftopper.

River Vibe (p107) Budget rooftop river views.

Park Society (p135) Gaze down at Lumphini Park from your 29th-floor perch.

Red Sky (p118) Peep on central Bangkok from 55 floors up.

Sky Train Jazz Club (p119) Hyper-casual rooftop bar.

Performing *kŏhn*, a traditional Thai dance-drama (p223)

⭐ Entertainment

Although Bangkok often seems to cater to the inner philistine in all of us, the city is home to a diverse but low-key art scene. Add to this dance performances, live music and, yes, the infamous go-go bars, and you have a city whose entertainment scene spans from – in local parlance – lo-so (low society) to hi-so (high society).

Cinemas

Hollywood movies are released in Bangkok's theatres in a relatively timely fashion. But as home-grown cinema grows bigger, more and more Thai films, often subtitled in English, fill the roster. Foreign films are sometimes altered by Thailand's film censors before distribution; this usually involves obscuring nude scenes.

The shopping-centre cinemas have plush VIP options. Despite the heat and humidity on the streets, keep in mind that Bangkok's movie theatres pump in the air-conditioning with such vigour that taking a jumper is an absolute necessity. Ticket prices range from 120B to 220B for regular seats, and more than 1000B for VIP seats.

Bangkok also hosts a handful of small annual film festivals, including the World Film Festival of Bangkok (www.worldfilmbkk. com; check the website for dates).

Gà·teu·i Cabaret

Over the last decade, choreographed stage shows featuring Broadway high kicks and lip-synched pop tunes performed by *gà·teu·i*

NEED TO KNOW

Opening Hours

Live-music venues generally close by 1am. A complicated zoning system sees venues in designated 'entertainment areas' open until 2am, but even these are subject to police discretion.

Reservations

Reservations are recommended for prominent theatre events. Tickets can often be purchased through Thai Ticket Major (www.thaiticketmajor.com).

Resources

To see what's on when you're in town, check local listings mags such as *BK* (www.bk.asia-city.com), *Bangkok 101* (www.bangkok101.com) or the *Bangkok Post's* Friday supplement, *Guru*.

(also spelt *kàthoey*) – Thai transgender and cross-dressing people – has become a 'must-do' fixture on the Bangkok tourist circuit.

Go-Go Bars

Although technically illegal, prostitution is fully 'out' in Bangkok, and the influence of organised crime and lucrative kickbacks mean that it will be a long while before the existing laws are ever enforced. Yet despite the image presented by much of the Western media, the underlying atmosphere of Bangkok's redlight districts is not one of illicitness and exploitation (although these do inevitably exist), but rather an aura of tackiness and boredom.

Patpong (p138) earned notoriety during the 1980s for its wild sex shows, involving everything from ping-pong balls and razors to midgets on motorbikes. Today it is more of a circus for curious spectators than sexual deviants. Soi Cowboy (p153) and Nana Entertainment Plaza (p153) are the real scenes of sex for hire. Not all of the sex business is geared towards Westerners: Th Thaniya, off Th Silom, is filled with massage parlours for Japanese expats and visitors, while the immense massage parlours outside central Bangkok service almost exclusively Thai customers.

Live Music

As Thailand's media capital, Bangkok is the centre of the Thai music industry, packaging and selling pop, crooners, *lôok tûng* (Thai-style country music) and the recent phenomenon of indie bands.

Music is a part of almost every Thai social gathering; the matriarchs and patriarchs like dinner with an easy-listening soundtrack – typically a Filipino band and a synthesiser. Patrons pass their request (on a napkin) up to the stage.

An indigenous rock style, *pleng pêu·a chee·wít* (songs for life), makes appearances at a dying breed of country-and-western bars decorated with buffalo horns and pictures of Native Americans. Several dedicated bars throughout the city feature blues and rock bands, but are relatively scant on live indie-scene performances. Up-and-coming garage bands occasionally pop up at free concerts where the kids hang out, often at Siam Square. For more subdued tastes, Bangkok also attracts grade-A jazz musicians to several hotel bars.

Bars and clubs with live music are allowed to stay open until 1am, but this is subject to police discretion. The drinking age is 20 years old.

Moo·ay tai (Thai Boxing)

Quintessentially Thai, almost anything goes in *moo·ay tai* (also spelt *muay Thai*), the martial art more commonly known elsewhere as Thai boxing or kickboxing. If you don't mind the violence, a Thai-boxing match is well worth attending for the pure spectacle: the wild musical accompaniment, the ceremonial beginning of each match and the frenzied betting.

The best of the best fight at Bangkok's two boxing stadiums. Built on royal land at the end of WWII, the art-deco-style Rajadamnern Stadium (p97) is the original and has a relatively formal atmosphere. The other main stage, Lumpinee Boxing Stadium (p165), has moved from its eponymous hood to a modern home north of Bangkok.

Admission fees vary according to seating. Ringside seats (from 2500B) are the most expensive and will be filled with subdued VIPs; tourists usually opt for the 2nd-class seats (from 1500B); diehard

oi Cowboy (p153)

'staff' outside the stadium, who practically tackle you upon arrival, will hand you a fight roster and steer you to the foreigners' ticket windows; they can also be helpful in telling you which fights are the best match-ups (some say that welterweights, between 61.2kg and 66.7kg, are the best). To avoid supporting scalpers, purchase your tickets from the ticket window or online, not from a person outside the stadium.

Traditional Theatre & Dance

The stage in Thailand typically hosts *kŏhn* performances, one of the six traditional dramatic forms. Performed only by men, *kŏhn* drama is based upon stories of the *Ramakian,* Thailand's version of India's epic *Ramayana,* and was traditionally staged only for royal audiences.

The less formal *lá·kon* dances, of which there are many dying subgenres, usually involve costumed dancers (of both sexes) performing elements of the *Ramakian* and traditional folk tales. If you hear the din of drums and percussion from a temple or shrine, follow the sound to see traditional *lá·kon gâa bon* (shrine dancing). At Lak Meuang (p73) and the Erawan Shrine (p112), worshippers commission costumed troupes to perform dance movements that are similar to classical *lá·kon,* but not as refined.

Another option for viewing Thai classical dance is at a dinner theatre. Most dinner theatres in Bangkok are heavily promoted through hotels to an ever-changing clientele, so standards are poor to fair.

moo·ay tai fans bet and cheer from 3rd class (1000B). If you're thinking these prices sound a bit steep for your average fight fan (taxi drivers are big fans and they make about 600B a day), then you're right – foreigners pay several times what the Thais do.

We recommend the 2nd- or 3rd-class seats. The 2nd-class area is filled with numbers-runners who take bets from fans in rowdy 3rd class, which is fenced off from the rest of the stadium. Akin to a stock-exchange pit, hand signals communicate bets and odds fly between the areas. Most fans in 3rd class follow the match (or their bets) too closely to sit down, and we've seen stress levels rise to near-boiling point. It's all very entertaining.

Most programs have eight to 10 fights of five rounds each. English-speaking

Entertainment by Neighbourhood

➡ **Thewet & Dusit** (p97) This is where you'll find the city's oldest Thai-boxing stadium.

➡ **Siam Square, Pratunam, Phloen Chit & Ratchathewi** (p119) Bangkok's best cinemas.

➡ **Riverside, Silom & Lumphini** (p137) Traditional Thai dinner theatre.

Lonely Planet's Top Choices

Brick Bar (p85) Live-music den, famous among locals, for whom dancing on the tables in practically obligatory.

Rajadamnern Stadium (p97) The country's premiere venue for Thai boxing.

The Living Room (p152) As the name implies, live jazz in a comfortable setting.

Parking Toys (p165) Far from the city centre is this eclectic shed, one of Bangkok's best venues for live music.

Bangkok Art & Culture Centre (p112) The city's grandest art gallery.

Best Cinemas

Paragon Cineplex (p118) The epitome of state-of-the-art cinema.

House (p165) The city's only real art-house theatre.

Scala (p118) Fantastical old-school cinema.

Friese-Greene Club (p152) Nine-seat private theatre.

Bangkok Screening Room (p137) Single-screen theatre hosting a revolving cast of classic films.

Best Commercial Private Art Galleries

Bangkok CityCity Gallery (p128) New, attention-grabbing art space.

100 Tonson Gallery (p114) Low-key hub for contemporary art.

Kathmandu Photo Gallery (p128) The city's only dedicated photography gallery.

Subhashok the Arts Centre (p144) One of the city's most ambitious galleries.

H Gallery (p128) Classy gallery/jumping-off point for domestic artists.

Jim Thompson Art Center (p111) Revolving, predominantly Southeast Asia–themed, art exhibitions.

Best State-Run Art Galleries

Museum of Contemporary Art (p161) The city's largest space dedicated to Thai contemporary art.

National Gallery (p73) Ground zero for domestic art.

Ratchadamnoen Contemporary Art Center (p79) Changing exhibitions of mixed-media contemporary domestic art.

Bangkok University Art Gallery (p145) The country's leading student gallery.

Silpakorn University Art Centre (p71) Venue for high quality student creations.

Best Thai-Style Live Music

Lam Sing (p152) Over-the-top glam cave for Thai-style country music.

Tawandang German Brewery (p133) Giant beer hall with even bigger stage shows.

Parking Toys' Watt (p152) Live Thai pop and rock.

Raintree (p119) Earthy, suburban pub that's a bastion of contemporary Thai folk music.

Best Traditional Performance

National Theatre (p75) State-sanctioned destination for traditional Thai performance.

Sala Chalermkrung (p107) Traditional Thai drama with contemporary twists.

Sala Rim Naam (p137) Classy venue for Thai-performance-themed dinner theatre.

Best Western-Style Live Music

SoulBar (p107) Intimate locale for live soul and funk.

Ad Here the 13th (p87) Tiny blues bar in the backpacker district.

Titanium (p152) Nightly performances by Unicorn, an all-girl band that's bound to get you bouncing.

Saxophone Pub & Restaurant (p119) One of Bangkok's most legendary live-music venues.

Bamboo Bar (p137) Classy, long-standing space for live jazz.

Rock Pub (p119) Bangkok's embassy of heavy metal.

Chatuchak Weekend Market (p158)

Shopping

Prime your credit card and shine your baht – shopping is serious business in Bangkok. Hardly a street corner in this city is free from a vendor, hawker or impromptu stall, and it doesn't stop there: Bangkok is also home to one of the world's largest outdoor markets, not to mention some of Southeast Asia's largest malls.

NEED TO KNOW

Opening Hours

Most family-run shops are open from 10am to 7pm daily. Malls are open 10am to 10pm approximately. Street markets are either daytime (9am to 5pm) or night-time (7pm to midnight). Note that city ordinance forbids streetside vendors from cluttering the pavements on Mondays, but they are present every other day.

Bargaining

At Bangkok's markets and at a handful of its malls, you'll have to bargain for most, if not all, items. In general, if you see a price tag, it means that the price is fixed and bargaining isn't an option.

Scams

Thais are generally so friendly and laid-back that some visitors are lulled into a false sense of security. While your personal safety is rarely at risk in Thailand, you may be unwittingly charmed out of the contents of your wallet or fall prey to a scam (p245).

Shopping Guide

Nancy Chandler's Map of Bangkok (www.nancychandler.net) tracks all sorts of small, out-of-the-way shopping venues and markets, and dissects the innards of the Chatuchak Weekend Market (p158). The colourful map is sold in bookshops throughout the city.

Antiques

Real Thai antiques are rare, costly and reserved primarily for serious collectors. Everything else is designed to look old and most shopkeepers are happy to admit it. Reputable antique dealers will issue an authentication certificate. Officially, a licence from the **Office of the National Museum** (Map p265; ☑ 02 224 1370; National Museum, 4 Th Na Phra That, Bangkok; ☉9am-4pm Tue-Fri; ☺Chang Pier, Maharaj Pier, Phra Chan Tai Pier) is required to export religious images and fragments, but really only high-profile antiques are scrutinised.

It's worth noting that trading in bona fide antiquities might not be either ethical or, in your country, legal. For more on this issue and the campaign to preserve Southeast Asia's cultural heritage, see Heritage Watch (www.heritagewatchinternational.org).

Gems & Jewellery

Countless tourists are sucked into the prolific and well-rehearsed gem scam in which they are taken to a shop by a helpful stranger and tricked into buying bulk gems that can supposedly be resold in their home country for 100% profit. The expert con artists (part of a well-organised cartel) seem trustworthy and convince tourists that they need a citizen of the country to circumvent tricky customs regulations. Unsurprisingly, the gem world doesn't work like that and what most tourists end up with are worthless pieces of glass. By the time you sort all this out, the shop has closed and changed names and the police can do little to help.

Counterfeits

One of the most ubiquitous aspects of shopping in Bangkok, and a drawcard for many visitors, is fake merchandise. Counterfeit clothes, watches and bags line sections of Th Sukhumvit and Th Silom, while there are entire malls dedicated to copied DVDs, music CDs and software. Fake IDs are available up and down Th Khao San, and there are even fake Lonely Planet guides – old editions made over with a new cover and 'publication date' to be resold (often before we've written the next edition!). Fakes are so prominent in Bangkok that there's even a **Museum of Counterfeit Goods** (☑02 653 5546; www.tilleke.com/firm/community/museum; Tilleke & Gibbins, 26th fl, Supalai Grand Tower, 1011 Rama III; ☉2pm Mon & 10am Thu, by appointment only; Ⓜ Khlong Toei exit 1 & taxi) **FREE**, where all the counterfeit booty that has been collected by law firm Tilleke & Gibbins over the years is on display.

The brashness with which fake goods are peddled in Bangkok gives the impression that black-market goods are fair game, which is and isn't true. Technically, knock-offs are illegal and periodic crackdowns by the Thai police have led to the closure of shops and the arrest of vendors. The shops typically open again after a few months, however, and the purchasers of fake merchandise are rarely the target of such crackdowns.

The tenacity of Bangkok's counterfeit goods trade is largely due to the fact that tourists aren't the only ones buying the stuff. A poll conducted by Bangkok University's research centre found that 80% of the 1104 people polled in Bangkok admitted to having purchased counterfeit goods (only 48% said they felt guilty for having bought fakes).

It's worth pointing out that some companies, including even a few luxury brands, argue that counterfeit goods can be regarded as a net positive. They claim that a preponderance of fake items inspires brand awareness and fosters a demand for 'real' luxury items while also acting as a useful gauge of what's hot. But the argument against fake goods points out that the industry supports organised crime and potentially exploitative and abusive labour conditions, circumvents taxes and takes jobs away from legitimate companies.

If the legal or moral repercussions aren't enough to convince you, keep in mind that in general, with fake stuff, you're getting exactly what you pay for. Consider yourself lucky if, after arriving home, the Von Dutch badge on your new hat hasn't peeled off within a week and your 'Rolex' is still ticking after the first rain.

Markets & Malls

Although the tourist brochures tend to tout the upmarket malls, Bangkok still lags slightly behind Singapore and Hong Kong in this arena, and the open-air markets are where the best deals and most original items are to be found.

Tailor-Made Clothes

Many tourists arrive in Bangkok with the notion of getting clothes custom-tailored at a bargain price. While this is entirely possible, there are a few things to be aware of. Prices are almost always lower than what you'd pay at home, but common scams such as commission-hungry túk-túk (pronounced *dúk dúk*) drivers, shoddy work and inferior fabrics make bespoke tailoring in Bangkok a potentially disappointing investment.

The golden rule of custom tailoring is that you get what you pay for. If you sign up for a suit, two pants, two shirts and a tie, with a silk sarong thrown in, for just US$199 (a very popular offer in Bangkok), chances are it will look and fit like a sub-US$200 wardrobe. Although an offer may seem great on the surface, the price may

Emquartier (p154)

fluctuate significantly depending on the fabric you choose. Supplying your own fabric won't necessarily reduce the price by much, but it should ensure you get exactly the look you're after.

Have a good idea of what you want before walking into a shop. If it's a suit you're after, should it be single- or double-breasted? How many buttons? What style trousers? Of course, if you have no idea, the tailor will be more than happy to advise. Alternatively, bring a favourite garment from home and have it copied.

Set aside a week to get clothes tailored. Shirts and trousers can often be turned around in 48 hours or less with only one fitting, but no matter what a tailor may tell you, it takes more than one and often more than two fittings to create a good suit. Most reliable tailors will ask for two to five sittings. Any tailor who can sew your order in less than 24 hours should be treated with caution.

Tax Refunds

A 7% Value Added Tax (VAT) applies to most purchases in Thailand, but if you spend enough and get the paperwork, the kindly Revenue Department will refund it at the airport when you leave. To qualify to receive a refund, you must not be a Thai citizen, part of an airline air crew or have spent more than 180 days in Thailand during the previous year. Your purchase must have been made at an approved shop; look for the blue-and-white VAT Refund sticker. Minimum purchases must add up to 2000B per shop in a single day and to at least 5000B total for the whole trip. Before you leave the shop, get a VAT Refund form and tax invoice. Most major malls in Bangkok will direct you to a dedicated VAT Refund desk, which will organise the appropriate paperwork (it takes about five minutes). Note that you won't get a refund on VAT paid in hotels or restaurants.

At the airport, your purchases must be declared at the customs desk in the departure hall, which will give you the appropriate stamp; you can then check them in. Smaller items (such as watches and jewellery) should be carried on your person, as they will need to be reinspected once you've passed immigration. You actually get your money at a VAT Refund Tourist Office; at Suvarnabhumi International Airport these are located on Level 4 in both the east and west wings. For how-to info, go to http://vrtweb.rd.go.th/index.php/en/.

Shopping by Neighbourhood

➡ **Banglamphu** (p87) Home to a couple of souvenir shops, not to mention the streetside wares of Th Khao San.

➡ **Chinatown** (p106) Street markets with a flea-market feel.

➡ **Siam Square, Pratunam, Phloen Chit & Ratchathewi** (p121) Simply put: malls, malls and more malls.

➡ **Riverside, Silom & Lumphini** (p137) The place to go for antiques and art.

➡ **Sukhumvit** (p153) Upscale malls and touristy street markets.

Lonely Planet's Top Choices

Chatuchak Weekend Market (p158) One of the world's largest markets.

MBK Center (p121) The Thai market in a mall.

Thanon Khao San Market (p87) Handicrafts, souvenirs and backpacker essentials.

Siam Square (p121) Ground zero for teen fashion in Bangkok.

Siam Discovery (p121) The recently renovated Discovery is the city's most image-conscious mall.

Best Antiques

River City (p139) The mall dedicated to beautiful ancient stuff.

House of Chao (p138) Shophouse full of one-of-a-kind aged items.

Talat Rot Fai 2 (p165) The kitschier side of the antique trade.

Best Cheap Stuff

Sampeng Lane (p103) Everything Made in China.

Baiyoke Garment Center (p123) Bargain-bin cloth and clothing.

Phahurat (p103) Bangkok's textile market.

Best Clothing

Siam Center (p121) The 3rd floor of this mall is one of the best locations to check out established local labels.

Gin & Milk (p123) One-stop shop for domestic menswear.

Baiyoke Garment Center (p123) More T-shirts than you've ever seen in one location, ever.

Platinum Fashion Mall (p122) Seemingly endless stalls of cheap togs.

Best Food & Drink

Nittaya Thai Curry (p87) Curry pastes, conveniently packaged for transit.

Chiang Heng (p139) Old-school shop proffering Thai kitchenwares.

Or Tor Kor Market (p161) The city's most upscale fresh market.

Best Gadgets

Pantip Plaza (p123) The city's biggest marketplace for computer goods.

Fortune Town (p165) Specialising in cameras and tech equipment.

Siam Paragon (p121) Basic tech needs can be satisfied here

Best Homewares & Handicrafts

ThaiCraft Fair (p153) A one-stop shop for Thai handicrafts.

Everyday by Karmakamet (p138) Candles and other scented items.

Heritage Craft (p87) High-quality handicrafts from upcountry.

Sop Moei Arts (p154) Handcrafted textiles and baskets from northern Thailand.

Thann (p122) Soaps, shampoos and other fragrant items.

Best Malls

Siam Paragon (p121) 'Mall' doesn't quite capture the essence of this immense, commerce-themed urban park.

CentralWorld (p122) One of the biggest malls in Southeast Asia: come for the shopping, stay for the ice rink.

Terminal 21 (p154) Wacky airport-themed mall equipped for both commerce and selfies.

Emquartier (p154) Where Bangkok's elite shop to be seen.

Best Markets

Pak Khlong Talat (p101) The capital's famous flower market; come late at night and don't forget your camera.

Talat Mai (p101) This frenetic fresh market is a slice of China.

Nonthaburi Market (p161) An authentic upcountry market only minutes from Bangkok.

Khlong Toey Market (p144) The city's largest fresh market.

Best One-of-a-Kind Souvenirs

Another Story (p153) Hip Thai fashion items and stationery.

it's going green (p122) Retro-themed domestic homewares.

ZudRangMa Records (p153) Pick up some vinyl or an exotic compilation at the headquarters of this eponymous music label.

Objects of Desire Store (p122) Unique design objects made by Thai hands.

The Selected (p122) Domestic clothing labels and other related knick-knacks.

Best Tailors

Tailor on Ten (p153) Has earned an excellent reputation for its quality work.

Pinky Tailors (p123) Long-standing, reliable stitcher.

Raja's Fashions (p153) Where ambassadors, foreign politicians and officers get suited.

July (p139) Tailor to Thailand's royalty.

Rajawongse (p153) Go-to venue for quality bespoke threads.

Duly (p153) Lauded shirtmakers utilising high-quality Itanlian fabrics.

Sports & Activities

Seen all the big sights? Eaten enough pàt tai for a lifetime? When you're done taking it all in, consider some of Bangkok's more active pursuits. Massages and spa visits are justifiably a huge draw, but the city is also home to some great guided tours and courses, the latter in subjects ranging from Thai cookery to meditation.

Jogging

Lumphini Park (p129) and Benjakiti Park (p144) host early-morning and late-evening runners. For something more social, one of Bangkok's longest-running sports groups is the **Hash House Harriers** (www.bangkok hhh.com), which puts on weekly runs.

Cycling

A bike path circles Benjakiti Park (p144) and cycling is allowed in Lumphini Park (p129) between 10am and 3pm. Cyclists also have their own hash, with the **Bangkok Hash House Bikers** (www.bangkokbikehash.org) meeting one Sunday a month for a 40km to 50km mountain-bike ride and post-ride refreshments.

Gyms

Bangkok has plenty of gyms, ranging in style from long-running, open-air affairs in spaces such as Lumphini Park to ultramodern mega-agyms complete with high-tech equipment. Most large hotels have gyms and swimming pools, as do a growing number of small hotels.

Yoga & Pilates

Yoga studios – and enormous accompanying billboards of smiling gurus – have popped up faster than mushrooms at a Full Moon Party. Expect to pay about 500B for a one-off class.

Golf

Bangkok's outer suburbs are well stocked with golf courses, with green fees ranging from 250B to 5000B, plus the customary 200B tip for caddies. The website Thai Golfer (www.thaigolfer.com) rates every course in Thailand (click through to 'Course Reviews').

Spas & Massage

According to the teachings of traditional Thai healing, the use of herbs and massage should be part of a regular health-and-beauty regimen, not just an excuse for pampering. In other words, you need no excuse to get a massage in Bangkok, and it's just as well, because the city could mount a strong claim to being the massage capital of the world. Exactly what type of massage you're after is another question. Variations range from store-front traditional Thai massage to an indulgent 'spa experience' with service and style. And even within the enormous spa category there are many options: there's plenty of pampering going around, but some spas now focus more on the medical than the sensory, while plush resort-style spas offer a menu of appealing beauty treatments.

Tours

GUIDED TOURS

If you're not travelling with a group but would like a guide, recommended outfits include **Tour with Tong** (☏081 835 0240; tours from 1000B), whose team of guides conducts tours in and around Bangkok, and **Thai Private Tour Guide** (☏082 799 1099; www.thaitourguide.com; tours from 2000B), whose guides have garnered heaps of positive feedback.

WALKING/SPECIALITY TOURS

Although the pollution and heat are significant obstacles, Bangkok is a fascinating city to explore on foot. If you'd rather do it with an expert guide, **Bangkok Private Tours** (www.bangkokprivatetours.com; tours from US$190) and Co van Kessel Bangkok Tours (p140) conduct themed walking tours of the city. Foodies will appreciate the offerings at **Bangkok Food Tours** (☏095 943 9222; www.bangkokfoodtours.com; tours from 1150B) or **Chili Paste Tours** (☏085 143 6779, 094 552 2361; www.foodtoursbangkok.com; tours from 2000B), both of which offer culinary tours of Bangkok's older neighbourhoods.

BICYCLE TOURS

You might be wondering who the hell would want to get on a bike and subject themself to the notorious traffic jams and sauna-like conditions of Bangkok's streets. But the fact that they sound so unlikely is part of what makes these trips so cool. The other part is that you discover a whole side of the city that's virtually off limits to four-wheeled transport. Routes include unusual circuits around Chinatown and Ko Ratanakosin, but the pick are journeys across the river to Thonburi and, in particular, to the Phrapradaeng Peninsula. Better known as Bang Kachao, this exquisite expanse of mangrove, banana and coconut plantations lies just a stone's throw from the frantic city centre, on the opposite side of Mae Nam Chao Phraya. You cycle to the river, take a boat to Bang Kachao and then follow elevated concrete paths that zigzag through the growth to a local village for lunch.

Several companies run regular, well-received tours starting at about 1000B for a half-day.

RIVER & CANAL TRIPS

The cheapest and most obvious way to commute between riverside attractions is on the commuter boats run by Chao Phraya Express Boat (p238). The terminus for most

NEED TO KNOW

....

Bookings

Long-term courses, like language or meditation, should ideally be booked a month or so in advance to ensure vacancies. Shorter courses, including cookery courses and most guided tours, can be arranged a few days in advance. Massage and spa treatments can often be booked on the same day.

Websites

➡ **BK** (www.bk.asia-city.com) Check this listings mag to see what active events are on when you're in town.

➡ **Bicycle Thailand** (www.bicyclethailand.com) The best resource for cycling in the kingdom.

northbound boats is Nonthaburi Pier, while for most southbound boats it's Sathon Pier (also called Central Pier), near the Saphan Taksin BTS station (although some boats run as far south as Wat Ratchasingkhon).

For a more personal view, you might consider chartering a long-tail boat along the city's canals. Alternatively, Pandan Tour (p76) offers 'small-boat', full-day private tours of Bangkok's canals. Another option is one of the dinner cruises that ply Mae Nam Chao Phraya at night.

Courses

MEDITATION

Although most of the time Bangkok seems like the most un-Buddhist place on earth, there are a few places where foreigners can practise Theravada Buddhist meditation. Some, like Center Meditation Wat Mahadhatu (p75) allow drop-ins on a daily basis, while others, such as House of Dhamma (p166), require advance notice.

THAI BOXING

Training in *moo·ay tai* (Thai boxing; also spelt *muay Thai*) for foreigners has increased in popularity in the last decade and many camps all over the country are tailoring their programs for English-speaking fighters of both sexes. Food and accommodation can often be provided for an extra charge. The website Muay Thai Camps (www.muaythaicampsthailand.com) contains detailed information on Thailand's various training centres.

BANGKOK BIKE CITY

Despite the obvious deterrents of heat, pollution, lack of proper infrastructure and deadly streets, over the last few years, cycling has exploded in popularity in Bangkok. Bike sales are booming, the 23km bicycle track that circles Suvarnabhumi International Airport was (yet again) being upgraded at the time of research, and a Bangkok cycling event in mid-2015 drew nearly 40,000 participants. And keen-eyed bicycle enthusiasts may have noticed a new, green, protected, bike-only lane that runs along parts of Banglamphu and Ko Ratanakosin.

The track is part of Pun Pun (www.punpunbikeshare.com), an initiative that includes 50 bicycle-hire stations across town and a clearly marked (although not always protected) bike path. To borrow a bike, you'll first need to register online. You then pick up a smartcard at one of eight staffed stations. The card costs 320B and includes 100B of credit; the bikes are free for the first 15 minutes, then cost approximately 10B per subsequent hour.

Alternatively, if you want to join Bangkok's two-wheeled revolution but are too intimidated to go at it alone, consider an excursion with one of the city's well-established bike touring outfits (p48).

COOKING

Having consumed everything Bangkok has to offer is one thing, but imagine the points you'll rack up if you can make the same dishes for your friends back at home. A visit to a Thai cooking school has become a must-do on many Bangkok itineraries and for some visitors it's a highlight of their trip.

Courses range in price and value, but a typical half-day course should include at least a basic introduction to Thai ingredients and flavours and a hands-on chance to both prepare and cook several dishes. Nearly all lessons include a set of printed recipes and end with a communal lunch consisting of your handiwork.

THAI LANGUAGE

Although their courses generally involve a pretty serious time commitment, several schools in Bangkok specialise in teaching Thai to foreigners, including Union Language School (p124) and AAA (p124).

THAI MASSAGE

Few places in Bangkok offer English-language instruction in Thai-style massage; the exceptions include Chetawan Traditional Massage School (p76) and Phussapa Thai Massage School (p155).

Sports & Activities by Neighbourhood

➡ **Ko Ratanakosin & Thonburi** (p75) Canal- and river-based boat tours and Thai massage.

➡ **Banglamphu** (p87) Bike tours.

➡ **Sukhumvit** (p155) This street is home to Bangkok's greatest variety of good-quality massage studios and spas.

➡ **Northern Bangkok** (p166) The suburbs are where you'll find Bangkok's most serious Thai boxing schools.

Lonely Planet's Top Choices

Amita Thai Cooking Class (p75) Thai cooking course led by charming hosts in a beautiful, home-based location.

Oriental Spa (p140) Riverside spa that sets the standard for luxury and pampering.

Eight Limbs (p155) A tiny but reputable ring for *moo·ay tai*.

Health Land (p140) Quite possibly one of the best-value massage studios in the world.

Co van Kessel Bangkok Tours (p140) Tours of Bangkok that span foot, bicycle and boat.

Best Courses

Chetawan Traditional Massage School (p76) Learn Thai massage steps at one of Bangkok's most famous temples.

Phussapa Thai Massage School (p155) A deep dive into Thai-style healing.

Union Language School (p124) Learn to talk to the locals.

MuayThai Institute (p166) A premier institution for instruction in Thai boxing.

Best Bicycle Tours

Grasshopper Adventures (p89) Lauded bike tours of Bangkok's lesser-known corners.

ABC Amazing Bangkok Cyclists (p155) Guided excursions in Bangkok's back alleys.

Velo Thailand (p89) Two-wheeled day and night tours of Bangkok.

Best for Kids

KidZania (p24) Impressively multi-faceted 'edutainment' for kids.

Fun-arium (p24) Play centre with a good rep.

Sea Life Ocean World (p122) For budding oceanographers.

Stanley MiniVenture (p25) The world in miniature for the little ones.

Dream World (p161) Bangkok's premier amusement park.

Children's Discovery Museum (p161) Where kids have fun and and learn in equal measure.

Best Moo·ay Tai (Thai Boxing)

MuayThai Institute (p166) Serious tuition in Thailand's national sport.

Fairtex Muay Thai (p166) Respected training centre for Thai boxing.

Jaroenthong Muay Thai Gym (p87) Shiny new training centre dedicated to *moo·ay tai*.

Best Spas

Spa 1930 (p124) Cosy spa located in an atmospheric traditional house.

Thann Sanctuary (p124) Chic, mall-bound spa employing the eponymous brand's fragrant herbal products.

Divana Massage & Spa (p154) Semi-concealed, classy spa.

Lavana (p154) Specialises in traditional Thai healing using herbal compresses.

Rakuten (p154) Japanese-themed spa.

Best Thai-Style Massage

Ruen-Nuad Massage Studio (p141) Charming, reputable massage studio.

Asia Herb Association (p154) Massage with an emphasis on Thai-style herbal compresses.

Coran (p154) Serious Thai massage in a homely-feeling villa.

LGBT Bangkok

Bangkok has a notoriously pink vibe to it. From kinky male-underwear shops mushrooming at street corners to lesbian-only get-togethers, as a LGBT person you could eat, shop and play here for days without ever leaving the comfort of gay-friendly venues. Unlike elsewhere in Southeast Asia, homosexuality is not criminalised in Thailand and the general attitude remains extremely laissez-faire.

The Scene

Gay people are out and ubiquitous in Bangkok. Yet gay and lesbian couples, like straight couples, do not show public affection, unless they are purposefully flouting social mores.

TRANSGENDER PEOPLE

Bangkok is famous for its open and visible communities of *gà·teu·i* (also spelt *kàthoey*), a term encompassing cross-dressers as well as some transgender people who may have had sex-reassignment surgery (Thailand is one of the leading countries for this procedure). *Gà·teu·i* cabarets aimed at tourists are common, fuelled by foreign fascination for *gà·teu·i*. Due to many references in popular culture, 'ladyboy' is often used to reference *gà·teu·i* in English, though the term is disliked by many. It's also worth noting that Thai transgender women may not refer to themselves as *gà·teu·i*.

LESBIANS

Although it would be a stretch to claim that Bangkok's lesbian scene is as vibrant as its male gay scene, lesbians have become more visible in recent years. It's worth noting that, perhaps because Thailand is still a relatively conservative place, lesbians in Bangkok generally adhere to rather strict gender roles. Overtly 'butch' lesbians, called *tom* (from 'tomboy'), typically have short hair, bind their breasts and wear men's clothing. Femme lesbians refer to themselves as *dêe* (from 'lady'). Visiting lesbians who don't fit into one of these categories may find themselves met with confusion.

Issues

Beneath the party vibe, serious issues remain for Bangkok's vast and visible population of LGBT people. After the government's initial success slowing the progression of HIV among the general population, there are new signs of an epidemic among young gay men. Transgender people are often treated as outcasts, same-sex couples enjoy no legal rights and lesbians have the added burden of negotiating a patriarchal society. In short, Bangkok's LGBT community may party as they please, sleep with whomever they want or even change their sex, but they do so without the protection, respect and rights enjoyed by heterosexuals – particularly heterosexual men.

Festivals

The single biggest event of the year is the Bangkok Pride Festival, slated for May, but sometimes held in October or November. An alternative is the annual party, coinciding with Songkran, that is put on by gCircuit (www.gcircuit.com).

LGBT by Neighbourhood

➡ **Riverside, Silom & Lumphini** (p136) Lower Th Silom is Bangkok's unofficial gaybourhood.

➡ **Greater Bangkok & Th Ratchadaphisek** (p164) Home to suburban Bangkok's gay scenes.

Lonely Planet's Top Choices

DJ Station (p136) One of the most iconic gay nightclubs in Asia.

Telephone Pub (p136) Long-standing bar right in the middle of Bangkok's pinkest zone.

Playhouse Magical Cabaret (p165) The city's premier drag show.

Best Gay & Lesbian Bars

The Stranger (p136) Probably the most low-key, sophisticated venue on Soi 4.

Balcony (p136) Streetside watering hole for local and visiting gays.

Maggie Choo's (p135) Sunday is gay day at this otherwise-hetero boozer.

Best Gay & Lesbian Dance Clubs

G Bangkok (p136) Where to go after all the other Silom bars have closed.

Fake Club The Next Gen (p164) Suburban megaclub in handsome new digs.

Banana Bar on 4 (p136) Chill dance club on the city's gayest street.

NEED TO KNOW

Websites

➡ Bangkok Lesbian (www.bangkoklesbian. com) is the city's premier website for ladies who love ladies.

➡ BK (www.bk.asia-city. com) and Siam2nite (www.siam2nite.com) are good sources for LGBT events in Bangkok.

➡ Trasher (www.face book.com/trasher bangkok) are noted pop parodists; they also organise gay-friendly parties – check the website to see if one's on when you're in town.

Other Resources

Look for entertainment tips in local listings rags such as BK (www.bk.asia-city. com) and the *Bangkok Post*'s Friday supplement, *Guru* (www.bangkokpost. com/guru).

Varying locales play host to weekend-long 'circuit parties'. See gCircuit (www. gcircuit.com).

PLAN YOUR TRIP LGBT BANGKOK

Explore Bangkok

BANGKOK'S
TOP SIGHTS

Neighbourhoods at a Glance

is a seemingly forgotten yet visit-worthy zone of sleepy residential districts connected by *klorng* (canals; also spelt *khlong*).

❶ Ko Ratanakosin & Thonburi p58

The artificial island of Ko Ratanakosin is Bangkok's birthplace, and the Buddhist temples and royal palaces here comprise some of the city's most important and most visited sights. By contrast, Thonburi, located across Mae Nam Chao Phraya (Chao Phraya River),

❷ Banglamphu p77

Leafy lanes, antique shophouses, buzzing wet markets and golden temples convene in Banglamphu – easily the city's most quintessentially 'Bangkok' neighbourhood. It's a quaint postcard picture of the city that

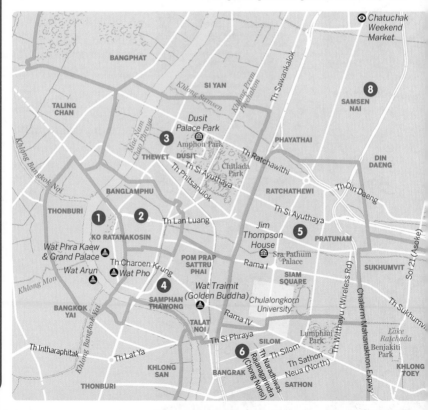

used to be, that is until you stumble upon Th Khao San, arguably the world's most famous backpacker enclave.

3 Thewet & Dusit p90

With its wide boulevards, manicured parks, imposing palaces and statues dedicated to former kings, Dusit has a knack for making you second-guess what city you're in. The reality check comes in neighbouring Thewet, where its soggy riverside setting, busy wet market and relentless traffic are classic Bangkok.

4 Chinatown p98

Although many generations removed from the motherland, Bangkok's Chinatown could be a bosom buddy of any Chinese city. The streets are crammed with bird's-nest restaurants, gaudy gold and jade shops, and flashing neon signs in Chinese characters.

It's Bangkok's most hectic neighbourhood, where half the fun is getting completely lost.

5 Siam Square, Pratunam, Phloen Chit & Ratchathewi p108

Multistorey malls, outdoor shopping precincts and never-ending markets leave no doubt that Siam Square, Pratunam and Phloen Chit combine to form Bangkok's commercial district. The BTS (Skytrain) interchange at Siam has also made this area the centre of modern Bangkok, while only a few blocks away, scruffy Ratchathewi has a lot more in common with provincial Thai cities.

6 Riverside, Silom & Lumphini p125

Although you may not see it behind the office blocks, high-rises and hotels, Mae Nam Chao Phraya forms a watery backdrop to these neighbourhoods. History is still palpable in the riverside area's crumbling architecture, while heading inland, Silom, Bangkok's de facto financial district, is frenetic and modern, Th Sathon is the much more subdued embassy zone and Lumphini is dominated by central Bangkok's largest green zone.

7 Sukhumvit p142

Japanese enclaves, burger joints, Middle Eastern nightlife zones, tacky 'sexpat' haunts: it's all here along Th Sukhumvit, Bangkok's unofficial international district. Where temples and suburban rice fields used to be, today you'll also find shopping centres, nightlife and other amenities that cater to middle-class Thais and resident foreigners.

8 Northern Bangkok p156

Once ringed by rice fields, modern Bangkok has since expanded in every possible direction with few concessions to agriculture or charm. Within northern Bangkok, other than some of the city's best markets, sights are relatively few, but the upside is that the area is a good place to get a taste of provincial Thailand if you don't have the time to go upcountry. If you're into Thai boxing, the Lumpinee Boxing Stadium relocated here in 2014.

Ko Ratanakosin & Thonburi

Neighbourhood Top Five

1 **Wat Pho** (p60) Trying to stop your jaw from dropping to the floor upon encountering the enormous Reclining Buddha for the first time.

2 **Wat Phra Kaew** (p64) Basking in the glow of the Emerald Buddha at Thailand's most sacred temple.

3 **Wat Arun** (p69) Getting up close and personal with this iconic riverside temple.

4 **Amulet Market** (p70) Picking up a unique souvenir at one of Bangkok's most unique markets.

5 **Museum of Siam** (p70) Learning about the origins of the Thai people and their culture.

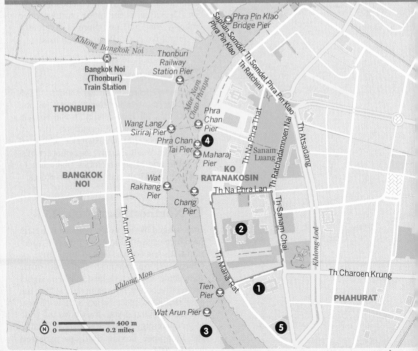

For more detail of this area see Map p265 ➡

Explore Ko Ratanakosin & Thonburi

The birthplace of Bangkok, the artificial island of Ko Ratanakosin is where it all started more than 200 years ago. The remnants of this history – today Bangkok's biggest sights – draw just about every visitor to the city. The big-hitters, the Wat Phra Kaew and Grand Palace complex and Wat Pho, are a short walk from the Chao Phraya Express Boat piers at Chang Pier, Maharaj Pier and Tien Pier, and are within walking distance of each other, although the hot sun may make doing this a more demanding task than it appears. Alternatively, túk-túk (pronounced *đúk đúk*) are a dime a dozen around here. If you're planning to visit several sights, it's a good idea to arrive early in the morning for the cooler weather and to avoid the crowds. Evening is best for photography, particularly if you're hoping for the classic sunset shot of Wat Arun.

Located across the river, neighbouring Thonburi has significantly less to offer in terms of sights, but is great for those who fancy urban exploration. The area is accessible via the 3B river-crossing ferries at Chang Pier and Tien Pier.

Local Life

➜ **Cross the River** Ko Ratanakosin is probably Bangkok's most touristy neighbourhood, but hop on any of the 3B river-crossing ferries and you'll be whisked to Thonburi, where regular Thai life carries on uninterrupted.

➜ **Dance Floor** Lak Meuang (p73) receives daily supplications from Thai worshippers, some of whom commission classical Thai dancers to perform *lá·kon gâa bon* (shrine dancing) as thanks for granted wishes.

➜ **Life Aquatic** Thonburi remains home to several *klorng* (canals; also spelt *khlong*) that once were responsible for Bangkok's former nickname, 'Venice of the East'. As Bangkok changes at a rapid pace, Thonburi's canals serve as something of a time capsule.

Getting There & Away

➜ **Chao Phraya Express Boat** To Ko Ratanakosin: Tien Pier, Chang Pier, Maharaj Pier and Phra Chan Tai Pier. To Thonburi: Wang Lang/Siriraj Pier, Thonburi Railway Station Pier and Phra Pin Klao Bridge Pier. Several cross-river ferries also connect to Bangkok piers.

➜ **BTS (Skytrain)** To Thonburi: Krung Thonburi and Wongwian Yai. To Ko Ratanakosin: National Stadium or Phaya Thai and taxi.

➜ **Bus** To Ko Ratanakosin: air-con 503, 508 and 511; ordinary 3, 25, 39, 47 and 53. To Thonburi: air-con 507 and 509; ordinary 21, 42 and 82.

➜ **Taxi** Best taken outside of rush hours.

Lonely Planet's Top Tip

Anyone standing outside any of the big sights in Ko Ratanakosin who claims that the sight is closed is either a gem tout or con artist – ignore them and proceed inside.

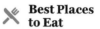

Best Places to Eat

➜ Tonkin-Annam (p74)
➜ Dao Tai (p74)
➜ Pa Aew (p74)
➜ Err (p74)
➜ Ming Lee (p74)
➜ Navy Club (p75)

For reviews, see p74 ➡

Best Drinking & Nightlife

➜ Roof (p75)
➜ Amorosa (p75)

For reviews, see p75 ➡

Best Museums

➜ Museum of Siam (p70)
➜ National Museum (p71)
➜ Siriraj Medical Museum (p70)

For reviews, see p70 ➡

TOP SIGHT
WAT PHO

Of all Bangkok's temples, Wat Pho is arguably the one most worth visiting, for both its remarkable Reclining Buddha image and its sprawling, stupa-studded grounds. The temple compound boasts a long list of credits: the oldest and largest *wát* in Bangkok; the longest Reclining Buddha and the largest collection of Buddha images in Thailand; and the country's first public education institution.

DON'T MISS

➡ Reclining Buddha
➡ Granite statues
➡ Massage pavilions

PRACTICALITIES

➡ วัดโพธิ์/วัดพระเชตุพน, Wat Phra Chetuphon
➡ Map p265, D5
➡ Th Sanam Chai
➡ admission 100B
➡ ⏱8.30am-6.30pm
➡ 🚢Tien Pier

Reclining Buddha

Located in the compound's main *wí·hǎhn* (sanctuary), the genuinely impressive Reclining Buddha, 46m long and 15m high, illustrates the passing of the Buddha into nirvana (ie the Buddha's death). Completed in 1848 and still holding the title of Bangkok's largest Reclining Buddha, the figure is modelled out of plaster around a brick core and is finished in gold leaf. Mother-of-pearl inlay ornaments the feet, displaying the 108 different *lák·sà·nà* (characteristics) of a Buddha. Continuing the numerical theme, behind the statue are 108 bronze monk bowls; for 20B you can buy 108 coins, each of which is dropped in a bowl for good luck.

Phra Ubosot

Though built during the reign of Rama I (King Phraphutthayotfa Chulalok; r 1782–1809) and influenced by the Ayuthaya school of architecture, the *bòht* (ordination hall) as it stands today is the result of extensive renovations dating back to the reign of Rama III (King Phranangklao; r 1824-51). Inside you'll find impressive murals and a three-tiered pedestal supporting Phra Buddha Deva Patimakorn, the compound's second-most noteworthy Buddha statue, as well as the ashes of Rama I.

Royal Chedi

On the western side of the grounds is a collection of four towering tiled *chedi* (stupa) commemorating the first four Chakri kings. Note the square bell shape with distinct corners, a signature of Ratanakosin style, and the titles emulating the colours of the Buddhist flag. The middle *chedi* is dedicated to Rama I and encases Phra Si Sanphet Dayarn, a 16m-high standing Buddha image from Ayuthaya. The compound's 91 smaller *chedi* include clusters containing the ashes of lesser royal descendants.

Ancient Inscriptions

Encircling Phra Ubosot is a low marble wall with 152 bas-reliefs depicting scenes from the *Ramakian,* the Thai version of the *Ramayana.* You'll recognise some of these figures when you exit the temple past the hawkers with mass-produced rubbings for sale: these are made from cement casts based on Wat Pho's reliefs.

Nearby, a small pavilion west of Phra Ubosot has Unesco-awarded inscriptions detailing the tenets of traditional Thai massage. These and as many as 2000 other stone inscriptions covering various aspects of traditional Thai knowledge led to Wat Pho's legacy as Thailand's first public university.

Phra Mondop

Also known as *hǒr đrai,* and serving as a depository for Buddhist scriptures, the elevated Phra Mondop is guarded by four *yaksha* (giants). Legend has it that an argument between the four led to the clearing of the area known today as Tha Tien. Just south of the Phra Mondop is the currently reptile-free Crocodile Pond.

Sala Kan Parian

Located in the southwestern corner of the compound is Sala Kan Parian, one of the few remaining structures that predates Rama III's extensive 19th-century renovation/expansion of then Wat Pho Tharam. Built in the Ayuthaya style, the structure formerly functioned as the wát's primary *bòht,* and held the temple compound's primary Buddha statue.

Top Tips

➡ Arrive early to avoid the crowds and to take advantage of the (relatively) cool weather.

➡ Don't just gawk at the Reclining Buddha and call it a day: Wat Pho's fantastical, almost mazelike grounds are also part of the experience, and are home to some less hyped but worthwhile treasures.

WAT PHO'S GRANITE STATUES

Aside from monks and sightseers, Wat Pho is filled with an altogether stiffer crowd: dozens of giants (*yaksha*) and figurines carved from granite. The rock giants first arrived in Thailand as ballast aboard Chinese junks and were put to work in Wat Pho (and other wát, including Wat Suthat), guarding the entrances of temple gates and courtyards.

At what other sacred religious sight in the world can you get a massage? Wat Pho is the national headquarters for the teaching of traditional Thai medicine, which includes Thai massage. The famous school has two massage pavilions (p76) located within the temple compound and additional rooms within a training facility (p76) outside the temple, providing a unique opportunity to combine relaxation with sightseeing.

TAKE A BREAK

You'd be wise to combine your visit to Wat Pho with lunch, specifically lunch at Pa Aew (p74), an open-air stall that serves tasty Bangkok-style curries and stir-fries.

Wat Pho

A WALK THROUGH THE BIG BUDDHAS OF WAT PHO

The logical starting place is the main *wi·hǎhn* (sanctuary), home to Wat Pho's centre piece, the immense **① Reclining Buddha**. In addition to its enormous size, note the **② mother-of-pearl inlay** on the soles of the statue's feet. The interior walls of the *wi·hǎhn* are covered with murals that depict previous lives of the Buddha, and along the south side of the structure there are 108 bronze monk bowls; for 20B you can buy 108 coins, each of which is dropped in a bowl for good luck.

Exit the *wi·hǎhn* and head east via the two **③ stone giants** who guard the gateway to the rest of the compound. Directly south of these are the four towering **④ royal chedi**.

Phra Ubosot
Built during the reign of Rama I, the imposing *bòht* (ordination hall) as it stands today is the result of renovations dating back to the reign of Rama III (r 1824–51).

Southern *wi·hǎhn*

Buddha Galleries
The two series of covered hallways that surround the Phra Ubosot feature no fewer than 394 gilded Buddha images, many of which display classic Ayuthaya or Sukhothai features.

Eastern *wi·hǎhn*

Massage Pavilions
If you're hot and footsore, the two air-conditioned massage pavilions are a welcome way to cool down while experiencing high-quality and relatively inexpensive Thai massage.

Phra Buddha Deva Patimakorn
On an impressive three-tiered pedestal that also holds the ashes of Rama I is this Ayuthaya-era Buddha statue originally brought to the temple by the monarch.

Northern *wi·hǎhn*

Western *wi·hǎhn*

Continue east, passing through two consecutive 5 **galleries of Buddha statues** linking four *wí·hăhn*, two of which contain notable Sukhothai-era Buddha statues; these comprise the exterior of 6 **Phra Ubosot**, the immense ordination hall that is Wat Pho's second-most noteworthy structure. The base of the building is surrounded by bas-relief inscriptions, and inside is the notable Buddha statue, 7 **Phra Buddha Deva Patimakorn**.

Wat Pho is often referred to as Thailand's first university, a tradition that continues today in an associated traditional Thai medicine school and, at the compound's eastern extent, two 8 **massage pavilions**.

Interspersed throughout the eastern half of the compound are several additional minor *chedi* and rock gardens.

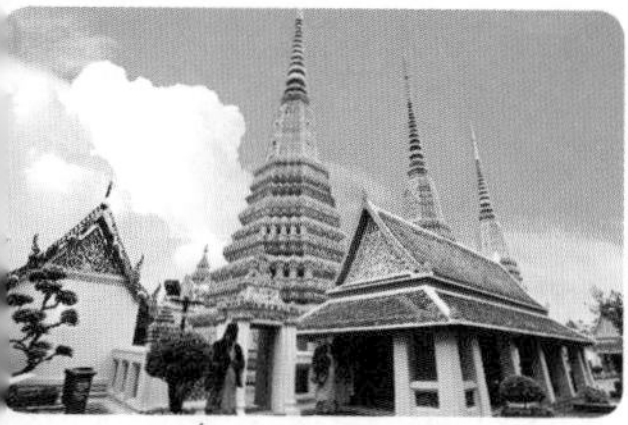

TAKEPICSFORFUN / GETTY IMAGES ©

Royal Chedi
Decorated in coloured tiles in a classic example of Ratanakosin style, these four *chedi* are meant to represent the first four kings of the Chakri dynasty.

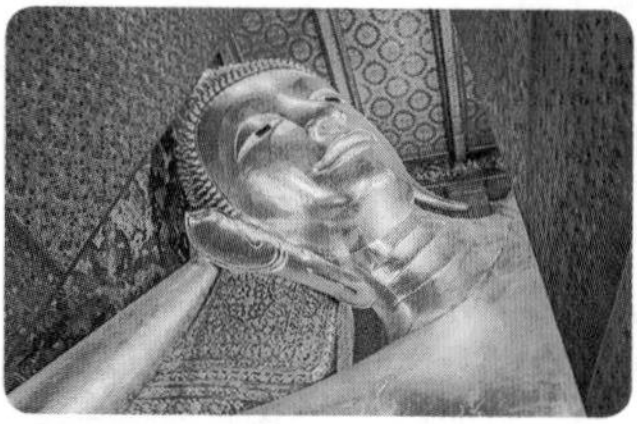

SAMART BOONYANG / GETTY IMAGES ©

Reclining Buddha
Modelled around a brick core 46m long and 15m high and finished in plaster and gold leaf, Wat Pho's Reclining Buddha is an imposing reminder of the Buddha's passing into nirvana (the Buddha's death).

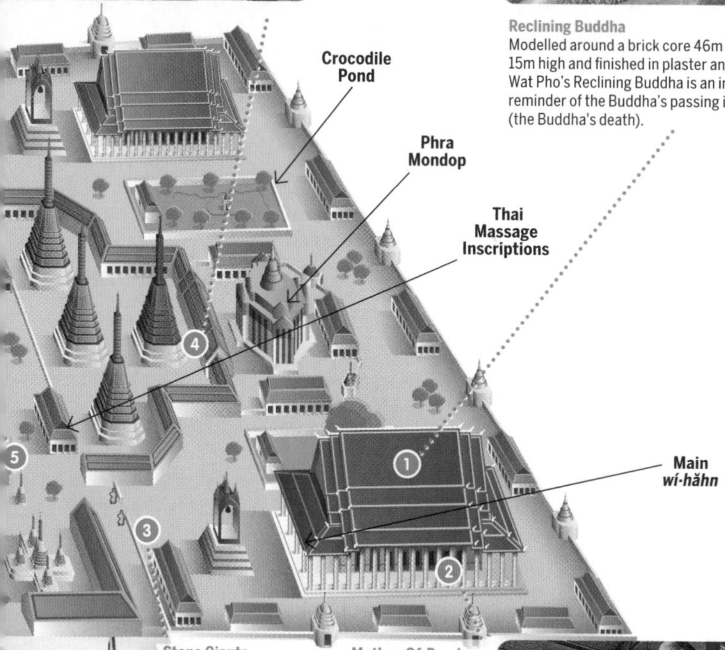
Crocodile Pond
Phra Mondop
Thai Massage Inscriptions
Main *wí·hăhn*
1
2
3
4
5

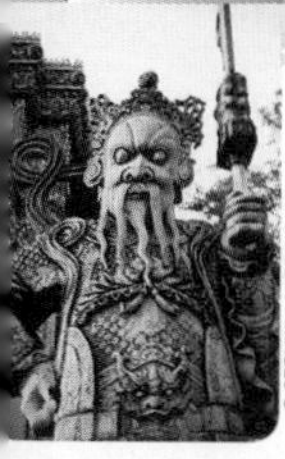

IMAGE SOURCE / GETTY IMAGES ©

Stone Giants
These huge granite figures – depictions range from Chinese opera characters to Marco Polo – originally arrived in Thailand in the 19th century as ballast aboard Chinese junks.

Mother-Of-Pearl Inlay
The 108 auspicious *lák·sà·nà*, physical characteristics of the Buddha, are depicted on the soles of the feet of the Reclining Buddha.

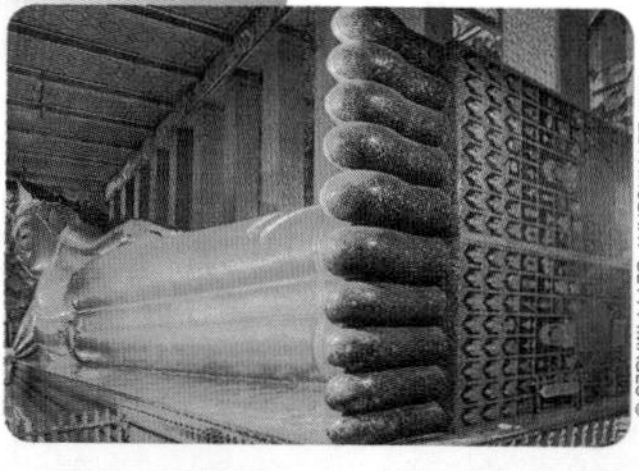

KAMPEE PATISENA / GETTY IMAGES ©

TOP SIGHT
WAT PHRA KAEW & GRAND PALACE

Also known as the Temple of the Emerald Buddha, Wat Phra Kaew is the colloquial name of the vast fairy-tale-like compound that also includes the former residence of the Thai monarch, the Grand Palace. The ground was consecrated in 1782, the first year of Bangkok rule, and is today Bangkok's biggest tourist attraction and a pilgrimage destination for devout Buddhists and nationalists.

Wat Phra Kaew

The Guardians of Wat Phra Kaew

The first sights you'll see upon entering Wat Phra Kaew are two 5m-high *yaksha* (giants or ogres) with origins in Hindu/Buddhist mythology. Other mythical creatures in the temple compound include the half-human, half-bird *kinnaree* and the sacred birds known as *garuda,* not to mention various hermits and elephants.

Ramakian Murals

Recently restored murals of the *Ramakian* (the Thai version of the Indian epic the *Ramayana*) line the inside walls of the Wat Phra Kaew compound. Originally painted during the reign of Rama I (King Phraphutthayotfa Chulalok; r 1782–1809), the 178 sections, beginning at the north gate and moving clockwise around the compound, describe the struggles of the hero Rama to rescue his kidnapped wife, Sita.

Phra Mondop

Commissioned by Rama I, this structure was built for the storage of sacred Buddhist manuscripts. The seven-tiered roof, floor woven from strands of silver, and intricate mother-of-pearl

DON'T MISS...

- ➡ Emerald Buddha
- ➡ *Ramakian* murals
- ➡ Grand Palace structures

PRACTICALITIES

- ➡ วัดพระแก้ว, พระบรมมหาราชวัง
- ➡ Map p265, C5
- ➡ Th Na Phra Lan
- ➡ admission 500B
- ➡ ⊘8.30am-3.30pm
- ➡ 🚤Chang Pier, Maharaj Pier, Phra Chan Tai Pier

door panels make it among the world's most decadent libraries. The interior of Phra Mondop is closed to the public.

Phra Mondop, along with the neighbouring Khmer-style peak of the Prasat Phra Thep Bidon and the gilded Phra Si Ratana *chedi* (stupa), are the tallest structures in the compound.

The Emerald Buddha

On a tall platform in Wat Phra Kaew's fantastically decorated *bòht* (ordination hall), the Emerald Buddha is the temple's primary attraction. The spectacular ornamentation inside and out does an excellent job of distracting first-time visitors from paying their respects to the image. Here's why: the Emerald Buddha is only 66cm tall and sits so high above worshippers in the main temple building that the gilded shrine is more striking than the small figure it cradles. Despite the name, the statue is actually carved from a single piece of nephrite, a type of jade.

No one knows exactly where it came from or who sculpted it, but it first appeared on record in 15th-century Chiang Rai in northern Thailand. Stylistically it seems to belong to Thai artistic periods of the 13th to 14th centuries.

The *bòht* itself is a notable example of the Rattanakosin school of architecture, which combines stylistic holdovers from Ayuthaya along with modern touches from China and the West.

Grand Palace

Borombhiman Hall

This French-inspired structure served as a residence for Rama VI (King Vajiravudh; r 1910–25). The palace was also where Rama VIII (King Ananda Mahidol; r 1935–46) was mysteriously killed in 1946, and in April 1981, General San Chitpatima used it as the headquarters for an attempted coup. Today the structure can only be viewed through iron gates.

Amarindra Hall

Originally a hall of justice, this large, mostly empty hall is used for coronation ceremonies – the most recent occasion being the current king's coronation in 2017. The golden, boat-shaped throne looks considerably more ornate than comfortable.

Chakri Mahaprasat

The largest of the palace buildings is the triple-winged Chakri Mahaprasat (Grand Palace Hall). Completed in 1882 following a plan by British

ROYAL FUNERAL

In October of 2017, the Grand Palace complex and adjacent Sanam Luang served as the setting for the funeral of King Rama IX – possibly one of the most ornate funerals in modern history. The ceremony took a year to plan, saw the construction of a nearly 50m-high gilded pyre, cost a total of US$90 million, and was attended by tens of thousands of mourners.

Because of its royal status, the Emerald Buddha is ceremoniously draped in monastic robes. There are now three royal robes: for the hot, rainy and cool seasons. The three robes are still solemnly changed by the king at the beginning of each season.

TAKE A BREAK

Cap off your visit to Wat Phra Kaew and the Grand Palace with lunch at Ming Lee (p74), a charmingly old-school Thai restaurant located virtually across the street from the complex's main entrance. Alternatively, enjoy a Thai-themed cocktail and a spicy drinking snack at Err (p74).

Wat Phra Kaew & Grand Palace

EXPLORE BANGKOK'S PREMIER MONUMENTS TO RELIGION & REGENCY

The first area tourists enter is the Buddhist temple compound generally referred to as Wat Phra Kaew. A covered walkway surrounds the area, the inner walls of which are decorated with the **1** **2 murals of the Ramakian**. Originally painted during the reign of Rama I (r 1782–1809), the murals, which depict the Hindu epic the *Ramayana*, span 178 panels that describe the struggles of Rama to rescue his kidnapped wife, Sita.

After taking in the story, pass through one of the gateways guarded by **3 yaksha** to the inner compound. The most important structure here is the **4 bòht, or ordination hall**, which houses the **5 Emerald Buddha**.

Kinaree
These graceful half-swan, half-women creatures from Hindu-Buddhist mythology stand outside Prasat Phra Thep Bidon.

Amarindra Hall

Borombhiman Hall

Prasat Phra Thep Bidon

Phra Si Ratana

The Murals of the Ramakian
These wall paintings, which begin at the eastern side of Wat Phra Kaew, often depict scenes more reminiscent of 19th-century Thailand than of ancient India.

Hanuman
Rows of these mischievous monkey deities from Hindu mythology appear to support the lower levels of two small *chedi* near Prasat Phra Thep Bidon.

Head east to the so-called Upper Terrace, an elevated area home to the **6 spires of the three primary chedi**. The middle structure, Phra Mondop, is used to house Buddhist manuscripts. This area is also home to several of Wat Phra Kaew's noteworthy mythical beings, including beckoning **7 kinaree** and several grimacing **8 Hanuman**.

Proceed through the western gate to the compound known as the Grand Palace. Few of the buildings here are open to the public. The most noteworthy structure is **9 Chakri Mahaprasat**. Built in 1882, the exterior of the hall is a unique blend of Western and traditional Thai architecture.

The Three Spires
The elaborate seven-tiered roof of Phra Mondop, the Khmer-style peak of Prasat Phra Thep Bidon, and the gilded Phra Si Ratana *chedi* are the tallest structures in the compound.

LEPNEVA IRINA / SHUTTERSTOCK ©

Emerald Buddha
Despite the name, this diminutive statue (it's only 66cm tall) is actually carved from nephrite, a type of jade.

ALEXEY STIOP / GETTY IMAGES ©

The Death of Thotsakan
The panels progress clockwise, culminating at the western edge of the compound with the death of Thotsakan, Sita's kidnapper, and his elaborate funeral procession.

Chakri Mahaprasat
This structure is sometimes referred to as *fa·ràng sài chá·dah* (Westerner in a Thai crown) because each wing is topped by a *mon·dòp*: a spire representing a Thai adaptation of a Hindu shrine.

DESIGN PICS / BLAKE KENT / GETTY IMAGES ©

Dusit Hall

Yaksha
Each entrance to the Wat Phra Kaew compound is watched over by a pair of vigilant and enormous *yaksha*, ogres or giants from Hindu mythology.

ZZVET / GETTY IMAGES ©

Bòht (Ordination Hall)
This structure is an early example of the Ratanakosin school of architecture, which combines traditional stylistic holdovers from Ayuthaya along with more modern touches from China and the West.

THE TRAVELS OF THE EMERALD BUDDHA

Some time in the 15th century, the Emerald Buddha is said to have been covered with plaster and gold leaf and placed in Chiang Rai's own Wat Phra Kaew. Many valuable Buddha images were masked in this way to deter potential thieves and marauders during unstable times. Often the true identity of the image was forgotten over the years until a 'divine accident' exposed its precious core. The Emerald Buddha experienced such a divine revelation while it was being transported to a new location. In a fall, the plaster covering broke off, revealing the brilliant green inside. But while this was seen as a divine revelation, the return of the Phra Kaew would prove anything but peaceful for the people of Siam and Laos.

During territorial clashes with Laos, the Emerald Buddha was seized and taken to Vientiane in the mid-16th century. Some 200 years later, after the fall of Ayuthaya and the ascension of the Bangkok-based kingdom, the Thai army marched up to Vientiane, razed the city and hauled off the Emerald Buddha. The Buddha was enshrined in the then capital, Thonburi, before the general who led the sacking of Vientiane assumed the throne and had it moved to its current location.

architects, the exterior shows a peculiar blend of Italian Renaissance and Thai architecture that earned it the Thai nickname *fa·ràng sài chá·dah* ('Westerner wearing a Thai classical dancer's headdress'). The central spire contains the ashes of Chakri kings; the flanking spires enshrine the ashes of the many Chakri princes who failed to inherit the throne.

Dusit Hall
The compound's westernmost structure is the Ratanakosin-style Dusit Hall, which initially served as a venue for royal audiences and, later, as a royal funerary hall.

Top Tips
➡ Enter Wat Phra Kaew and the Grand Palace complex through the clearly marked third gate from the river pier. Tickets are purchased inside the complex; anyone telling you it's closed is a gem tout or a con artist.

➡ At Wat Phra Kaew and the Grand Palace grounds, dress rules are strictly enforced. If you're flashing a bit too much skin, expect to be shown into a dressing room and issued with a shirt or sarong (rental is free, but you must provide a refundable 200B deposit).

➡ Admission to the complex includes entrance to Dusit Palace Park.

◉ TOP SIGHT
WAT ARUN

The missile-shaped temple that rises from Mae Nam Chao Phraya's banks is known as Temple of Dawn, and was named after the Indian god of dawn, Aruna. It was here that, after the destruction of Ayuthaya, King Taksin stumbled upon a small local shrine and interpreted the discovery as an auspicious sign that this should be the site of the new capital of Siam.

The Spire

The central feature of Wat Arun is the 82m-high Khmer-style *þrahng* (spire), constructed during the first half of the 19th century by Rama II (King Phraphutthaloetla Naphalai; r 1809–24). From the river it is not apparent that this corn-cob-shaped steeple is adorned with colourful floral murals made of glazed porcelain, a common temple ornamentation in the early Ratanakosin period, when Chinese ships calling at Bangkok used the stuff as ballast.

At the time of research, the spire of Wat Arun was closed due to renovation. Visitors can enter the compound, but cannot, as in previous years, climb the tower.

The Ordination Hall

The compound's primary *bòht* (ordination hall) contains a Buddha image that is said to have been designed by Rama II himself, as well as beautiful murals that depict Prince Siddhartha (the Buddha) encountering examples of birth, old age, sickness and death outside his palace walls, an experience that led him to abandon the worldly life.

The Grounds

In addition to the central spire and ordination hall, the Wat Arun compound includes two *wí·hǎhn* (sanctuaries) and a *hǒr đrai* (depository for Buddhist scriptures), among other structures. Adjacent to the river are six *sǎhlah* (often spelt as *sala*), open-air pavilions traditionally meant for relaxing or study, but increasingly used these days as docks for tourist boats.

Take a Break

If you're visiting the temple during the day, consider a lunch break at Tonkin-Annam (p74), an excellent Vietnamese restaurant just across the river. Sunset views of the temple compound can be caught from Roof (p75) or Amorosa (p75), rooftop bars located directly across from the temple.

Top Tips

➡ You must wear appropriate clothing to visit Wat Arun. If you are flashing too much flesh, you'll have to rent a sarong for 20B (and a 100B refundable deposit).

➡ For our money, it's best to visit Wat Arun in the late afternoon, when the sun shines from the west, lighting up the spire and river behind it.

➡ Sunset views of the temple can be caught from across the river at the warehouses that line Th Maha Rat – although be forewarned that locals may ask for a 20B 'fee'.

➡ Many people visit Wat Arun on long-tail boat tours, but it's dead easy and more rewarding to just jump on the 3B cross-river ferry from Tien Pier (from 5am to 9pm, frequent). Once across, consider taking a stroll away from the river on Th Wang Doem, a quiet tiled street of wooden shophouses.

DON'T MISS...

➡ The Khmer-style *þrahng* (spire)

➡ Buddhist murals inside the main *bòht*

➡ Historic surrounding neighbourhood

PRACTICALITIES

➡ วัดอรุณฯ

➡ Map p265, B6

➡ www.watarun.net

➡ off Th Arun Amarin

➡ admiss50B

➡ ⏱8am-6pm

➡ 🚢cross-river ferry from Tien Pier

⊙ SIGHTS

Nearly all of Bangkok's big-hitter sights are found in the two linked neighbourhoods of Ko Ratanakosin and Thonburi. Combined, they cover a relatively small area, and it's possible to tackle most if not all sights in one (hot and sweaty) day.

WAT PHO   BUDDHIST TEMPLE
See p60.

WAT PHRA KAEW & GRAND PALACE   BUDDHIST TEMPLE
See p64.

WAT ARUN   BUDDHIST TEMPLE
See p69.

MUSEUM OF SIAM   MUSEUM
Map p265 (สถาบันพิพิธภัณฑ์การเรียนรู้แห่งชาติ; www.museumsiam.org; Th Maha Rat; 300B; ⊙10am-6pm Tue-Sun; 🚼; 🛳Tien Pier) Although temporarily closed for renovation when we stopped by, this fun museum's collection employs a variety of media to explore the origins of the Thai people and their culture. Housed in a European-style; 19th-century building that was once the Ministry of Commerce, the exhibits are presented in a contemporary, engaging and interactive fashion not typically found in Thailand's museums. They are also refreshingly balanced and entertaining, with galleries dealing with a range of questions about the origins of the nation and its people.

Each room has an informative narrated video started by a sensory detector, keeping waiting to a minimum. An Ayuthaya-era

ℹ️ DRESS FOR SUCCESS

Most of Bangkok's biggest tourist attractions are in fact sacred places, and visitors should dress and behave appropriately. In particular, at Wat Phra Kaew and the Grand Palace, you won't be allowed to enter unless you're well covered. Shorts, sleeveless shirts or spaghetti-strap tops, cropped pants – basically anything that reveals more than your arms and head – are not allowed. Those who aren't dressed appropriately can expect to be shown into a dressing room and issued with a sarong before being allowed in.

battle game, a room full of traditional Thai toys and a street vending cart where you can be photographed pretending to whip up a pan of *pàt tai* (fried noodles) will help keep kids interested for at least an hour, adults for longer. Check out the attached shop for some innovative gift ideas.

SIRIRAJ MEDICAL MUSEUM   MUSEUM
Map p265 (พิพิธภัณฑ์นิติเวชศาสตร์สงกรานต์นิยมเสน; 2nd fl, Adulyadejvikrom Bldg, Siriraj Hospital; 200B; ⊙10am-4pm Wed-Mon; 🛳Wang Lang/Siriraj Pier, Thonburi Railway Station Pier) Various appendages, murder weapons and crime-scene evidence, including a bloodied T-shirt from a victim stabbed to death with a dildo, are on display at these linked museums – collectively dubbed the Museum of Death – dedicated to anatomy, pathology and forensic science.

Although the intent is ostensibly to educate rather than nauseate, exhibits such as the preserved body of Si Ouey, a serial killer who murdered – and then ate – more than 30 children in the 1950s before being executed, often do the latter. (For decades Si Ouey has functioned as a Thai bogeyman, his name used to scare misbehaving children into submission: 'Behave yourself or Si Ouey will come for you!'.) If you're still with us at this point, you'll probably also enjoy the adjacent **Parasite Museum**.

The easiest way to reach the Siriraj museum is by taking the river-crossing ferry from Chang Pier to Wang Lang/Siriraj Pier in Thonburi. At the exit to the pier, turn right (north) to enter Siriraj Hospital and follow the green Museum signs.

AMULET MARKET   MARKET
Map p265 (ตลาดพระเครื่องวัดมหาธาตุ; Th Maha Rat; ⊙7am-5pm; 🛳Chang Pier, Maharaj Pier, Phra Chan Tai Pier) This arcane and fascinating market claims both the footpaths along Th Maha Rat and Th Phra Chan, as well as a dense network of covered market stalls that runs south from Phra Chan Pier; the easiest entry point is clearly marked 'Trok Maha That'. The trade is based around small talismans carefully prized by collectors, monks, taxi drivers and people in dangerous professions.

Potential buyers, often already sporting many amulets, can be seen bargaining and flipping through magazines dedicated to the amulets, some of which command astronomical prices. It's a great place to just wander and watch men (because it's

ARTIST'S HOUSE

Sort of a gallery, kind of a coffee shop, seemingly a cultural centre...it's hard to pin down **Artist's House** (บ้านศิลปิน; www.facebook.com/baansilapin; Khlong Bang Luang; ⊙9am-6pm; §Wongwian Yai exit 2) FREE, an old wooden house on Khlong Bang Luang, in Thonburi. There's food available on weekends, as well as a free traditional Thai puppet show scheduled at 2pm, but the best excuse to come is simply to soak up the old-world canalside vibe.

Artist's House can be reached on canal boat tours of Thonburi, or on land via Soi 3, Th Charansanitwong; cross the canal at the bridge by the 7-Eleven, turn left and it's about 100m down.

rarely women) looking through magnifying glasses at the tiny amulets, seeking hidden meaning and, if they're lucky, hidden value.

NATIONAL MUSEUM   MUSEUM

Map p265 (พิพิธภัณฑสถานแห่งชาติ; 4 Th Na Phra That; 200B; ⊙9am-4pm Wed-Sun; §Chang Pier, Maharaj Pier, Phra Chan Tai Pier) Often touted as Southeast Asia's biggest museum, Thailand's National Museum is home to an impressive, albeit occasionally dusty, collection of items, best appreciated on one of the museum's free twice-weekly guided **tours** (National Museum, 4 Th Na Phra That; free with museum admission; ⊙9.30am Wed & Thu; §Chang Pier, Maharaj Pier).

Most of the museum's structures were built in 1782 as the palace of Rama I's viceroy, Prince Wang Na. Rama V turned it into a museum in 1874, and today there are three permanent exhibitions spread out over several buildings.

The recently renovated **Gallery of Thai History** is home to some of the country's most beautiful Buddha images.

The **history wing** has made impressive bounds towards contemporary curatorial aesthetics with a succinct chronology of prehistoric, Sukhothai-, Ayuthaya- and Bangkok-era events and figures. Gems include King Ramkhamhaeng's inscribed stone pillar, said to be the oldest record of Thai writing (although this has been contested); King Taksin's throne; the Rama V section; and the screening of a movie about Rama VII, *The Magic Ring.*

The **decorative arts and ethnology exhibit** covers seemingly every possible handicraft including traditional musical instruments, ceramics, clothing and textiles, woodcarving, regalia and weaponry. The **archaeology and art history wing** has exhibits ranging from prehistory to the Bangkok period.

In addition to the main exhibition halls, the **Bhuddhaisawan (Phutthaisawan) Chapel** includes some well-preserved murals and one of the country's most revered Buddha images, Phra Phuttha Sihing. Legend claims the image came from Sri Lanka, but art historians attribute it to the 13th-century Sukhothai period.

When we stopped by, several of the exhibition halls were being renovated.

SILPAKORN UNIVERSITY ART CENTRE   GALLERY

Map p265 (หอศิลป์ มหาวิทยาลัยศิลปากร; www.facebook.com/ArtCentre.SilpakornUniversity; 31 Th Na Phra Lan; ⊙9am-7pm Mon-Fri, to 4pm Sat; §Chang Pier, Maharaj Pier) FREE This gallery – located inside Thailand's most prestigious arts school, Silpakorn University (p74) – showcases faculty and student exhibitions. There's also an accompanying courtyard cafe and art shop.

SANAM LUANG   PARK

Map p265 (สนามหลวง; bounded by Th Na Phra That, Th Ratchadamnoen Nai & Th Na Phra Lan; ⊙daylight hours; §Chang Pier, Maharaj Pier, Phra Chan Tai Pier) On a hot day, Sanam Luang (Royal Field) is far from charming: a shadeless expanse of dying grass and concrete pavement ringed by flocks of pigeons and homeless people. Yet despite its shabby appearance, it has been at the centre of royal ceremony since Bangkok was founded.

Large funeral pyres are constructed here during elaborate, but infrequent, royal cremations, and explain the field's alternative name, Thung Phra Men (Cremation Ground). The most recent was in October of 2017, for the elaborate funeral of King Rama IX. Sanam Luang also draws the masses in December for Constitution Day (10 December) and New Year.

TAXI ALTARS: INSURANCE ON THE DASHBOARD

As your taxi races into Bangkok from the airport, your delight at being able to do the 30km trip for less than US$15 might soon be replaced by uneasiness, anxiety and eventually outright fear – 150km/h is fast, you're tailgating the car in front and there's no seatbelt. You can rest assured (or not), however, that your driver will share none of these concerns.

All of this makes the humble taxi trip an instructive introduction to Thai culture. Buddhists believe in karma and thus that their fate is, to a large extent, predestined. Unlike Western ideas, which take a more scientific approach to road safety, many Thais believe factors such as speed, concentration, seatbelts and actual driving skills have no bearing whatsoever on your chances of being in a crash. Put simply, if you die a horrible death on the road, karma says you deserved it. The trouble is that when a passenger gets into a taxi they bring their karma and any bad spirits they might have along for the ride, which could upset the driver's own fate.

To counteract such bad influences, most Bangkok taxi drivers turn the dashboard and ceiling into a sort of life-insurance shrine. The ceiling will have a *yantra* diagram drawn in white powder by a monk as a form of spiritual protection. This will often be accompanied by portraits of notable royals. Below this a red box dangling red tassels, beads and amulets hangs from the rear-vision mirror, while the dashboard is populated by Buddhist and royal statuettes, and quite possibly banknotes with the king's image prominent, and more amulets. With luck (such as it exists in Thailand), the talismans will protect your driver from any bad karma you bring into the cab. Passengers, meanwhile, must simply hope that their driver's number is not up. If you feel like it might be, try saying *cháh cháh* soothingly – that is, ask your driver to slow down. For a peek inside some of Bangkok's 100,000 or so taxis, check out Still Life in Moving Vehicles (www.lifeinmovingvehicle.blogspot.com).

Less dramatic events staged here include the annual Royal Ploughing Ceremony, in which the king officially initiates the rice-growing season, an appropriate location given that Sanam Luang was used to grow rice for almost 100 years after the royals moved into Ko Ratanakosin. After the rains, the kite-flying season (mid-February to April) sees the air above filled with butterfly-shaped Thai kites. Matches are held between teams flying either a 'male' or 'female' kite in a particular territory; points are won if they can force a competitor into their zone.

ROYAL BARGES
NATIONAL MUSEUM   MUSEUM

Map p265 (พิพิธภัณฑสถานแห่งชาติ เรือพระราชพิธี/เรือ
พระที่นั่ง; Khlong Bangkok Noi or 80/1 Th Arun Amarin; admission 100B, camera 100B; ⊙9am-5pm; ⛴Phra Pin Klao Bridge Pier) The royal barges are slender, fantastically ornamented vessels used in ceremonial processions. The tradition dates back to the Ayuthaya era, when travel (for commoners and royals) was by boat. When not in use, the barges are on display at this Thonburi museum.

Suphannahong, the king's personal barge, is the most important of the six boats on display here. Made from a single piece of timber, it's said to be the largest dugout in the world. The name means Golden Swan, and a huge swan head has been carved into the bow. Lesser barges feature bows that are carved into other Hindu-Buddhist mythological shapes such as the *naga* (mythical sea serpent) and *garuda* (Vishnu's bird mount).

Historic photos help envision the grand processions in which the largest of the barges would require a rowing crew of 50 men, plus seven umbrella bearers, two helmsmen and two navigators, as well as a flagsman, rhythm keeper and chanter. Today, the royal barge procession is an infrequent occurrence, most recently performed in 2012 in honour of the late King Bhumibol Adulyadej's 85th birthday.

The most convenient way to get here is by motorcycle taxi from Phra Pin Klao Bridge Pier (ask the driver to go to *reu·a prá têe nâng*). The museum is also an optional stop on long-tail boat trips through Thonburi's canals.

SARANROM ROYAL GARDEN   PARK

Map p265 (สวนสราญรมย์; bounded by Th Ratchini, Th Charoen Krung & Th Sanam Chai; ⊙5am-9pm; ⛴Tien Pier) Easily mistaken for a European public garden, this Victorian-era green space was originally designed as a royal residence in the time of Rama IV. After Rama VII abdicated in 1935, the palace served as the headquarters of the People's Party, the political organisation that orchestrated the handover of the government. The open space remained and in 1960 was opened to the public.

Today a wander through the garden reveals a Victorian gazebo, paths lined with frangipani and a moat around a marble monument built in honour of one of Rama V's favourite wives, Queen Sunantha, who died in a boating accident in 1880. The queen was on her way to Bang Pa-In Summer Palace in Ayuthaya when her boat began to sink. The custom at the time was that commoners were forbidden to touch royalty, which prevented her attendants from saving her from drowning.

NATIONAL GALLERY   GALLERY
Map p265 (พิพิธภัณฑ์สถานแห่งชาติหอศิลป์/หอ
ศิลป์เจ้าฟ้า; www.facebook.com/thenationalgallery
thailand; 4 Th Chao Fa; 200B; ⊘9am-4pm Wed-
Sun; ⛴Chang Pier, Maharaj Pier, Phra Chan Tai
Pier) Housed in a building that was the Royal Mint during the reign of Rama V, the National Gallery's permanent exhibition is admittedly a rather dusty and dated affair. Secular art is a relatively new concept in Thailand and most of the country's best examples of fine art reside in the temples for which they were created – much as historic Western art is often found in European cathedrals. As such, most of the permanent collection here documents Thailand's homage to modern styles.

More interesting are the rotating exhibits held in the spacious rear galleries; take a look at the Facebook page or the posters out front to see what's on.

LAK MEUANG   MONUMENT
Map p265 (ศาลหลักเมือง; cnr Th Sanam Chai & Th
Lak Meuang; ⊘6.30am-6.30pm; ⛴Chang Pier,
Maharaj Pier, Phra Chan Tai Pier) Serving as the spiritual keystone of Bangkok, Lak Meuang is a phallus-shaped wooden pillar erected by Rama I during the foundation of the city in 1782. Part of an animistic tradition, the city pillar embodies the city's guardian spirit (Phra Sayam Thewathirat) and also lends a practical purpose as a marker of a town's crossroads and measuring point for distances between towns.

If you're lucky, *lá·kon gâa bon* (a commissioned dance) may be in progress. Brilliantly costumed dancers measure out subtle movements as gratitude to the guardian spirit for granting a worshipper's wish.

THAMMASAT UNIVERSITY   UNIVERSITY
Map p265 (มหาวิทยาลัยธรรมศาสตร์; www.tu.ac.
th; 2 Th Phra Chan; ⛴Chang Pier, Maharaj Pier,
Phra Chan Tai Pier) Much of the drama that followed Thailand's transition from monarchy to democracy has unfolded on this quiet riverside campus. Thammasat University was established in 1934, two years after the bloodless coup that deposed the absolute monarchy. Its remit was to instruct students in law and political economy, considered to be the intellectual necessities for an educated democracy.

The university was founded by Dr Pridi Phanomyong, whose statue stands in Pridi Court at the centre of the campus. Pridi was the leader of the civilian People's Party that successfully advocated a constitutional monarchy during the 1920s and '30s. He went on to serve in various ministries, organised the Seri Thai movement (a Thai resistance campaign against the Japanese during WWII) and was forced into exile when the postwar government was seized by a military dictatorship in 1947.

Pridi was unable to counter the dismantling of democratic reforms, but the university he established continued his crusade. Thammasat was the hotbed of pro-democracy activism during the student uprising era of the 1970s. On 14 October 1973, an estimated 10,000 protesters convened on the parade grounds beside the university's Memorial Building demanding the government reinstate the constitution. From the university the protest grew and moved to the Democracy Monument, where the military and police opened fire on the crowd, killing 77 and wounding 857. The massacre prompted the king to revoke his support of the military rulers and for a brief period a civilian government was reinstated. On 6 October 1976, Thammasat itself was the scene of a bloody massacre, when at least 46 students were shot dead while rallying against the return from exile of former dictator Field Marshal Thanom Kittikachorn. Near the southern entrance to the university is the Bodhi Court, where a sign beneath the Bodhi tree explains more about the democracy movement that germinated at Thammasat.

KO RATANAKOSIN & THONBURI SIGHTS

LOCAL KNOWLEDGE

THONBURI'S SOUTHERN THAI RESTAURANTS

The area around Thonburi's Siriraj Hospital is one of the best places in Bangkok for southern-Thai food, the theory being that the cuisine took root here because of the nearby train station that served southern destinations. In particular, between Soi 8 and Soi 13 of Th Wang Lang there is a knot of authentic, southern Thai-style curry shops: **Dao Tai** (508/26 Th Wang Lang, no Roman-script sign; mains from 30B; ⊙7am-8.30pm; 🚤Wang Lang/Siriraj Pier), **Ruam Tai** (376/4 Th Wang Lang, no Roman-script sign; mains from 30B; ⊙7am-9pm; 🚤Wang Lang/Siriraj Pier) and **Chawang** (375/5-6 Th Wang Lang; mains from 30B; ⊙7am-7pm; 🚤Wang Lang/Siriraj Pier). A menu isn't necessary as all feature bowls and trays of prepared curries, soups, stir-fries and relishes; simply point to whatever looks tastiest. And when eating, don't feel ashamed if you're feeling the heat; even Bangkok Thais tend to find southern Thai cuisine spicy.

SILPAKORN UNIVERSITY   UNIVERSITY
Map p265 (มหาวิทยาลัยศิลปากร; www.su.ac.th; 31 Th Na Phra Lan; 🚤Chang Pier, Maharaj Pier, Phra Chan Tai Pier) Thailand's universities aren't usually repositories for interesting architecture, but Silpakorn (pronounced *sĭn lá pà gorn*), the country's premier art school, breaks the mould. The classical buildings form the charming nucleus of what was an early Thai aristocratic enclave, and the traditional artistic temperament still survives.

The building immediately facing the Th Na Phra Lan gate was once part of a palace and now houses the Silpakorn University Art Centre (p71). To the right of the building is a shady sculpture garden displaying the work of Corrado Feroci (also known as Silpa Bhirasri), the Italian art professor and sculptor who came to Thailand at royal request in the 1920s and later established the university (which is named after him), sculpted parts of the Democracy Monument and, much to his own annoyance, the Victory Monument.

EATING

PA AEW   THAI $
Map p265 (Th Maha Rat; mains 20-60B; ⊙10am-5pm Tue-Sat; 🚤Tien Pier) Pull up a plastic stool for some rich, seafood-heavy, Bangkok-style fare. It's a bare-bones, open-air curry stall, but for taste, Pa Aew is one of our favourite places to eat in this part of town. There's no English-language sign; look for the exposed trays of food directly in front of the Krung Thai Bank near the corner with Soi Pratu Nokyung.

MING LEE   THAI, CHINESE $
Map p265 (28-30 Th Na Phra Lan, no Roman-script sign; mains 70-100B; ⊙11.30am-6pm; 🚤Chang Pier, Maharaj Pier, Phra Chan Tai Pier) Hidden in plain sight across from Wat Phra Kaew is this decades-old shophouse restaurant. The menu spans Western/Chinese dishes (stewed tongue, for example) and Thai standards (such as the impossibly tart and garlicky 'beef spicy salad', Ming Lee). Often closed before 6pm, Ming Lee is best approached as a post-sightseeing lunch option. There's no English-language sign here; look for the last shophouse before Silpakorn University.

WANG LANG MARKET   THAI $
Map p265 (Trok Wang Lang; mains 30-80B; ⊙10am-3pm Mon-Fri; 🚤Wang Lang/Siriraj Pier) Running south from Siriraj Hospital is this busy market bringing together takeaway stalls and basic restaurants. Options range from noodles to curries ladled over rice, and come lunch, the area is positively mobbed by the area's office staff.

⭐TONKIN-ANNAM   VIETNAMESE $$
Map p265 (📱093 469 2969; www.facebook.com/tonkinannam; 69 Soi Tha Tien; mains 140-300B; ⊙10am-10pm Wed-Mon; ❄; 🚤Tien Pier) The retro-minimalist interior here might be a red flag for hipster ethnic cuisine, but Tonkin-Annam serves some of the best Vietnamese food in Bangkok. Come for the deliciously tart and peppery banana blossom salad, or dishes you won't find elsewhere, such as *bánh bèo* (steamed cups of rice flour topped with pork), a speciality of Hue.

ERR   THAI $$
Map p265 (www.errbkk.com; off Th Maha Rat; mains 65-360B; ⊙11am-late Tue-Sun; ❄; 🚤Tien Pier) Think of all those different smoky, spicy, crispy, meaty bites you've encountered on the street. Now imagine them assembled in one funky, retro-themed locale, and coupled with tasty Thai-themed cocktails and

domestic microbrews. If Err (a Thai colloquialism for agreement) seems too good to be true, we empathise, but insist that it's true.

NAVY CLUB
THAI $$

Map p265 (77 Th Maha Rat; mains 70-450B; ◷11am-10pm; ❄; ⛴Chang Pier, Maharaj Pier, Phra Chan Tai Pier) The restaurant of the Royal Navy Association has one of the few coveted riverfront locations along this stretch of Mae Nam Chao Phraya. Locals come for the combination of views and cheap and tasty seafood-based eats – not for the cafeteria-like atmosphere.

SAVOEY
THAI $$

Map p265 (www.savoey.co.th; 1st fl, Maharaj Pier, Th Maha Rat; mains 125-1800B; ◷10am-10pm; ❄; ⛴Maharaj Pier, Chang Pier) A chain with other branches across town, you're not going to find heaps of character here, but you will get consistency, river views, air-con, and a seafood-heavy menu that should appeal to just about everybody. Come cool evenings, take advantage of the open-air, riverside deck.

SALA RATTANAKOSIN
EATERY & BAR
THAI $$$

Map p265 (☏02 622 1388; www.salaresorts.com/rattanakosin; Sala Rattanakosin, 39 Th Maha Rat; mains 240-1100B; ◷11am-4.30pm & 5.30-11pm; ❄; ⛴Tien Pier) Located on an open-air deck next to the river with Wat Arun virtually towering overhead, the Sala Rattanakosin hotel's signature restaurant has nailed the location. The food – largely central and northern Thai dishes with occasional Western twists – doesn't necessarily live up to the scenery.

🍷 DRINKING & NIGHTLIFE

ROOF
BAR

Map p265 (www.salaresorts.com/rattanakosin; 5th fl, Sala Rattanakosin, 39 Th Maha Rat; ◷5pm-midnight Mon-Thu, to 1am Fri-Sun; ⛴Tien Pier) The open-air bar on top of the Sala Rattanakosin hotel has upped the stakes for sunset views of Wat Arun – if you can see the temple at all through the wall of selfie-snapping tourists. Be sure to get there early for a good seat.

AMOROSA
BAR

Map p265 (www.arunresidence.com; rooftop, Arun Residence, 36-38 Soi Pratu Nokyung; ◷5pm-midnight Mon-Thu, to 1am Fri-Sun; ⛴Tien Pier) Perched above the Arun Residence, Amorosa takes advantage of a location directly above the river and opposite Wat Arun. The cocktails aren't going to blow you away, but watching boats ply their way along the royal river as Wat Arun glows is a beautiful reminder that you're not home any more.

☆ ENTERTAINMENT

NATIONAL THEATRE
THEATRE

Map p265 (☏02 224 1342; 2 Th Ratchini; tickets 60-100B; ⛴Chang Pier, Maharaj Pier, Phra Chan Tai Pier) The National Theatre holds performances of *kŏhn* (masked dance-drama based on stories from the *Ramakian*) at 2pm on the first and second Sundays of the month from January to September, and *lá·kon* (classical dance-dramas) at 2pm on the first and second Sundays of the month from October to December. Tickets go on sale an hour before performances begin.

🏃 SPORTS & ACTIVITIES

★ AMITA THAI COOKING CLASS
COOKING

Map p265 (☏02 466 8966; www.amitathaicooking.com; 162/17 Soi 14, Th Wutthakat, Thonburi; classes 3000B; ◷9.30am-1pm Thu-Tue; ⛴klorng boat from Maharaj Pier) One of Bangkok's most charming cooking schools is held in this canalside house in Thonburi. Taught by the delightfully enthusiastic Piyawadi 'Tam' Jantrupon, a course here includes a romp through the garden and instruction in four dishes. The fee covers transport, which in this case takes the form of a boat ride from Maharaj Pier.

CENTER MEDITATION
WAT MAHADHATU
MEDITATION

Map p265 (☏02 222 6011, 02 223 3813; Section 5, Wat Mahathat, Th Maha Rat; donations accepted; ◷classes 7am, 1pm & 6pm; ⛴Chang Pier, Maharaj Pier, Phra Chan Tai Pier) Located within Wat Mahathat, this small centre offers informal daily meditation classes. Taught by English-speaking Prasuputh Chainikom (Kosalo), classes last three hours. Longer periods of study, which include accommodation and food, can be arranged, but students are expected to follow a strict regimen of conduct.

KO RATANAKOSIN & THONBURI DRINKING & NIGHTLIFE

WORTH A DETOUR

EXPLORING THONBURI'S CANALS

Bangkok was formerly known as the Venice of the East, as the city used to be criss-crossed by an advanced network of *klorng* (also spelt *khlong*), artificial canals that inhabitants used both for transport and to ship goods. Today cars and motorcycles have superseded boats, and the majority of Bangkok's canals have been filled in and covered by roads, or are fetid and drying up. Yet a peek into the watery Bangkok of yesteryear can still be had west of Mae Nam Chao Phraya, in Thonburi.

Thonburi's network of canals and river tributaries still carries a motley fleet of watercraft, from paddle canoes to rice barges. Homes, trading houses and temples are built on stilts with front doors opening out to the water. According to residents, these waterways protect them from the seasonal flooding that plagues the capital. **Khlong Bangkok Noi** is lined with greenery and historic temples; smaller **Khlong Mon** is largely residential. **Khlong Bangkok Yai** was in fact the original course of the river until a canal was built to expedite transits. Today long-tail boats that ply these and other Thonburi canals are available for charter at Chang Pier and Tien Pier, both on Ko Ratanakosin. Prices at these piers are slightly higher than elsewhere and allow little room for negotiation, but you stand the least chance of being conned or hit up for tips and other unexpected fees.

Trips generally traverse Khlong Bangkok Noi and Khlong Mon, taking in the Royal Barges National Museum, Wat Arun and a riverside temple with fish feeding. Longer trips diverge into Khlong Bangkok Yai, and can include a visit to an orchid farm. On weekends, you have the option of visiting the **Taling Chan Floating Market** (ตลาดน้ำ ตลิ่งชัน; Khlong Bangkok Noi, Thonburi; ☉7am-4pm Sat & Sun; Ⓢ Wongwian Yai exit 3 & taxi). However, it's worth pointing out that to actually disembark and explore any of these sights, the most common tour of one hour (1000B, up to six people) is simply not enough time; you'll most likely need 1½ or two hours (1300B or 1500B respectively). Most operators have set tour routes, but if you have a specific destination in mind, you can request it. Tours are generally conducted from 8am to 5pm.

If you'd prefer something longer or more personalised, **Pandan Tour** (🖉02 689 1232, 087 109 8873; www.thaicanaltour.com; tours from 2395B) conducts a variety of mostly full-day tours. And a budget alternative is to take the one-way-only **commuter long-tail boat** (Map p265; Chang Pier, off Th Maha Rat; 25B; ☉4.30am-7.30pm; 🚢Chang Pier) from Chang Pier to Bang Yai, at the distant northern end of Khlong Bangkok Noi, although foreigners are sometimes discouraged from doing so.

MASSAGE PAVILIONS   MASSAGE

Map p265 (Wat Pho, Th Sanam Chai; Thai massage per hour 420B; ☉9am-4pm; 🚢Tien Pier) These two air-conditioned *săh·lah* (pavilions; often spelt *Sala*) near the eastern entrance to the temple grounds are run by the school (p76) affiliated with Wat Pho, which is the country's primary training centre for Thai traditional massage. The menu is short but the quality is guaranteed, and after a day of temple sightseeing it's hard to think of a better way to cool down and chill out.

CHETAWAN TRADITIONAL MASSAGE SCHOOL   HEALTH & WELLBEING

Map p265 (🖉02 622 3551; www.watpomassage. com; 392/32-33 Soi Phen Phat; lessons from 2500B, Thai massage per hour 420B; ☉lessons 9am-4pm, massage 9am-8pm; 🚢Tien Pier) Associated with the nearby temple of the same name, this institute offers basic and advanced courses in traditional massage; basic courses offer 30 hours spread over five days and cover either general massage or foot massage. Thai massage is also available for non-students.

The school's advanced level course spans 165 hours, requires the basic course as a prerequisite, and covers therapeutic and healing massage. Other advanced courses include oil massage and aromatherapy, and infant and child massage.

The school is outside the temple compound in a restored Bangkok shophouse in Soi Phen Phat.

Banglamphu

Neighbourhood Top Five

1 **Th Khao San** (p88) Exploring Bangkok's most famous street, a unique cultural melting pot with something for everyone.

2 **Golden Mount** Taking in the panoramic views of old Bangkok from this artificial summit.

3 **Krua Apsorn** (p83) Tasting classic Bangkok-style nosh at this and other similarly classic restaurants.

4 **Brick Bar** (p85) Dancing on the tables with Thai hipsters, sipping cocktails riverside or dancing the

night away in Banglamphu's fun nightlife scene.

5 **Wat Suthat** (p80) Sitting and gazing at the huge Buddha and sky-high murals inside this lesser-known yet gorgeous temple.

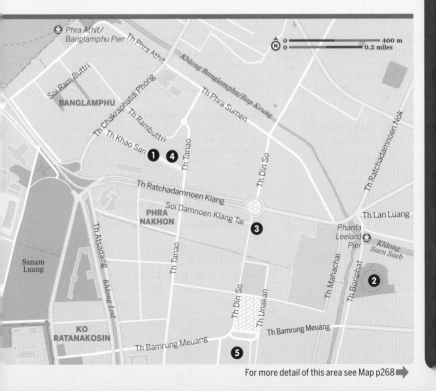

For more detail of this area see Map p268 ➡

Lonely Planet's Top Tip

Boats – both the Chao Phraya Express and *klorng* boats – are a steady, if slow, way to reach Banglamphu, but remember that most only run until about 7pm.

✗ Best Places to Eat

➡ Krua Apsorn (p83)

➡ Jay Fai (p83)

➡ Shoshana (p83)

➡ Thip Samai (p82)

➡ Somsong Phochana (p84)

➡ Baan Nual (p83)

For reviews, see p82➡

◉ Best Drinking & Nightlife

➡ Brick Bar (p85)

➡ Ku Bar (p84)

➡ The Club (p85)

➡ Hippie de Bar (p85)

➡ Madame Musur (p85)

➡ Phra Nakorn Bar & Gallery (p85)

For reviews, see p84➡

🛍 Best Places to Shop

➡ Thanon Khao San Market (p87)

➡ Heritage Craft (p87)

➡ Lofty Bamboo (p87)

➡ Nittaya Thai Curry (p87)

For reviews, see p87➡

Explore Banglamphu

Antique shophouses, classic restaurants, ancient temples: Banglamphu is old Bangkok encapsulated in one leafy, breezy district. If you've come for the sights, arrive early, while the heat is still tolerable and the touts few. It's worth sticking around Banglamphu for lunch, as this is when the majority of the area's street stalls and shophouse restaurants are operating. Come evening, young locals flood the area in search of a cheap meal and a cold Chang, giving the area an entirely different vibe, but there are enough restaurants and bars here that there's no need to consider another destination for the night.

Despite being one of Bangkok's best areas for accommodation, sights, eating and nightlife, Banglamphu is not very well linked up with the rest of the city by public transport networks. During the day, a good strategy is to approach the area via the river ferry at Phra Athit/ Banglamphu Pier – most of the sights are within walking distance. At night, most of the action is centered on Th Khao San, which can be accessed via taxi from the BTS stop at National Stadium or the MRT stop at Hua Lamphong.

Local Life

➡ **Local Cuisine** Bangkok's most traditional district is not surprisingly one of the best places to try authentic central Thai- and Bangkok-style food.

➡ **Streetside Shopping** The spectrum of goods available in this district ranges from backpacker staples along Th Khao San to delicious Thai curry pastes and high-quality handicrafts in the more traditional areas nearby.

➡ **Les Champs Élysées de Bangkok** The royal boulevard of Th Ratchadamnoen Klang links the Grand Palace in Ko Ratanakosin with newer palaces in Dusit, and is suitably adorned with billboard-sized pictures of the king and other royal family members.

Getting There & Away

➡ **Chao Phraya Express Boat** Phra Athit/Banglamphu Pier.

➡ **Taxi** From the BTS stops at National Stadium or Phaya Thai, or from the MRT stop at Hua Lamphong.

➡ **Klorng boat** Phanfa Leelard Pier.

➡ **Bus** Air-con 44, 79, 503 and 511; ordinary 2, 15, 49, 59, 60, 69 and 70.

⊙ SIGHTS

**TH BAMRUNG MEUANG
RELIGIOUS SHOPS** AREA

Map p268 (ถนนบำรุงเมือง; Th Bamrung Meuang; ☉9am-6pm; ⛴klorng boat to Phanfa Leelard Pier) The stretch of Th Bamrung Meuang (one of Bangkok's oldest streets and originally an elephant path leading to the Grand Palace) from Th Mahachai to Th Tanao is lined with shops selling all manner of Buddhist religious paraphernalia. You probably don't need a car-sized Buddha statue or an eerily lifelike effigy of a famous monk, but browsing is fun, and who knows when you might need to do a great deal of Thai-style merit making?

KING PRAJADHIPOK MUSEUM MUSEUM

Map p268 (พิพิธภัณฑ์พระบาทสมเด็จพระปกเกล้าเจ้าอยู่หัว; www.kingprajadhipokmuseum.org; 2 Th Lan Luang; ☉9am-4pm Tue-Sun; ⛴klorng boat to Phanfa Leelard Pier) **FREE** This museum assembles old photos and memorabilia to illustrate the rather dramatic life of Rama VII (King Prajadhipok; r 1925–35), Thailand's last absolute monarch. It occupies a grand neocolonial-style building constructed on the orders of Rama V for his favourite firm of Bond St merchants – the only foreign business allowed on the royal road linking Bangkok's two palace districts.

The exhibitions reveal that Prajadhipok did not expect to become king, but once on the throne showed considerable diplomacy in dealing with what was, in effect, a revolution fomented by a new intellectual class of Thais. The 1st floor deals with the life of Queen Rambhai Barni, while the upper two floors cover the king's own life, revealing, for example, that the army-officer-turned-king spent many of his formative years in Europe where he became fond of British democracy. (Ironically, those plotting his downfall had themselves learned of democracy during years of European education.) A coup, carried out while the king and queen were playing golf, ended Thailand's absolute monarchy in 1932. Prajadhipok's reign eventually ended when he abdicated while in England in 1935; he died there in 1941.

WAT BOWONNIWET BUDDHIST TEMPLE

Map p268 (วัดบวรนิเวศวิหาร; www.watbowon.org; Th Phra Sumen; ☉8.30am-5pm; ⛴Phra Athit/Banglamphu Pier) **FREE** Founded in 1826, Wat Bowonniwet (known colloquially as Wat Bowon) is the national headquarters for the Thammayut monastic sect, a reformed version of Thai Buddhism. The rest of us should visit the temple for the noteworthy murals in its *bòht* (ordination hall), which include Thai depictions of Western life (possibly copied from magazine illustrations) during the early 19th century.

Because of its royal status, visitors should be particularly careful to dress properly for admittance; shorts and sleeveless clothing are not allowed.

Rama IV (King Mongkut; r 1851–68), who set out to be a scholar, not a king, founded the Thammayut sect and began the royal tradition of ordination at this temple. In fact, Mongkut was the abbot of Wat Bowon for several years. Rama IX (King Bhumibol Adulyadej; r 1946–2016) and Rama X (King Maha Vajiralongkorn; r 2016–), as well as several other males in the royal family, have been ordained as monks here.

**RATCHADAMNOEN
CONTEMPORARY ART CENTER** GALLERY

Map p268 (หอศิลป์ร่วมสมัยราชดำเนิน, RCAC; www.facebook.com/Ratchadamnone; Th Ratchadamnoen Klang; ☉10am-7pm Tue-Sun; ⛴klorng boat to Phanfa Leelard Pier) **FREE** This new, three-storey structure hosts changing exhibitions of mixed-media contemporary domestic art.

BAN BAAT AREA

Map p268 (บ้านบาตร, Monk's Bowl Village; off Soi Ban Bat; ☉9am-5pm; ⛴klorng boat to Phanfa Leelard Pier) The residents of Ban Baat inhabit the only remaining village of three established in Bangkok by Rama I (King Phraphutthayotfa Chulalok; r 1782–1809) to produce *bàht*, the distinctive bowls used by monks to receive morning food donations. Tourists – not temples – are among the customers these days, and a bowl purchase is usually rewarded with a bowl-making demonstration.

As cheaper factory-made bowls are now the norm, the artisanal tradition has shrunk to one extended family. You can

LOCAL KNOWLEDGE
WHAT'S IN A NAME?
Banglamphu means 'Place of Lamphu', a reference to the *lam·poo* tree (*Duabanga grandiflora*) that was once prevalent in the area.

observe the process of hammering the bowls together from eight separate pieces of steel, said to represent Buddhism's eightfold path. The joints are then fused with melted copper wire, and the bowl is beaten, polished and coated with several layers of black lacquer. To find the village – today just a single alleyway – from Th Bamrung Meuang, turn down Soi Ban Bat, then take the first right.

SAO CHING-CHA   MONUMENT

Map p268 (เสาชิงช้า, Giant Swing; Th Bamrung Meuang; ⛴klorng boat to Phanfa Leelard Pier) This spindly red arch – a symbol of Bangkok – formerly hosted a Brahman festival in honour of Shiva, in which participants would swing in ever higher arcs in an effort to reach a bag of gold suspended from a 15m-high bamboo pole. Whoever grabbed the gold could keep it, but that was no mean feat, and deaths were as common as successes. A black-and-white photo illustrating the risky rite can be seen at the ticket counter at adjacent Wat Suthat.

The Brahmans once enjoyed a mystical position within the royal court, primarily in the coronation rituals. But after the 1932 revolution the Brahmans' waning power was effectively terminated and the festival, including the swinging, was discontinued during the reign of Rama VII (King Prajadhipok; r 1925–35).

In 2007, the Giant Swing was replaced with the current model, which was made from six giant teak logs from Phrae, in northern Thailand. The previous version is kept at the National Museum.

WAT RATCHANATDARAM   BUDDHIST TEMPLE

Map p268 (วัดราชนัดดาราม; Th Mahachai; ⊙8am-5pm; ⛴klorng boat to Phanfa Leelard Pier) **FREE** This temple was built for Rama III (King Phranangklao; r 1824-51) in the 1840s, and its design is said to derive from metal temples built in India and Sri Lanka more than 2000 years ago.

The temple is most stunning at night when the 37 spires – representing the 37 virtues that lead to enlightenment – of the

---

⊙ TOP SIGHT
WAT SUTHAT

The main attraction at this temple compound is Thailand's biggest *wí·hǎhn* (sanctuary) and the imperious yet serene 8m-high **Phra Si Sakayamuni** that resides within. The Buddha image is Thailand's largest surviving Sukhothai-period bronze, cast in the former capital in the 14th century. Today the ashes of Rama VIII (King Ananda Mahidol; r 1935–46) are contained in the base of the image.

Colourful, if now somewhat faded, *Jataka* (murals depicting scenes from the Buddha's life) cover every wall and pillar. The deep-relief wooden doors are also impressive and were carved by artisans including Rama II (King Phraphutthaloetla Naphalai; r 1809–24) himself.

Behind the *wí·hǎhn*, the *bòht* (ordination hall) is the largest of its kind in the country. To add to its list of 'largests', Wat Suthat holds the rank of Rachavoramahavihan, the highest royal temple grade. It maintains a special place in the national religion because of its association with the Brahman priests who perform important ceremonies, such as the Royal Ploughing Ceremony in May. These priests also perform religious rites at two Hindu shrines near the *wát* – **Dhevasathan** (เทวสถาน/โบสถ์พราหมณ์; Map p268; Th Din So; ⊙daylight hours) **FREE** on Th Din So, and the smaller **Vishnu Shrine** (ศาลเทวาลัย พระวิษณุนารายณ์; Map p268; Th Unakan; ⊙daylight hours) **FREE** on Th Unakan.

DON'T MISS

➜ Phra Si Sakayamuni
➜ Temple murals

PRACTICALITIES

➜ วัดสุทัศน์
➜ Map p268, E7
➜ Th Bamrung Meuang
➜ admission 20B
➜ ⊙8.30am-9pm
➜ ⛴klorng boat to Phanfa Leelard Pier

all-metal **Loha Prasat** (Metal Palace) are lit up like a medieval birthday cake. The interior is relatively unadorned by Thai temple standards, but the hallways and square edges contribute to a symmetry reminiscent of the much earlier temples at Angkor, in Cambodia.

At the back of the compound, behind the formal gardens, is a well-known market selling prá krêu·ang (Buddhist amulets) in all sizes, shapes and styles.

PHRA SUMEN FORT & SANTI CHAI PRAKAN PARK   NOTABLE BUILDING, PARK

Map p268 (ป้อมพระสุเมรุ, สวนสันติชัยปราการ; Th Phra Athit; ⏱5am-9pm; 🚤Phra Athit/Banglamphu Pier) **FREE** Formerly the site of a sugar factory, today Santi Chai Prakan Park is a tiny patch of greenery with a great river view and lots of evening action, including comical communal aerobics classes. The riverside pathway heading southwards makes for a serene promenade. The park's most prominent landmark is the blindingly white Phra Sumen Fort, which was built in 1783 to defend the city against a river invasion.

Named for the mythical Phra Sumen (Mt Meru) of Hindu–Buddhist cosmology, the octagonal brick-and-stucco bunker was one of 14 city watchtowers that formerly punctuated the old city wall alongside Khlong Rop Krung (now Khlong Banglamphu but still called Khlong Rop Krung on most signs). Apart from Mahakan Fort (p81), this is the only one still standing.

OCTOBER 14 MEMORIAL   MONUMENT

Map p268 (อนุสรณ์สถาน ๑๔ ตุลา; cnr Th Ratchadamnoen Klang & Th Tanao; ⏱24hr; 🚤klorng boat to Phanfa Leelard Pier) **FREE** A peaceful amphitheatre commemorates the civilian demonstrators who were killed by the military during a pro-democracy rally on 14 October 1973. Over 200,000 people had assembled at the Democracy Monument and along the length of Th Ratchadamnoen to protest against the arrest of political campaigners and continuing military dictatorship. Although some in Thailand continue to deny it, photographs confirm that more than 70 demonstrators were killed when the tanks met the crowd.

The complex is an interesting adaptation of Thai temple architecture for a secular and political purpose. A central *chedi* (stupa) is dedicated to the fallen and a gallery of historic photographs lines the interior wall.

THA OR PIER?

Tâh, often transliterated as *tha*, is the Thai word for 'pier', which explains why some of the signs for the Chao Phraya Express Boat stops say Tha XXX instead of XXX Pier.

MAHAKAN FORT   NOTABLE BUILDING

Map p268 (ป้อมมหากาฬ; Th Ratchadamnoen Klang; ⏱24hr; 🚤klorng boat to Phanfa Leelard Pier) **FREE** Dating back to the late 18th century, white-washed Mahakan Fort is one of two surviving citadels that defended the old walled city. The octagonal fort is a picturesque, if brief and hot, stop en route to Golden Mount, but the neighbouring village is more interesting. This small community of wooden houses has been here for more than 100 years, but since the mid-1990s it has fought the Bangkok municipal government's plan to demolish it and create a 'tourist' park.

In 2016, some of the homes were demolished, but as of press time the community had proposed the area as a Living Heritage Museum and the situation was at a terse standstill. Visitors are welcome. Climb the ramparts (not for children) running away from the fort and walk to the far end, where stairs lead down and into the village.

DEMOCRACY MONUMENT   MONUMENT

Map p268 (อนุสาวรีย์ประชาธิปไตย; Th Ratchadamnoen Klang; 🚤klorng boat to Phanfa Leelard Pier) The Democracy Monument is the focal point of the grand, European-style boulevard that is Th Ratchadamnoen Klang. As the name suggests, it was erected to commemorate Thailand's momentous transformation from absolute to constitutional monarchy.

It was designed by Thai architect Mew Aphaiwong and the relief sculptures were created by Italian Corrado Feroci who, as Silpa Bhirasri, gives his name to Silpakorn University. Feroci combined the square-jawed 'heroes of socialism' style popular at the time with Mew Aphaiwong's art deco influences.

There are 75 cannonballs around the base to signify the year BE (Buddhist Era) 2475 (AD 1932); the four wings of the monument stand 24m tall, representing 24 June, the day the constitution was signed; and the central plinth stands 3m high (June was

BANGLAMPHU SIGHTS

then the third month in the Thai calendar) and supports a chiselled constitution. Each wing has bas-reliefs depicting soldiers, police and civilians who helped usher in the modern Thai state.

EATING

KARIM ROTI-MATABA
THAI **$**

Map p268 (136 Th Phra Athit; mains 40-130B; ⊗9am-10pm Tue-Sun; ✱🖉; 🚤Phra Athit/Banglamphu Pier) This classic Bangkok eatery may have grown a bit too big for its britches in recent years, but it still serves tasty Thai-Muslim dishes such as roti, *gaang màt·sà·màn* ('Muslim curry'), tart fish curry and *má·đà·bà* (something of a stuffed pancake). An upstairs air-con dining area and a couple of outdoor tables provide barely enough seating for loyal fans and curious tourists alike.

THIP SAMAI
THAI **$**

Map p268 (313 Th Mahachai; mains 50-250B; ⊗5pm-2am; 🚤klorng boat to Phanfa Leelard Pier) Brace yourself: you should be aware that the fried noodles sold from carts along Th Khao San have little to do with the dish known as *pàt tai*. Luckily, less than a five-minute túk-túk ride away lies Thip Samai, home to some of the most legendary fried noodles in town.Note that Thip Samai is closed on alternate Wednesdays.

NUTTAPORN
THAI **$**

Map p268 (94 Th Phraeng Phuthon; mains from 20B; ⊗9am-4pm Mon-Sat; 🖉; 🚤Phra Athit/Banglamphu Pier) A crumbling shophouse that for the last 70 years has been churning out some of Bangkok's most famous coconut ice cream – in our opinion, the ideal palate cleanser after a bowl of spicy noodles. Other uniquely domestic flavours include mango, Thai tea, and for the daring, durian.

KIMLENG
THAI **$**

Map p268 (158-160 Th Tanao; mains 60-150B; ⊗10am-10pm Mon-Sat; ✱; 🚤klorng boat to Phanfa Leelard Pier) This tiny family-run restaurant specialises in the dishes and flavours of central Thailand. It's a good place to dip your toes in the local cuisine via an authentic *yam* (Thai-style salad), such as *yam plah dùk foo,* a mixture of catfish deep-fried until crispy and strands of tart, green mango.

TOP SIGHT
GOLDEN MOUNT & WAT SAKET

Before glass and steel towers began growing out of Bangkok's flat riverine plain, the massive **Golden Mount** was the only structure to make any significant impression on the horizon. The mount was commissioned by Rama III (King Phranangklao; r 1824–51), who ordered that the earth dug out to create Bangkok's expanding *klorng* (canal) network be piled up to build a 100m-high, 500m-wide *chedi* (stupa). As the hill grew, however, the weight became too much for the soft soil beneath and the project was abandoned until his successor built a small gilded *chedi* on its crest and added trees to stave off erosion. Rama V (King Chulalongkorn; r 1868–1910) later added to the structure and interred a Buddha relic from India in the *chedi*. The concrete walls were added during WWII. At the peak, you'll find a breezy 360° view of Bangkok's most photogenic side.

Next door, seemingly peaceful **Wat Saket** contains murals that are among both the most beautiful and the goriest in the country; proceed directly to the pillar behind the Buddha statue for explicit depictions of Buddhist hell.

DON'T MISS

➡ View from the summit of Golden Mount
➡ Temple paintings at Wat Saket

PRACTICALITIES

➡ ภูเขาทอง & วัดสระเกศ
➡ Map p268, H6
➡ Th Boriphat
➡ admission to summit of Golden Mount 10B
➡ ⊗7.30am-5.30pm
➡ 🚤klorng boat to Phanfa Leelard Pier

CHOTE CHITR

THAI $

Map p268 (146 Th Phraeng Phuthon; mains 60-200B;
⊗11am-10pm; 🚢klorng boat to Phanfa Leelard Pier)
This third-generation shophouse restaurant
boasting just six tables is a Bangkok foodie
landmark. The kitchen can be inconsistent
and the service is consistently grumpy, but
when they're on, dishes like *mèe gròrp* (crispy
fried noodles) and *yam tòo·a ploo* (wing-bean
salad) are in a class of their own.

★ KRUA APSORN

THAI $$

Map p268 (www.kruaapsorn.com; Th Din So; mains
100-450B; ⊗10.30am-8pm Mon-Sat; 🅰; 🚢klorng
boat to Phanfa Leelard Pier) This cafeteria-like
dining room is a favourite of members of
the Thai royal family and restaurant critics
alike. Just about all of the central and south-
ern Thai dishes are tasty, but regulars never
miss the chance to order the decadent stir-
fried crab with yellow pepper chili or the
tortilla Española–like fluffy crab omelette.
There's another branch (p96) on Th Samsen
in Thewet and Dusit.

SHOSHANA

ISRAELI $$

Map p268 (88 Th Chakraphatdi Phong; mains
80-320B; ⊗10am-midnight; 🅰🅰; 🚢Phra
Athit/Banglamphu Pier) One of Khao San's
longest-running Israeli restaurants, Shoshana resembles your grandparents' living
room right down to the tacky wall art and
plastic placemats. Feel safe in ordering
anything deep-fried – staff do an excellent
job of it – and don't miss the deliciously
garlicky eggplant dip.

BAAN NUAL

THAI $$

Map p268 (📞081 889 7403; 372 Soi 2, Th Sam-
sen, no Roman-script sign; mains 70-390B;
⊗noon-9pm Tue-Fri, 4-9pm Sat & Sun; 🚢Phra
Athit/Banglamphu Pier) It's come full circle:
the restaurateurs of today are design-
ing venues that resemble the holes-in-
the-wall of yesteryear. With three tables
and retro charm in spades, Baan Nual
is the epitome of this trend. But rest as-
sured that the rich, rather meaty central
Thai fare delivers. The English-language
menu is limited, but you can hop onto the
restaurant's Instagram feed (@baannual
372) for more options.

BANGKOK POUTINE

INTERNATIONAL $$

Map p268 (www.facebook.com/bangkokpoutine;
Th Samsen; mains 70-200B; ⊗noon-midnight
Tue-Sun; 🅰🅰; 🚢Phra Athit/Banglamphu Pier)
You've conquered the deep-fried scorpion,

❶ VEGGING OUT IN BANGLAMPHU

Due to the strong foreign influence,
there's an abundance of vegetarian
restaurants in the Banglamphu area. In
addition to **Hemlock**, **Shoshana** and
Bangkok Poutine, all of which have
generous meat-free menus, other vegie dining destinations include **Arawy
Vegetarian Food** (152 Th Din So; mains
from 30B; ⊗7am-8pm; 🅰; 🚢klorng boat
to Phanfa Leelard Pier), with heaps of
prepared meat-free curries, dips and
stir-fries; and **May Kaidee's** (Map 268;
www.maykaidee.com; 59 Th Tanao; mains
80-120B; ⊗9am-10pm; 🅰🅰; 🚢Phra
Athit/Banglamphu Pier), a long-standing
restaurant that also houses a vegie
Thai cooking school.

now wrangle with poutine: French fries
topped with cheese curds and gravy. Run
by guys from Québec, this is the place to go
for Francophone pop and the latest hockey
game, as well as dishes ranging in cuisine
from Thai to Lebanese, including lots of
meat-free items.

HEMLOCK

THAI $$

Map p268 (56 Th Phra Athit; mains 75-280B;
⊗4pm-midnight Mon-Sat; 🅰🅰; 🚢Phra Athit/
Banglamphu Pier) Taking full advantage of
its cosy shophouse location, this perennial
favourite has enough style to feel like a spe-
cial night out, but doesn't skimp on flavour
or preparation. The eclectic menu reads like
an ancient literary work, reviving old dishes
from aristocratic kitchens across the coun-
try, not to mention several meat-free items.

POJ SPA KAR

THAI $$

Map p268 (443 Th Tanao; mains 65-200B;
⊗12.30-8.30pm; 🅰; 🚢klorng boat to Phanfa
Leelard Pier) Pronounced *pôht sà·pah kahn,*
this is allegedly the oldest restaurant in
Bangkok, and it continues to maintain
recipes handed down from a former palace cook. Be sure to order the simple but
tasty lemongrass omelette or the deliciously
sour-sweet *gaang sôm*, a traditional central
Thai soup.

★ JAY FAI

THAI $$$

Map p268 (327 Th Mahachai; mains 180-1000B;
⊗3pm-2am Mon-Sat; 🚢klorng boat to Phanfa
Leelard Pier) With its bare-bones dining

LOCAL KNOWLEDGE

A NOODLE TOUR OF TH PHRA ATHIT

Despite being virtually next door to touristy Th Khao San, Th Phra Athit remains a microcosm of noodle dishes from Bangkok – and beyond. If you're interested in sampling some of Thailand's more obscure noodle dishes, consider one of the following:

Soy (Map p268; 100/2-3 Th Phra Athit, no Roman-script sign; mains 80-100B; ⏲7am-5.30pm; ⛴Phra Athit/Banglamphu Pier) Long-standing and lauded Soy serves big, hearty bowls of beef noodle soup. Choose between the fall-apart tender braised beef, fresh beef, beef balls, or all of the above. There's no English-language sign here; look for the open-fronted shophouse with red plastic chairs.

Khun Daeng (Map p268; Th Phra Athit, no Roman-script sign; mains 45-55B; ⏲11am-9.30pm Mon-Sat; ⛴Phra Athit/Banglamphu Pier) This popular place does *gŏo·ay jáp yoo·an*, identified on the English-language menu as 'Vietnamese noodle'. Introduced to northeastern Thailand via Vietnamese immigrants, the dish combines peppery pork sausage, a quail egg, thin rice noodles and a garnish of crispy fried shallots in a slightly viscous broth. Khun Daeng has no English-language sign; look for the white-and-green shopfront.

Somsong Phochana (Map p268; off Th Lamphu; mains from 30B; ⏲9.30am-4pm; ⛴Phra Athit/Banglamphu Pier) This is one of the few places in Bangkok that serves *gŏo·ay đĕe·o sù·kŏh·tai*, Sukhothai-style noodles: slices of barbecued pork and thin rice noodles in a clear pork broth seasoned with a little sugar, supplemented with sliced green beans and garnished with ground peanuts. To find Somsong, enter Th Lamphu, then take the first left, opposite Watsungwej School; the restaurant is on the right.

Pua-Kee (Map p268; Th Phra Sumen, no Roman-script sign; mains 50-90B; ⏲9am-4pm; ⛴Phra Athit/Banglamphu Pier) Come here for the central Thai classic, *gŏo·ay đĕe·o đôm yam* ('rice noodle soup hotspicy with mixed ball' on the menu), fishball noodles pre-seasoned with sugar, lime and dried chilli, and served with a crispy deep-fried wonton. There's no English-language sign here, but it's located next door to the clearly labelled Makalin Clinic.

room, it's hard to believe Jay Fai is renowned for serving Bangkok's most expensive *pàt kêe mow* ('drunkard's noodles': wide rice noodles fried with seafood and Thai herbs). The price, however, is justified by the copious fresh seafood, plus a distinct frying style resulting in an almost oil-free finished dish.It's in a virtually unmarked shophouse, opposite a 7-Eleven.

RARB — THAI $$$

Map p268 (49 Th Phra Athit; mains 300-500B; ⏲5pm-midnight Tue-Sun; [S] Saphan Taksin) Sip a potent R-rated cocktail (their names might make you blush) crafted by award-winning bartender Karn Liangsrisuk, formerly of the next-door burger institution Escapade, while '70s Thai funk plays. This resto-bar is tiny, but their *lâhp mŏo* (spicy pork salad) is outstanding when paired with house-toasted rice and the chef's secret blend of spices and chillies. A truly local joint in an up-and-coming hood.

DRINKING & NIGHTLIFE

Rowdy Th Khao San is one of the city's best areas for a night out. And although Banglamphu used to be an almost exclusively foreign scene, in recent years, locals have joined the mix, especially along Th Phra Athit. If the main drag is too intense, consider the (slightly) quieter places along Soi Ram Buttri and Th Samsen.

KU BAR — BAR

Map p268 (www.facebook.com/ku.bangkok; 3rd fl, 469 Th Phra Sumen; ⏲7pm-midnight Thu-Sun) Tired of buckets and cocktails that revolve around Red Bull? Head to Ku Bar, in almost every way the polar opposite of the Khao San party scene. Climb three floors of stairs (look for the tiny sign) to emerge at an almost comically minimalist interior where sophisticated fruit- and food-heavy cocktails (sample names: Lychee, Tomato,

Pineapple/Red Pepper) and obscure music augment the underground vibe.

COMMÉ
BAR

Map p268 (100/4-5 Th Phra Athit; ⏱6pm-1am; 🚇Phra Athit/Banglamphu Pier) The knot of vintage motorcycles is your visual cue, but most likely you'll hear Commé before you see it. A staple for local hipsters, this classic Th Phra Athit semi-open-air bar is the place to go for a loud, boozy, Thai-style night out.

HIPPIE DE BAR
BAR

Map p268 (www.facebook.com/hippie.debar; 46 Th Khao San; ⏱3pm-2am; 🚇Phra Athit/Banglamphu Pier) Hippie boasts a funky retro vibe and indoor and outdoor seating, all set to the type of indie-pop soundtrack that you're unlikely to hear elsewhere in town. Despite being located on Th Khao San, there are surprisingly few foreign faces, and it's a great place to make some new Thai friends.

THE BANK
BAR

Map p268 (3rd fl, 44 Th Chakraphatdi Phong; ⏱6pm-late; 🚇Phra Athit/Banglamphu Pier) This vaguely Middle Eastern–themed bar represents the posh alter ego of Th Khao San. There's live music, lounges for puffing on *shisha* (waterpipes), and a dark club. And the bar's elevated setting appears to lend it some leniency with the city's strict closing times.

MADAME MUSUR
BAR

Map p268 (www.facebook.com/madamemusur; 41 Soi Ram Buttri; ⏱8am-midnight; 🚇Phra Athit/Banglamphu Pier) Saving you the trip north to Pai, Madame Musur pulls off that elusive combination of northern Thailand meets *The Beach* meets Th Khao San. It's a fun place to chat, drink and people-watch, and it's also not a bad place to eat, with a short menu of northern Thai dishes priced from 100B to 200B.

THE CLUB
CLUB

Map p268 (www.facebook.com/theclubkhaosan-bkk; 123 Th Khao San; admission Fri & Sat 120B; ⏱9pm-2am; 🚇Phra Athit/Banglamphu Pier) Located right in the middle of Th Khao San, this cavern-like dance hall hosts a good mix of locals and backpackers; check the Facebook page for upcoming events and guest DJs.

PHRA NAKORN BAR & GALLERY
BAR

Map p268 (www.facebook.com/Phranakornbarandgallery; 58/2 Soi Damnoen Klang Tai; ⏱6pm-1am; 🚇klorng boat to Phanfa Leelard Pier) Located an ambivalent arm's length from the hype of Th Khao San, Phra Nakorn Bar and Gallery is a home away from hovel for Thai students and arty types, with eclectic decor and changing gallery exhibits. Our tip: head directly for the breezy rooftop and order some of the bar's cheap and tasty Thai food.

ROLLING BAR
BAR

Map p268 (Th Prachathipatai; ⏱5pm-midnight; 🚇klorng boat to Phanfa Leelard Pier) An escape from hectic Th Khao San is a good enough excuse to schlep to this quiet canalside boozer. Live music and salty bar snacks are reasons to stay.

JHAM JUN
BAR

Map p268 (rooftop, Fortville Guesthouse, 9 Th Phra Sumen; ⏱6pm-1am; 🚇Phra Athit/Banglamphu Pier) Boasting a rooftop address, a casual, loungey vibe, live music and an emphasis on food, Jham Jun is a characteristically Thai-style drinking spot a short walk from Th Khao San.

LAVA GOLD
CLUB

Map p268 (www.facebook.com/Lava.Gold.Club; 249 Th Khao San; ⏱7pm-4am; 🚇Tha Phra Athit/Banglamphu) Descend the stairs to this long-standing, perpetually packed, Th Khao San disco. The DJs are probably not going to win international acclaim, but that's the way the boozy crowd likes it.

☆ ENTERTAINMENT

★ BRICK BAR
LIVE MUSIC

Map p268 (www.brickbarkhaosan.com; basement, Buddy Lodge, 265 Th Khao San; admission Sat & Sun 150B; ⏱7pm-1.30am; 🚇Phra Athit/Banglamphu Pier) This basement pub, one of our favourite destinations in Bangkok for live music, hosts a nightly revolving cast of bands for an almost exclusively Thai crowd – many of whom will end the night dancing on the tables. Brick Bar can get infamously packed, so be sure to get there early.

BROWN SUGAR
LIVE MUSIC

Map p268 (www.brownsugarbangkok.com; 469 Th Phra Sumen; ⏱5pm-1am Tue-Thu & Sun, to 2am Fri & Sat; 🚇klorng boat to Phanfa Leelard Pier, Phra Athit/Banglamphu Pier) Located in a cavernous shophouse is this long-standing live-music staple. The music, which spans from funk to

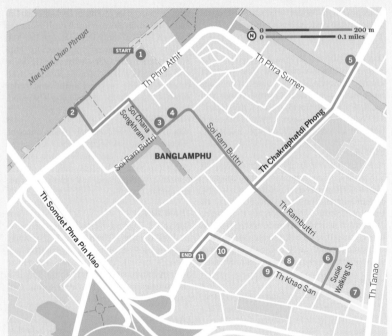

🏃 Neighbourhood Walk
Banglamphu Pub Crawl

START SHEEPSHANK
END THE BANK
LENGTH 1.5KM; THREE TO SIX HOURS

You don't need to go too far to find a bar in Banglamphu, but why limit yourself to one? With this in mind, we've assembled a pub crawl that spans river views, people-watching, live music and late-night shenanigans.

Begin your crawl in sophisticated, air-conditioned comfort at ❶ **Sheepshank**, a gastropub with an intriguing menu of bar snacks and classic cocktails. If you still have space for tapas, head west along the riverfront promenade until you reach ❷ **Babble & Rum**, the Riva Surya hotel's open-air restaurant-bar.

From Th Phra Athit, enter Soi Chana Songkhram and take a left on Soi Ram Buttri, where you begin phase two of your crawl: people-watching. ❸ **Gecko Bar** is a fun and frugal place to gawk at other patrons and passers-by, while a few doors down, ❹ **Madame Musur** (p85) offers the

same perks, but with a bit more sophistication and tasty northern-style eats.

It's time to add some music to the mix, so for phase three, head north on Th Chakraphatdi Phong to the long-standing blues bar ❺ **Ad Here the 13th** (p87) or to one of the open-air live music bars along Th Rambuttri, such as ❻ **Molly Bar**.

At this point, you should be lubricated enough for the main event, so, crossing via Susie Walking St, proceed to Th Khao San. If you need a bathroom or a blast of air-con, make a pit stop at ❼ **Mulligans**, an Irish-themed bar in the Buddy Lodge. Otherwise, get a bird's-eye view of the human parade from elevated ❽ **The Roof Bar**, or ringside at the noisy and buzzy ❾ **Center Khao Sarn**.

End the night on a good note by planting yourself at ❿ **Hippie de Bar** (p85), one of Banglamphu's best bars. Or if 2am is too early to call it a night, crawl over to ⓫ **The Bank** (p85), a rooftop lounge and nightclub that stays open until late.

jazz, starts at 8pm most nights, and on weekends in particular, draws heaps of locals.

JAZZ HAPPENS! LIVE MUSIC

Map p268 (www.jazzhappens.org; 62 Th Phra Athit; ☺7pm-1am; ☏; ⛴Phra Athit/Banglamphu Pier) Linked with Silpakorn University, Thailand's most famous arts university, jazz happens! is a stage for aspiring musical talent. With four acts playing most nights of the week and a huge selection of bar snacks, you'll be thoroughly entertained.

AD HERE THE 13TH LIVE MUSIC

Map p268 (www.facebook.com/adhere13thbluesbar; 13 Th Samsen; ☺6pm-midnight; ⛴Phra Athit/Banglamphu Pier) This closet-sized blues bar is everything a neighbourhood joint should be: lots of regulars, cold beer and heart-warming tunes delivered by a masterful house band (starting at 10pm). Everyone knows each other, so don't be shy about mingling.

🛍 SHOPPING

★ THANON KHAO

SAN MARKET GIFTS & SOUVENIRS

Map p268 (Th Khao San; ☺10am-midnight; ⛴Phra Athit/Banglamphu Pier) The main guesthouse strip in Banglamphu is a day-and-night shopping bazaar peddling all the backpacker 'essentials': profane T-shirts, bootleg MP3s, hemp clothing, fake student ID cards, knock-off designer wear, selfie sticks, orange juice and, of course, those croaking wooden frogs.

HERITAGE CRAFT ARTS & CRAFTS

Map p268 (35 Th Bamrung Meuang; ☺11am-6pm Mon-Fri; ⛴klorng boat to Phanfa Leelard Pier) Handicrafts with a conscience: this new boutique is an atmospheric showcase for the quality domestic wares of ThaiCraft (p153), some of which are produced via fairtrade practices. Items include silks from Thailand's northeast, baskets from the south and jewellery from the north, and there's also an inviting on-site cafe.

MOWAAN HEALTH & WELLBEING

Map p268 (www.mowaan.com/en; 9 Soi Thesa; ☺9am-5pm; ⛴klorng boat to Phanfa Leelard Pier) With nearly a century under its belt, this brand makes lozenges, inhalers, oils and balms rooted in Thai herbal medicine. Even if you are in satisfactory health, a visit

to the immaculately preserved showroom is akin to a trip back in time.

LOFTY BAMBOO ARTS & CRAFTS

Map p268 (ground fl, Buddy Lodge, 265 Th Khao San; ☺10.30am-8pm; ⛴Phra Athit/Banglamphu Pier) No time to make it to northern Thailand? No problem. At this shop you can get the type of colourful, hill-tribe-inspired clothes, cloth items and other handicrafts you'd find at the markets in Chiang Mai and Chiang Rai. And best of all, a purchase supports economic self-sufficiency in upcountry villages.

NITTAYA THAI CURRY FOOD & DRINKS

Map p268 (136-40 Th Chakraphatdi Phong; ☺9am-7pm Mon-Sat; ⛴Phra Athit/Banglamphu Pier) Follow your nose: Nittaya is famous throughout Thailand for her pungent, high-quality curry pastes. Pick up a couple of takeaway canisters for prospective dinner parties or peruse the snack and gift sections, where visitors to Bangkok load up on local specialities for friends and family back in the provinces.

TAEKEE TAEKON ARTS & CRAFTS

Map p268 (118 Th Phra Athit; ☺9am-5pm Mon-Sat; ⛴Phra Athit/Banglamphu Pier) This atmospheric shop has a decent selection of Thai textiles from the country's main silk-producing areas, especially northern Thailand, as well as interesting postcards not widely available elsewhere.

🏃 SPORTS & ACTIVITIES

BANGKOK BOLD

COOKING STUDIO COOKING

Map p268 (☎098 829 4310; www.facebook.com/bangkokboldcookingstudio; 503 Th Phra Sumen; classes 2500-4500B; ☺11am-2pm; ⛴klorng boat to Phanfa Leelard Pier) The newest venture by a team that previously ran a popular cooking school on Th Khao San, Bold offers daily courses ranging in difficulty from beginner to intermediate in three Thai dishes, with lessons taught in a chic shophouse setting.

JAROENTHONG

MUAY THAI GYM MARTIAL ARTS

Map p268 (☎02 629 2313; www.jaroenthongmuaythaikhaosan.com; Th Phra Athit; lessons from 600B; ☺drop-in hours 10-11.30am &

WHAT'S SO LONELY ABOUT THE KHAO SAN ROAD?

Th Khao San, better known as Khao San Rd, is genuinely unlike anywhere else on earth. It's an international clearing house of people either entering the liberated state of travelling in Southeast Asia or returning to the coddling bonds of 'real' life, all coming together in a neon-lit melting pot in Banglamphu. Its uniqueness is probably best illustrated by a question: apart from airports, where else could you share space with the citizens of dozens of countries at the same time, people ranging from first-time backpackers scoffing banana pancakes to 75-year-old grandparents ordering G&Ts, and everyone in between, including hippies, hipsters, nerds, glamazons, package tourists, global nomads, people on a week's holiday and those taking a gap year, people of every colour and creed looking at you looking at them looking at everyone else?

Th Khao San (*kâw săhn*, meaning 'uncooked rice') is perhaps the most high-profile bastard child of the age of independent travel. Of course, it hasn't always been this way. For its first two centuries or so it was just another unremarkable road in old Bangkok. To see what it was like back in the day, you can stop into the **Khaosan Museum** (ข้าวสารมิวเซียม; Map p268; 1st fl, 201 Th Khao San; ⊙9am-9pm; 호Phra Athit/Banglamphu Pier) `FREE`. The first guesthouses appeared in 1982, and as more backpackers arrived through the '80s the old wooden homes were converted one by one into low-rent dosshouses. By the time Alex Garland's novel *The Beach* was published in 1997, with its opening scenes set in the seedier side of Khao San, staying here had become a rite of passage for backpackers coming to Southeast Asia.

The publicity from Garland's book and the movie that followed pushed Khao San into the mainstream, romanticising the seedy, and stereotyping the backpackers it attracted as unwashed and counterculturalist. It also brought the long-simmering debate about the relative merits of Th Khao San to the top of backpacker conversations across the region. Was it cool to stay on KSR? Was it uncool? Was this 'real travel' or just an international anywhere surviving on the few baht Western backpackers spent before they headed home to start their high-earning careers? Was it really Thailand at all?

Perhaps one of Garland's characters summed it up most memorably when he said: 'You know, Richard, one of these days I'm going to find one of those Lonely Planet writers and I'm going to ask him, what's so fucking lonely about the Khao San Road?'

Today more than ever the answer would have to be: not that much. With the help of all that publicity, Khao San continued to evolve, with bedbug-infested guesthouses replaced by boutique hotels, and downmarket TV bars showing pirated movies transformed into hip design bars peopled by flashpackers in designer threads. But the most interesting change has been in the way Thais see Khao San.

Once written off as home to cheap, dirty *fa·ràng kêe ngók* (stingy foreigners), Banglamphu has become just about the coolest district in Bangkok. Attracted in part by the long-derided independent traveller and their modern ideas, the city's own counterculture kids have moved in and brought with them a tasty selection of small bars, organic cafes and shops. Indeed, Bangkok's indie crowd has proved to be the Thai spice this melting pot always lacked.

Not that Khao San has moved completely away from its backpacker roots. The strip still anticipates every traveller need: meals to soothe homesickness, cafes and bars for swapping travel tales about getting to the Cambodian border, tailors, travel agents, teeth whitening, secondhand books, hair braiding and, of course, the perennial Akha women trying to harass everyone they see into buying wooden frogs. No, it's not very lonely at all...

2-9pm; 호Phra Athit/Banglamphu Pier) With branches around the country, this lauded gym has opened up an outlet a short walk from Th Khao San. Beginners can drop in and train in air-conditioned comfort, or the more experienced can opt for longer training regimens.

GRASSHOPPER ADVENTURES   CYCLING

Map p268 (☑02 280 0832; www.grasshopperadventures.com; 57 Th Ratchadamnoen Klang; half-/full-day tours from 1350/2400B; ☺8.30am-6.30pm; ⚑klorng boat to Phanfa Leelard Pier) This lauded outfit runs a variety of unique bicycle tours in and around Bangkok, including a night tour and a tour of the city's historic zone.

VELO THAILAND   CYCLING

Map p268 (☑02 628 8628, 089 201 7782; www.velothailand.com; 29 Soi 4, Th Samsen; tours from 1000B; ☺10am-7pm; ⚑Phra Athit/Banglamphu Pier) Velo is a small and personal bike-tour outfit based out of Banglamphu. Day and night tours to Thonburi and further afield are on offer.

BAAN CHAO YOGA   YOGA

Map p268 (☑062 007 4796; ASTV Bldg, Th Phra Athit; courses 300B; ☺lessons 5.30-6.30pm Mon-Fri; ⚑Phra Athit/Banglamphu Pier) A yoga studio with daily hour-long sessions and English-language instruction, located a brief walk from Th Khao San. Walk-ins are encouraged.

SOR VORAPIN GYM   MARTIAL ARTS

Map p268 (☑02 282 3551; www.thaiboxings.com; 13 Th Kasab; per session/month 500/9000B; ☺lessons 7.30-9.30am & 3-5pm; ⚑Phra Athit/Banglamphu Pier) Conveniently located steps from Th Khao San, this gym offers training in *moo·ay tai* (Thai boxing) for foreign students of both genders.

Thewet & Dusit

Neighbourhood Top Five

1 Dusit Palace Park
(p92) Witnessing Victorian sense and Thai sensibilities merge in this fairy-tale-like former royal enclave.

2 Rajadamnern Stadium
(p97) Cheering on Thai boxing – the sport that makes Steven Seagal look

as soft as a pillow – at the county's most venerable and prestigious venue.

3 Khinlom Chom Sa-Phan
(p96) Enjoying tasty, breezy, open-air dining at the area's riverside restaurants.

4 Wat Benchamabophit
(p94) Wondering what

country you're in while among the Carrara marble, European-style frescoes and red carpet of this unique Buddhist temple.

5 Krua Apsorn (p96) Sampling homestyle Thai food good enough for royalty at this lauded restaurant.

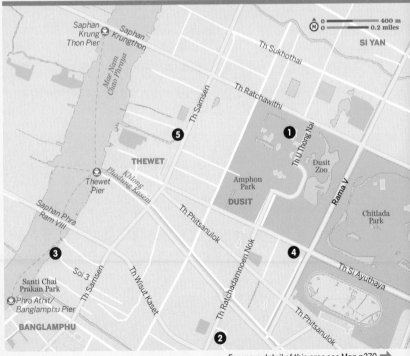

For more detail of this area see Map p270 ➡

Explore Thewet & Dusit

Thewet, particularly the area near Th Samsen, has the hectic, buzzy feel often associated with Bangkok: relentless traffic, throngs of civil servants and schoolkids, and a soggy market. The adjacent river is the only respite from the action, and it also functions as a good point from which to approach the area, as most sights and restaurants are a short walk from the river ferry pier. Plan to visit this area at lunch or dinner time to best take advantage of the riverside restaurants.

Dusit, on the other hand, is possibly Bangkok's most orderly district, home to the kind of tree-lined avenues and regal monuments you'd expect to find in Paris. Set aside a few hours – ideally in the cool morning – to visit the area's gems: Dusit Palace Park and Wat Benchamabophit.

Local Life

→ **Local Hero** Visit the Rama V Memorial (p94) on any Tuesday (the day of his birth) to witness worshippers make offerings. An even larger celebration is on 23 October, the anniversary of the former monarch's death.

→ **Boxing Day Dinner** Planning to watch Thai boxing at Rajadamnern Stadium (p97)? Do as the locals do: grab a plate of *gài yâhng* (grilled chicken) beforehand from the restaurants surrounding the stadium, such as Likhit Kai Yang (p96).

→ **Royal Digs** Chitlada Palace (p95) is the official residence of the royal family. The compound is generally closed to the public, and you're not likely to see any royals, but it's worth taking a peek through the gates.

→ **Time Machine** Nang Loeng Market (p96) provides a glimpse into Bangkok's yesteryear. Particularly emblematic is the market area's wooden movie theatre, allegedly the city's oldest, slated to be renovated in time for its 2018 centenary.

Getting There & Away

→ **Chao Phraya Express Boat** One way to approach the Thewet and Dusit areas is via the river ferry stop at Thewet Pier. From here it's a brief walk through shady walkways to the riverside restaurants, or a short túk-túk or taxi ride to Dusit Palace Park and other attractions.

→ **Bus** Air-con 505, 510 and 510; ordinary 3, 16, 18, 32, 53, 70 and 72.

→ **BTS** An option best attempted outside of rush hours is to take the BTS to Phaya Thai before continuing by taxi.

Lonely Planet's Top Tip

If you're keen to see a Thai boxing match at Rajadamnern Stadium, go on a Thursday night, when aficionados say the best-matched bouts are on.

✕ Best Places to Eat

→ Likhit Kai Yang (p96)
→ Krua Apsorn (p96)
→ Nang Loeng Market (p96)
→ Khinlom Chom Sa-Phan (p96)
→ Steve Café & Cuisine (p96)

For reviews, see p96 →

☕ Best Drinking & Nightlife

→ Hazel's Ice Cream Parlor & Fine Drinks (p97)
→ Post Bar (p97)
→ Khinlom Chom Sa-Phan (p96)

For reviews, see p97 →

⊙ Best Historical Structures

→ Vimanmek Teak Mansion (p93)
→ Wat Benchamabophit (p94)
→ Abhisek Dusit Throne Hall Ananta (p93)
→ Ananta Samakhom Throne Hall (p94)

For reviews, see p93 →

THEWET & DUSIT

AJISAI13 / SHUTTERSTOCK ©

TOP SIGHT
DUSIT PALACE PARK

Following his first European tour in 1897, Rama V (King Chulalongkorn; r 1868–1910) returned with visions of European castles and set about transforming these styles into a uniquely Thai expression, today's Dusit Palace Park.

At the time of research, Dusit Palace Park was closed for renovations.

Vimanmek Teak Mansion

Originally constructed on Ko Si Chang in 1868 and moved to the present site in 1910, Vimanmek Teak Mansion (pictured above) contains 81 rooms, halls and anterooms, and is said to be the world's largest golden-teak building, allegedly built without the use of a single nail. The interior of the mansion contains various personal effects of the king and a treasure trove of early Ratanakosin-era art objects and antiques. Compulsory tours (in English) leave every 30 minutes between 9.45am and 3.15pm, and last about an hour.

Abhisek Dusit Throne Hall

Originally built as a throne hall for Rama V in 1904, the smaller Abhisek Dusit Throne Hall is typical of the finer architecture of the era. Victorian-influenced gingerbread architecture and Moorish porticoes blend to create a striking and distinctly Thai exterior. The hall houses an excellent display of regional handiwork crafted by members of the Promotion of Supplementary Occupations & Related Techniques (Support)

DON'T MISS...

- Vimanmek Teak Mansion
- Abhisek Dusit Throne Hall
- Royal Thai Elephant Museum
- Ancient Cloth Museum

PRACTICALITIES

- วังสวนดุสิต
- Map p270, C2
- bounded by Th Ratchawithi, Th U Thong Nai & Th Nakhon Ratchasima
- adult/child 100/20B, or free with Grand Palace ticket
- ⏲9.30am-4pm Tue-Sun
- ⛴Thewet Pier, [S]Phaya Thai exit 2 & taxi

foundation, a charity organisation sponsored by Queen Sirikit. The hall was closed for renovations when we visited.

Royal Thai Elephant Museum

Think 'white elephant' and something like Howard Hughes' Spruce Goose comes to mind. But why is it that this and other supposedly valuable but hugely expensive and basically useless items are known as white elephants? The answer lies in the sacred status given to albino elephants by the kings of Thailand, Cambodia, Laos and Myanmar.

The tradition derives from the story in which the Buddha's mother is said to have dreamt of a white elephant presenting her with a lotus flower – a symbol of purity and wisdom – just before she gave birth. Extrapolating from this, a monarch possessing a white elephant was regarded as a just and benign ruler.

Across the region any genuinely albino elephant automatically became crown property; the physical characteristics used to identify and rank white elephants are outlined in the Royal Thai Elephant Museum.

Near the Th U Thong Nai entrance of Dusit Palace Park, two large stables that once housed three white elephants. One of the structures contains artefacts and photos outlining the importance of elephants in Thai history and explaining their various rankings according to physical characteristics. The second stable holds a sculptural representation of a living royal white elephant. Draped in royal vestments, the statue is more or less treated as a shrine by the visiting Thai public.

In contemporary Thailand, the white elephant has retained its sacred status – indeed, the animal was prominently featured on the flag of Siam from 1855 to 1916 – and the late King Bhumibol Adulyadej possessed 11 of them, more than any previous monarch. The elephants were once kept at Chitlada Palace in Bangkok, but now reside at three different locations upcountry.

Ancient Cloth Museum

The Ancient Cloth Museum contains a beautiful – and informative – assemblage of traditional silks and cottons from across the Thai-speaking world, although at the time of research it was closed for renovations.

TOP TIPS

➡ Admission to Dusit Palace Park is included with the Grand Palace ticket fee.

➡ Because Dusit Palace Park is royal property, visitors should wear long pants (no cropped pants) or long skirts and sleeved shirts.

TAKE A BREAK

If you find yourself at Dusit Palace Park at lunchtime, head to Likhit Kai Yang (p96) for some of the city's best grilled chicken. If it's evening, get a craft beer or a boozy ice cream coke at Hazel's Ice Cream Parlor & Fine Drinks (p97).

THEWET & DUSIT DUSIT PALACE PARK

⊙ SIGHTS

DUSIT PALACE PARK   MUSEUM, HISTORIC SITE
See p92.

WAT BENCHAMABOPHIT   BUDDHIST TEMPLE
Map p270 (วัดเบญจมบพิตร/วัดเบญจะฯ; cnr Th Si Ayuthaya & Rama V; 20B; ⊙8am-6pm; 🚲Thewet Pier, 🚊Phaya Thai exit 3 & taxi) You might recognise this temple from the back of the 5B coin. Made of white marble imported from Italy, the distinctive *bòht* (ordination hall) of Wat Ben, as it's colloquially known, was built in the late 19th century under Rama V. The base of the central Buddha image, a copy of the revered Phra Phuttha Chinnarat in Phitsanulok, northern Thailand, contains his ashes.

The structure is a unique example of modern Thai temple architecture, as is the interior design, which melds Thai features with European influences: the red carpets, the gold-on-white motifs painted repetitively on the walls, the walls painted like stained-glass windows and the royal blue wall behind the central Buddha image are strongly reminiscent of a European palace. It's not all that surprising when you consider how enamoured Rama V was with Europe – just walk across the street to Dusit Palace Park for further evidence.

The courtyard behind the *bòht* has 53 Buddha images (33 originals and 20 copies) representing every *mudra* (gesture) and style from Thai history, making this the ideal place to compare Buddhist iconography. If religious imagery isn't your thing, this temple still offers a pleasant stroll beside landscaped canals filled with blooming lotus and Chinese-style footbridges.

**ANANTA SAMAKHOM
THRONE HALL**   MUSEUM
Map p270 (พระที่นั่งอนันตสมาคม; www.artsof thekingdom.com; Th U Thong Nai; 150B; ⊙10am-5pm Tue-Sun; 🚲Thewet Pier, 🚊Phaya Thai exit 3 & taxi) The domed neoclassical building behind the Rama V Memorial was originally built as a royal reception hall during the reign of Rama V, but wasn't completed until 1915, five years after his death. Today the building houses an exhibit called Arts of the Kingdom, which, like the nearby Abhisek Dusit Throne Hall, displays the products of Queen Sirikit's Support foundation.

The hall was designed as a place to host – and impress – foreign dignitaries, and on occasion it still serves this purpose, most notably during celebrations of King Bhumibol Adulyadej's 60th year on the throne, when royals from around the world converged here in full regalia (you may encounter a much-published picture of this meeting while in Bangkok). The first meeting of the Thai parliament was held in the building before moved to a facility nearby.

NATIONAL LIBRARY   LIBRARY
Map p270 (หอสมุดแห่งชาติ; Th Samsen; ⊙9am-6.30pm Mon-Fri, to 5pm Sat & Sun; 🚲Thewet Pier) FREE The country's largest repository of books has few foreign-language resources, but its strength is in its astrological books and star charts; the collection also holds recordings by the late King Bhumibol Adulyadej, sacred palm-leaf writings and ancient maps.

DUSIT ZOO   ZOO
Map p270 (สวนสัตว์ดุสิต/เขาดิน; www.dusitzoo. org; Th Ratchawithi; adult/child 150/70B; ⊙8am-6pm; 🚲Thewet Pier, 🚊Phaya Thai exit 3 & taxi) Originally a private botanic garden for Rama V, Dusit Zoo (Suan Sat Dusit or *kŏw din*) was opened in 1938 and is now one of the premier zoological facilities in Southeast Asia. Squeezed into the 19 hectares are more than 300 mammals, 200 reptiles and 800 birds, including relatively rare indigenous species. The shady grounds feature trees labelled in English, plus a lake in the centre with paddle boats for rent.

RAMA V MEMORIAL   MONUMENT
Map p270 (พระบรมรูปทรงม้า; Th U Thong Nai; 🚲Thewet Pier, 🚊Phaya Thai exit 3 & taxi) The bronze figure on horseback is Rama V (King Chulalongkorn; r 1868–1910), the monarch widely credited for steering the country into the modern age and for preserving Thailand's independence from European colonialism. He is also considered a champion of the common person for his abolition of slavery and corvée (the requirement that every citizen be available for state labour when called on).

Rama V's accomplishments are so revered, especially by the middle class, that his statue attracts worshippers (particularly on Tuesdays, the day of his birth),

LOCAL KNOWLEDGE

KICKING & SCREAMING

More formally known as Phahuyut (from the Pali-Sanskrit *bhahu* or 'arm' and *yodha* or 'combat'), Thailand's ancient martial art of *moo·ay tai* (or *muay Thai*) is one of the kingdom's most striking national icons. Overflowing with colour and ceremony as well as exhilarating moments of clenched-teeth action, the best matches serve up a blend of such skill and tenacity that one is tempted to view the spectacle as emblematic of Thailand's centuries-old devotion to independence in a region where most other countries fell under the European colonial yoke.

Many martial-arts aficionados agree that *moo·ay tai* is the most efficient, effective and generally unbeatable form of ring-centred, hand-to-hand combat practised today. According to legend, it has been for a while. After the Siamese were defeated at Ayuthaya in 1767, several expert *moo·ay boh·rahn* (from which *moo·ay tai* is derived) fighters were among the prisoners hauled off to Burma. A few years later a festival was held; one of the Thai fighters, Nai Khanom Tom, was ordered to take on prominent Burmese boxers for the entertainment of the king and to determine which martial art was most effective. He promptly dispatched nine opponents in a row and, as legend has it, was offered money or beautiful women as a reward; he promptly took two new wives. Today a *moo·ay tai* festival in Ayuthaya is named after Nai Khanom Tom.

In the early days of the sport, combatants' fists were wrapped in thick horsehide for maximum impact with minimum knuckle damage; tree bark and seashells were used to protect the groin from lethal kicks. But the high incidence of death and physical injury led the Thai government to ban *moo·ay tai* in the 1920s; in the 1930s the sport was revived under a modern set of regulations. Bouts were limited to five three-minute rounds separated by two-minute breaks. Contestants had to wear international-style gloves and trunks, and their feet were taped – to this day no shoes are worn. In spite of all these concessions to safety, today all surfaces of the body remain fair targets, and any part of the body except the head may be used to strike an opponent. Common blows include high kicks to the neck, elbow thrusts to the face and head, knee hooks to the ribs and low kicks to the calf. Punching is considered the weakest of all blows, and kicking merely a way to 'soften up' one's opponent; knee and elbow strikes are decisive in most matches.

Unlike some martial disciplines, such as kung fu or *qi gong*, *moo·ay tai* doesn't entertain the idea that martial-arts techniques can be passed only from master to disciple in secret. Thus the *moo·ay tai* knowledge base hasn't fossilised – in fact, it remains ever open to innovation, refinement and revision. Thai champion Dieselnoi, for example, created a new approach to knee strikes that was so difficult to defend that he retired at 23 because no one dared to fight him anymore.

Another famous *moo·ay tai* champion is Parinya Kiatbusaba, aka Nong Thoom, a *gà·teu·i* (transgender person) from Chiang Mai who arrived for weigh-ins wearing lipstick and rouge. After a 1998 triumph at Lumphini, Parinya used the prize money to pay for sex reassignment surgery; in 2003, the movie *Beautiful Boxer* was made about her life.

While Bangkok has long attracted foreign fighters, it wasn't until 1999 that French fighter Mourad Sari became the first non-Thai fighter to take home a weight-class championship belt from a Bangkok stadium. Several Thai *nák moo·ay* (fighters) have gone on to triumph in world championships in international-style boxing. Khaosai Galaxy, one of the greatest Asian boxers of all time, successfully defended his World Boxing Association super-flyweight world title 19 times before retiring in 1991.

who make offerings of candles, flowers (predominantly pink roses) and bottles of whisky. The statue is also the site of a huge celebration on 23 October, the anniversary of the monarch's death.

CHITLADA PALACE NOTABLE BUILDING

Map p270 (พระราชวังจิตรลดา; cnr Th Ratchawithi & Rama V; ⛴Thewet Pier, [S]Phaya Thai exit 3 & taxi) Formerly the official residence of the Thai royal family, Chitlada Palace is also

RIVERSIDE DINING

Dinner beside Mae Nam Chao Phraya, where the breezes are cool and aquariums serve as your menu, is a local tradition and a classic Bangkok experience. And while Thewet and Dusit may lack in culinary diversity, they excel in riverfront views. So to narrow your choices, here's the scoop on the areas' riverside restaurants:

Khinlom Chom Sa-Phan (Map p270; ☎02 628 8382; www.khinlomchomsaphan.com; 11/6 Soi 3, Th Samsen; mains 100-2500B; ⏰11.30am-midnight; ⛴Thewet Pier) Probably the best all-around riversider, locals crowd this covered deck just about every night for seafood and live music; as such, you'll need to book ahead for the best tables.

Steve Café & Cuisine (Map p270; www.stevecafeandcuisine.com; 68 Soi 21, Th Si Ayuthaya; mains 180-1900B; ⏰11.30am-2.30pm Mon-Fri, to 11pm Sat & Sun; ⛴Thewet Pier) Despite the cheesy name, Steve is the most sophisticated of the area's riverside restaurants. The menu spans a diverse selection of Thai dishes, and service is friendly and efficient, even when the place is mobbed. To get here, enter Th Si Ayuthaya and walk through Wat Thevaratkunchong until you reach the river; locals will point the way.

Kaloang Home Kitchen (Map p270; Th Si Ayuthaya; mains 80-300B; ⏰10am-10pm; ⛴Thewet Pier) Don't be alarmed by the peeling paint and dilapidated deck at this charmingly unrefined riverside staple – the return customers at Kaloang Home Kitchen certainly aren't. To reach the restaurant, follow the final windy stretch of Th Si Ayuthaya all the way to the river.

In Love (Map p270; Th Krung Kasem; mains 80-280B; ⏰11.30am-midnight; ❄; ⛴Thewet Pier) The budget option for a riverside night out, In Love charms with its great views of Saphan Phra Ram VIII and approachable prices.

a royally funded agriculture centre demonstrating the late King Bhumibol Adulyadej's commitment to the progress of the country's major industry. The palace is not open to the general public and it's pretty difficult to see much from the outside, but you can spot rice paddies and animal pastures – smack in the middle of Bangkok – through the perimeter fence.

EATING

NANG LOENG MARKET — THAI $

Map p270 (btwn Soi 8-10, Th Nakhon Sawan; mains 30-80B; ⏰10am-2pm Mon-Fri; ⛴Thewet Pier, [S]Phaya Thai exit 3 & taxi) Dating back to 1899, this atmospheric fresh market offers a charming glimpse of old Bangkok – not to mention a great place to grab a bite. Nang Loeng is renowned for its Thai sweets, and at lunchtime it's also an excellent place to fill up on central-Thai-style curries or Chinese-influenced noodles.

★LIKHIT KAI YANG — THAI $$

Map p270 (off Th Ratchadamnoen Nok; mains 50-300B; ⏰9am-9pm; ❄; ⛴Thewet Pier, [S]Phaya Thai exit 3 & taxi) Located just behind Rajadamnern Stadium (avoid the grotty branch directly adjacent to the stadium), this decades-old restaurant is where locals come for a northeastern-Thai-style meal before a Thai boxing match. The friendly English-speaking owner will steer you through the ordering process, but don't miss the deliciously herbal, eponymous 'charcoal roasted chicken'. There's no English-language sign; look for the huge yellow banner.

★KRUA APSORN — THAI $$

Map p270 (www.kruaapsorn.com; 503-505 Th Samsen; mains 100-450B; ⏰10.30am-7.30pm Mon-Fri, to 6pm Sat; ❄; ⛴Thewet Pier) This is the original branch of this homey, award-winning and royally patronised restaurant. Expect a clientele of fussy families and big-haired, middle-aged ladies, and a cuisine revolving around full-flavoured, largely seafood- and vegetable-heavy central and southern Thai dishes. If you have dinner in mind, be sure to note the early closing times.

SEVEN SPOONS — INTERNATIONAL $$

Map p270 (☎084 539 1819, 02 629 9214; 22-24 Th Chakraphatdi Phong; mains 200-680B; ⏰11am-3pm & 6-11.30pm Tue-Sat, 6-11.30pm

Sun; ✈; 🚢Thewet Pier, 🚇Phaya Thai exit 3 & taxi) Dark woods, smooth concrete, a menu with influences ranging from Montreal to Morocco, including lots of vegetarian options – one doesn't expect a place this modern and cosmopolitan in such an antiquated corner of Bangkok.

THAMNA
VEGETARIAN **$$**

Map p270 (175 Th Samsen; mains 100-290B; ⊙11am-3pm & 5-9pm Mon-Sat; ✳✈; 🚢Thewet Pier) This self-professed 'hometaurant' specialises in fusiony vegetarian dishes that will make even the meat-eaters smile.

🍷 DRINKING & NIGHTLIFE

HAZEL'S ICE CREAM PARLOR & FINE DRINKS
BAR

Map p270 (www.facebook.com/HazelsParlor; 171 Th Chakraphatdi Phong; ⊙5-11pm Tue-Sat, noon-11pm Sun; 🚢Thewet Pier, 🚇Phaya Thai exit 3 & taxi) Occupying a former publishing house (the original 1950s-era press still prints beautiful documents) is this charming bar-cum-ice cream parlour. Come for adult flavours, boozy shakes, craft beer and live music. And lest you think Hazel's is big

kids-only, Sunday's extended hours make it a family-friendly weekend destination.

POST BAR
BAR

Map p270 (161 Th Samsen; ⊙7pm-1am; 🚢Thewet Pier) If 'Chinese pawn shop' can be considered a legitimate design theme, Post Bar has nailed it. The walls of this narrow, shophouse-bound bar are decked with retro Thai kitsch, the soundtrack is appropriately classic rock, and the clientele overwhelmingly Thai.

☆ ENTERTAINMENT

★RAJADAMNERN STADIUM
SPECTATOR SPORT

Map p270 (สนามมวยราชดำเนิน; www.rajadamnern.com; off Th Ratchadamnoen Nok; tickets 3rd class/2nd class/ringside 1000/1500/2500B; ⊙Matches Mon-Thur from 6.30-11pm, Sun 3pm & 6.30pm; 🚢Thewet Pier, 🚇Phaya Thai exit 3 & taxi) Rajadamnern Stadium, Bangkok's oldest and most venerable venue for *moo·ay tai* (Thai boxing; also spelt *muay Thai*), hosts matches on Monday, Wednesday and Thursday from 6.30pm to around 11pm, and Sunday at 3pm and 6.30pm. Be sure to buy tickets from the official ticket counter or online, not from the touts and scalpers who hang around outside the entrance.

Chinatown

Neighbourhood Top Five

❶ Nay Hong (p104) Dining alfresco at this and the dozens of other decades-old street-food stalls that define this neighbourhood.

❷ Wat Traimit (p100) Feasting your eyes on 5.5 tonnes of solid gold Buddha at what is arguably one of the country's grandest and most famous temples.

❸ Talat Mai (p101) Watching chaos and commerce battle it out in Chinatown's frenetic, photogenic fresh-food market.

❹ Talat Noi (p101) Getting lost among the oil-stained machine shops, hidden Chinese temples and twisting lanes of this unique neighbourhood.

❺ Phahurat (p103) Taking in the Bollywood-style markets and Indian food of the city's Little India.

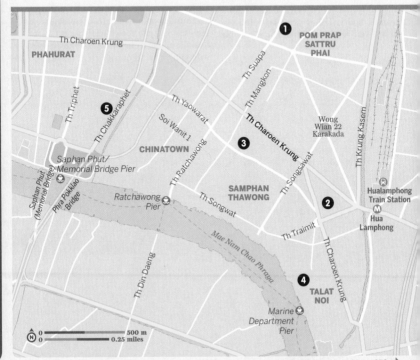

For more detail of this area see Map p272 ➡

Explore Chinatown

Chinatown embodies everything that's hectic, noisy and polluted about Bangkok, but that's what makes it such a fascinating area to explore. The area's big sights – namely Wat Traimit (Golden Buddha) and the street markets – are worth hitting, but be sure to set aside enough time to do some map-free wandering among the neon-lit gold shops, hidden temples, crumbling shop fronts and pencil-thin alleys, especially the tiny winding lanes that extend from Soi Wanit 1 (aka Sampeng Lane).

For ages, Chinatown was home to Bangkok's most infamous traffic jams, but the arrival of the MRT (Metro) in 2005 finally made the area a sane place to visit. Still, the station is about 1km from many sights, so you'll have to take a longish walk or a short taxi ride. An alternative is to take the Chao Phraya Express Boat to the stop at Ratchawong Pier, from where it's a brief walk to most restaurants and a bit further to most sights.

Local Life

→ **Street Food** Although Chinatown can appear dominated by restaurants serving shark-fin and bird's-nest soup, the true Chinatown meal is what's usually prepared by the street vendors lining Th Yaowarat after dark. Locals come from all over Bangkok to eat at Chinatown's stalls, and so should you.

→ **Markets** The Phahurat (p103) and Chinatown districts have interconnected markets selling fabrics, clothes and household wares, as well as wholesale shops for every imaginable bulk item and a few places selling gems and jewellery.

→ **Living on a Prayer** In many of Chinatown's temples, you'll see locals shaking cans of thin sticks called *see·am see*. When a stick falls to the floor, look at its number and find the corresponding paper that gives a no-nonsense appraisal of your future in Thai, Chinese and English.

→ **Nightlife** Or should we say, lack thereof... Other than a few new bars on Soi Nana, there's little in the realm of non-dodgy nightlife in Chinatown. Instead, eat here first then head to nearby Banglamphu or Silom for drinks.

Getting There & Away

→ **MRT** Hua Lamphong.

→ **Chao Phraya Express Boat** Marine Department Pier, Ratchawong Pier, Saphan Phut/Memorial Bridge Pier and Pak Klong Taladd Pier.

→ **Bus** Air-con 507 and 508; ordinary 1, 4, 25, 33, 37, 49 and 53.

Lonely Planet's Top Tip

Most of Bangkok's street-food vendors close up shop on Monday, so don't plan on eating in Chinatown on this day.

✕ Best Places to Eat

→ Nay Hong (p104)
→ 80/20 (p105)
→ Th Phadungdao Seafood Stalls (p105)
→ Khun Yah Cuisine (p104)
→ Fou de Joie (p105)

For reviews, see p104

☐ Best Drinking & Nightlife

→ Tep Bar (p105)
→ Teens of Thailand (p105)
→ River Vibe (p107)
→ Pijiu Bar (p105)
→ El Chiringuito (p105)

For reviews, see p107 →

◉ Best Markets

→ Talat Mai (p101)
→ Pak Khlong Talat (p101)
→ Sampeng Lane (p103)

For reviews, see p101 →

CHINATOWN

TOP SIGHT
WAT TRAIMIT (GOLDEN BUDDHA)

Wat Traimit, also known as the Temple of the Golden Buddha, is home to the world's largest gold statue, a gleaming, 3m-tall, 5.5-tonne Buddha with a mysterious past. The image is thought to date from as long ago as the 13th century, but if it's possible for a Buddha image to live a double life, this one has done so.

The Golden Buddha
The star attraction at Wat Traimit is the gold Buddha image. Located on the 4th floor of the temple compound's marble structure, the gold statue was originally 'discovered' some 60 years ago beneath a stucco or plaster exterior when it fell from a crane while being moved. It's thought that the covering was added to protect the statue from marauding hordes, either during the late Sukhothai period or later in the Ayuthaya period when the city was under siege by the Burmese.

Phra Maha Mondop
In 2009 a new home for the Buddha statue was built. Combining marble, Chinese-style balustrades and a steep Thai-style roof, it's now one of the taller buildings in Chinatown, and the golden spire can be seen from blocks away.

Yaowarat Chinatown Heritage Center
On the 3rd floor of Phra Maha Mondop is this small but engaging **museum** (ศูนย์ประวัติศาสตร์เยาวราช; Map p272; 40B; ⊗8am-5pm Tue-Sun), which houses multimedia exhibits on Chinese immigration to Thailand, as well as on the history of Bangkok's Chinatown and its residents. Particularly fun are the miniature dioramas that depict cultural facets of Thai-Chinese life.

Phra Buddha Maha Suwanna Patimakorn Exhibition
This 2nd-floor **exhibition** (นิทรรศการพระพุทธมหาสุวรรณปฏิมากร; ; Map p272; 40B; ⊗8am-5pm Tue-Sun) recounts how Wat Traimit's Buddha statue was made, discovered and came to arrive at its current home. If you've ever wondered how to make – or move – a 5.5-tonne gold Buddha statue, your questions will be answered here.

DON'T MISS...
➡ The Golden Buddha
➡ Phra Buddha Maha Suwanna Patimakorn Exhibition
➡ Yaowarat Chinatown Heritage Center

PRACTICALITIES
➡ วัดไตรมิตร, Temple of the Golden Buddha
➡ Map p272, F3
➡ Th Mittaphap Thai-China
➡ admission 100B
➡ ⊗8am-5pm
➡ 🚢Ratchawong Pier, Ⓜ Hua Lamphong exit 1

SIGHTS

Chinatown's most touted sights are its temples, but if you're willing to do some self-guided exploration, its winding streets and frenetic fresh markets are additional reasons to visit.

WAT TRAIMIT
(GOLDEN BUDDHA)   BUDDHIST TEMPLE
See p100.

TALAT MAI   MARKET
Map p272 (ตลาดใหม่; Soi Yaowarat 6/Charoen Krung 16; ⊙6am-6pm; ⛴Ratchawong Pier, ⓂHua Lamphong exit 1 & taxi) With nearly two centuries of commerce under its belt, New Market is no longer an entirely accurate name for this strip of commerce. Regardless, this is Bangkok's, if not Thailand's, most Chinese market, and the dried goods, seasonings, spices and sauces will be familiar to anyone who's ever spent time in China. Even if you're not interested in food, the hectic atmosphere (be on guard for motorcycles squeezing between shoppers) and exotic sights and smells create something of a surreal sensory experience.

While much of the market centres on cooking ingredients, the section north of Th Charoen Krung (equivalent to Soi 21, Th Charoen Krung) is known for selling incense, paper effigies and ceremonial sweets – the essential elements of a traditional Chinese funeral.

WAT MANGKON
KAMALAWAT   BUDDHIST TEMPLE
Map p272 (วัดมังกรกมลาวาส; cnr Th Charoen Krung & Th Mangkon; ⊙6am-6pm; ⛴Ratchawong Pier, ⓂHua Lamphong exit 1 & taxi) FREE Clouds of incense and the sounds of chanting form the backdrop at this Chinese-style Mahayana Buddhist temple. Surrounding the temple are vendors selling food for the gods – steamed lotus-shaped dumplings and oranges – which are donated to the temple in exchange for merit. Dating back to 1871, it's the largest and most important religious structure in the area, and during the annual **Vegetarian Festival** (⊙Sep or Oct), religious and culinary activities are particularly active here.

TALAT NOI   AREA
Map p272 (ตลาดน้อย; off Th Charoen Krung; ⊙7am-7pm; ⛴Marine Department Pier) This microcosm of soi life is named after a small (*nóy*) market (*dà·làht*) that sets up between Soi 22 and Soi 20, off Th Charoen Krung. Wandering here you'll find streamlike soi turning in on themselves, weaving through noodle shops, grease-stained machine shops and people's living rooms.

CHURCH OF SANTA CRUZ   CHURCH
Map p272 (โบสถ์สังตาครูส; Soi Kuti Jiin; ⊙7am-noon Sat & Sun; ⛴river-crossing ferry from Atsadang Pier) Centuries before Sukhumvit became Bangkok's international district, the Portuguese claimed *fa·ràng* (Western) supremacy on a riverside plot of land given to them by King Taksin in appreciation for their support after the fall of Ayuthaya. Located on this concession, the Church of Santa Cruz dates to 1913.

Very little activity occurs on the grounds itself, but small and fascinating village streets break off from the main courtyard into the area known as Kuti Jiin, the local name for the church. On Soi Kuti Jiin 3, a few houses continue to sell Portuguese-inspired cakes and sweets.

PAK KHLONG TALAT   MARKET
Map p272 (ปากคลองตลาด, Flower Market; Th Chakkaraphet; ⊙24hr; ⛴Pak Klong Taladd Pier, Saphan Phut/Memorial Bridge Pier) As of 2016, Bangkok's famous and formerly streetside flower market has been moved indoors. In the markets and shophouses that line Th Chakkaraphet, you'll still find piles of delicate orchids, rows of roses and stacks of button carnations, but the vibe isn't as exciting as it used to be. The best time to come is late at night, when the goods arrive from upcountry. During the daytime, Pak Khlong Talat is one of the city's largest wholesale vegetable markets.

HUALAMPHONG
TRAIN STATION   HISTORIC BUILDING
Map p272 (สถานีรถไฟหัวลำโพง; off Rama IV; ⓂHua Lamphong exit 2) At the southeastern

CHINATOWN SIGHTS

ⓘ GAME PLAN

Bangkok's street stalls and family-run restaurants operate frustratingly inconsistent business hours. So if you're heading to Chinatown with the intent of eating at a specific stall, it's always a good idea to have a Plan B.

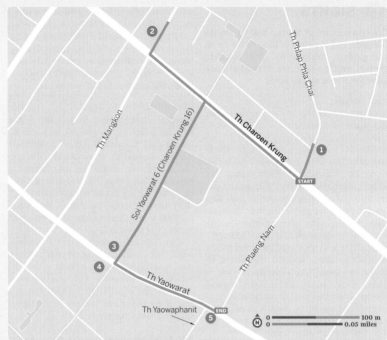

🏃 Neighbourhood Walk
A Taste of Chinatown

START CNR TH PLAENG NAM
& TH CHAROEN KRUNG
END CNR TH YAOWAPHANIT
& TH YAOWARAT
LENGTH 1KM; TWO TO THREE HOURS

Street food rules in Chinatown, making the area ideal for a culinary adventure. Although many vendors stay open late, the more popular stalls tend to sell out quickly, so the best time to feast in this area is from 7pm to 9pm. Don't try this walk on a Monday, when most of the city's street vendors stay at home. Bringing a friend (or three) and sharing is a good way to ensure that you can try as many dishes as possible.

Start your walk at the intersection of Th Plaeng Nam and Th Charoen Krung. Head north along Th Phlap Phla Chai, staying on the right-hand side for about 50m, until you reach **1 Nai Mong Hoi Thod** (p104), a shophouse restaurant renowned for its delicious *hŏy tôrt* (oysters fried with egg and a sticky batter).

Backtrack to Th Charoen Krung and turn right. Upon reaching Th Mangkon make a right; on your left-hand side you'll see **2 Jék Pûi**, a table-less stall famous for its Chinese-style Thai curries.

Cross Th Charoen Krung again, turn left, and continue east until you reach Soi Yaowarat 6/Charoen Krung 16, also known as Talat Mai, the area's most famous strip of commerce. At the end of the alley you'll see a gentleman making **3 gŏo·ay dĕe·o kôo·a gài**, rice noodles fried with chicken, egg and garlic oil.

Upon emerging at Th Yaowarat, cross over to the busy market area directly across the street. The first vendor on the right, **4 Nay Lék Ûan** (p104), sells *gŏo·ay jáp nám săi*, an intensely peppery broth containing noodles and pork offal.

Returning back to Th Yaowarat, turn right and continue until the next intersection. On the corner of Th Yaowaphanit and Th Yaowarat you'll see **5 Mangkorn Khăo**, a stall selling *bà·mèe* (Chinese-style wheat noodles) and barbecued pork, and wontons.

edge of Chinatown, Bangkok's main train station was built by Dutch architects and engineers between 1910 and 1916.

It was designed in a neoclassical style by Italian architect-and-engineer combination Mario Tamagno and Annibale Rigotti, who were working at the same time on the grand Ananta Samakhom Throne Hall (p94) at Dusit. It also embraces other influences, such as the patterned, two-toned skylights that exemplify nascent De Stijl Dutch modernism – it is through these that it is known as an early example of the shift towards Thai art deco. If you can zone out of the chaos for a moment, look for the vaulted iron roof and neoclassical portico, which were a state-of-the-art engineering feat.

HOLY ROSARY CHURCH CHURCH

Map p272 (วัดแม่พระลูกประคำกาลหว่าร์; cnr Th Yotha & Soi Charoen Phanit; ⊙Thai-language mass 7.30pm Mon-Sat, 8am, 10am & 7.30pm Sun; ⊠Marine Department Pier) Portuguese seafarers were among the first Europeans to establish diplomatic ties with Siam, and their influence in the kingdom was rewarded with prime riverside real estate. When a Portuguese contingent moved across the river to the present-day Talat Noi area (p101) of Chinatown in 1787, they were given this piece of land and built the Holy Rosary Church, known in Thai as Wat Kalawan, from the Portuguese 'Calvario' (Calvary).

Over the years the Portuguese community dispersed and the church fell into disrepair. However, Vietnamese and Cambodian Catholics displaced by the Indochina wars adopted it, and together with Chinese speakers now constitute much of the parish. Of particular note are the splendid Romanesque stained-glass windows, gilded ceilings and a statue of Christ that is carried through the streets during Easter celebrations.

PHAHURAT AREA

Map p272 (พาหุรัด; Th Chakkaraphet; ⊙9am-5pm; ⊠Saphan Phut/Memorial Bridge Pier, Pak Klong Taladd Pier) Heaps of South Asian traders set up shop in Bangkok's small but bustling Little India, where everything from Bollywood movies to bindis is sold by enthusiastic, small-time traders. It's a great area to just wander through, stopping for masala chai and a Punjabi sweet as you go.

The bulk of the action unfolds along unmarked Soi ATM, which runs alongside the large **India Emporium** (Map p272; Th Chakkaraphet; ⊙10am-10pm; ⊠Saphan Phut/Memorial Bridge Pier) shopping centre.

The emphasis is on cloth, and Phahurat proffers boisterously coloured textiles, traditional Thai dance costumes, tiaras, sequins, wigs and other accessories to make you look like a cross-dresser, a *mŏr lam* (Thai country music) performer, or both. Amid the spectacle of colour there are also good deals on machine-made Thai textiles and children's clothes.

SAMPENG LANE MARKET

Map p272 (สำเพ็ง; Soi Wanit 1; ⊙8am-6pm; ⊠Ratchawong Pier, ⊠Hua Lamphong exit 1 & taxi) Soi Wanit 1 – colloquially known as Sampeng Lane – is a narrow artery running parallel to Th Yaowarat and bisecting the commercial areas of Chinatown and Phahurat. The Chinatown portion of Sampeng Lane is lined with wholesale shops of hair

---

WAVING THE YELLOW FLAG

During the annual Vegetarian Festival in September/October, Bangkok's Chinatown becomes a virtual orgy of non-meat cuisine. The festivities centre on Chinatown's main street, Th Yaowarat, and the Talat Noi (p101) area, but food shops and stalls all over the city post yellow flags to announce their meat-free status.

Celebrating alongside the ethnic Chinese are Thais who look forward to the special dishes that appear during the festival period. Most restaurants put their normal menus on hold and instead prepare soy-based substitutes for standard Thai dishes like *ðôm yam* (Thai-style spicy/sour soup) and *gaang kĕe·o wăhn* (green curry). Even Thai regional cuisines are sold (without the meat, of course). Yellow Hokkien-style noodles often make an appearance in the special festival dishes, usually in stir-fries along with meaty mushrooms and big hunks of vegetables.

Along with abstinence from meat, the 10-day festival is celebrated with special visits to the temple, often requiring worshippers to dress in white.

BIRD'S NEST SOUP

Most of the ostentatious, neon-signed shops you'll see along Th Yaowarat, Chinatown's main drag, do business in gold, but a few deal in two other more obscure, but similarly valued commodities: birds' nests and shark fins.

The birds' nests in question don't consist of twigs or grass, but rather are the hardened saliva of a type of swiftlet. Pried from the walls of island-bound caves in southern Thailand, the nests are rehydrated and cleaned of impurities before being combined with broth and served in the form of a soup. Despite consisting of jellylike, tasteless strands (the soup is often supplemented with honey and egg to provide it with some flavour), the dish is considered a delicacy by the Chinese, who also believe it benefits the skin. Depending on the colour and purity of the bird's nest, a bowl of the soup can cost as much as 2000B or more. The nests can be harvested sustainably, but over-exploitation does occur.

Many of the same restaurants that sell bird's-nest soup also serve shark-fin soup. Yet another Chinese delicacy that is believed to have healing properties, shark-fin soup has become highly stigmatised in recent years, as many animal welfare experts have pointed out that the fins are gathered via a process that is unsustainable and cruel – the sharks are often caught and stripped of their fins, then dumped in the water to die. Compared to other countries in the region, including even China, Thailand has done little to discourage the consumption of shark's fin soup, and the dish remains a popular item in Bangkok's Chinatown and at Thai-Chinese banquets.

accessories, pens, stickers, household wares and beeping, flashing knick-knacks. Near Th Chakrawat, gem and jewellery shops abound. Weekends are horribly crowded, and it takes a gymnast's flexibility to squeeze past the pushcarts, motorcycles and other roadblocks.

EATING

NAY HONG
STREET FOOD **$**

Map p272 (off Th Yukol 2; mains 35-50B; ⊙4-10pm; ⏩Ratchawong Pier, Ⓜ Hua Lamphong exit 1 & taxi) The reward for locating this hole-in-the-wall is one of Bangkok's best fried noodle dishes – *gŏo·ay dĕe·o kôo·a gài* (flat rice noodles fried with garlic oil, chicken and egg). No English-language menu.

There's no English-language sign. To find Nay Hong, proceed north from the corner of Th Suapa and Th Luang, then turn right into the first side street; it's at the end of the narrow alleyway.

NAY LÉK ÛAN
STREET FOOD **$**

Map p272 (Soi Yaowarat 11; mains from 40B; ⊙5pm-midnight; ⏩Tha Ratchawong, Ⓜ Hua Lamphong exit 1 & taxi) Nay Lék Ûan sells *gŏo·ay jáp nám săi,* an intensely peppery broth

containing noodles and pork offal. No English-language menu.

NAI MONG HOI THOD
CHINESE **$**

Map p272 (539 Th Phlap Phla Chai; mains 50-70B; ⊙5-10pm Tue-Sun; ⏩Ratchawong Pier, Ⓜ Hua Lamphong exit 1) A shophouse restaurant renowned for its delicious *hŏy tôrt* (oysters fried with egg and a sticky batter) and a decent crab fried rice. No English-language menu.

KHUN YAH CUISINE
THAI **$**

Map p272 (off Th Mittaphap Thai-China, no roman-script sign; mains from 40B; ⊙6am-1.30pm Mon-Fri; ⏩Ratchawong Pier, Ⓜ Hua Lamphong exit 1) Strategically located for a lunch break after visiting Wat Traimit (Golden Buddha), Khun Yah specialises in the full-flavoured curries, relishes, stir-fries and noodle dishes. Be sure to get here early; come noon many dishes are already sold out. Khun Yah has no English-language sign (nor an English-language menu) but is located just east of the Golden Buddha, in the same compound.

OLD SIAM PLAZA
SWEETS **$**

Map p272 (cnr Th Phahurat & Th Triphet; mains 30-90B; ⊙10am-7pm; ❖; ⏩Saphan Phut/Memorial Bridge Pier, Pak Klong Taladd Pier) Sugar junkies, be sure to include this stop on your Bangkok eating itinerary. The ground floor of this shopping centre is a candyland of traditional Thai sweets and snacks, most made right before your eyes.

80/20 — INTERNATIONAL $$

Map p272 (🖂02 639 1135; www.facebook.com/8020bkk; 1052-1054 Th Charoen Krung; mains from 240B; ⏱6pm-midnight Wed-Mon; ❄; 🚢Ratchawong Pier, Ⓜ️Hua Lamphong exit 1) Don't call it fusion; rather, 80/20 excels at taking and blending Thai and Western ingredients and dishes, arriving at something altogether unique. The often savoury-leaning desserts, overseen by a Japanese pastry chef are especially worth the trip. A progressive breath of air in otherwise conservative Chinatown.

FOU DE JOIE — FRENCH $$

Map p272 (🖂085 527 3511; 831 Soi 31, Th Charoen Krung; mains from 200B; ⏱6pm-midnight Wed-Sun; ❄; 🚢Ratchawong Pier, Ⓜ️Hua Lamphong exit 1) Dining at the retro Hong Kong–themed Fou de Joie is like being an extra in a Wong Kar-Wai film. Better yet, the French-style crêpes and cheese platters – not to mention the upstairs barbecue – are more than just set pieces, and also offer terrific value.

HOON KUANG — CHINESE $$

Map p272 (381 Th Yaowarat; mains 90-240B; ⏱11am-7.45pm Mon-Sat; ❄; 🚢Ratchawong Pier, Ⓜ️Hua Lamphong exit 1 & taxi) Serving the food of Chinatown's streets in air-con comfort is this low-key, long-standing staple. The must-eat dishes are pictured on the door, but it'd be a pity to miss the 'prawn curry flat rice noodle', a unique mash-up of two Chinese-Thai dishes – crab in curry powder and flash-fried noodles – that will make you wonder why they were ever served apart.

THANON PHADUNGDAO SEAFOOD STALLS — STREET FOOD $$

Map p272 (cnr Th Phadungdao & Th Yaowarat; mains 100-600B; ⏱4pm-midnight Tue-Sun;

SOI NANA'S DRINKING SCENE

No, not that **Nana** (p153); at this emerging strip of shophouse-based bar/galleries you'll get custom cocktails, contemporary art installations and cute cafes, not go-go dancing. To witness a neighbourhood that appears to be at the cusp of gentrification, pop into one of the following hot spots.

Tep Bar (Map p272; www.facebook.com/tepbar; 69-71 Soi Nana; ⏱5pm-midnight Tue-Sun; Ⓜ️Hua Lamphong exit 1) We never expected to find a bar this sophisticated – yet this fun – in Chinatown. Tep does it with a Thai-tinged, contemporary interior, tasty signature cocktails, Thai drinking snacks, and, come Friday to Sunday, raucous live Thai music performances.

Pijiu Bar (Map p272; www.facebook.com/pijiubar; 16 Soi Nana; ⏱5pm-midnight Tue-Sun; 🚢Ratchawong Pier, Ⓜ️Hua Lamphong exit 1) Old West meets old Shanghai at this new yet classic-feeling bar. The emphasis here is on beer (*pijiu* is Chinese for beer), with four revolving craft brews on tap, but perhaps even more enticing are the charcuterie platters (300B) that unite a variety of smoked and preserved meats from some of the best vendors in Chinatown.

Ba Hao (Map p272; www.ba-hao.com; 8 Soi Nana; ⏱6pm-midnight Tue-Sun; 🚢Ratchawong Pier, Ⓜ️Hua Lamphong exit 1) At this point, there's little original about this retro Chinese-themed refurbished shophouse on Soi Nana, but domestic craft beer, inventive cocktails and really excellent Chinese-style bar snacks (don't miss the Chinese pancake with braised pork belly, herbs and fried egg) make Ba Hao stand out.

Teens of Thailand (Map p272; 76 Soi Nana; ⏱7pm-midnight Tue-Sun; Ⓜ️Hua Lamphong exit 1) Probably the edgiest of the new bars in Soi Nana; squeeze through the tiny wooden door of this refurbished shophouse to emerge at an artsy warehouse-like interior, with hipster barkeeps serving creative gin-based drinks, and an upright piano we're guessing doesn't get too much play time.

El Chiringuito (Map p272; 🖂086 340 4791; www.facebook.com/elchiringuitobangkok; 221 Soi Nana; ⏱6pm-midnight Thu-Sun; Ⓜ️Hua Lamphong exit 1) Come to this retro-feeling bar for sangria, Spanish gin and bar snacks, or the revolving art exhibitions. Opening hours can be sporadic, so call or check the Facebook page before heading out.

CHINATOWN EATING

CHINATOWN'S STREETS OF COMMERCE

Chinatown might be the city's most commerce-heavy hood, although it must be said that the bulk of wares are utilitarian, and will hold little interest for most travellers. The neighbourhood is essentially is a megastore divided up into categories of commerce, with streets as aisles; here's your in-store guide:

Th Charoen Krung Starting on the western end of the street, near the intersection of Th Mahachai, is a collection of old record shops. **Talat Khlong Ong Ang** (ตลาด คลองโอ่งอ่าง; Map p272; Th Charoen Krung; ⏰9am-5pm; 🚢Ratchawong Pier, Ⓜ Hua Lamphong exit 1 & taxi) consumes the next block, selling all sorts of used and new electronic gadgets. Further east, near Th Mahachak, is **Talat Khlong Thom** (ตลาดคลอง ถม; Map p272; off Th Charoen Krung; ⏰9am-5pm; 🚢Ratchawong Pier, Ⓜ Hua Lamphong exit 1 & taxi), a hardware centre. West of Th Ratchawong is everything you'd need to give a Chinese funeral.

Th Yaowarat A hundred years ago this was a poultry farm; now it's gold street, the biggest trading centre of the precious metal in the country. Along Th Yaowarat, gold is sold by the *baht* (a unit of weight equivalent to 15g) from neon-lit shopfronts that look more like shrines than shops. Near the intersection of Th Ratchawong, shops shift to Chinese and Singaporean tourists' tastes: dried fruit and nuts, chintzy talismans and accoutrements for Chinese festivals. The multistorey buildings around here were some of Bangkok's first skyscrapers and a source of wonder for the local people. Bangkok's skyline has grown and grown, but this area retains a few Chinese apothecaries, smelling of wood bark and ancient secrets.

Thanon Mittraphan (ถนนมิตรพันธ์; Map p272; Th Mittraphan; ⏰9am-5pm; 🚢Ratchawong Pier, Ⓜ Hua Lamphong exit 2) Sign-makers can be found along this street, which branches off Wong Wian 22 Karakada; Thai and roman letters are typically cut out by a hand-guided lathe placed prominently beside the pavement.

Thanon Santiphap (ถนนสันติภาพ; Map p272; Th Santiphap; ⏰9am-5pm; 🚢Ratchawong Pier, Ⓜ Hua Lamphong exit 2) Car parts and other automotive gear make this the place for kicking tyres.

Sampeng Lane (p103) Plastic cuteness in bulk, from pencil cases to pens, stuffed animals, hair flotsam and enough bling to kit out a rap video – it all hangs out near the eastern end of the alley.

Talat Mai (p101) This ancient produce market splays along the cramped alley between Th Yaowarat and Th Charoen Krung.

🚢Ratchawong Pier, Ⓜ Hua Lamphong exit 1 & taxi) After sunset, these two opposing open-air restaurants – each of which claims to be the original – become a culinary train wreck of outdoor barbecues, screaming staff, iced seafood trays and messy pavement seating. True, the vast majority of diners are foreign tourists, but this has little impact on the cheerful setting, the fun experience and the cheap bill.

ROYAL INDIA   INDIAN $$
Map p272 (392/1 Th Chakkaraphet; mains 135-220B; ⏰10am-10pm; ❄🖊; 🚢Saphan Phut/ Memorial Bridge Pier, Pak Klong Taladd Pier) Yes, we're aware that this hole-in-the-wall has

been in every edition of our guide since the beginning, but after all these years it's still the most reliable place to eat in Bangkok's Little India. Try any of the delicious breads or rich curries, and don't forget to finish with a homemade Punjabi sweet.

SAMSARA   JAPANESE, THAI $$
Map p272 (Soi Khang Wat Pathum Khongkha; mains 110-320B; ⏰4pm-midnight Tue-Thu, to 1am Fri-Sun; 🖊; 🚢Ratchawong Pier, Ⓜ Hua Lamphong exit 1 & taxi) Combining Japanese and Thai dishes, Belgian beers and an artfully ramshackle atmosphere, Samsara is one of Chinatown's most eclectic places to eat. Its food is also tasty, and the generous

riverside breezes and views simply add to the package.

The restaurant is at the end of tiny Soi Khang Wat Pathum Khongkha, just west of the temple of the same name.

🍷 DRINKING & ⚓ ENTERTAINMENT

SOULBAR   LIVE MUSIC

Map p272 (www.facebook.com/livesoulbarbangkok; 945 Th Charoen Krung; ☺7pm-midnight Tue-Sun; 🚢Marine Department Pier, Ⓜ Hua Lamphong exit 1) An unlikely venue – and neighbourhood – for live music, this converted shophouse nonetheless plays host to live blues, jazz and soul from 9pm just about every night.

RIVER VIBE   BAR

Map p272 (8th fl, River View Guesthouse, off Soi Charoen Phanit; ☺7.30-11pm; 🚢Marine Department Pier, Ⓜ Hua Lamphong exit 1) Can't afford the overpriced cocktails at Bangkok's upscale rooftop bars? The excellent river views from the top of this guesthouse will hardly feel like a compromise. We suggest getting dinner elsewhere, though.

SALA CHALERMKRUNG   THEATRE

Map p272 (🖉02 224 4499; www.salachalermkrung.com; 66 Th Charoen Krung; tickets 800-1200B; ☺shows 7.30pm Thu & Fri; 🚢Saphan Phut/Memorial Bridge Pier, Ⓜ Hua Lamphong exit 1 & taxi) This art deco Bangkok landmark, a former cinema dating to 1933, is one of the few remaining places *kŏhn* (masked dance-drama based on stories from the *Ramakian,* the Thai version of the Indian epic *Ramayana*) can be witnessed. The traditional dance-drama is enhanced here by laser graphics, high-tech audio and English subtitles. Concerts and other events are also held; check the website for details.

SOY SAUCE FACTORY   ARTS CENTRE

Map p272 (www.facebook.com/soysaucefactory; Soi 24, Th Charoen Krung; ☺10am-7pm Tue-Sun; Ⓜ Hua Lamphong exit 1) A former soy sauce factory turned gallery/event space/bar/photo studio... Whatever it is, check the Facebook page to see what's currently on at this artsy, open-ended gathering place, indicative of the kind of changes currently underfoot in Bangkok's Chinatown.

Siam Square, Pratunam, Phloen Chit & Ratchathewi

Neighbourhood Top Five

❶ Jim Thompson House (p110) Visiting the teak mansion that put Thai style on the map...before its ex-spy owner disappeared off that map.

❷ MBK Center (p121) Shopping at this and the other mega-malls, depart-ment stores and shops that practically engulf Siam Sq.

❸ Baan Khrua (p113) Exploring the pencil-thin lanes of the canal-side Muslim village where Jim Thompson first encountered Thai silk.

❹ Erawan Shrine (p112) Making a wish or catching a traditional dance performance at this one-of-a-kind crossroads of commerce and faith.

❺ Paragon Cineplex (p118) Reclining in the decadence of what must be one of the world's best-value cinemas.

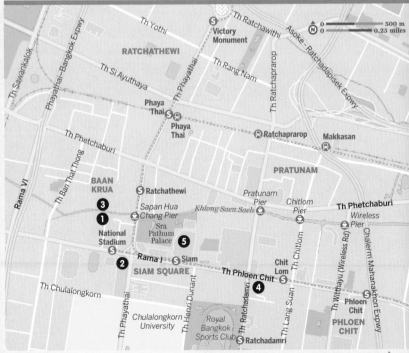

For more detail of this area see Map p271 and p274 ➡

Explore Siam Square, Pratunam, Phloen Chit & Ratchathewi

Siam Sq, Pratunam and Phloen Chit combine to form the de facto geographical and commercial centre of modern Bangkok. Huge malls, towering hotels, international fast-food chains and open-air shopping centres dominate this area, and if you're serious about shopping, set aside the better part of a day to burn your baht here.

Ratchathewi, on the other hand, has a lot less to offer – unless of course you have a specific sight in mind or simply want to check out a more suburban/workday side of Bangkok. The attractions in this area can be covered in a couple hours, and most are all within walking distance of the BTS stop at Victory Monument.

Local Life

➡ **Mall-hopping** On weekends a significant part of Bangkok's population is drawn to this area's malls to socialise in stylish settings and air-con comfort.

➡ **Air-conditioned dining** A mall-based food court may not seem like the most authentic place to eat *pàt tai* (fried noodles), but several of Bangkok's most famous restaurants and stalls maintain branches at the various Siam Sq area malls.

➡ **Wholesale retail** For local penny-pinchers and visiting wholesalers the ultimate destination is Pratunam district, where a seemingly never-ending clothing bazaar stocks both locally made and cheap import items.

➡ **Keeping it real** For a view of Bangkok without the malls, cup-cake bakeries, fashionistas and tourists, take the BTS north to the Victory Monument in Ratchathewi district, where you'll find ordinary Thais doing ordinary Thai things.

Getting There & Away

➡ **BTS** To Siam Sq, Pratunam and Phloen Chit: Siam, National Stadium, Chit Lom, Phloen Chit and Ratchadamri. To Ratchathewi: Ratchathewi, Phaya Thai and Victory Monument.

➡ **Canal boat** To Siam Sq, Pratunam and Phloen Chit: Sapan Hua Chang Pier, Pratunam Pier and Wireless Pier. To Ratchathewi: Pratunam Pier.

➡ **Bus** To Siam Sq, Pratunam and Phloen Chit: air-con 141, 183, 204, 501, 508 and 547; ordinary 15, 16, 25, 47 and 73. To Ratchathewi: air-con 503, 513 and 536; ordinary 29, 36, 54, 59 and 112.

Lonely Planet's Top Tip

They may lack street cred, but the mall-based food courts that abound in this part of town are among the most user-friendly introductions to Thai food in Bangkok. They're generally clean and convenient, and also have the benefit of using English-language menus, so ordering is a snap.

Best Places to Eat

➡ MBK Food Island (p115)

➡ Nuer Koo (p115)

➡ Din Tai Fung (p115)

➡ Toy (p116)

➡ Food Republic (p116)

➡ Eathai (p116)

For reviews, see p116 ➡

Best Drinking & Nightlife

➡ Hyde & Seek (p118)

➡ Hair of the Dog (p118)

➡ Red Sky (p118)

➡ Saxophone Pub & Restaurant (p119)

➡ Sky Train Jazz Club (p119)

➡ Wine Pub (p119)

For reviews, see p118 ➡

Best Places to Shop

➡ MBK Center (p121)

➡ Siam Discovery (p121)

➡ Siam Square (p121)

➡ Siam Center (p121)

➡ Siam Paragon (p121)

➡ Platinum Fashion Mall (p122)

For reviews, see p121 ➡

COWARDLION / SHUTTERSTOCK ©

TOP SIGHT
JIM THOMPSON HOUSE

In 1959, 12 years after he single-handedly turned Thai silk into a hugely successful export business, American Jim Thompson bought a piece of land next to Khlong Saen Saeb and built himself a house. It wasn't, however, any old house. Thompson's love of all things Thai saw him buy six traditional wooden homes and reconstruct them in his garden.

The Man

Born in Delaware, USA, in 1906, Jim Thompson served in a forerunner of the CIA in Thailand during WWII. When in 1947 he spotted some silk in a market and was told it was woven in Baan Khrua, he found the only place in Bangkok where silk was still woven by hand.

Thompson's Thai silk eventually attracted the interest of fashion houses in New York, Milan, London and Paris, and he gradually built a worldwide clientele for a craft that had, just a few years before, been in danger of dying out.

By 1967 Thai silk had annual sales of almost US$1.5 million. In March that year Thompson went missing while out for an afternoon walk in the Cameron Highlands of western Malaysia; his business success, spy background and the fact that his sister was also murdered in the same year made it an international mystery. Thompson has never been heard from since, but the conspiracy theories have never stopped. Was it communist spies? Business rivals? A hungry tiger? Although the mystery has never been solved, evidence revealed by American journalist Joshua Kurlantzick in his profile of Thompson, The Ideal Man, suggests that

DON'T MISS...

→ Thompson's art and antique collection
→ A walk in the jungle-like garden
→ Jim Thompson Art Center

PRACTICALITIES

→ เรือนไทยจิมทอมป์สัน
→ Map p274, A2
→ www.jimthompson house.com
→ 6 Soi Kasem San 2
→ adult/student 150/100B
→ 9am-6pm, z tours every 20min
→ klorng boat to Sapan Hua Chang Pier, S National Stadium exit 1

the vocal anti-American stance Thompson took later in his life may have made him a potential target of suppression by the CIA.

The House

Thompson adapted the six Thai structures to create a larger home in which each room had a more familiar Western function. Another departure from tradition is the way Thompson arranged each wall with its exterior side facing the house's interior. Some of the homes were brought from the old royal capital of Ayuthaya; others were pulled down and floated across the canal.

Thompson's Art Collection

Thompson's small but splendid Asian art collection is also on display in the main house: pieces include rare Chinese porcelain and Burmese, Cambodian and Thai artefacts. Thompson had a particularly astute eye for somewhat less flashy but nonetheless charming objects, such as the 19th-century mouse maze that resembles a home.

The Grounds

After the tour, be sure to poke around the house's jungle-like gardens, which include ponds filled with exotic fish. The compound also includes a cafe/restaurant and a shop flogging Jim Thompson–branded silk goods.

Jim Thompson Art Center

The compound also includes the **Jim Thompson Art Center** (Map p274; ⏱9am-8pm) FREE, a museum with revolving displays spanning a variety of media; recent exhibitions have seen contributions from the likes of Palme d'Or-winning Thai film-maker, Apichatpong Weerasethakul.

TOP TIPS

➜ Beware of well-dressed touts in the soi near the Jim Thompson House who will tell you it is closed and then try to haul you off on a dodgy buying spree.

➜ The house can only be viewed via a guided tour, which is available in Chinese, English, French, Japanese and Thai.

➜ Photography is not allowed inside any of the buildings.

TAKE A BREAK

The compound is home to the **Thompson Bar & Restaurant** (Map p274; mains 160-480B; ⏱11am-5pm & 6-10pm; ❄ 🥢), which serves somewhat gentrified Thai food. Alternatively, head over to MBK Food Island (p115), one of the city's best food courts, for cheap Thai eats.

SIGHTS

Emerge from the malls and there's relatively little in terms of visit-worthy sights in this part of town, the exceptions being Jim Thompson House and a couple of art galleries.

JIM THOMPSON HOUSE — HISTORIC BUILDING

See p110.

BANGKOK ART & CULTURE CENTRE — GALLERY

Map p274 (BACC; หอศิลปวัฒนธรรมแห่งกรุงเทพมหานคร; www.bacc.or.th; cnr Th Phayathai & Rama I; ⏲10am-9pm Tue-Sat; [S]National Stadium exit 3) [FREE] This large, modern building in the centre of Bangkok has become one of the more significant players in the city's contemporary arts scene. As well as its three floors and 3000 sq metres of gallery space, the centre also contains shops, private galleries, cafes and an art library. Visit the website to see what exhibitions are on when you're in town.

ERAWAN SHRINE — MONUMENT

Map p274 (ศาลพระพรหม; cnr Th Ratchadamri & Th Phloen Chit; ⏲6am-11pm; [S]Chit Lom exit 8) [FREE] The Erawan Shrine was originally built in 1956 as something of a last-ditch effort to end a string of misfortunes that occurred during the construction of a hotel, at that time known as the Erawan Hotel.

After several incidents ranging from injured construction workers to the sinking of a ship carrying marble for the hotel, a Brahman priest was consulted. Since the hotel was to be named after the elephant escort of Indra in Hindu mythology, the priest determined that Erawan required a passenger, and suggested it be that of Lord Brahma. A statue was built and, lo and behold, the misfortunes miraculously ended.

Although the original Erawan Hotel was demolished in 1987, the shrine still exists, and today remains an important place of pilgrimage for Thais, particularly those in need of some material assistance. Those making a wish from the statue should ideally come between 7am and 8am, or 7pm and 8pm, and should offer a specific list of items that includes candles, incense, sugar cane or bananas, all of which are almost exclusively given in multiples of seven. Particularly popular are teak elephants, with

TOP SIGHT
SUAN PAKKAD PALACE MUSEUM

Everyone loves the Jim Thompson House, but few have even heard of Suan Pakkad Palace Museum, another noteworthy traditional Thai house-museum. Once the residence of Princess Chumbon of Nakhon Sawan, the museum is a collection of eight traditional wooden Thai houses linked by elevated walkways containing varied displays of art, antiques and furnishings. The landscaped grounds are a peaceful oasis complete with ducks, swans and a semi-enclosed, Japanese-style garden.

The diminutive **Lacquer Pavilion** at the back of the complex dates from the Ayuthaya period (the building originally sat in a monastery compound on the banks of Mae Nam Chao Phraya, just south of Ayuthaya) and features gold-leaf *Jataka* and *Ramayana* murals as well as scenes from daily Ayuthaya life. Larger residential structures at the front of the complex contain displays of Khmer, Hindu and Buddhist art, Ban Chiang ceramics and a collection of historic **Buddhas**, including a beautiful late U Thong–style image. Amid the noise and confusion of Bangkok, the gardens offer a tranquil retreat.

DON'T MISS

- Lacquer Pavilion
- Buddha statue collection

PRACTICALITIES

- วังสวนผักกาด
- Map p271, B3
- Th Si Ayuthaya
- 100B
- ⏲9am-4pm
- [S]Phaya Thai exit 4

BAAN KHRUA

The canalside neighbourhood of **Baan Khrua** (บ้านครัว; Map p274; ⚲klorng boat to Sapan Hua Chang Pier, ⓈRatchathewi exit 1, National Stadium exit 1) dates back to the turbulent years at the end of the 18th century, when Cham Muslims from Cambodia and Vietnam fought on the side of the new Thai king and were rewarded with this plot of land east of the new capital. The immigrants brought their silk-weaving traditions with them, and the community grew when the residents built Khlong Saen Saeb to better connect them to the river.

The 1950s and '60s were boom years for Baan Khrua after Jim Thompson hired the weavers and began exporting their silks across the globe. The last 50 years, however, haven't been so great. Silk production was moved elsewhere following Thompson's disappearance, and the community spent 15 years successfully fighting to stop a freeway being built right through it. Through all this, many Muslims moved out of the area; today it is estimated that only about 30% of the population is Muslim, the rest primarily immigrants from northeast Thailand. Today's Baan Khrua consists of old, tightly packed homes threaded by tiny paths barely wide enough for two people to pass. There's a mosque, and two family-run outfits, **Phamai Baan Krua** (ผ้าไหมบ้านครัว; Map p274; www.phamaibaankrua.com; Soi 9, Soi Phaya Nak; ⊙8.30am-5pm; ⚲klorng boat to Sapan Hua Chang Pier, ⓈRatchathewi exit 1, National Stadium exit 1) and **Aood Bankrua Thai Silk** (ลุงอู๊ดบ้านครัวไหมไทย; Map p274; 📞02 215 9864; Soi 9, Soi Phaya Nak; ⊙9am-8pm; ⚲klorng boat to Sapan Hua Chang Pier, ⓈRatchathewi exit 1, National Stadium exit 1), continue to be involved in every step of silk cloth production, from the dyeing of threads to weaving the cloth by hand on old wood looms. Of the two, Phamai Baan Krua claims to be the original. Run by English- and German-speaking Niphon Manuthas, the company continues to produce the type of high-quality handwoven silk that originally attracted Jim Thompson, at much cheaper prices than a certain more famous shop across the klorng.

Baan Khrua is an easy stop after visiting Jim Thompson House; simply cross the bridge over the canal at the end of Soi Kasem San 3. Alternatively, from the BTS stop at Ratchathewi, enter Soi Phaya Nak, take the third left (the street that leads to Da-Ru-Fa-Lah Mosque), following it to the canal; turn right and look for the signs.

money from the sale of these items donated to a charity run by the current hotel, the Grand Hyatt Erawan. And as the tourist brochures depict, it is also possible to charter a classical Thai dance, often done as a way of giving thanks if a wish is granted. A bomb exploded near the shrine in August 2015, killing 20 and slightly damaging the shrine. It was repaired and reopened just two days later.

YELO HOUSE   GALLERY
Map p274 (www.yelohouse.com; 20/2 Soi Kasem San 1; ⊙11am-8pm Tue-Sun) An art gallery? Vintage-clothing market? Co-working space? Cafe/restaurant? YELO House is so cool, it's hard to pin down what it actually is. So we'll go with the website's claim that it's a multi-function space for creative people. In practical terms, this means it's a place to dig through vintage clothes and ceramics, check out the latest exhibition, or enjoy an espresso in the canalside cafe.

LINGAM SHRINE   MONUMENT
Map p274 (ศาลเจ้าแม่ทับทิม; Swissôtel Nai Lert Park, Th Witthayu/Wireless Rd; ⊙24hr; ⚲klorng boat to Wireless Pier, ⓈPhloen Chit exit 1) FREE Every village-neighbourhood has a local shrine, either a sacred banyan tree tied up with coloured scarves or a spirit house. But it isn't every day you see a phallus garden like this lingam shrine, tucked back behind the staff quarters of the Swissôtel Nai Lert Park. When facing the entrance of the hotel, follow the small concrete pathway to the right, which winds down into the building beside the car park. The shrine is at the end of the building next to the *klorng*.

Clusters of carved stone and wooden shafts surround a spirit house and shrine built by millionaire businessman Nai Loet to honour Jao Mae Thap Thim, a female deity thought to reside in the old banyan tree on the site. Someone who made an offering shortly after the shrine was built had a baby, and the shrine has received a steady stream of worshippers ever since.

LOCAL KNOWLEDGE

TOUGH TIMES AT THE ERAWAN SHRINE

One of the more clichéd tourist images of Bangkok is that of elaborately dressed classical Thai dancers performing at the Hindu shrine in front of the Grand Hyatt Erawan hotel. Although not a fabrication, as with many things in Thailand, there is great deal hidden behind the serene facade.

After 50 years of largely benign existence, the Erawan Shrine became a point of focus when just after midnight on 21 March 2006, 27-year-old Thanakorn Pakdeepol, a man with a history of mental illness and depression, destroyed the highly revered, gilded plaster image of Brahma with a hammer. Thanakorn was almost immediately attacked and beaten to death by two Thai rubbish collectors in the vicinity. Although the government ordered a swift restoration of the statue, the incident became a galvanising omen for the protest movement opposing then Prime Minister Thaksin Shinawatra, which was in full swing at the time. At a rally the following day, protest leader Sondhi Limthongkul suggested that the prime minister had masterminded the image's destruction in order to replace the deity with a 'dark force'. Rumours spreading through the capital claimed that Thaksin had hired Cambodian shamans to put spells on Thanakorn so that he would perform the unspeakable deed. In response, Thanakorn's father was quoted as saying that Sondhi was a 'liar'. Thaksin, when asked to comment on Sondhi's accusations, simply replied, 'That's insane.' A new statue, which incorporated pieces of the previous one, was installed a month later, and Thaksin has remained in exile since 2008.

In 2010, the Ratchaprasong Intersection, where the shrine is located, became the main gathering point for anti-government Red Shirt protesters, who occupied the area for several months. Images of the predominantly lower-class rural protesters camped out in front of the Ratchaprasong's luxury shopfronts became a media staple. When the Red Shirts were forcibly cleared out by the military on 19 May, five people were killed and fleeing protesters set fire to the nearby CentralWorld mall.

CentralWorld was renovated in 2012, but a year later Ratchaprasong Intersection yet again became a major protest site, this time occupied by opponents of Thaksin's sister, then Prime Minister Yingluck Shinawatra. The protests were known colloquially as Shutdown Bangkok (complete with protest merchandise featuring the computer shutdown button icon), and this time media images of the largely middle- and upper-class urban protesters in front of chic malls drew comparisons rather than contrasts. On 20 May 2014, the Thai Army declared martial law and took over the government in a coup d'état, leading the protesters to disperse.

Yet undoubtedly the most significant event in the shrine's history came on the evening of 17 August 2015, when a bomb planted in the Erawan Shrine compound exploded, killing 20 and injuring more than 120 people, an apparent act of terrorism that Prime Minister Prayut Chan-o-cha described as the 'worst incident that has ever happened' in Thailand. Two years on, two suspects have been arrested and are undergoing trial, although their motives remain unclear and a verdict has yet to be reached.

Why so much turmoil associated with a shrine that most believe to have positive powers? Some feel that the Erawan Shrine sits on land that carries long-standing and potentially conflicting supernatural powers. Others feel that the area is currently spiritually overcrowded, as other nearby structures also have their own, potentially competing, Hindu shrines. What's certain is that in Thailand, politics, faith, fortune and tragedy are often linked.

100 TONSON GALLERY GALLERY

Map p274 (www.100tonsongallery.com; 100 Th Ton Son; ⏰11am-7pm Thu-Sun; [S]Chit Lom exit 4) [FREE] Housed in a spacious residential villa, and regarded as one of the city's top commercial galleries, 100 Tonson hosts a variety of exhibitions of all genres by local and international artists.

BAIYOKE TOWER II NOTABLE BUILDING

Map p271 (ตึกใบหยก ๒; 22 Th Ratchaprarop; 300B; ⏰9am-11pm; ⛴klorng boat to Pratunam Pier) Cheesiness and altitude run in equal parts at Baiyoke Tower II, Bangkok's tallest building (to be usurped by a 'super tower' slated to be finished in 2021). Ascend through a corridor decked with aliens and planets (and the *Star Wars* theme song) to emerge at the 84th-floor, open-air revolving platform that looks over a city whose concrete sprawl can appear never-ending.

JAMJUREE ART GALLERY
GALLERY

Map p274 (หอศิลป์จามจุรี; www.chamchuriartgallery.chula.ac.th; Jamjuree Bldg, Chulalongkorn University, Th Phayathai; ⊘10am-7pm Mon-Fri, 11am-6pm Sat & Sun; S Siam exit 2 & taxi) FREE This gallery, part of Chulalongkorn University's Faculty of Arts, emphasises modern spiritual themes and brilliantly coloured abstracts from emerging student artists.

TANG CONTEMPORARY ART
GALLERY

Map p274 (www.tangcontemporary.com; 2nd fl, Golden Place Plaza, 153 Th Ratchadamri; ⊘11am-7pm Tue-Sat; S Ratchadamri exit 4) Bangkok's primary venue for modern artists from China has edged its way to become one of the city's top contemporary galleries. Check the website to see what's on display.

VICTORY MONUMENT
MONUMENT

Map p271 (อนุสาวรีย์ชัย; cnr Th Ratchawithi & Th Phayathai; ⊘24hr; S Victory Monument exit 2) This obelisk monument was built by the then military government in 1941 to commemorate a 1940 campaign against the French in Laos. Today the monument is primarily a landmark for observing the social universe of local university students and countless commuters. It's worth exploring the neighbourhood around Victory Monument, which is reminiscent of provincial Thai towns, if not exactly hicksville.

CHULALONGKORN UNIVERSITY
UNIVERSITY

Map p274 (จุฬาลงกรณ์มหาวิทยาลัย; ☎02 215 0871; www.chula.ac.th; 254 Th Phayathai; M Sam Yan exit 2, S Siam exit 2 or 6) Thailand's oldest and most prestigious university is nestled in a leafy enclave south of busy Rama I.

The centrepiece of the campus is the promenade ground on the east side of Th Phayathai where a seated statue of Rama V (King Chulalongkorn; r 1868–1910) is surrounded by purple bougainvillea and offerings of pink carnations. The showcase buildings display the architectural fusion the monarch favoured, a mix of Italian revival and Thai traditional. The campus has a parklike quality, with noble tropical trees considerately labelled for plant geeks. Of the many species that shade the campus, the rain trees with their delicate leaves are considered symbolic of the university; they

are commemorated in a school song, and their deciduous cycle matches the beginning and ending of each school year.

✕ EATING

If you find yourself hungry in this part of central Bangkok, you're largely at the mercy of shopping-mall food courts and chain restaurants. However, this is still Thailand, and if you can ignore the prefabricated atmosphere, the food can often be quite good.

★ MBK FOOD ISLAND
THAI $

Map p274 (6th fl, MBK Center, cnr Rama I & Th Phayathai; mains 35-150B; ⊘10am-9pm; ✷ ✎; S National Stadium exit 4) With dozens of vendors offering exceedingly cheap and tasty regional Thai, international and even vegetarian dishes, MBK Food Island fiercely clings to its crown as the grandaddy of Bangkok food courts.

NUER KOO
CHINESE $

Map p274 (4th fl, Siam Paragon, 991/1 Rama I; mains 85-970B; ⊘11.30am-9.15pm; ✷; S Siam exits 3 & 5) Is this the future of the noodle stall? Mall-bound Nuer Koo does a luxe version of the formerly humble bowl of beef noodles. Choose your cut of beef (including Kobe beef from Japan), enjoy the rich broth and cool air-con, and quickly forget about the good old days.

DIN TAI FUNG
CHINESE $$

Map p274 (7th fl, CentralWorld, Th Ratchadamri; mains 65-350B; ⊘11am-10pm; ✷ ✎; S Chit Lom exit 9 to Sky Walk, Siam exit 6 to Sky Walk) Most come to this lauded Taiwanese chain for the *xiao long bao* (broth-filled 'soup' dumplings). And so should you. But the other northern-Chinese-style dishes are just as good, and justify exploring the more remote regions of the menu.

ⓘ MAKING SENSE OF BANGKOK STREET NAMES

Street names often seem unpronounceable, and the inconsistency of romanised Thai spellings doesn't help. For example, the street Th Ratchadamri can be spelt 'Rajdamri'. And one of the most popular locations for foreign embassies is known both as Wireless Rd and Th Witthayu (*wí·tá·yú* is Thai for 'radio').

LOCAL KNOWLEDGE

FOOD COURT FRENZY

The Siam Square area is home to some of Bangkok's biggest malls, which means that it's also home to more than its share of mall-based food courts. They're a great way to dip your toe in the sea of Thai food as they're generally cheap, clean, air-conditioned and have English-language menus. At most, paying is done by exchanging cash for vouchers or a temporary credit card at one of several counters; your change is refunded at the same desk.

MBK Food Island (p115) The grandaddy of the genre offers dozens of vendors selling Thai-Chinese, regional Thai and international dishes.

Food Republic (Map p274; 4th fl, Siam Center, cnr Rama I & Th Phayathai; mains 30-200B; ⏲10am-10pm; ❄ 🍴; [S]Siam exit 1) The city's handsomest food court has a good mix of Thai and international (mostly Asian) outlets in an open, modern-feeling locale.

Eathai (Map p274; www.facebook.com/EathaibyCentral; basement, Central Embassy, 1031 Th Phloen Chit; mains 60-360B; ⏲10am-10pm; ❄ 🍴; [S]Phloen Chit exit 5) This expansive food court spans Thai – and only Thai – dishes from just about every corner of the country, including those from several lauded Bangkok restaurants and stalls.

Gourmet Paradise (Map p274; ground fl, Siam Paragon, 991/1 Rama I; mains 35-500B; ⏲10am-10pm; ❄ 🍴; [S]Siam exits 3 & 5) The perpetually busy Gourmet Paradise unites international fast-food chains, domestic restaurants and food-court-style stalls, with a particular emphasis on the sweet stuff.

Food Loft (Map p274; www.centralfoodloft.com; 6th fl, Central Chidlom, 1027 Th Phloen Chit; mains 65-950B; ⏲10am-10pm; ❄ 🍴; [S]Chit Lom exit 5) This department-store-bound food court pioneered the concept of the upscale food court, and mock-ups of the Indian, Italian, Japanese and other international cuisines aid in the decision-making process.

FoodPark (Map p274; 4th fl, Big C, 97/11 Th Ratchadamri; mains 30-90B; ⏲9am-9pm; ❄; [S]Chit Lom exit 9 to Sky Walk) The selections here may not inspire you to move here, but they are abundant and cheap, and are representative of the kind of 'fast food' Thais enjoy eating.

GAA — INTERNATIONAL $$

Map p274 (☎091 419 2424; www.gaabkk.com; 68/4 Soi Langsuan; set menu 1800-2400B; ⏲6-9.30pm; ❄; [S]Ratchadamri) A bright yellow and pink shophouse opposite **Gaggan** (☎02 652 1700; www.eatatgaggan.com; 68/1 Th Langsuan; set menu 5000B; ⏲6-11pm; ❄ 🍴; [S]Ratchadamri exit 2) has been taken over by Gaggan's former sous chef, Garima Arora, who also honed her craft at Copenhagen's famed Noma. Classic Indian and Thai dishes are the specialities here, upgraded with modern cooking techniques and presented in artful 8-12-course tasting menus. Reservations are strongly recommended.

TOY — THAI $

Map p271 (Soi 18, Th Ratchawithi, no Roman-script sign; mains from 15B; ⏲8am-5pm; [S]Victory Monument exit 3) The area surrounding the Victory Monument is home to heaps of simple restaurants selling spicy, rich 'boat noodles' – so-called because they used to be sold directly from boats that plied central Thailand's rivers and canals. Our pick of the lot is Toy, located at the edge of the canal at the northern end of Soi 18, Th Ratchawithi. No English-language menu.

SANEH JAAN — THAI $$$

Map p274 (☎02 650 9880; www.facebook.com/sanehjaan; Glasshouse at Sindhorn, 130-132 Th Withayu/Wireless Rd; set lunch 690B, mains 320-780B; ⏲11.30am-2pm & 6-10pm) A new restaurant with an old-school feel, Saneh Jaan features a menu of intriguing, unusual – and delicious – Thai dishes, many with a southern Thai accent. The prices reflect the semi-formal vibe of the dining room, but serves are generous.

GINZA SUSHI-ICHI — JAPANESE $$$

Map p274 (☎02 250 0014; www.ginza-sushi ichi.jp/english/shop/bangkok.html; ground fl, Erawan Bangkok, 494 Th Phloen Chit; set lunch 1300-4000B, set dinner 4000-10,000B; ⏲noon-2.30pm Tue-Sun, 6-11pm Tue-Sat, to 10pm Sun; ❄; [S]Chit Lom exit 8) This closet-sized restaurant – the Bangkok branch of a Tokyo-based recipient of a Michelin star – is arguably the city's premier place for sushi. The set menus depend on what was purchased at Tokyo's Tsukiji Market the previous day, which means that Ginza Sushi-Ichi does not open immediately following public holidays in Japan; check the website calendar for details.

SOMTAM NUA THAI $

Map p274 (392/14 Soi 5, Siam Sq; mains 75-120B; ⏰10.45am-9.30pm; ❄; [S]Siam exit 4) It can't compete with the street stalls for flavour and authenticity, but if you need to be seen, particularly while in air-con and trendy surroundings, this is a good place to sample northeastern Thai specialities. Expect a line at dinner.

ERAWAN TEA ROOM THAI $$

Map p274 (2nd fl, Erawan Bangkok, 494 Th Phloen Chit; mains 180-640B; ⏰10am-10pm; ❄✍; [S]Chit Lom exit 8) The oversized chairs, panoramic windows and variety of hot drinks make this one of Bangkok's best places to catch up with the paper. The lengthy menu of Thai standards will likely encourage you to linger a bit longer, and the selection of jams and teas to take away allows you to recreate the experience at home.

KOKO THAI $$

Map p274 (262/2 Soi 3, Siam Sq; mains 75-250B; ⏰11am-9pm; ❄✍; [S]Siam exit 2) Perfect for omnivores and vegetarians alike, this casual cafe-like restaurant offers a lengthy vegie menu, not to mention a short but solid repertoire of meat-based Thai dishes, such as a Penang curry served with tender pork, or fish deep-fried and served with Thai herbs.

LA MONITA MEXICAN $$

Map p274 (www.lamonita.com; 888/26 Mahatun Plaza, Th Phloen Chit; mains 120-550B; ⏰11.30am-10pm; ❄✍; [S]Phloen Chit exit 2) Admittedly, the menu here is more Texas than Tijuana, but of all the places that have attempted Mexican in Bangkok over the years, we reckon La Monita has done the best job. Come for an inviting, pleasant atmosphere and a repertoire of hearty dishes such as *queso fundido* (a skillet of melted cheese) and burritos.

BANGKOK'S PLASTIC ADDICTION

Buy a can of beer at any shop in Bangkok, and it will be presented to you in a tiny plastic bag, usually accompanied by a plastic straw (a container of yoghurt will be accompanied by a plastic spoon – wrapped in plastic). Do your shopping at any Bangkok supermarket, and you'll find that your groceries have been thematically divided (toiletries must never come in contact with edibles) into a comical and inconvenient-to-carry number of plastic bags of all sizes. We once bought a backpack that was wrapped in plastic, which a clerk then inserted into a thick plastic sack. A futile exercise: next time when shopping in Bangkok, make a point of telling your checkout person *mâi sài tǔng* ('no bag, please'), and we guarantee that the response will be a blank stare, followed by the person putting your purchase in a plastic bag, insisting *mâi ben rai* ('it's no big deal').

In Thailand, a huge producer of plastic products, bags are ubiquitous They're also very cheap, and even street vendors who run razor-thin profit margins can afford to be generous with the plastic. As a result, the country – in particular Bangkok – is seemingly addicted to plastic bags. A survey conducted by the country's Department of Environmental Quality Promotion (DEQP) estimated that the average Thai uses eight plastic bags per day. And like most addictions, it's proving harmful. The DEQP estimates that plastic bags form 20% of the country's rubbish. Bangkok's landfills, which receive nearly 10,000 tonnes of rubbish every day, are already overcrowded, and bags that aren't disposed of properly often obstruct drainage systems, contributing to already problematic flooding.

Over the last decade, retailers, such as 7-Eleven and Tesco Lotus, and municipal and government authorities have kick-started numerous informal initiatives to reduce the distribution of plastic bags. Indeed, a 2015 campaign initiated by the Thai Ministry of Natural Resources and Environment pleaded with Thais to part with their precious plastic bags – for one day a month. Yet without the mandate of strict anti-plastic-bag policies seen in countries like Bangladesh, it's likely that Thais will continue to consume as much plastic as ever.

SIAM SQUARE'S SILVER SCREENS

Each Bangkok mall has its own cinema, but few can rival **Paragon Cineplex** (Map p274; ☎02 129 4635; www.paragoncineplex.com; 5th fl, Siam Paragon, 991/1 Rama I; [S]Siam exits 3 & 5). In addition to 16 screens, more than 3000 seats and Thailand's largest IMAX screen, the options here include the Blue Ribbon Screen, a cinema with a maximum of 72 seats, where you're plied with pillows, blankets, complimentary snacks and drinks, and of course, a 15-minute massage; and Enigma, where in addition to a sofa-like love seat designed for couples, you'll be served cocktails and food (as well as blankets and a massage).

If you're looking for something with less glitz and a bit more character, consider the old-school stand-alone theatres just across the street, such as **Scala** (Map p274; ☎02 251 2861; Soi 1, Siam Sq; [S]Siam exit 2) and **Lido** (Map p274; ☎02 252 6498; www.apexsiam-square.com; btwn Soi 2 & Soi 3, Siam Sq; [S]Siam exit 2). For film showtimes at theatres across Bangkok, check in with moveedoo (www.moveedoo.com).

COCA SUKI CHINESE, THAI $$

Map p274 (416/3-8 Th Henri Dunant; mains 100-800B; ⏲11am-11pm; ❄✍; [S]Siam exit 6) Immensely popular with Thai families, *sù·gêe* takes the form of a bubbling hotpot of broth and the raw ingredients to dip therein. Coca is one of the oldest purveyors of the dish, and this branch reflects the brand's efforts to appear more modern. Insider tip for fans of spice: be sure to request the tangy *tom yam* broth.

SRA BUA BY KIIN KIIN THAI $$$

Map p274 (☎02 162 9000; www.kempinski.com/en/bangkok/siam-hotel/dining; ground fl, Siam Kempinski Hotel, 991/9 off Rama I; mains 550-890B, set meals 1350-3100B; ⏲noon-3pm & 6-10.30pm; ❄✍; [S]Siam exits 3 & 5) Helmed by a Thai and a Dane whose Copenhagen restaurant, Kiin Kiin, snagged a Michelin star, Sra Bua takes a correspondingly international approach to Thai food. Putting local ingredients through the wringer of molecular gastronomy, the couple have created unconventional Thai dishes such as 'tom kha snow, mushrooms and picked lemon'.

SANGUAN SRI THAI $

Map p274 (59/1 Th Witthayu/Wireless Rd, no Roman-script sign; mains 70-200B; ⏲10am-3pm Mon-Sat; ❄; [S]Phloen Chit exit 5) The English-language menu is limited at this old-school Thai eatery, but simply pointing to the delicious dishes being consumed around you is almost certainly a wiser ordering strategy. There's no English-language sign here; look for the bunker-like concrete structure.

PATHÉ THAI, INTERNATIONAL $$

Map p271 (www.patherestaurant.com; 507 Th Ratchawithi; mains 95-275B; ⏲10am-midnight; ❄; [S]Victory Monument exit 4) The modern Thai equivalent of a 1950s-era American diner, this popular place combines solid Thai food, a fun atmosphere and a jukebox playing scratched records. The menu is equally eclectic, and combines Thai and Western dishes and ingredients; be sure to save room for the deep-fried ice cream.

🍷 DRINKING & NIGHTLIFE

Bangkok's most central zone is home to a scant handful of bars.

HAIR OF THE DOG BAR

Map p274 (www.hairofthedogbkk.com; 1st fl, Mahathun Plaza, 888/26 Th Phloen Chit; ⏲5pm-midnight; [S]Phloen Chit exit 2) The craft-beer craze that has swept Bangkok over the last few years is epitomised at this semi-concealed bar. With a morgue theme, dozens of bottles and 13 rotating taps, it's a great place for a weird, hoppy night.

HYDE & SEEK BAR

Map p274 (www.hydeandseek.com; ground fl, Athenee Residence, 65/1 Soi Ruam Rudi; ⏲4.30pm-1am; [S]Phloen Chit exit 4) The tasty and comforting English-inspired bar snacks and meals here have earned Hyde & Seek the right to call itself a 'gastro bar'. But we reckon the real reasons to come are one of Bangkok's best-stocked liquor cabinets and some of the city's tastiest and most sophisticated cocktails.

RED SKY BAR

Map p274 (www.centarahotelsresorts.com; 55th fl, Centara Grand, CentralWorld, Th Ratchadamri; ⏲6pm-1am; [S]Chit Lom exit 9 to Sky Walk, Siam exit 6 to Sky Walk) Perched on the 55th floor of a skyscraper smack-dab in the modern centre of Bangkok, Red Sky provides one of Bangkok's most stunning rooftop views. The dramatic arch and all that glass provide the bar with a more upscale feel than Bangkok's other rooftoppers.

SKY TRAIN JAZZ CLUB BAR

Map p271 (cnr Th Rang Nam & Th Phayathai; 🕐5pm-2am; [S]Victory Monument exit 2) An evening at this comically misnamed bar is more like chilling on the rooftop of your stoner buddy's flat than any jazz club we've ever been to. But there are indeed views of the BTS, jazz on occasion and a scrappy speakeasy atmosphere. To find it, look for the sign and proceed up the graffiti-strewn stairway until you reach the roof.

MIXX CLUB

Map p274 (www.mixx-discotheque.com; basement, InterContinental Hotel, 973 Th Phloen Chit; 300B; 🕐10pm-2am; [S]Chit Lom exit 7) As the name suggests, Mixx draws a relatively wide swath of Bangkok's partiers, from newly arrived backpackers to hardened working girls, making it the least dodgy (a relative term) of the city's late-night discos.

ROOF BAR

Map p274 (www.siamatsiam.com/dining/roof; 25th fl, Siam@Siam, 865 Rama I; 🕐6pm-12.30am; [S]National Stadium exit 1) In addition to views of central Bangkok from 25 floors up, the Roof offers a dedicated personal martini sommelier and an extensive wine and champagne list. Party House One, on the ground floor of the same building, offers live music most nights.

WINE PUB BAR

Map p271 (www.winepubbangkok.com; 1st fl, Pullman Bangkok King Power, 8/2 Th Rang Nam; 🕐6.30pm-2am; [S]Victory Monument exit 2) If the upmarket but chilled setting and spinning DJ aren't compelling enough reasons to venture from your Sukhumvit comfort zone, consider that this is probably the least expensive place in town to drink wine. Check the website for revolving nibbles promotions that span everything from imported cheeses and cold cuts to tapas.

CO-CO WALK BAR

(87/70 Th Phayathai; 🕐5pm-midnight; [S]Ratchathewi exit 2) This covered compound is a loud, messy smorgasbord of pubs, bars and live music popular with Thai university students on a night out. We'd list a few specific locales here, but they'd most likely all have changed names by the time you read this – it's just that kinda place.

FOREIGN CORRESPONDENTS' CLUB OF THAILAND BAR

Map p274 (FCCT; www.fccthai.com; Penthouse, Maneeya Center, 518/5 Th Phloen Chit; 🕐noon-2.30pm & 6pm-midnight Mon-Fri; [S]Chit Lom exit 2) A bar-restaurant, not to mention a bona fide gathering place for the city's hacks and photogs, the FCCT also hosts art exhibitions ranging in genre from photojournalism to contemporary painting (and there's live jazz on Friday nights). Check the website to see what's on when you're in town.

☆ ENTERTAINMENT

Mall-based movie theatres provide the bulk of entertainment options in this part of Bangkok.

SAXOPHONE PUB & RESTAURANT LIVE MUSIC

Map p271 (www.saxophonepub.com; 3/8 Th Phayathai; 🕐7.30pm-1.30am; [S]Victory Monument exit 2) After 30 years, Saxophone remains Bangkok's premier live-music venue – a dark, intimate space where you can pull up a chair just a few metres away from the band and see their every bead of sweat. If you prefer some mystique in your musicians, watch the blues, jazz, reggae or rock from the balcony.

RAINTREE LIVE MUSIC

Map p271 (Soi Ruam Chit; 🕐6pm-1am Mon-Sat; [S]Victory Monument exit 2) This rustic pub is one of the few remaining places in town to hear 'songs for life', Thai folk music with roots in the political movements of the 1960s and '70s. Tasty bar snacks also make it a clever place to have a bite to eat.

ROCK PUB LIVE MUSIC

Map p274 (www.facebook.com/therockpub; 93/26-28 Th Phayathai; 🕐7pm-1am; [S]Ratchathewi exit 2) With posters of Iron Maiden as interior design, and black jeans and long hair as the dress code, this long-standing, cave-like, live-music bar is Thailand's unofficial Embassy of Heavy Metal.

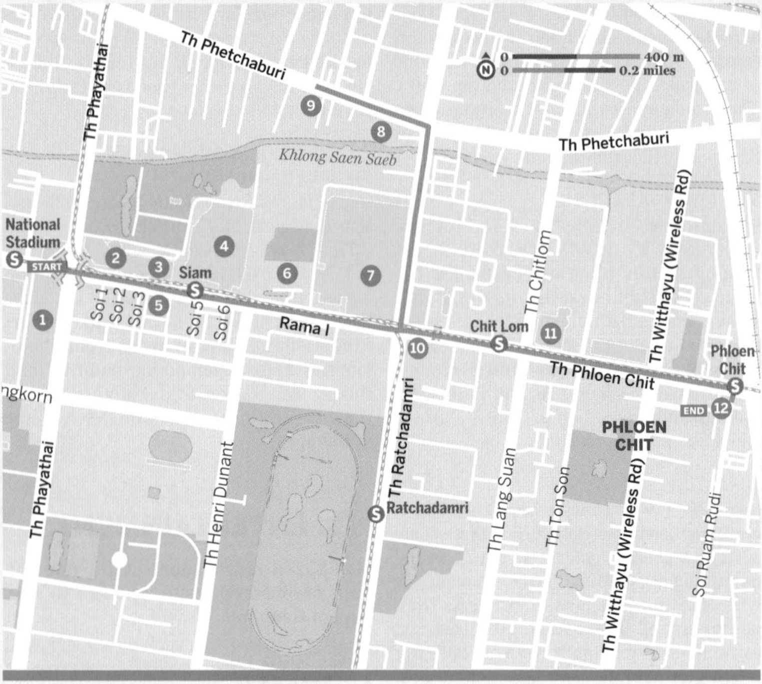
Th Phetchaburi
0 400 m
0 0.2 miles
Th Phayathai
Khlong Saen Saeb
Th Phetchaburi
National Stadium
START
Siam
Soi 1
Soi 2
Soi 3
Soi 5
Soi 6
Rama I
Th Chitlom
Th Witthayu (Wireless Rd)
Chit Lom
Th Phloen Chit
Phloen Chit
END
PHLOEN CHIT
Th Phayathai
Th Henri Dunant
Th Ratchadamri
Ratchadamri
Th Lang Suan
Th Ton Son
Th Witthayu (Wireless Rd)
Soi Ruam Rudi

Neighbourhood Walk
Siam Square Shopping Spree

START MBK CENTER
END HYDE & SEEK
LENGTH 3KM; TWO TO FOUR HOURS

This walk cuts across the heart of Bangkok's most commercial district via elevated walkways, escalators and air-conditioned malls. Start no earlier than 10am, when most shopping centres open.

Begin your walk at 1 **MBK Center** (p121), where you can pick up anything ranging from a used smartphone to new sneakers, or fuel up for the rest of the walk at the mall's 6th-floor food court.

From MBK, it's possible to continue, more or less, without touching street level again. Following the elevated walkway to the recently renovated 2 **Siam Discovery**, continue to 3 **Siam Center** and 4 **Siam Paragon** via linking walkways. If you're missing the heat and exhaust, make a detour across Rama I to the teen-themed shops and restaurants of 5 **Siam Square**, an open-air shopping centre.

From Siam BTS station, continue east along the Sky Walk. After a couple of minutes, on your left you'll see 6 **Wat Pathum**, an incongruously located Buddhist temple. Turn left on the bridge that connects to 7 **CentralWorld** (p122), one of the largest malls in Southeast Asia.

From CentralWorld, head north along yet another elevated walkway, this time terminating at 8 **Platinum Fashion Mall** (p122), a one-stop, multi-storey hall for cheap couture. If you're so inclined, you could tack on a stop at 9 **Pantip Plaza** (p123), the city's most famous destination for tech goods.

Returning to Rama I, continue east until you reach the 10 **Erawan Shrine** (p112), a buzzy tourist destination that was tragically bombed in 2015.

If there's anything you've forgotten, you can most likely pick it up at 11 **Central Chidlom** (p123), a seven-storey department store. Otherwise, end your walk, simultaneously checking your credit-card balance and sipping one of Bangkok's best mixed drinks, at 12 **Hyde & Seek** (p118).

LOCAL KNOWLEDGE

WHAT'S YOUR NUMBER?

The 4th floor of **MBK Center** resembles something of a digital produce market. A confusing maze of stalls sell all the components to send you into the land of cellular: a new phone, a new number and a SIM card. Even if you'd rather keep yourself out of reach, do a walk-through to observe the chaos and the mania over phone numbers. Computer print-outs displaying all the available numbers for sale turn the phone numbers game into a commodities market. The luckier the phone number, the higher the price; the equivalent of thousands of dollars have been paid for numbers composed mostly of nines, considered lucky in honour of the former king, Rama IX (King Bhumibol Adulyadej; r 1946–2016), and because the Thai word for 'nine' is similar to the word for 'progress'.

DIPLOMAT BAR LIVE MUSIC

Map p274 (ground fl, Conrad Hotel, 87 Th Witthayu/Wireless Rd; ⏲7pm-1am Mon-Thu, to 2am Fri & Sat; [S]Phloen Chit exit 5) Named for its location in the middle of the embassy district, this is one of the few hotel lounges that locals make a point of visiting. Choose from an expansive list of innovative martinis, and sip to live jazz, played gracefully at conversation level. The live music starts at 8pm from Monday to Thursday, and at 8.30pm on Friday and Saturday.

SHOPPING

The area around Siam Sq is home to the city's greatest concentration of malls; if name brands are your thing, this is your place. Cheap stuff, namely clothes, is found just north, in the Pratunam area.

★SIAM DISCOVERY SHOPPING CENTRE

Map p274 (www.siamdiscovery.co.th; cnr Rama I & Th Phayathai; ⏲10am-10pm; [S]Siam exit 1) With an open, almost-market-like feel and an impressive variety of unique goods ranging from housewares to clothing (including lots of items by Thai designers), the recently renovated Siam Discovery is hands down the most design-conscious mall in town.

★MBK CENTER SHOPPING CENTRE

Map p274 (www.mbk-center.com; cnr Rama I & Th Phayathai; ⏲10am-10pm; [S]National Stadium exit 4) This eight-storey market in a mall has emerged as one of Bangkok's top attractions. On any given weekend half of Bangkok's residents (and most of its tourists) can be found here combing through a seemingly inexhaustible range of small stalls, shops and merchandise.

MBK is Bangkok's cheapest place to buy mobile phones and accessories (4th floor). It's also one of the better places to stock up on camera gear (ground floor and 5th floor), and the expansive food court (6th floor) is one of the best in town.

★SIAM SQUARE SHOPPING CENTRE

Map p274 (Rama I; ⏲11am-9pm; [S]Siam exits 2, 4 & 6) This open-air shopping zone is ground zero for teenage culture in Bangkok. Pop music blares out of tinny speakers, and gangs of hipsters in various costumes ricochet between fast-food restaurants and closet-sized boutiques. It's a great place to pick up labels and designs you're guaranteed not to find anywhere else, though most outfits require a barely there waistline.

SIAM CENTER SHOPPING CENTRE

Map p274 (www.siamcenter.co.th; Rama I; ⏲10am-9pm; [S]Siam exit 1) Siam Center, Thailand's first shopping centre, was built in 1976 but, since a recent nip and tuck, hardly shows its age. Its 3rd floor is one of the best locations to check out established local labels such as Flynow III, Theatre and Tango.

SIAM PARAGON SHOPPING CENTRE

Map p274 (www.siamparagon.co.th; 991/1 Rama I; ⏲10am-10pm; [S]Siam exits 3 & 5) As much air-conditioned urban park as it is a shopping centre, Siam Paragon is home to **Sea Life Ocean World** (Map p274; www.sealifebangkok.com; basement, Siam Paragon, 991/1 Rama I; adult/child from 490/350B; ⏲10am-9pm; [S]Siam exits 3 & 5), Paragon Cineplex (p118) and Gourmet Paradise (p116), a huge basement-level food court. Then there are shops: on the 3rd floor is Kinokuniya, Thailand's largest English-language bookshop.

LOCAL BRANDS WORTH BUYING

Bangkok's malls are dominated by international brands, but there are some unique local labels to consider.

The Selected (Map p274; www.facebook.com/theselected; 3rd fl, Siam Center, Rama I; ⊙10am-9pm; Ⓢ Siam exit 1) A carefully curated assemblage of modern, mostly Thai-made housewares, knick-knacks, clothing and accessories for the *Kinfolk* generation.

Thann (Map p274; www.thann.info; ground fl & 2nd fl, CentralWorld, Th Ratchadamri; ⊙10am-10pm; Ⓢ Chit Lom exit 9 to Sky Walk, Siam exit 6 to Sky Walk) Smell good enough to eat with these botanical-based spa products. The soaps, shampoos and lotions are all natural, rooted in Thai traditional medicine, and stylish enough to share space with brand-name beauty.

Tango (Map p274; www.tangothailand.com; 3rd fl, Siam Center, Rama I; ⊙10am-9pm; Ⓢ Siam exit 1) This home-grown brand specialises in leather goods, but you may not even recognise the medium under the layers of bright embroidery and chunky jewels.

Karmakamet (Map p274; www.karmakamet.co.th; 3rd fl, CentralWorld, Th Ratchadamri; ⊙10am-9.30pm; Ⓢ Chit Lom exit 9 to Sky Walk, Siam exit 6 to Sky Walk) This brand's scented candles, incense, essential oils and other fragrant and non-fragrant items double both as classy housewares and unique souvenirs.

it's going green (Map p274; ground fl, Bangkok Art & Culture Center, cnr Th Phayathai & Rama I; ⊙10.30am-8pm; Ⓢ National Stadium exit 3) Ostensibly a shop selling gardening equipment, this boutique is also a good place to pick up retro Thai-style homewares (check out the enamel dishes), soaps and other items that double as one-of-a-kind souvenirs.

Viera by Ragazze (Map p274; www.facebook.com/vierabyragazze; 2nd fl, CentralWorld, Th Ratchadamri; ⊙10am-10pm; Ⓢ Chit Lom exit 9 to Sky Walk, Siam exit 6 to Sky Walk) Handsome, high-quality leather items, ranging from shoes to bags.

Objects of Desire Store (Map p274; ODS; www.facebook.com/objectsofdesirestore; 3rd fl, Siam Discovery, cnr Rama I & Th Phayathai; ⊙10am-10pm; Ⓢ Siam exit 1) An open-air boutique specialising in design-focused contemporary ceramics, paper products, furniture and other homewares, most of which are made by Thai artisans.

Flynow III (Map p274; www.flynowiii.com; 3rd fl, Siam Center, Rama I; ⊙10am-9pm; Ⓢ Siam exit 1) A long-standing leader in Bangkok's home-grown fashion scene, Flynow creates feminine couture that has appeared in several international shows.

Doi Tung (Map p274; www.doitung.org; 3rd fl, Siam Discovery, cnr Rama I & Th Phayathai; ⊙10am-9pm; Ⓢ Siam exit 1) Beautiful hand-woven carpets, rustic ceramics and domestic coffee beans are some of the items available at this royally sponsored enterprise.

Elephant Parade (Map p274; www.elephantparade.com; 4th fl, Siam Discovery, cnr Rama I & Th Phayathai; ⊙10am-10pm; Ⓢ Siam exit 1) Instead of visiting that elephant show – which animal-welfare activists claim can harm the animals – consider a purchase at this stall. The elephant-themed toys and knick-knacks are attractive and fun, and 20% of the proceeds go to help elephant causes.

CENTRALWORLD SHOPPING CENTRE

Map p274 (www.centralworld.co.th; Th Ratchadamri; ⊙10am-10pm; Ⓢ Chit Lom exit 9 to Sky Walk, Siam exit 6 to Sky Walk) Spanning eight storeys of more than 500 shops and 100 restaurants, CentralWorld is one of Southeast Asia's largest shopping centres. In addition to an ice rink, you'll find an extra-huge branch of bookshop B2S, and you could spend an hour sniffing around the fragrances at Karmakamet on the 3rd floor.

PLATINUM FASHION MALL CLOTHING

Map p274 (www.platinumfashionmall.com; 644/3 Th Phetchaburi; ⊙9am-8pm; ⓫ klorng boat to Pratunam Pier, Ⓢ Ratchathewi exit 4) Linked with Bangkok's garment district, which lies just north across Th Phetchaburi, is this five-storey mall stocked with a seemingly never-ending selection of cheap, no-name couture.

GIN & MILK CLOTHING

Map p274 (www.facebook.com/ginandmilkstore; 3rd fl, Siam Center, Rama I; ⏰10am-9pm; [S]Siam exit 1) A one-stop shop for domestic menswear, with items ranging from leather shoes to accessories, in looks ranging from traditional to edgy.

CENTRAL EMBASSY SHOPPING CENTRE

Map p274 (www.centralembassy.com; Th Phloen Chit; ⏰10am-10pm; [S]Phloen Chit exit 5) A flashy new shopping centre in central Bangkok.

CENTRAL CHIDLOM SHOPPING CENTRE

Map p274 (www.central.co.th; 1027 Th Phloen Chit; ⏰10am-10pm; [S]Chit Lom exit 5) Generally regarded as the country's best department store for quality and selection, Central has 13 branches across Bangkok in addition to this, the chain's chichi flagship.

NARAI PHAND GIFTS & SOUVENIRS

Map p274 (www.naraiphand.com; ground fl, President Tower, 973 Th Phloen Chit; ⏰10am-8pm; [S]Chit Lom exit 7) Souvenir-quality handicrafts are given fixed prices and comfortable air-conditioning at this government-run facility. You won't find anything here that you haven't already seen at all of the tourist street markets, but it is a good stop if you're pressed for time or are spooked by haggling.

PANTIP PLAZA SHOPPING CENTRE

Map p274 (www.pantipplaza.com; 604 Th Phetchaburi; ⏰10am-9pm; [S]Ratchathewi exit 4) If you can tolerate the crowds and annoying pornography vendors ('DVD sex? DVD sex?'), Pantip, a multistorey computer and electronics warehouse might just be your kinda paradise. Technorati will find pirated software and music, gear for hobbyists to enhance their machines, flea-market-style peripherals, and other odds and ends.

BAIYOKE GARMENT CENTER CLOTHING

Map p274 (cnr Th Phetchaburi & Th Ratchaprarop; ⏰10am-10pm; ⛴klorng boat to Pratunam Pier, [S]Ratchathewi exit 4) This rabbit warren of stalls is the undisputed epicentre of Bangkok's garment district. The vendors spill from the covered market area to dozens of nearby shops selling similarly cheap T-shirts, bags and other no-brand clothing items.

PINKY TAILORS CLOTHING

Map p274 (www.pinkytailor.com; 888/40 Mahatun Plaza, Th Phloen Chit; ⏰10am-7pm Mon-Sat; [S]Phloen Chit exits 2 & 4) Suit jackets have been Mr Pinky's speciality for 35 years. His custom-made dress shirts, for both men and women, also have dedicated fans. Pinky is located behind the Mahatun Building.

FASHION MALL SHOPPING CENTRE

Map p271 (Th Ratchawithi; ⏰10.30am-midnight; [S]Victory Monument exit 2) A suburban destination for no-name, cut-rate clothing.

MARCO TAILOR CLOTHING

Map p274 (430/33 Soi 7, Siam Sq; ⏰9am-7pm Mon-Fri; [S]Siam exit 2) Dealing solely in men's suits, this long-standing and reliable tailor has a wide selection of banker-sensibility wools. If you're considering getting suited, be sure to set aside time over at least a week for the various fittings.

SPORTS & ACTIVITIES

ISSAYA COOKING STUDIO COOKING

Map p274 (☎02 160 5636; www.issayastudio.com; Eatthai, level LG, Central Embassy, 1031 Th Phloen Chit; classes 2000-3000B; ⏰11am-2pm, 3-6pm & 6-8pm; [S]Phloen Chit exit 5) Started up by home-grown celebrity chef Pongtawat 'Ian' Chalermkittichai, morning lessons here include instruction in four dishes from his linked restaurant, Issaya Siamese

[i] LIVING LARGE

At home you may be considered average or even petite but, based on the Thai measuring stick, you're an extra large, clearly marked in the tag as 'LL' or, worse still, 'XL'. If that batters the body image, then skip the street markets, where you'll bust the seams from the waist up – if you can squirm that far into the openings. If you're larger than a US size 10 or an Australian size 14, you strike out altogether. Men will find that they exceed Thai clothes in length and shoulder width, as well as shoe sizes. For formal wear, many expats turn to custom orders through tailors. For ready-to-wear, many of the vendors at Pratunam Market and several stalls on the 6th floor of MBK Center stock the larger sizes.

Club (p134), while afternoon and evening lessons focus on desserts and mixology; check the calendar to see what's coming up. Specialised and private lessons can also be arranged.

THANN SANCTUARY SPA

Map p274 (☎02 658 6557; www.thannsanctuaryspa.info; 2nd fl, CentralWorld, Th Ratchadamri; Thai massage from 2000B, spa treatments from 2800B; 🕐10am-9pm; [S]Chit Lom exit 9 to Sky Walk, Siam exit 6 to Sky Walk) This local brand of herbal-based cosmetics also has a series of mall-based spas – perfect for post-shopping therapy.

SPA 1930 SPA

Map p274 (☎02 254 8606; www.spa1930.com; 42 Th Ton Son; Thai massage from 1000B, spa packages from 3500B; 🕐9.30am-9.30pm; [S]Chit Lom exit 4) Discreet and sophisticated, Spa 1930 rescues relaxers from the contrived spa ambience of New Age music and ingredients you'd rather see at a dinner party. The menu is simple (face, body care and body massage) and the scrubs and massage oils are logical players.

ABSOLUTE YOGA YOGA

Map p274 (☎02 252 4400; www.absoluteyogabangkok.com; 4th fl, Amarin Plaza, Th Phloen Chit; classes from 750B; [S]Chit Lom exit 6) This is the largest of Bangkok's yoga studios, teaching Bikram hot yoga plus a host of other styles.

UNION LANGUAGE SCHOOL LANGUAGE

Map p274 (☎02 214 6033; www.unionlanguage.com; 7th fl, 328 CCT Office Bldg, Th Phayathai; tuition from 7000B; [S]Ratchathewi exit 1) Generally recognised as having the best and most rigorous Thai-language courses (many missionaries study here), Union employs a balance of structure- and communication-oriented methodologies in 80-hour, four-week modules.

PILATES STUDIO HEALTH & FITNESS

Map p274 (☎02 650 7797; www.pilates.co.th; 888/58-59 Mahatun Plaza, Th Phloen Chit; classes from 550B; 🕐8am-7pm; [S]Phloen Chit exit 2) The first choice for those in Bangkok looking for Pilates instruction and training.

AAA LANGUAGE

Map p271 (Advance Alliance Academy Thai Language School; ☎02 045 1427; www.aaathai.school; 10th fl, Wannasorn Tower, 35 Th Phaya Thai; tuition from 7000B; [S]Phaya Thai exit 4) Opened by a group of experienced Thai-language teachers from various schools, good-value AAA has a loyal following.

Riverside, Silom & Lumphini

RIVERSIDE | SILOM | LUMPHINI

Neighbourhood Top Five

1 **nahm** (p133) Indulging in a meal at what is quite possibly the best Thai restaurant in the city and – if you believe the critics – one of the best restaurants in the world.

2 **Moon Bar** (p135) Soaking up the views at this

and the area's other tower-top bars.

3 **Lumphini Park** (p129) Relaxing Bangkok-style among the exercisers and exercise-observers in the 'lungs of the city'.

4 **Bangkok's Gaybourhood** (p136) Partying with

the LGBT crowd in the city's pinkest zone.

5 **Dinner Cruise** (p132) Ending the day (or kicking off the night) with drinks or a meal on Mae Nam Chao Phraya.

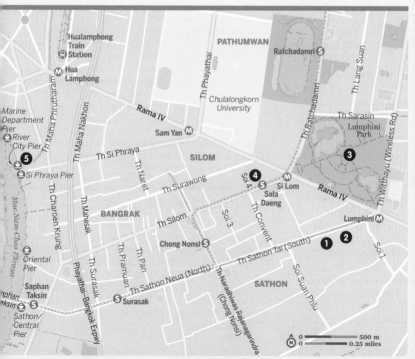

For more detail of this area see Map p277, p278 and p280 ➡

Lonely Planet's Top Tip

Getting out on Mae Nam Chao Phraya is a great way to escape Bangkok's traffic. So it's fortunate that the city's riverside hotels also have some of the most attractive boats on the river (technically for hotel guests, but staff don't check). These free services mostly run from Sathon/Central Pier to their mother hotel, departing every 10 or 15 minutes. There's no squeeze and a crew to help you on and off.

✕ Best Places to Eat

➡ nahm (p133)

➡ Eat Me (p132)

➡ Muslim Restaurant (p129)

➡ Jay So (p131)

➡ Kai Thort Jay Kee (p133)

➡ Le Normandie (p130)

For reviews, see p129➡

◉ Best Drinking & Nightlife

➡ Smalls (p134)

➡ Moon Bar (p135)

➡ DJ Station (p136)

➡ Vesper (p134)

➡ Namsaah Bottling Trust (p135)

➡ Wong's Place (p137)

For reviews, see p134➡

🔒 Best Places to Shop

➡ Asiatique (p139)

➡ Everyday by Karmakamet (p138)

➡ River City (p139)

➡ Tamnan Mingmuang (p139)

➡ House of Chao (p138)

➡ Chiang Heng (p139)

For reviews, see p137➡

Explore Riverside, Silom & Lumphini

Th Silom, with its towering hotel and office buildings, is Bangkok's de facto financial district, while adjacent Th Sathon is home to many of the city's embassies. Incongruously, lower Th Silom functions as Bangkok's gaybourhood. There's a dearth of proper sights in this part of town, so unless you're heading to Lumphini Park – at its best in the early morning – take advantage of the area's street stalls and upscale restaurants and combine your visit with lunch or dinner. The BTS stop at Sala Daeng and the MRT stop at Si Lom put you at lower Th Silom, perfect jumping-off points for either Lumphini Park or the area's restaurants and sights.

The Riverside area is significantly less flashy, and is great for an aimless wander among old buildings. This stretch of Mae Nam Chao Phraya was formerly Bangkok's international zone, and today retains a particularly Chinese and Muslim feel. Most of the sights in this area can be seen in a morning; the BTS stop at Saphan Taksin is a good starting point.

Local Life

➡ **Halal Hood** The area around the intersection of Th Silom and Th Charoen Krung is home to a handful of Thai-Muslim and Indian restaurants.

➡ **Rainbow Flag** Lower Th Silom, particularly the strip from Soi 2 to Soi 4, is Bangkok's pinkest district, and is popular with both local and visiting gay men.

➡ **Good Morning** Pretend you're Thai-Chinese by getting up at 5am and taking part in the early morning stretching rituals at Lumphini Park. Or you can just show up at a slightly saner hour and watch.

➡ **Art Attack** Those looking for a painting by a contemporary Burmese artist or an Ayuthaya-era Buddhist manuscript cabinet will undoubtedly find something interesting in one of Th Silom area's art galleries and antique shops.

Getting There & Away

➡ **BTS** To Riverside: Saphan Taksin. To Silom: Sala Daeng (interchange with MRT Si Lom). To Lumphini: Ratchadamri, Sala Daeng, Chong Nonsi and Surasak.

➡ **MRT** To Silom: Si Lom (interchange with BTS Sala Daeng). To Lumphini: Lumphini.

➡ **Chao Phraya Express Boat** To Riverside: River City Pier, Si Phraya Pier, Oriental Pier and Sathon/Central Pier. To Lumphini: Sathon/Central Pier.

➡ **Bus** To Silom: air-con 76 and 77; ordinary 1, 15, 33 and 27.

⊙ SIGHTS

⊙ Riverside

OLD CUSTOMS HOUSE HISTORIC BUILDING

Map p280 (กรมศุลกากร; Soi 36, Th Charoen Krung; ⛴Oriental Pier) The country's former Customs House was once the gateway to Thailand, levying taxes on traders moving in and out of the kingdom. It was designed by an Italian architect and built in the 1890s; the front door opened onto its source of income (the river) and the grand facade was ceremoniously decorated in columns and transom windows.

Today, with its sagging shutters, peeling yellow paint and laundry flapping on the balconies, the crumbling yet hauntingly beautiful building serves as a residence for members of Bangkok's fire brigade, not to mention a popular destination for wedding shoots. And hard-core movie buffs with a keen eye will recognise the Old Customs House from its cameo appearance in Wong Kar-Wai's film *In the Mood for Love* (2000).

ASSUMPTION CATHEDRAL CHURCH

Map p280 (อาสนวิหารอัสสัมชัญ; 23 Soi 40/Oriental, Th Charoen Krung; ⊙7am-7pm; ⛴Oriental Pier) **FREE** Marking the ascendancy of the French missionary influence in Bangkok during the reign of Rama II (King Phraphutthaloetla Naphalai; r 1809–24), this current incarnation of this Romanesque church with its rich golden interior dates from 1910, and hosted a mass by Pope John Paul II in 1984; his statue now stands outside the main door. The schools associated with the cathedral are considered some of the best in Thailand.

THAILAND CREATIVE & DESIGN CENTER LIBRARY

Map p280 (TCDC, ศูนย์สร้างสรรค์งานออกแบบ; ☎02 105 7400; www.tcdc.or.th; 1160 Th Charoen Krung; ⊙10.30am-9pm Tue-Sun) Taking up a sizeable chunk of Bangkok's art deco main post office is this new 'playground for creativity'. In practical terms, that means an art- and design-heavy research library, work spaces, gallery space and a cafe, all in a package that screams to be Instagrammed. Non-members can purchase a day pass to the facilities for 100B.

⊙ Silom

MR KUKRIT PRAMOJ HOUSE HISTORIC BUILDING

Map p278 (บ้านหม่อมราชวงศ์คึกฤทธิ์ปราโมช; ☎02 286 8185; Soi 7, Th Naradhiwas Rajanagarindra/ Chong Nonsi; adult/child 50/20B; ⊙10am-4pm;

⊙ TOP SIGHT
BANGKOKIAN MUSEUM

A collection of three antique structures built during the early 20th century, the Bangkokian Museum illustrates an often-overlooked period of Bangkok's history. The main building was constructed in 1937 as a home for the Surawadee family and, as the signs inform us, was finished by Chinese carpenters on time and for less than the budgeted 2400B (which would barely buy a door handle today). It is filled with beautiful wooden furniture and the detritus of postwar family life, and offers a fascinating window into the period. An adjacent two-storey shophouse contains themed displays of similar items on the ground floor (don't miss the replicated traditional Thai kitchen), while the upper level **Bang Rak Museum** profiles Khet Bang Rak, the district in which the compound is located. The third building, at the back of the block, was built in 1929 as a surgery for a British doctor, though he died soon after arriving in Thailand. A visit takes the form of an informal guided tour in halting English, and photography is encouraged.

DON'T MISS

➡ Antique wooden buildings
➡ Bang Rak Museum

PRACTICALITIES

➡ พิพิธภัณฑ์ชาวบางกอก
➡ Map p280, D2
➡ 273 Soi 43, Th Charoen Krung
➡ admission by donation
➡ ⊙10am-4pm Wed-Sun
➡ ⛴Si Phraya/River City Pier

LOCAL KNOWLEDGE

SILOM'S ART GALLERIES

Upper Th Silom and around is home to some of Bangkok's better art galleries. Located within walking distance of each other, it's possible to stop into several of the area's galleries in a leisurely afternoon and gain a good overview of the Thai contemporary art scene.

Kathmandu Photo Gallery (Map p278; www.kathmanduphotobkk.com; 87 Th Pan; ⏲11am-7pm Tue-Sun; [S]Surasak exit 3) [FREE] Bangkok's only gallery wholly dedicated to photography is housed in a charmingly restored Sino-Portuguese shophouse. The owner, photographer Manit Sriwanichpoom, wanted Kathmandu to resemble photographers' shops of old, where customers could flip through photographs for sale. Manit's own work is on display on the ground floor, and the small upstairs gallery has changing exhibitions by local and international artists and photographers.

Bangkok CityCity Gallery (Map p277; ☎083 087 2725; www.bangkokcitycity.com; 13/3 Soi 1, Th Sathon Tai/South; ⏲1-7pm Wed-Sun; [M]Lumphini exit 2) [FREE] This small, modern-feeling gallery hosts changing exhibitions featuring the work of domestic, often pop-inspired artists, as well as the occasional performance. Check the website to see what's on when you're in town.

Number 1 Gallery (Map p278; www.number1gallery.com; 19 Soi 21, Th Silom; ⏲10am-7pm Mon-Sat; [S]Surasak exit 3) [FREE] This relatively new gallery has established itself by featuring the often attention-grabbing contemporary work of Thai artists such as Vasan Sitthiket, Sutee Kunavichayanont and Thaweesak Srithongdee.

Gallery VER (☎02 103 4067; www.vergallery.com; 10 Soi 22, Th Narathiwat Ratchanakharin/Chong Nonsi; ⏲noon-6pm Tue-Sun; [S]Chong Nonsi exit 2 & taxi) [FREE] This vast art space has hosted a variety of work by both established and emerging domestic artists, sometimes with a subversive lean; in 2017 the gallery was raided by the Thai military and five pieces deemed 'threatening to the peace and security of the nation' were removed.

H Gallery (Map p278; www.hgallerybkk.com; 201 Soi 12, Th Sathon Neua/North; ⏲10am-6pm Wed-Sat, by appointment Tue; [S]Chong Nonsi exit 1) [FREE] Housed in a refurbished wooden building, H is generally considered among the city's leading private galleries. It's also regarded as a jumping-off point for Thai artists with international ambitions, such as Jakkai Siributr and Somboon Hormthienthong.

Thavibu Art Gallery (Map p278; www.thavibuart.com; 4th fl, Suite 435, Jewelry Trade Center Bldg, 919/1 Th Silom; ⏲11am-6.30pm Mon-Sat; [S]Surasak exit 3) [FREE] This gallery specialises in contemporary paintings by younger and emerging artists from Thailand, Vietnam and Myanmar.

[S]Chong Nonsi exit 2) Author and statesman Mom Ratchawong Kukrit Pramoj (1911–95) once resided in this charming complex now open to the public. Surrounded by a manicured garden, the five teak buildings introduce visitors to traditional Thai architecture, arts and the former resident, who served as prime minister of Thailand in 1974 and '75, wrote more than 150 books and spent 20 years decorating the house.

SRI MARIAMMAN TEMPLE HINDU TEMPLE

Map p278 (วัดพระศรีมหาอุมาเทวี/วัดแขก, Wat Phra Si Maha Umathewi; cnr Th Silom & Th Pan; ⏲6am-8pm Mon-Thu, to 9pm Fri, to 8.30pm Sat & Sun; [S]Surasak exit 3) [FREE] Arrestingly flamboyant, the Sri Mariamman Hindu temple is a wild collision of colours, shapes and deities. It was built in the 1860s by Tamil immigrants and features a 6m facade of intertwined, full-colour Hindu deities. While most of the people working in the temple hail from the Indian subcontinent, you will likely see plenty of Thai and Chinese devotees praying here as well. This is because the Hindu gods figure just as prominently in their individualistic approach to religion.

The official Thai name of the temple is Wat Phra Si Maha Umathewi, but it's often referred to as Wat Khaek – *kàak* being a common expression for people of Indian descent. The literal translation is 'guest', an obvious euphemism for any group of people not particularly wanted as permanent residents; hence most Indian Thais aren't fond of the term.

NEILSON HAYS LIBRARY LIBRARY

Map p278 (www.neilsonhayslibrary.com; 195 Th Surawong; non-members 50B; ⏲9.30am-5pm Tue-Sun; [S]Surasak exit 3) The oldest English-language library in Thailand, the Neilson Hays dates back to 1922, and today remains the city's noblest place for a read – with the added benefit of air-con. It has a good selection of children's books and a decent range of titles on Thailand.

Lumphini

QUEEN SAOVABHA MEMORIAL INSTITUTE ZOO

Map p277 (สถานเสาวภา, Snake Farm; cnr Rama IV & Th Henri Dunant; adult/child 200/50B; ⏲9.30am-3.30pm Mon-Fri, to 1pm Sat & Sun; 👪; [M]Si Lom exit 1, [S]Sala Daeng exit 3) Thailand's snake farms tend to gravitate towards carnivalesque rather than humanitarian, except at the Queen Saovabha Memorial Institute. Founded in 1923, the snake farm gathers antivenom by milking the snakes' venom, injecting it into horses, and harvesting and purifying the antivenom they produce. The antivenoms are then used to treat human victims of snake bites. Regular milkings (11am Monday to Friday) and snake-handling performances (2.30pm Monday to Friday and 11am Saturday and Sunday) are held at the outdoor amphitheatre.

The leafy grounds are home to a few caged snakes (and a soundtrack of Western rock music), but the bulk of the attractions are found in the Simaseng Building, at the rear of the compound. The ground floor houses several varieties of snakes in glass cages.

EATING

Riverside

MUSLIM RESTAURANT THAI $

Map p280 (1354-6 Th Charoen Krung; mains 40-140B; ⏲6.30am-5.30pm; ⛴Oriental Pier, [S]Saphan Taksin exit 1) Plant yourself in any random wooden booth of this ancient eatery

TOP SIGHT
LUMPHINI PARK

Named after the Buddha's birthplace in Nepal (Lumbini), Lumphini Park is central Bangkok's largest and most popular park. Its 58 hectares are home to an artificial lake surrounded by broad, well-tended lawns, wooded areas, walking paths and startlingly large monitor lizards to complement the shuffling Bangkokians. It's the best outdoor escape from Bangkok without actually leaving town.

The park was originally a royal reserve but in 1925 Rama VI (King Vajiravudh; r 1910–25) declared it a public space. One of the best times to visit is early morning, when the air is (relatively) fresh and legions of Thai-Chinese are practising t'ai chi, doing their best to mimic the aerobics instructor or doing the half-run half-walk version of jogging that makes a lot of sense in oppressive humidity. There are paddleboats for lovers, playgrounds for the kids and ramshackle weight-lifting areas for stringy old men. Cold drinks are available at the entrances and street-food vendors set up tables outside the park's northwest corner from about 5pm. Late at night the borders of the park are frequented by streetwalking prostitutes, both male and female.

DON'T MISS

- Enormous monitor lizards
- Early morning t'ai chi and evening aerobics

PRACTICALITIES

- สวนลุมพินี
- Map p277, B1
- bounded by Th Sarasin, Rama IV, Th Witthayu/Wireless Rd & Th Ratchadamri
- ⏲4.30am-9pm
- 👪
- [M]Lumphini exit 3, Si Lom exit 1, [S]Sala Daeng exit 3, Ratchadamri exit 2

LOCAL KNOWLEDGE

SATHON UNIQUE TOWER

The Asian financial crisis of the late 1990s left Thailand with a hobbled currency, a crippled economy and seemingly insurmountable debts to the International Monetary Fund. It left an even more tangible mark on the streets of Bangkok: hundreds of unfinished buildings. As banks crashed and investors bailed, huge construction jobs were simply abandoned, and the city's skyline became an almost post-apocalyptic blend of slick glass and concrete skyscrapers mingling with bare structural elements, exposed rebar and unintentionally edgy (read unfinished) architectural flourishes. Although in the subsequent two decades many of these structures have been torn down or even completed, arguably the most famous example of the genre, the unfinished, 49-storey **Sathorn Unique Tower** (Map p280; Soi 51, Th Charoen Krung; [♿]Sathon/Central Pier, [S]Saphan Taksin), remains almost exactly as it was when abandoned in 1997.

Known colloquially as the Ghost Tower, as locals believe the plot of land it occupies to be a former cemetery, construction began on Sathorn Unique in 1990. The building was slated to be a luxury condominium, and like its sister structure, the State Tower, it incorporates a gaudy hodgepodge of architectural influences, from Roman columns to neoclassical domes, a style that was popular in Thailand during this period. In 1997, with an estimated 75% of the tower completed, the Asian crisis reached its peak, funds disappeared, and construction on the tower was simply halted, leaving it in its partially finished state ever since.

Today, Sathorn Unique is both a cringe-worthy reminder of that era and a popular destination for urban explorers. It is officially off-limits to the public, although the building's guards have been known to look the other way for payment. (Though the tower's structural elements were completed, it's worth noting that huge holes, a lack of walls and falling debris make exploring the tower an extremely risky activity.)

for a glimpse into what restaurants in Bangkok used to be like. The menu, much like the interior design, doesn't appear to have changed much in the restaurant's 70-year history, and the biryanis, curries and samosas remain more Indian-influenced than Thai.

LE NORMANDIE   FRENCH $$$
Map p280 ([✆]02 659 9000; www.mandarinoriental.com; Mandarin Oriental, 48 Soi 40/Oriental, Th Charoen Krung; mains 2100-3300B; [⏰]noon-2.30pm & 7-11pm Mon-Sat, 7-11pm Sun; [❄]; [⛴]Oriental Pier or hotel shuttle boat from Sathon/Central Pier) Although today's Bangkok boasts a plethora of upmarket choices, Le Normandie has maintained its niche and is still the only place to go for a genuinely old-world 'Continental' dining experience. A revolving cast of Michelin-starred guest chefs and some of the world's most decadent ingredients keep up the standard, and appropriately formal attire (including jacket) is required. Book ahead.

NEVER ENDING SUMMER   THAI $$$
Map p280 ([✆]02 861 0953; www.facebook.com/theneverendingsummer; 41/5 Th Charoen

Nakhon; mains 200-1000B; [⏰]11am-11pm; [❄]; [⛴]river-crossing ferry from River City Pier) The cheesy name doesn't do justice to this surprisingly sophisticated Thai restaurant located in a former warehouse by the river. Join Bangkok's beautiful crowd for antiquated Thai dishes such as cubes of watermelon served with a dry 'dressing' of fish, sugar and deep-fried shallots, or fragrant green curry with pork and fresh bird's-eye chilli.

CHINA HOUSE   CHINESE $$$
Map p280 ([✆]02 659 9000 ext 7393; www.mandarinoriental.com/bangkok/fine-dining/the-china-house; Mandarin Oriental, 48 Soi 40/Oriental, Th Charoen Krung; mains 1000-1500B; [⏰]11.30am-2.30pm, 7-10.30pm Tue-Sun; [❄]; [⛴]Oriental Pier or hotel shuttle boat from Sathon/Central Pier) Art deco Shanghai comes to life in this refurbished colonial-style house in Bangkok, located in the compound of the Mandarin Oriental hotel. The big draw here is the unlimited dim sum lunch Tuesday through Friday and weekend brunch buffet, but under the guidance of a five Michelin star chef, the Peking duck wrapped in light-as-air pancakes shines.

LORD JIM'S
INTERNATIONAL $$$

Map p280 (📞02 659 9000; www.mandarinoriental.com/bangkok/fine-dining/lord-jims; Mandarin Oriental hotel, 48 Soi 40/Oriental, Th Charoen Krung; buffet 2050-2945B; ⊘noon-2.30pm Mon-Fri, 11.30am-2.30pm Sat, 11am-2.30pm Sun; ❄️ 🎵; 🚢Oriental Pier or hotel shuttle boat from Sathon/Central Pier) Even if you can't afford to stay at the Oriental, you should save up for the hotel's decadent riverside buffet. Dishes such as foie gras are standard, and weekends, when reservations are recommended, see additional seafood stations.

✖️ Silom

JAY SO
THAI $

Map p278 (146/1 Soi Phiphat 2; mains 45-80B; ⊘10am-4pm Mon-Sat; MSi Lom exit 2, SSala Daeng exit 2) Jay So has no menu, but a mortar and pestle and a huge grill are the telltale signs of ballistically spicy sôm·đam (green papaya salad), sublime herb-stuffed, grilled catfish and other northeastern Thai specialities.

There's no English signage (nor English-language menu), so look for the ramshackle, white and green, Coke-decorated shack about halfway down Soi Phiphat 2.

CHENNAI KITCHEN
INDIAN $

Map p278 (107/4 Th Pan; mains 70-150B; ⊘10am-3pm & 6-9.30pm; ❄️ 🎵; SSurasak exit 3) This thimble-sized mum-and-dad restaurant puts out some of the best southern Indian vegetarian food in town. The metre-long dosai (a crispy southern Indian bread) is always a good choice, but if you're feeling indecisive (or exceptionally famished) go for the banana-leaf thali (set meal) that seems to incorporate just about everything in the kitchen.

SOI 10 FOOD CENTRES
THAI $

Map p278 (Soi 10, Th Silom; mains 20-60B; ⊘8am-3pm Mon-Fri; MSi Lom exit 2, SSala Daeng exit 1) These two adjacent hangar-like buildings tucked behind Soi 10 are the main lunchtime fuelling stations for the area's office staff. Choices range from southern-style kôw gaang (point-and-choose curries ladled over rice) to just about every incarnation of Thai noodle.

SOMTAM CONVENT
THAI $

Map p278 ('Hai'; 2/4-5 Th Convent; mains 60-160B; ⊘11am-9pm Mon-Fri, to 5pm Sat; ❄️; MSi Lom

exit 2, SSala Daeng exit 2) Northeastern-style Thai food is usually relegated to less-than-hygienic stalls perched by the side of the road with no menu or English-speaking staff in sight. A less intimidating introduction to the wonders of lâhp (a minced meat 'salad'), sôm·đam (papaya salad) and other Isan (northeastern Thai) delights can be had at this popular and long-standing restaurant.

KRUA 'AROY-AROY'
THAI $

Map p278 (Th Pan; mains 40-100B; ⊘8am-8pm; SSurasak exit 3) Krua 'Aroy-Aroy' (Delicious Kitchen) is the kind of family-run Thai restaurant where nobody seems to notice the cat slumbering on the cash register. Stop by for some of the richest curries around, as well as the interesting daily specials including, on Thursdays, kôw klúk gà·þì (rice cooked in shrimp paste and served with sweet pork, shredded green mango and other toppings).

DAIMASU
JAPANESE $$

Map p278 (www.facebook.com/shichirinizakaya-daimasu; 9/3 Soi Than Tawan; mains 49-300B; ⊘5.30pm-1am; ❄️🎵; MSi Lom exit 2, SSala Daeng exit 1) The emphasis at this cosy, retro-themed Japanese restaurant is yakiniku (DIY grilled meat). But we also love the tiny, tasty sides ranging from crispy spears of cucumber in a savoury marinade to a slightly bitter salad of paper-thin slices of eggplant.

SUSHI TSUKIJI
JAPANESE $$

Map p278 (62/19-20 Th Thaniya; sushi per item 60-700B; ⊘11.30am-2.30pm & 5.30-10.30pm; ❄️; MSi Lom exit 2, SSala Daeng exit 1) Our pick of the numerous Japanese joints along Th Thaniya is Tsukiji, named after Tokyo's famous seafood market. Dinner at this sleek sushi joint will leave a significant dent in the wallet, so instead come for lunch on a weekday, when Tsukiji does generous set meals for a paltry 300B.

INDIAN HUT
INDIAN $$

Map p278 (www.indianhutbangkok.com; 414-420 Th Surawong; mains 160-380B; ⊘11am-11pm; ❄️🎵; 🚢Oriental Pier) Despite the fast-food overtones in the name and logo, this long-standing restaurant is classy and popular with visiting businesspeople. The emphasis is on northern Indian cuisine, including excellent flatbreads and tandoor-baked meats, and dishes such as homemade paneer in a tomato and onion curry.

KALAPAPRUEK THAI $$

Map p278 (27 Th Pramuan; mains 90-330B; ⊙8am-6pm Mon-Sat, to 3pm Sun; ❋ ✐; ⓈSurasak exit 3) This venerable Thai eatery has numerous branches and mall spin-offs around town, but we still fancy the original branch. The diverse menu spans Thai specialities from just about every region, daily specials and, occasionally, seasonal treats as well.

TALING PLING THAI $$

Map p278 (Baan Silom, Soi 19, Th Silom; mains 110-275B; ⊙11am-10pm; ❋ ✐; ⓈSurasak exit 3) Don't be fooled by the flashy interior; long-standing Taling Pling continues to serve a thick menu of homey, full-flavoured Thai dishes. It's a good starting point for rich, southern and central Thai fare such as *gaang kôo·a* (crabmeat curry with wild betel leaves), with tasty pies and cakes and refreshing drinks rounding out the choices.

BONITA CAFE
& SOCIAL CLUB VEGETARIAN $$

Map p278 (www.bonitacafesocialclub.wordpress. com; 100 Soi 26, Th Silom; mains 100-300B; ⊙9.30am-9.30pm Wed-Mon; ❋ 🛜 ✐; ⓈSurasak exit 3) Resembling grandma's living room, this homey restaurant serves predominantly Western-style vegan and raw dishes.

★**EAT ME** INTERNATIONAL $$$

Map p278 (✆02 238 0931; www.eatmerestaurant. com; Soi Phiphat 2; mains 300-1400B; ⊙3pm-1am; ❋ ✐; ⓂSi Lom exit 2, ⓈSala Daeng exit 2) With descriptions like 'charred witlof and mozzarella salad with preserved lemon and dry-aged Cecina beef', the dishes may sound all over the map or perhaps somewhat pretentious, but they're actually just plain tasty. A casual yet sophisticated atmosphere, excellent cocktails, a handsome wine list and some of the city's best desserts also make this one of our favourite places in Bangkok to dine.

INDIGO FRENCH $$$

Map p278 (✆02 235 3268; 6 Th Convent; mains 390-1850B; ⊙11.30am-midnight; ❋ ✐; ⓂSi Lom exit 2, ⓈSala Daeng exit 2) Indigo is set in a former schoolhouse, and while the charming atmosphere appears to be the main draw here, the food actually delivers. Think your neighbourhood French place, if your neighbourhood French place had oysters flown in from Les Halles on a weekly basis, and an

DINNER CRUISES

A dinner cruise along Mae Nam Chao Phraya is touted as an iconic Bangkok experience, and several companies cater to this. Yet it's worth mentioning that, in general, the vibe can be somewhat cheesy, with loud live entertainment and mammoth boats so brightly lit inside you hardly know you're on the water. The food, typically served as a buffet, usually ranges from mediocre to forgettable. But the atmosphere of the river at night, bordered by illuminated temples and skyscrapers, and the cool breeze chasing the heat away, is usually enough to trump all of this.

A good one-stop centre for all your dinner cruise needs is the **River City Boat Tour Check-In Center** (www.rivercity.co.th; ground fl, River City, 23 Th Yotha; ⊙10am-10pm; 🚢Si Phraya/River City Pier, or shuttle boat from Sathon/Central Pier), where tickets can be purchased for **Grand Pearl** (Map p280; ✆02 861 0255; www.grandpearlcruise. com; cruises 2000B; ⊙cruise 7.30-9.30pm; 🚢Si Phraya/River City Pier), **Chaophraya Cruise** (Map p280; ✆02 541 5599; www.chaophrayacruise.com; cruises 1700B; ⊙cruise 7-9pm; 🚢Si Phraya/River City Pier), **Wan Fah** (Map p280; ✆02 622 7657; www.wanfah. in.th; cruises 1500B; ⊙cruise 7-9pm; 🚢Si Phraya/River City Pier), **Chao Phraya Princess** (Map p280; ✆02 860 3700; www.thaicruise.com; cruises 1500B; ⊙cruise 7-9.30pm; 🚢Si Phraya/River City Pier) and **White Orchid** (Map p280; ✆02 438 8228; www.whiteorchidrivercruise.com; cruises 1400B; ⊙cruise 7.20-9.45pm; 🚢Si Phraya/River City Pier). All cruises depart from River City Pier; take a look at the websites to see exactly what's on offer.

For something slightly more upmarket, consider **Manohra Cruises** (✆02 476 0022; www.manohracruises.com; cruises 2300B; 🚢hotel shuttle boat from Sathon/Central Pier) or **Supanniga Cruise** (Map p280; ✆02 714 7608; www.supannigacruise.com; cruises 1250-3250B; ⊙cruises 4.45-5.45pm & 6.15-8.30pm; 🚢Si Phraya/River City Pier), more intimate experiences that also get positive feedback for their food.

WORTH A DETOUR

TAWANDANG GERMAN BREWERY

A German beer hall may seem like an odd destination in Bangkok, but the long-standing **Tawandang German Brewery** (www.tawandang.co.th; cnr Rama III & Th Narathiwat Ratchanakharin/Chong Nonsi; ⏲5pm-1am; [S]Chong Nonsi exit 2 & taxi) is a bona fide local institution – not to mention a one-stop venue for a guaranteed fun night out. The Thai-German food is tasty (don't miss the 'deep-fried pork knuckle served with spicy sauce', a Thai-German fusion staple), the house-made brews are potable, and the nightly stage shows make singing along a necessity. Music starts at 8.30pm.

interesting cheese selection. It doesn't come cheap, but daily set lunches start at 380B.

L'ATELIER DE JOËL ROBUCHON INTERNATIONAL **$$$**

Map p278 (☎02 001 0698; www.robuchon-bangkok.com; 5th fl, Mahanakorn Cube, 96 Th Naradhiwas Rajanagarindra/Chong Nonsi; set lunch 950-1950B, set dinner 7500-11,500B, mains 1350-3200B; ⏲11.30am-2pm & 6.30-10pm; ❄🍷; [S]Chong Nonsi exit 3) We'd like to think that you came to Bangkok to eat Thai, but we'd be remiss not to mention this place. Helmed by the chef who holds more Michelin stars than anyone else, it's one of the biggest openings in the city's recent past. Expect modern, French-inspired dishes, some with local touches, served in a sexy, sultry atmosphere where counter-top 'atelier' seating is encouraged.

SOMBOON SEAFOOD CHINESE **$$$**

Map p278 (☎02 233 3104; www.somboonseafood.com; cnr Th Surawong & Th Naradhiwas Rajanagarindra/Chong Nonsi; mains 120-900B; ⏲4-11pm; ❄; [S]Chong Nonsi exit 3) Somboon, a hectic seafood hall with a reputation far and wide, is known for doing the best curry-powder crab in town. Soy-steamed sea bass *(ɓlah grà·pong nêung see·éw)* is also a speciality and, like all good Thai seafood, should be enjoyed with an immense platter of *kôw pàt ɓoo* (fried rice with crab) and as many friends as you can gather together.

BUNKER AMERICAN **$$$**

Map p278 (☎02 234 7749; www.bunkerbkk.com; 118/2 Soi 12, Th Sathon Nuea; mains 450-900B; ⏲5.30-11pm; [S]Chong Nonsi exit 3) Bunker's menu, vibe, ace cocktail menu and swish service make you feel like you're in Manhattan, except that here in Bangkok, the dining room is spacious, not elbow-to-elbow. Tapas, sharing plates and hearty mains range from plant-based (endive and sunchoke salad) to high-quality meats (wagyu short ribs), and make this a good spot for a special occasion. Snap a selfie in the trippy mirror-covered bathroom before leaving.

🍴 Lumphini

KAI THORT JAY KEE THAI **$$**

Map p277 (Polo Fried Chicken; 137/1-3 Soi Sanam Khli/Polo; mains 50-350B; ⏲11am-9pm; ❄; [M]Lumphini exit 3) Although the *sôm·đam* (spicy green papaya salad), sticky rice and *lâhp* (a spicy salad of minced meat) of this former street stall give the impression of a northeastern-Thai-style eatery, the restaurant's namesake deep-fried bird is more southern in origin. Regardless, smothered in a thick layer of crispy deep-fried garlic, it is none other than a truly Bangkok experience.

★**NAHM** THAI **$$$**

Map p277 (☎02 625 3388; www.comohotels.com; ground fl, Metropolitan Hotel, 27 Th Sathon Tai/South; set lunch 600-1600B, set dinner 2500B, mains 310-800B; ⏲noon-2pm Mon-Fri, 7-10.30pm daily; ❄; [M]Lumphini exit 2) Australian chef-author David Thompson is the man behind one of Bangkok's – and if you believe the critics, the world's – best Thai restaurants. Using ancient cookbooks as his inspiration, Thompson has given new life to previously extinct dishes with exotic descriptions such as 'smoked fish curry with prawns, chicken livers, cockles, chillies and black pepper'.

Dinner is best approached via the multicourse set meal, while lunch means *kà·nŏm jeen,* thin rice noodles served with curries.

If you're expecting bland, gentrified Thai food meant for foreigners, prepare to be disappointed. Reservations essential.

LOCAL KNOWLEDGE

SILOM'S SWEET STUFF

Perhaps due to its legacy as Bangkok's former international district, the area around Th Silom has a disproportionately wide selection of sweets, both domestic and imported. Here's a selection of the highlights.

Chocolate Buffet (Map p277; www.sukhothai.com; Sukhothai Hotel, 13/3 Th Sathon Tai/South; buffet 900B; ⊙2-5pm Fri-Sun; ❄ ✎; MLumphini exit 2) For those with an insatiable sweet tooth, the Sukhothai Hotel offers a unique and almost entirely cocoa-based high tea.

Boonsap Thai Desserts (Map p280; www.boonsap.com; 1478 Th Charoen Krung, no Roman-script sign; desserts from 15B; ⊙7am-5pm Mon-Sat; ❄Sathon/Central Pier, ⓈSaphan Taksin exit 3) Dating back to the 1940s is this legendary producer of Thai sweets. Couple their sweetened sticky rice with mangoes or coconut custard. There's no English-language sign; look for the white shopfront with the gold letters near Soi 44.

iBerry (Map p278; www.iberryhomemade.com; 2nd fl, Silom Complex, Th Silom; ice cream from 69B; ⊙10am-9pm; ✎; MSi Lom exit 3, ⓈSala Daeng exit 4) A domestic chain with correspondingly Thai flavours such as guava and salted plum, santol sorbet and, for the daring, durian.

Duc de Praslin (Map p278; www.facebook.com/DucDePraslin; 2nd fl, Silom Complex, Th Silom; chocolates from 28B; ⊙10am-10pm; MSi Lom exit 3, ⓈSala Daeng exit 4) A mall-bound cafe featuring domestically made, Belgian-style chocolates. Combine your coffee – or the delicious hot chocolate – with one of the huge variety of bonbons or a bar of chocolate with an exotic pedigree.

Mashoor (Map p278; 38 Th Pan; mains 50-120B; ⊙9am-9pm; ❄ ✎; ⓈSurasak exit 3) This and a couple of other similar cafes near the Hindu temple do Indian-style sweets.

Eat Me (p132) We reckon that this restaurant does some of the best desserts in Bangkok; folks are known to have crossed town for the sticky date pudding alone.

ISSAYA SIAMESE CLUB   THAI $$$
Map p277 (☎02 672 9040; www.issaya.com; 4 Soi Sri Aksorn; mains 150-600B; ⊙11.30am-2.30pm & 6-10.30pm; ❄ ✎; MKhlong Toei exit 1 & taxi) Housed in a charming 1920s-era villa, Issaya is Thai celebrity-chef Ian Kittichai's first effort at a domestic outpost serving the food of his homeland. Dishes alternate between somewhat saucy, meaty items and lighter dishes using produce from the restaurant's organic garden.

The restaurant can be a bit tricky to find, and is best approached in a taxi via Soi Ngam Du Phli.

🍷 DRINKING & NIGHTLIFE

🍷 Riverside

VIVA & AVIV   BAR
Map p280 (www.vivaaviv.com; ground fl, River City, 23 Th Yotha; ⊙11am-midnight; ❄Si Phraya/River City Pier) An enviable riverside location,

casual open-air seating and a funky atmosphere make this restaurant-ish bar a contender for one of Bangkok's better sunset cocktail destinations.

🍷 Silom

★**SMALLS**   BAR
Map p278 (www.facebook.com/smallsbkk; 186/3 Soi Suan Phlu; ⊙8.30pm-late; MLumphini exit 2 & taxi) Even though it only opened its doors in 2014, Smalls is the kind of bar that feels like it's been here forever. Fixtures include a cheekily decadent interior, an inviting rooftop, food-themed nights (check the Facebook page) and live jazz on Wednesdays. The eclectic house cocktails are strong, if sweet, and bar snacks range from rillettes to quesadillas.

VESPER   BAR
Map p278 (www.vesperbar.co; 10/15 Th Convent; ⊙noon-2.30pm & 6pm-1am Mon-Fri, 6pm-midnight Sat, noon-2.30pm Sun; MSi Lom exit 2, ⓈSala Daeng exit 2) One of the freshest faces on Bangkok's drinking scene is this deceptively classic-feeling bar-restaurant. As the

name suggests, the emphasis here is on cocktails, including several revived classics and mixed drinks mellowed by ageing for six weeks in white-oak barrels.

CERESIA
CAFE

(ground fl, Tisco Tower, 48/2 Th Sathon Neua/North; ☺8am-6pm Mon-Fri, 9am-6pm Sat; Ⓜ Lumphini exit 2) Finally, a local roastery to rescue us from the caffeinated shackles of you-know-who. And best of all, boasting high-quality exotic and domestic beans, expertly prepared drinks and good pastries, Ceresia is more than just an alternative.

NAMSAAH BOTTLING TRUST
BAR

Map p278 (www.namsaah.com; 401 Soi 7, Th Silom; ☺5pm-2am; Ⓜ Si Lom exit 2, Ⓢ Sala Daeng exit 2) Namsaah is all about twists. From its home (a former mansion incongruously painted hot pink) to the cocktails (classics with a tweak or two) and the bar snacks and dishes (think *pàt tai* with foie gras), everything's a little bit off in just the right way.

MADRID
BAR

Map p278 (78/3 Th Patpong; ☺10am-1am; Ⓜ Si Lom exit 2, Ⓢ Sala Daeng exit 1) Shelve any notion of tapas or sangria here; dating back to 1969, Bangkok's oldest bar is all about late-'60s kitsch and Vietnam War–era intrigue. It's also known for its pizzas, and is really the only reason to consider a night out on Patpong.

MAGGIE CHOO'S
BAR

Map p278 (www.facebook.com/maggiechoos; basement, Novotel Bangkok Fenix Silom, 320 Th Silom; ☺7.30pm-2am Sun-Thu, to 3am Fri & Sat; Ⓢ Surasak exit 1) A former bank vault with a Chinatown-opium-den vibe, secret passageways and lounging women in silk dresses. With all this going on, it's easy to forget that Maggie Choo's is actually a bar, although you'll be reminded by the creative and somewhat sweet cocktails, and a crowd that blends selfie-snapping locals and curious tourists.

THE BAR
BAR

Map p278 (www.whotelbangkok.com/en/thehouse onsathorn; The House on Sathorn, W Bangkok, 106 Th Sathon Neua/North; ☺noon-midnight; Ⓢ Chong Nonsi exit 1) Located in one of Bangkok's more famous addresses – a registered historical landmark that in previous lives was a mansion, a hotel, and most recently, the Cold War–era Russian Embassy – is this atmospheric bar. The signature drinks are creative and pricey, yet worth it to gain access to the decadent surroundings.

UP ON THE ROOF

In Bangkok, nobody seems to mind if you slap the odd bar on top of a skyscraper. Indeed, the city has become associated with open-air rooftop bars, and the area around Th Sathon and Th Silom is home to some of its best, with locales boasting views that range from riverside to hyper-urban.

Note that nearly all of Bangkok's hotel-based rooftop bars have strictly enforced dress codes barring access to those wearing shorts and/or sandals.

Moon Bar (Map p277; www.banyantree.com; 61st fl, Banyan Tree Hotel, 21/100 Th Sathon Tai/South; ☺5pm-1am; Ⓜ Lumphini exit 2) An alarmingly low barrier at this rooftop bar is all that separates patrons from the street, 61 floors down. Located on top of the Banyan Tree Hotel, Moon Bar claims to be among the highest alfresco bars in the world. It's also a great place from which to see the Phrapradaeng Peninsula, the vast green area that's colloquially known as Bangkok's green lung.

Park Society (Map p277; 29th fl, Sofitel So, 2 Th Sathon Neua/North; ☺5pm-2am; Ⓜ Lumphini exit 2) Gazing down at the green expanse of Lumphini Park, abruptly bordered by tall buildings on most sides, you can be excused for thinking that Bangkok almost, kinda, sorta feels like Manhattan. The drink prices at Park Society, 29 floors above the ground, may also remind you of New York City, although there are monthly promotions.

Sky Bar (Map p280; www.lebua.com; 63rd fl, State Tower, 1055 Th Silom; ☺6pm-1am; Ⓢ Sathon/Central Pier, Ⓢ Saphan Taksin exit 3) Descend the Hollywood-like staircase to emerge at this bar that juts out over the city's skyline and Mae Nam Chao Phraya. This is the classic Bangkok rooftop bar – scenes from *The Hangover Part II* were filmed here – and the views are breathtaking, although the excessive drink prices and photo-snapping crowds have made it an increasingly hectic destination.

VOGUE LOUNGE BAR
(Map p278; www.voguelounge.com; 5th fl, Mahanakorn Cube, 96 Th Naradhiwas Rajanagarindra/Chong Nonsi; ⏲5pm-late; [S]Chong Nonsi exit 3) An extension of the eponymous magazine, brand placement is thankfully at a minimum here. Instead, you get a classy, classic-feeling bar in marble and brass, with an engaging menu of signature drinks and high-end nibbles. Happy hours that extend beyond dark and a terrace equipped with air-con make Vogue a clever late-night alternative.

BANGKOK'S GAYBOURHOOD

The side streets off lower Th Silom are so gay that they make San Francisco look like rural Texas. Every night, a pink tractor beam draws gay locals and tourists to the in-your-face sex shows in nearby Duangthawee Plaza, the chilled open-air bars on Soi 4 and the booming clubs in and around Soi 2.

Bars

Soi 4 is a tiny alleyway packed with gay bars, most with strategically positioned seats to best observe the nightly parade.

Telephone Pub (Map p278; www.telephonepub.com; 114/11-13 Soi 4, Th Silom; ⏲6pm-1am; 📶; [M]Si Lom exit 2, [S]Sala Daeng exit 1) Telephone is famous for the phones that used to sit on every table, allowing you to ring up that hottie sitting across the room. Its popularity remains even if most of the phones are gone. The clientele is mostly 30-plus white men with their Thai 'friends'.

The Stranger (Map p278; www.facebook.com/thestrangerbar; Soi 4, Th Silom; ⏲5.45pm-2am; [M]Si Lom exit 2, [S]Sala Daeng exit 1) Probably the most low-key, sophisticated venue on Soi 4 – except during the drag shows on Monday, Friday and Saturday nights.

Balcony (Map p278; www.balconypub.com; 86-88 Soi 4, Th Silom; ⏲5.30pm-2am; 📶; [M]Si Lom exit 2, [S]Sala Daeng exit 1) Located directly across from Telephone, this is yet another long-standing cafe-like pub that features the occasional drag-queen performance.

Duangthawee Plaza (Map p278; Soi Twilight; Soi Pratuchai; ⏲7pm-1am; [M]Si Lom exit 2, [S]Sala Daeng exit 3) This strip of male-only go-go bars is the gay equivalent of nearby Th Patpong. Expect tacky sex shows by bored-looking men.

Banana Bar on 4 (Map p278; 114/17-18 Soi 4, Th Silom; ⏲7pm-2am; [M]Si Lom exit 2, [S]Sala Daeng exit 1) An inviting open-air balcony, sultry, curtained private lounges, and an intimate club, Banana Bar is a one-stop-shop for a fabulously gay night out.

Clubs

The area's clubs are located in dead-end Soi 2 and Soi 2/1; if the following are too packed, alternatives are just steps away.

DJ Station (Map p278; www.dj-station.com; 8/6-8 Soi 2, Th Silom; admission from 150B; ⏲10pm-2am; [M]Si Lom exit 2, [S]Sala Daeng exit 1) One of Bangkok's – indeed Asia's – most legendary gay dance clubs, here the crowd is a mix of Thai guppies (gay professionals), money boys and a few Westerners.

G Bangkok (Map p278; G.O.D. (Guys on Display); www.facebook.com/pg/gbangkok; 60/18-21 Soi 2/1, Th Silom; from 300B; ⏲8pm-late; [M]Si Lom exit 2, [S]Sala Daeng exit 1) Also known as Guys on Display; as the name suggests, this three-storey club is not averse to a little shirtless dancing. Open late, this is where to go after the other clubs have closed.

Saunas

In Bangkok, there's a fine line – often no line at all – between male massage and prostitution. Saunas, on the other hand, don't involve any transaction past the entrance fee.

Babylon (Map p277; www.babylonbangkok.com; 34 Soi Nantha-Mozart; sauna 230-350B; ⏲10.30am-10.30pm; [M]Lumphini exit 2) Bangkok's most famous gay sauna remains extremely popular with visitors, many from neighbouring Singapore and Hong Kong. B&B-style accommodation is also available.

HANAKARUTA BAR

Map p278 (www.facebook.com/hanakaruta; Soi 10, Th Sathon Neua/North; ⏰6pm-2am Mon-Sat; [S]Chong Nonsi exit 1) The floor-to-ceiling wall of bottles here is proof of Hanakaruta's dedication to booze. Sake and *shochu* are specialities, but we love the house-made *umeshu* (plum wine). There's a menu of bar snacks (from 60B to 680B) that, like the drinks, is served with Japanese efficiency.

CRAFT BAR

Map p278 (www.craftbangkok.com; ground fl, Holiday Inn, cnr Th Silom & Th Surasak; ⏰noon-midnight; [S]Surasak exit 3) The microbrew trend that has swept across Sukhumvit has finally reached this part of town. Craft has 20, mostly American, beers on tap and even more bottles in the fridge.

CÉ LA VI CLUB

Map p278 (www.bkk.celavi.com; 38th & 39th fl, Sathorn Sq Complex, 98 Th Sathon Neua/North; ⏰11am-1am Mon-Thu, to 3am Fri & Sat; [S]Chong Nonsi exit 1) Spanning multiple bars, three restaurants and two clubs, Cé La Vi remains the biggest thing on Bangkok's club scene – literally and figuratively – although it must be said that there are more sophisticated places in town. Expect an entry fee of 300B after 10pm on Fridays and Saturdays.

Lumphini

WONG'S PLACE BAR

Map p277 (27/3 Soi Si Bamphen; ⏰9pm-late Tue-Sun; [M]Lumphini exit 1) This dusty den is a time warp into the backpacker world of the early 1980s. The namesake owner died several years ago, but a relative removed the padlock and picked up where Wong left off. It works equally well as a destination or a last resort, but don't bother knocking until 1am, keeping in mind that it stays open until the last person crawls out.

☆ ENTERTAINMENT

BAMBOO BAR LIVE MUSIC

Map p280 (☎02 236 0400; www.mandarinoriental.com; ground fl, Mandarin Oriental, 48 Soi 40/Oriental, Th Charoen Krung; ⏰5pm-1am Sun-Thu, to 2am Fri & Sat; ⛴Oriental Pier or hotel shuttle boat from Sathon/Central Pier) After more than 60 years of service, the Mandarin Oriental's Bamboo Bar remains one of the city's premier locales for live jazz. Guest vocalists are flown in from across the globe – check the website to see who's in town – and the music starts at 9pm nightly.

WHITELINE BAR

Map p278 (☎087 061 1117; www.facebook.com/whitelinebangkok; Soi 8, Th Silom; ⏰7pm-midnight Thu-Sun; [M]Si Lom exit 2, [S]Sala Daeng exit 1) This six-storey shophouse-turned-art-space in bustling Silom has something for everyone: film screenings, indie concerts, gallery nights displaying local talent and parties that rage late into the night. Drinks are simple Thai lagers and house spirits, with a few standout bottles of imported IPAs. Check the Facebook page for a current list of events.

BANGKOK SCREENING ROOM CINEMA

Map p277 (www.bkksr.com; 8-9 Soi Sala Deang 1; [M]Si Lom exit 2, [S]Sala Daeng exit 4) Bangkok has heaps of attractions that draw tourists in — great weather, fantastic bars, unbeatable food, low prices – but it's not known for being an arts haven. This cinema is trying to change that, one indie film at a time. Check the website for the revolving list of films, but expect the roster to showcase the work of budding Thai filmmakers.

Book tickets a day in advance to score one of the 50 seats in the single screen theatre and grab a craft beer before settling in.

SALA RIM NAAM THEATRE

Map p280 (☎02 437 3080; www.mandarinoriental.com/bangkok/fine-dining/sala-rim-naam; Mandarin Oriental hotel, Soi 40/Oriental, Th Charoen Krung; tickets adult/child 2000/1700B; ⏰dinner & show 8.15-9.30pm; ⛴Oriental Pier or hotel shuttle boat from Sathon/Central Pier) The historic Mandarin Oriental hosts dinner theatre in a sumptuous Thai pavilion located across the river in Thonburi. The price is well above the average, reflecting the means of the hotel's client base, but the performance gets positive reviews.

🛍 SHOPPING

A handful of high-quality souvenir and antique shops and the vast Asiatique market (p139) make these areas a solid option for shopping.

HOUSE OF CHAO ANTIQUES

Map p278 (9/1 Th Decho; ⏲9.30am-7pm; [S]Chong Nonsi exit 3) This three-storey antique shop, appropriately located in an antique shophouse, has everything necessary to deck out your fantasy colonial-era mansion. Particularly interesting are the various weather-worn doors, doorways, gateways and trellises that can be found in the covered area behind the showroom.

EVERYDAY BY KARMAKAMET GIFTS & SOUVENIRS

Map p278 (Soi Yada; ⏲10am-10pm; [M]Si Lom exit 2, [S]Sala Daeng exit 1) Part cafe, part showroom for the eponymous brand's vast selection of scented candles, incense, essential oils and other fragrant and non-fragrant items, Karmakamet is the ideal gift stop.

WAREHOUSE 30 HOMEWARES

Map p280 (52-60 Soi 30, Th Charoen Krung; ⏲11am-8pm Mon-Fri, 10am-9pm Sat & Sun) The latest trend in Bangkok seems to be converting formerly utilitarian structures into hyper-cool destinations that blend artsy sophistication and commerce. Warehouse 30, the newest and most impressive of the lot, takes the form of a string of World War II–era godowns housing a cafe, a high-end florist, and

PATPONG: TOURISTS IN THE GO-GO BAR ZONE

The neon signs leave little doubt about the dominant industry in Patpong, arguably the world's most infamous strip of go-go bars and clubs running 'exotic' shows.

For years opinion on Patpong has been polarised between those people who see it as an exploitative, immoral place that is the very definition of sleaze, and others for whom a trip to Bangkok is about little more than immersing themselves in planet Patpong. But Patpong has become such a caricature of itself that in recent times a third group has emerged: the curious tourist.

Prostitution is technically illegal in Thailand but there are as many as two million sex workers, the vast majority of whom – women and men – cater to Thai men. Many come from poorer regional areas, such as Isan in the northeast, while others might be students helping themselves through university. Sociologists suggest Thais often view sex through a less moralistic or romantic filter than Westerners. That doesn't mean Thai wives like their husbands employing the services of sex workers, but it's only recently that the gradual empowerment of women through education and employment has led to a more vigorous questioning of this very widespread practice.

Patpong actually occupies two soi that run between Th Silom and Th Surawong in Bangkok's financial district. The two streets are privately owned by – and named for – the Thai-Chinese Patpongpanich family, who bought the land in the 1940s and initially built Th Phat Phong and its shophouses; Soi Phat Phong 2 was laid later. During the Vietnam War the first bars and clubs opened to cater to American soldiers on 'R&R'. The scene and its international reputation grew through the '70s and peaked in the '80s, when official Thai tourism campaigns made the sort of 'sights' available in Patpong a pillar of their marketing.

These days Patpong has mellowed considerably, if not matured. Thanks in part to the popular night market that fills the street after 5pm, it draws so many tourists that it has become a sort of sex theme park. There are still plenty of the stereotypical middle-aged men ogling pole dancers, sitting in dark corners of the so-called 'blowjob bars' and paying 'bar fines' to take girls to hotels that charge by the hour. But you'll also be among other tourists and families who come to see what all the fuss is about.

Most tourists go no further than stolen glances into the ground-floor go-go bars, where women in bikinis drape themselves around stainless-steel poles. Others will be lured to the dimly lit upstairs clubs by men promising sex shows. But it should be said that the so-called 'ping pong' shows usually feature bored-looking women performing acts that feel not so much erotic as demeaning to everyone involved. Several of these clubs are also infamous for their scams, usually involving the nonperforming (ie clothed, if just barely) staff descending on wide-eyed tourists like vultures on fresh meat. Before you know it you've bought a dozen drinks, racked up a bill for thousands of baht, followed up with a loud, aggressive argument flanked by menacing-looking bouncers.

WORTH A DETOUR

ASIATIQUE

One of Bangkok's more popular night markets, **Asiatique** (Soi 72-76, Th Charoen Krung; ⏰4-11pm; 🚤shuttle boat from Sathon/Central Pier) takes the form of warehouses of commerce next to Mae Nam Chao Phraya. Expect clothing, handicrafts, souvenirs and several dining and drinking venues. There's a 60m-high Ferris wheel, and for those curious to see a performance of *gà·teu·i* (also spelt *kàthoey*) cabaret – featuring crossdresser and/or transgender performers – there's also a branch of **Calypso Bangkok** (📞02 688 1415; www.calypsocabaret.com; Asiatique, Soi 72-76, Th Charoen Krung; adult/child 900/600B; ⏰show times 8.15pm & 9.45pm; 🚤shuttle ferry from Sathon/Central Pier).

To get here, take one of the frequent, free shuttle boats from Sathon/Central Pier that run from 4pm to 11.30pm.

---

a shop selling curated vintage items, locally made homewares and a tiny organic grocery.

RIVER CITY
ANTIQUES

Map p280 (www.rivercity.co.th; 23 Th Yotha; ⏰10am-10pm; 🚤Si Phraya/River City Pier, or shuttle boat from Sathon/Central Pier) Several upscale art and antique shops occupy the 3rd and 4th floors of this riverside mall, but, as with many antique shops in Bangkok, the vast majority of pieces appear to come from Myanmar and, to a lesser extent, Cambodia.

A free shuttle boat to River City departs from Sathon/Central Pier every 30 minutes, from 10am to 8pm.

JULY
CLOTHING

Map p278 (📞02 233 0171; www.julytailor.com; 30/6 Th Sala Daeng; ⏰9am-6pm Mon-Sat; Ⓜ Si Lom exit 2, Ⓢ Sala Daeng exit 4) Suits at this tailor to Thailand's royalty and elite don't come cheap and the cuts can be somewhat conservative, but the quality is unsurpassed.

JIM THOMPSON
FASHION & ACCESSORIES

Map p278 (www.jimthompson.com; 9 Th Surawong; ⏰9am-9pm; Ⓜ Si Lom exit 2, Ⓢ Sala Daeng exit 3) The surviving business of the international promoter of Thai silk, the largest Jim Thompson shop sells colourful silk handkerchiefs, place mats, wraps and cushions. The styles and motifs appeal to older, somewhat more conservative tastes.

TAMNAN MINGMUANG
ARTS & CRAFTS

Map p278 (2nd fl, Thaniya Plaza, Th Thaniya; ⏰10am-7pm; Ⓜ Si Lom exit 2, Ⓢ Sala Daeng exit 1) As soon as you step through the doors of this museum-like shop, the earthy smell of dried grass and stained wood rushes to meet you. Rattan, *yahn lí·pow* (a fern-like vine) and water hyacinth woven into patterns, and coconut shells carved into delicate bowls are among the exquisite pieces that will outlast flashier souvenirs available on the streets.

TR GIFT SHOP LIMITED
HOMEWARES

Map p280 (📞02 234 5773; www.facebook.com/t.r.giftshopthailand; 2-4 Soi 40/Oriental, Th Charoen Krung; ⏰9am-7pm Mon-Sat, 10am-6pm Sun; Ⓢ Saphan Taksin exit 3) TR Gift Shop has been selling hammered stainless-steel trays, pitchers, bowls and other accessories since 1977. Shop specialities include water pitchers with buffalo-horn handles, serving pieces with mother-of-pearl inlay and cute items like olive picks. Paying in cash will earn you a substantial discount.

CHIANG HENG
HOMEWARES

Map p280 (1466 Th Charoen Krung; ⏰10.30am-7pm; 🚤Sathon/Central Pier, Ⓢ Saphan Taksin exit 3) In need of a handmade stainless-steel wok or a manually operated coconut-milk strainer? Then we suggest you stop by this third-generation family-run kitchen-supply shop. Even if your cabinets are already stocked, a visit here is a glance into the type of specialised shops that are quickly disappearing from Bangkok. There's no English-language sign; look for the blue doors.

THAI HOME INDUSTRIES
ARTS & CRAFTS

Map p280 (35 Soi 40/Oriental, Th Charoen Krung; ⏰9am-6.30pm Mon-Sat; 🚤Oriental Pier) Much more fun than the typically faceless Bangkok handicraft shop, the selection at this temple-like structure includes attractive woven baskets, cotton farmer shirts, handsome stainless-steel flatware and delicate mother-of-pearl spoons.

PATPONG
NIGHT MARKET
GIFTS & SOUVENIRS

Map p278 (Th Phat Phong & Soi Phat Phong 2; ⏰6pm-midnight; Ⓜ Si Lom exit 2, Ⓢ Sala Daeng

LOCAL KNOWLEDGE

7-ELEVEN FOREVER

Be extremely wary of any appointment that involves the words 'meet me at 7-Eleven'. In Bangkok alone, there are nearly 4000 branches of the convenience store (known in Thai as *sair·wên*) – indeed, Thailand, with more than 10,000 locations, ranks only behind the United States and South Korea in total number of 7-Elevens. In central Bangkok, 7-Elevens are so ubiquitous that it's not uncommon to see two branches staring at each other from across the street.

Although the company claims its stores carry more than 2000 items, the fresh flavours of Thai cuisine are not reflected in the wares of a typical Bangkok 7-Eleven, the food selections of which are even junkier than those of its counterpart in the West. Like all shops in Thailand, alcohol is only available from 11am to 2pm and 5pm to midnight, and branches of 7-Elevens located near hospitals, temples and schools are not allowed to sell alcohol or cigarettes at all (but do continue to sell unhealthy snack food).

7-Eleven stores carry a wide selection of drinks, a godsend in sweltering Bangkok. You can conveniently pay most of your bills at the service counter, and all manner of phonecards, prophylactics and 'literature' (although very few English-language newspapers) are also available. And sometimes the blast of air-conditioning alone is enough reason to stop by. But our single favourite item must be the dirt-cheap chilled scented towels for wiping away the accumulated grime and sweat before your next appointment.

exit 1) You'll be faced with the competing distractions of strip-clubbing and shopping in this infamous area. And true to the area's illicit leanings, pirated goods (in particular watches) make a prominent appearance even amid a wholesome crowd of families and straight-laced couples. Bargain with determination, as first-quoted prices tend to be astronomically high.

🏃 SPORTS & ACTIVITIES

ORIENTAL SPA   SPA

Map p280 (☑02 659 9000; www.mandarinorien tal.com; Mandarin Oriental, 48 Soi 40/Oriental, Th Charoen Krung; massage & spa packages from 2900B; ◎9am-10pm; 🚢Oriental Pier or hotel shuttle boat from Sathon/Central Pier) Regarded as among the premier spas in the world, the Oriental Spa sets the standard for Asian-style spa treatment. Depending on where you flew in from, the jet-lag massage might be a good option, but all treatments require advance booking.

HEALTH LAND   MASSAGE

Map p278 (☑02 637 8883; www.healthlandspa. com; 120 Th Sathon Neua/North; 2hr massage 550B; ◎9am-11pm; 🚇Surasak exit 3) This, the

main branch of a long-standing Thai massage mini-empire, offers good-value, no-nonsense massage and spa treatments in a tidy environment.

BANYAN TREE SPA   SPA

Map p277 (☑02 679 1052; www.banyantreespa. com; 21st fl, Banyan Tree Hotel, 21/100 Th Sathon Tai/South; massage/spa packages from 2800/6000B; ◎9am-10pm; 🚇Lumphini exit 2) A combination of highly trained staff and high-tech facilities have provided this hotel spa with a glowing reputation. Come for pampering regimens based on Thai traditions, or unique signature treatments.

CO VAN KESSEL
BANGKOK TOURS   CYCLING

Map p280 (☑02 639 7351; www.covankessel.com; ground fl, River City, 23 Th Yotha; tours from 950B; ◎6am-7pm; 🚢River City Pier) This originally Dutch-run outfit offers a variety of tours in Chinatown, Thonburi and Bangkok's green zones, many of which also involve boat rides. Tours depart from the company's office in the River City shopping centre.

BLUE ELEPHANT
THAI COOKING SCHOOL   COOKING

Map p278 (☑02 673 9353; www.blueelephant cookingschool.com; 233 Th Sathon Tai/South; classes from 3295B; ◎8.45am-1pm & 1.30-

4.30pm Mon-Sat; [S]Surasak exit 2) Bangkok's most chichi Thai cooking school offers two lessons daily. The morning class squeezes in a visit to a local market, while the afternoon session includes a detailed introduction to Thai ingredients.

RUEN-NUAD MASSAGE STUDIO MASSAGE

Map p278 (☎02 632 2662; 42 Th Convent; massage per hour 350B; ⏲10am-9pm; [M]Si Lom exit 2, [S]Sala Daeng exit 2) Set in a refurbished wooden house, this charming place successfully avoids both the tackiness and New Agedness that characterise most Bangkok Thai-massage joints. Prices are relatable, too.

SILOM THAI COOKING SCHOOL COOKING

Map p278 (☎084 726 5669; www.bangkokthaicooking.com; 68 Soi 13, Th Silom; classes from 900B; ⏲9am-12.20pm, 1.40-5pm & 6-9pm; [S]Chong Nonsi exit 3) This cooking school is spread over two simple but charming facilities and offers lessons that include a visit to a local market and instruction for six dishes, making it the best bang for your baht. Hotel pick-up in central Bangkok is available.

ORIENTAL HOTEL THAI COOKING SCHOOL COOKING

Map p280 (☎02 659 9000; www.mandarinoriental.com; Mandarin Oriental, 48 Soi 40/Oriental, Th Charoen Krung; classes from 3735B; ⏲9am-1pm Wed-Mon, to 2pm Sat & Sun; ⛴Oriental Pier or hotel shuttle boat from Sathon/Central Pier) Located across the river in an antique wooden house, the Oriental's cooking classes span a daily revolving menu of four Thai dishes, and in some cases, excursions to a local market. It's worth noting that the courses here are less 'hands on' compared to others in Bangkok.

Sukhumvit

Neighbourhood Top Five

❶ **WTF** (p149) Sipping a classic cocktail and checking out the art exhibition at what we reckon is Bangkok's best bar.

❷ **Health Land** (p154) Recovering from all that sightseeing at one of Th Sukhumvit's numerous and

excellent-value spas and massage parlours.

❸ **Jidori Cuisine Ken** (p147) Sampling from Th Sukhumvit's generous and delicious buffet of international restaurants.

❹ **Ban Kamthieng** (Kamthieng House) (p144)

Taking a trip back to ancient northern Thailand – smack dab in the middle of modern Bangkok.

❺ **Khlong Toey Market** (p144) Getting lost among the stacks of durians and piles of herbs in what is the city's largest fresh market.

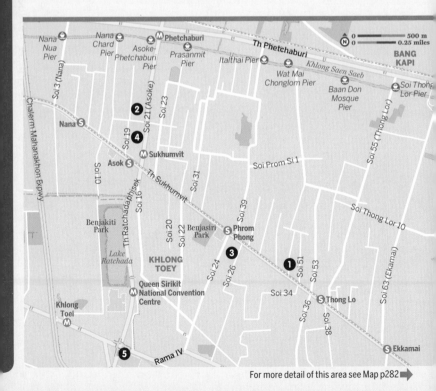

For more detail of this area see Map p282 ➡

Explore Sukhumvit

You'll probably spend more time on Th Sukhumvit eating, drinking and perhaps sleeping (there's a high concentration of hotels here), rather than sightseeing. Thankfully the BTS (Skytrain) runs along the length of Th Sukhumvit, making it a snap to reach just about anywhere around here. BTS stops are also a convenient way to define the street's various vibes. Lower Sukhumvit, particularly the area around Nana BTS station, is a discombobulating mix of sexpats and Middle Eastern tourists; street markets and touts make this a frustrating zone to navigate nearly any time of day or night. Middle Sukhumvit, around BTS Asok/MRT Sukhumvit, is dominated by midrange hotels, upscale condos, international restaurants and businesses meant to appeal to both tourists and resident foreigners. Near BTS Phrom Phong is where you'll find the well-concealed compounds of wealthy Thai residents and tidy Japanese enclaves, while extending east from BTS Ekkamai, the area feels more provincial and more Thai.

Local Life

→ **Hi-So Hangouts** Th Sukhumvit is Bangkok's ritziest zone, and is *the* area to observe *hi-so* (high society) Thais in their natural environment: chatting at a wine bar on Soi 55/Thong Lor or topping up on Fendi bags at Emquartier.

→ **International Dining** Th Sukhumvit's various ethnic enclaves are a logical destination if you've grown tired of Thai food. Known colloquially as Little Arabia, Soi 3/1 is home to several Middle Eastern restaurants, while Korean restaurants can be found at Soi 12, and several Japanese restaurants are located near BTS Phrom Phong. Not surprisingly, there's relatively little interesting Thai food in the area.

Getting There & Away

→ **BTS** Nana, Asok (interchange with MRT Sukhumvit), Phrom Phong, Thong Lo, Ekkamai, Phra Khanong, On Nut, Bang Chak, Punnawithi, Udom Suk, Bang Na and Bearing.

→ **MRT** Queen Sirikit National Convention Centre, Sukhumvit (interchange with BTS Asok) and Phetchaburi.

→ **Canal Boat** Asoke-Phetchaburi Pier, Nana Nua Pier and Nana Chard Pier.

→ **Bus** Air-con 501, 508, 511 and 513; ordinary 2, 25, 30, 48 and 72.

Lonely Planet's Top Tip

All odd-numbered soi branching off Th Sukhumvit head north, while even numbers run south. Unfortunately, they don't line up sequentially (eg Soi 11 lies directly opposite Soi 8). Also, some larger soi are better known by alternative names, such as Soi 3/Nana, Soi 21/Asoke, Soi 55/Thong Lor and Soi 63/Ekamai.

✗ Best Places to Eat

→ Jidori Cuisine Ken (p147)
→ Sri Trat (p145)
→ Ginzado (p147)
→ Soul Food Mahanakorn (p145)
→ Appia (p147)
→ Little Beast (p148)

For reviews, see p145 →

♈ Best Drinking & Nightlife

→ WTF (p149)
→ Q&A Bar (p149)
→ Studio Lam (p149)
→ Tuba (p149)
→ A R Sutton & Co Engineers Siam (p149)
→ Mikkeller (p149)

For reviews, see p149 →

☆ Best Dance Clubs

→ Beam (p150)
→ Glow (p150)
→ Demo (p151)
→ Sing Sing Theater (p151)
→ Narz (p152)
→ Levels (p151)

For reviews, see p149 →

SUKHUMVIT

👁 SIGHTS

SUBHASHOK THE ARTS CENTRE   GALLERY

Map p282 (SAC; www.sac.gallery; 160/3 Soi 33, Th Sukhumvit; ⏰10am-5.30pm Sat, noon-6pm Sun; Ⓢ Phrom Phong exit 6 & taxi) Tucked deep in a residential Th Sukhumvit side street is this vast new gallery, one of the city's most ambitious art spaces. A collaboration with Paris' Galerie Adler, so far the artists have largely stemmed from the big-name, often politically motivated, Thai art world.

KHLONG TOEY MARKET   MARKET

Map p282 (ตลาดคลองเตย; cnr Th Ratchadaphisek & Rama IV; ⏰5-10am; Ⓜ Khlong Toei exit 1) This wholesale market, one of the city's largest, is the origin of many of the meals you'll eat during your stay in Bangkok. Get there early, and bring a camera; although some corners of the market can't exactly be described as photogenic, the cheery fishmongers and stacks of durians make great happy snaps. By 10am, most vendors have already packed up and left.

CHUVIT GARDEN   PARK

Map p282 (สวนชูวิทย์; Th Sukhumvit; ⏰6-10am & 4-8pm; Ⓢ Nana exit 4) The eponymous benefactor of this park ran unsuccessfully for Bangkok governor in 2004, and successfully for the Thai parliament in 2005 and 2011. This park was one of his early campaign promises. It's a pretty green patch in a neighbourhood lean on trees.

Yet the story behind the park is shadier than the plantings. Chuvit Kamolvisit was Bangkok's biggest massage-parlour owner, and was arrested in 2003 for illegally bulldozing, rather than legally evicting, tenants off the land where the park now stands. With all the media attention, he sang like a bird about the police bribes he handed out during his career and became an unlikely activist against police corruption. In 2016, the cops got the last laugh when Chuvit was found guilty of three different charges related to the bulldozing and was sentenced to two years in prison.

BENJAKITI PARK   PARK

Map p282 (สวนเบญจกิติ; Th Ratchadaphisek; ⏰5am-8pm; 🚲; Ⓜ Queen Sirikit National Convention Centre exit 3) This 130-*rai* (20.8-hectare) park is built on what was once a part of the Tobacco Monopoly, a vast, crown-owned expanse of low-rise factories and warehouses.

👁 TOP SIGHT
SIAM SOCIETY & KAMTHIENG HOUSE

Stepping off cacophonous Soi 21/Asoke and into the Siam Society's Kamthieng House is as close to visiting a northern Thai village as you'll come in Bangkok. Kamthieng House is a traditional 19th-century home that was located on the banks of Mae Nam Ping in Chiang Mai. Now relocated to Bangkok, the house presents the daily customs and spiritual beliefs of the Lanna tradition. Communicating all the hard facts as well as any sterile museum (with detailed English signage and engaging video installations), Kamthieng House also instills in the visitor a palpable sense of place, from the attached rice granary and handmade tools to the wooden loom and woven silks. You can't escape the noise of Bangkok completely, but the houses are refreshingly free of concrete and reflecting glass, and make a brief but interesting break.

Next door are the headquarters of the prestigious Siam Society, publisher of the renowned *Journal of the Siam Society* and a valiant preserver of traditional Thai culture. Those with a serious interest can use the **reference library**, which has the answers to almost any question you might have about Thailand (outside the political sphere, since the society is sponsored by the royal family).

DON'T MISS

➡ Ban Kamthieng (Kamthieng House)

➡ Siam Society's reference library

PRACTICALITIES

➡ สยามสมาคม & บ้านคำเทียง

➡ Map p282, C3

➡ www.siam-society.org

➡ 131 Soi 21/Asoke, Th Sukhumvit

➡ adult/child 100B/free

➡ ⏰9am-5pm Tue-Sat

➡ Ⓜ Sukhumvit exit 1, Ⓢ Asok exit 3 or 6

There's an artificial lake that's good for jogging and cycling around its 2km track where bikes can be **hired** (Map p282; per hour 40B; ⏰8am-7pm; 👪).

BANGKOK UNIVERSITY ART GALLERY GALLERY

(BUG; www.facebook.com/bangkokuniversitygallery; 3rd fl, Bldg 9, City Campus, Rama IV; ⏰10am-7pm Tue-Sat; [S]Ekkamai exit 4 & taxi) [FREE] This spacious, modern compound is part of the country's most cutting-edge art school. Recent exhibitions have encompassed a variety of media by some of the country's top names, as well as the work of internationally recognised artists.

🍴 EATING

GOKFAYUEN CHINESE $

Map p282 (www.facebook.com/wuntunmeen; 161/7 Soi Thong Lor 9; mains 70-140B; ⏰11am-11.30pm; ❄; [S]Thong Lo exit 3 & taxi) Gokfayuen has gone to great lengths to re-create classic Hong Kong dishes in Bangkok. Couple your house-made wheat-and-egg noodles with roasted pork, steamed vegetables with oyster sauce, or the Hong Kong–style milk tea.

KLANG SOI RESTAURANT THAI $

Map p282 (Soi 49/9, Th Sukhumvit; mains 80-250B; ⏰11am-2.30pm & 5-10pm Tue-Sun; ❄; [S]Phrom Phong exit 3 & taxi) If you had a Thai grandma who lived in the Sukhumvit area, this is where she'd eat. The mimeographed menu spans old-school specialities from central and southern Thailand, as well as a few Western dishes. Located at the end of Soi 49/9, in the Racquet Club complex.

PIER 21 THAI $

Map p282 (5th fl, Terminal 21, cnr Th Sukhumvit & Soi 21/Asoke; mains 40-200B; ⏰10am-10pm; ❄🌿; [M]Sukhumvit exit 3, [S]Asok exit 3) Ascend a seemingly endless series of escalators to arrive at this noisy food court made up of vendors from across the city. The selection is vast (and includes a large vegetarian stall) and the dishes are exceedingly cheap, even by Thai standards.

SARAS INDIAN $

Map p282 (www.saras.co.th; Soi 20, Th Sukhumvit; mains 90-200B; ⏰9am-10.30pm; ❄🌿; [M]Sukhumvit exit 2, [S]Asok exit 4) Describing your restaurant as a 'fast-food feast' may not be the cleverest PR strategy we've encountered, but it's a pretty spot-on description of this Indian restaurant. Order at the counter to be rewarded with *dosai* (crispy southern Indian bread), meat-free regional set meals or rich curries (dishes are brought to your table).

BHARANI THAI $

Map p282 (Sansab Boat Noodle; 96/14 Soi 23, Th Sukhumvit; mains 60-250B; ⏰11am-10pm; ❄; [M]Sukhumvit exit 2, [S]Asok exit 3) This cosy Thai restaurant dabbles in a bit of everything, from ox-tongue stew to rice fried with shrimp paste, but the real reason to come is for the rich, meaty 'boat noodles' – so called because they used to be sold from boats plying the *klorng* (canals; also spelt *khlong*) of central Thailand.

BOON TONG KIAT SINGAPORE CHICKEN RICE SINGAPOREAN $

Map p282 (440/5 Soi 55/Thong Lor, Th Sukhumvit; mains 65-300B; ⏰10am-10pm; ❄; [S]Thong Lo exit 3 & taxi) After taking in the detailed and ambitious chicken rice manifesto written on the walls, order a plate of the restaurant's namesake and witness how a dish can be so simple, yet so delicious. The ideal accompaniment is *rojak* (a spicy/sour fruit 'salad'), referred to here as 'Singapore Som Tam'.

★SOUL FOOD MAHANAKORN THAI $$

Map p282 (☎02 714 7708; www.soulfoodmahanakorn.com; 56/10 Soi 55/Thong Lor, Th Sukhumvit; mains 140-290B; ⏰5.30pm-midnight; ❄🌿; [S]Thong Lo exit 3) This contemporary staple gets its interminable buzz from its dual nature as both an inviting restaurant – the menu spans tasty interpretations of rustic Thai dishes – and a bar serving deliciously boozy, Thai-influenced cocktails. Reservations recommended.

★SRI TRAT THAI $$

Map p282 (www.facebook.com/sritrat; 90 Soi 33, Th Sukhumvit; mains 180-450B; ⏰noon-11pm Wed-Mon; ❄; [S]Phrom Phong exit 5) This new restaurant specialises in the unique fare of Thailand's eastern provinces, Trat and Chanthaburi. What this means is lots of rich, slightly sweet, herbal flavours, fresh seafood and dishes you won't find anywhere else in town. Highly recommended.

DANIEL THAIGER AMERICAN $$

Map p282 (☎084 549 0995; www.facebook.com/danielthaiger; Soi 11, Th Sukhumvit; mains from 140B; ⏰11am-late; [S]Nana exit 3) Bangkok's best burgers are served from this American-run stall that, at the time of research, had a long-standing location on Soi 11. Check the Facebook page to see where the food truck will be when you're in town.

CHARCOAL TANDOOR GRILL & MIXOLOGY INDIAN $$

Map p282 (☎089 307 1111; www.charcoalbkk.com; 5th fl, Fraser Suites Sukhumvit, Soi 11, Th Sukhumvit; mains 290-1050B; ⏲6pm-midnight; ❄✍; [S]Nana exit 3) Indian food in Bangkok is gaining speed, and this kebab and tandoor grill restaurant is indicative of the trend. Almost every dish is slow-cooked in a clay oven, and menu standouts are the buttery charcoal dahl; lamb kebabs blended with ginger, green chillies, coriander and royal cumin; and *murgh malai kabab*. Cut the smoke with a signature South Asian-influenced cocktail.

PEPPINA PIZZA $$

Map p282 (☎02 119 7677; www.peppinabkk.com; 27/1 Soi 33, Th Sukhumvit; pizzas 160-415B; ⏲11.30am-3pm & 6pm-midnight Mon-Thu, 11.30am-2.30pm & 6pm-midnight Fri-Sun; ❄; [S]Phrom Phong exit 5) You'll be hard-pressed to find a better pizza in town. The flour, sea salt and yeast dough is risen for 24 hours before it is opened by hand and turned into mouth-watering Neapolitan pizzas. The wood-fired pies are topped with a sweet San Marzano tomato sauce that sings on simpler pizzas like the Napoletana.

PRAI RAYA THAI $$

Map p282 (Soi 8, Th Sukhumvit; mains 150-600B; ⏲10.30am-10.30pm; ❄; [S]Nana exit 4) This Phuket institution has opened a branch in Bangkok, bringing to the city the southern Thai island's uniquely spicy, occasionally Chinese-influenced cuisine. Although the English-language-menu descriptions may not always make sense, you can't go wrong choosing from the 'Prai Raya's popular dishes' section of the menu.

GAME OVER AMERICAN $$

Map p282 (www.gameover.co.th; Liberty Plaza, 1000/39 Soi 55/Thong Lor, Th Sukhumvit; mains 160-340B; ⏲5.30pm-2am Tue-Fri, 11.30am-2am Sat & Sun; ❄; ⛴Soi Thong Lor Pier, [S]Thong Lo exit 3 & taxi) Indulge your inner teen by playing *Call of Duty* while downing burgers and truffle fries at this video-game centre/restaurant. For the old at heart, there's Scrabble and an impressive selection of imported microbrews.

PIZZA ROMANA PALA ITALIAN $$

Map p282 (www.palapizzabangkok.com; cnr Th Sukhumvit & Soi 21/Asoke; pizza per slice 60-105B, mains 190-240B; ⏲8am-11.30pm; ❄✍; [M]Sukhumvit exit 3, [S]Asok exit 3) Strategically located at the intersection of the BTS and MRT – perfect for that rush-hour snack – this place serves some of Bangkok's best pies. Pizzas are sold by the slice and are made using almost exclusively imported ingredients. Pala also boasts a deli, and in addition to antipasti and simple pasta dishes you can also pick up a chunk of Pecorino Romano or some salami.

SUPANNIGA EATING ROOM THAI $$

Map p282 (www.supannigaeatingroom.com; 160/11 Soi 55/Thong Lor, Th Sukhumvit; mains 120-580B; ⏲11.30am-2.30pm & 5.30-11pm; ❄✍; [S]Thong Lo exit 3 & taxi) Thais are finally starting to take a serious interest in their own cuisine,

[i] SUPER MARKETS

Are you an American in need of a peanut-butter fix or an Aussie craving Vegemite? Don't fret: Th Sukhumvit is home to Bangkok's best-stocked international grocery stores.

Villa Market (Map p282; www.villamarket.com; Soi 33/1, Th Sukhumvit; ⏲24hr; [S]Phrom Phong exit 5) The main branch of this long-standing international grocery store is the place to pick up culinary 'necessities' from Cheerios to cheddar cheese. There are additional Th Sukhumvit branches at **Soi 11** (Map p282; Soi 11, Th Sukhumvit; ⏲24hr; [S]Nana exit 3), **Soi 49** (Map p282; Soi 49, Th Sukhumvit; ⏲24hr; [S]Phrom Phong exit 3 & taxi) and off **Soi 55/Thong Lor** (Map p282; Soi 55/Thong Lor 15; ⏲24hr; [S]Thong Lo exit 3 & taxi). Check the website for other locations.

Gourmet Market (Map p282; 5th fl, Emporium, cnr Soi 24 & Th Sukhumvit; ⏲10am-10pm; [S]Phrom Phong exit 2) Emporium's Gourmet Market carries a wide range of Western-style staples.

Foodland (Map p282; www.foodland.co.th; 87 Soi 5, Th Sukhumvit; ⏲24hr; [S]Nana exit 1) Well-stocked grocery store with several branches across town.

LOCAL KNOWLEDGE

JAPANESS VILLAGE

Bangkok is home to a huge Japanese expat population, many of whom live around mid-Sukhumvit (indeed, on Google Maps this area is labelled as 'Japaness [sic] Village'). Along with these Japanese expats has come a sophisticated array of restaurants, some representing the only branches of certain chains outside of Japan. Not surprisingly, the dining options go way beyond sushi. Here's some of our favourites.

Jidori Cuisine Ken (Map p282; ☎02 661 3457; www.facebook.com/jidoriken; off Soi 26, Th Sukhumvit; mains 60-350B; 🕒5pm-midnight Mon-Sat, to 10pm Sun; ❄; [S]Phrom Phong exit 4) This cosy restaurant does excellent tofu dishes, delicious salads and great desserts – basically everything here is above average – but the highlight is the sublimely smoky, perfectly seasoned chicken skewers.

Ginzado (Map p282; ☎02 392 3247; Panjit Tower, 117 Soi 55/Thong Lor, Th Sukhumvit; mains 120-900B; 🕒5-11pm; ❄; [S]Thong Lo exit 3) Make a reservation or queue for some really excellent *yakitori* (DIY grilled beef) not to mention a mean *bibimbap* (rice and toppings served in a sizzling stone bowl). Ginzado is located between Soi Thong Lor 3 and Soi Thong Lor 5, through the large white archway.

Teppen (Map p282; www.facebook.com/TeppenThailand; 14/2 Soi 61, Th Sukhumvit; dishes 140-960B; 🕒6pm-midnight; ❄; [S]Ekkamai exit 1) This is one of our favourite Bangkok *izakaya* (Japanese-style gastropubs), and the menu here has a bit of everything, from Western-influenced salads to Japanese-style beef offal stew.

Ippudo (Map p282; www.ippudo.co.th/en; 4th fl, Emporium, cnr Soi 24 & Th Sukhumvit; mains 130-310B; 🕒10.30am-10pm; ❄; [S]Phrom Phong exit 2) This Japanese ramen chain with a cult-like following has reached Thailand. Come for vast, rich bowls that adventurous eaters are encouraged to season with raw, pressed garlic.

Nirai-Kanai (Map p282; www.facebook.com/niraikanaibangkok; Soi Thong Lor 13; dishes 80-480B; 🕒5pm-midnight; ❄; [S]Phrom Phong exit 3 & taxi) Think you know Japanese food? Prepared to be schooled at this open-air restaurant serving the specialities of the southern island of Okinawa. With ingredients such as bitter gourd and yes, Spam, you're in for a surprise.

Imoya (Map p282; 3rd fl, Terminal Shop Cabin, 2/17-19 Soi 24, Th Sukhumvit; mains 40-400B; 🕒6pm-midnight; ❄; [S]Phrom Phong exit 4) A visit to this well-hidden Japanese restaurant, with its antique ads, wood panelling and wall of sake bottles, is like taking a trip in a time machine. Even the prices of the Japanese-style pub grub haven't caught up with modern times.

Fuji Super (Map p282; www.ufmfujisuper.com; 593/29-39, Soi 33/1, Th Sukhumvit; 🕒8am-10pm; [S]Phrom Phong exit 5) Central Bangkok or suburban Tokyo? It's hard to tell when inside this well-stocked supermarket; it has additional branches around town.

Gateway Ekamai (Map p282; www.gatewayekamai.com; 982/22 Th Sukhumvit; 🕒10am-10pm; ❄; [S]Ekkamai exit 4) Much of this huge mall is dedicated to Japanese-style fast food, including several restaurant outlets and shops selling Japanese snacks and sweets.

and over the last few years Bangkok has seen an explosion of sophisticated-feeling places serving regional Thai dishes. A standout is Supanniga, which focuses on the typically seafood-based, herb-forward dishes of Chanthaburi and Trat in eastern Thailand.

CABBAGES & CONDOMS THAI $$

Map p282 (www.pda.or.th; Soi 12, Th Sukhumvit; mains 120-470B; 🕒11am-11pm; ❄ 🍷; [M]Sukhumvit exit 3, [S]Asok exit 2) 🌿 This long-standing garden restaurant is a safe place to gauge the Thai staples. It also stands for a safe cause: instead of after-meal mints, diners receive packaged condoms, and all proceeds go towards the Population and Community Development Association (PDA), a sex education/AIDS prevention organisation.

★APPIA ITALIAN $$$

Map p282 (☎02 261 2056; www.appia-bangkok.com; 20/4 Soi 31, Th Sukhumvit; mains 400-1000B;

LOCAL KNOWLEDGE

SUNDAY BRUNCH

Sunday brunch has become a modern Bangkok tradition, particularly among members of the city's expat community, and the hotels along Th Sukhumvit offer some of the city's best – and most diverse – spreads. Here are some of our favourites.

Rang Mahal (Map p282; ☎02 261 7100; www.facebook.com/Rangmahal; 26th fl, Rembrandt Hotel, 19 Soi 20, Th Sukhumvit; buffet 850B; ⊙11am-2.30pm Sun; ❄✍; ⓂSukhumvit exit 2, ⓈAsok exit 6) Combine views from this restaurant's 26th floor with an all-Indian buffet and a live band, and you have one of the most popular Sunday destinations for Bangkok's South Asian expat community.

Sunday Jazzy Brunch (Map p282; ☎02 649 8888; www.sheratongrandesukhumvit. com/sundayjazzybrunch; 1st fl, Sheraton Grande Sukhumvit, 250 Th Sukhumvit; buffet adult 2500-3700B, child 1250B; ⊙noon-3pm Sun; ❄✍; ⓂSukhumvit exit 3, ⓈAsok exit 2) If you require more than just victuals, then consider the Sheraton's Sunday brunch, which unites all the hotel's dining outlets to a live jazz theme.

Marriott Café (Map p282; ☎02 656 7700; ground fl, JW Marriott, 4 Soi 2, Th Sukhumvit; buffet 2345B; ⊙noon-3pm Sun; ❄✍; ⓈNana exit 3) The feast-like Sunday brunch at this American hotel chain is likened to Thanksgiving year-round.

Scandinavian Smorgaas Buffet (Map p282; Stable Lodge, 39 Soi 8, Th Sukhumvit; buffet 585B; ⊙noon-3pm Sat & Sun; ❄✍; ⓈNana exit 4) Swap out the usual seafood station for pickled fish, and the roast beef for Swedish meatballs, and you'll get an idea of this unique, excellent-value weekend buffet option.

⊙6.30-11pm Tue-Sat, 11.30am-2.30pm & 6.30-11pm Sun; ❄✍; ⓈPhrom Phong exit 5) Handmade pastas, slow-roasted meats and a carefully curated and relatively affordable wine list are the selling points of this restaurant serving Roman-style cuisine – for our baht, one of the best places in town for non-Thai dinner. Reservations recommended.

LITTLE BEAST INTERNATIONAL $$$
Map p282 (☎02 185 2670; www.facebook.com/littlebeastbar; 44/9-10 Soi Thong Lor 13; mains 300-750B; ⊙5.30pm-1am Tue-Sat, 11am-4pm Sun; ❄☎; ⓈPhrom Phong exit 3 & taxi) With influences stemming from modern American cuisine, Little Beast isn't very Bangkok, but it is very good. Expect meaty mains, satisfying salads and some of the best desserts in town.

THE COMMONS MARKET $$$
Map p282 (www.thecommonsbkk.com; 335 Soi 17, Soi 55/Thong Lor, Th Sukhumvit; mains 500-2000B; ⊙8am-midnight; ❄✍; ⓈThong Lo exit 3 & taxi) Trendy Thong Lor gets even cooler with this marketplace-style eatery that is packed with reliable names such as Soul Food 555, Peppina and Meat & Bones, along with a coffee roaster, a craft beer bar and wine vendor. It's an ideal place to idle away an evening listening to Jack Johnson wannabes strum acoustic sets.

BEI OTTO GERMAN $$$
Map p282 (☎02 260 0869; www.beiotto.com; 1 Soi 20, Th Sukhumvit; mains 200-1000B; ⊙11am-midnight; ❄✍; ⓂSukhumvit exit 2, ⓈAsok exit 4) Claiming a Bangkok residence for more than 30 years, Bei Otto's culinary bragging point is its pork knuckles, reputedly the best in town. A good selection of German beers and an attached delicatessen with brilliant breads and super sausages make it even more attractive to go Deutsch.

QUINCE INTERNATIONAL $$$
Map p282 (☎02 662 4478; www.quincebangkok. com; Soi 45, Th Sukhumvit; mains 150-3900B; ⊙11.30am-1am; ❄✍; ⓈPhrom Phong exit 3) Back in 2011, Quince made an audible splash in Bangkok's dining scene with its retro/industrial interior and eclectic, internationally influenced menu. The formula has since been copied ad nauseam, but Quince continues to put out the type of vibrant, full-flavoured dishes, many with palpable Middle Eastern or Spanish influences, that made it stand out in the first place.

BO.LAN THAI $$$
Map p282 (☎02 260 2962; www.bolan.co.th; 24 Soi 53, Th Sukhumvit; set meals 1200-3500B; ⊙6-10.30pm Tue-Sun, noon-2.30pm Sat & Sun; ❄✍; ⓈThong Lo exit 1) Upscale Thai is often more garnish than flavour, but Bo.lan has proved

to be the exception. Bo and Dylan (Bo.lan is a play on words that means Ancient) take a scholarly approach to Thai cuisine, and generous set meals featuring full-flavoured Thai dishes are the results of this tuition (à la carte is not available; meat-free meals are). Reservations recommended.

NASIR AL-MASRI   MIDDLE EASTERN $$$

Map p282 (4/6 Soi 3/1, Th Sukhumvit; mains 160-370B; ⊘24hr; ✳ ☌; Ⓢ Nana exit 1) One of several Middle Eastern restaurants on Soi 3/1, Nasir Al-Masri is easily recognisable by its floor-to-ceiling stainless-steel 'theme'. Middle Eastern food often means meat, meat and more meat, but the menu here also includes several delicious vegie-based *mezze* (small dishes).

MYEONG GA   KOREAN $$$

Map p282 (ground fl, Sukhumvit Plaza, cnr Soi 12 & Th Sukhumvit; mains 200-950B; ⊘11am-10pm Tue-Sun, 4-10pm Mon; ✳; Ⓜ Sukhumvit exit 3, Ⓢ Asok exit 2) Located on the ground floor of Sukhumvit Plaza (the multistorey complex also known as Korean Town), this restaurant is the city's best destination for authentic Seoul food. Go for the tasty prepared dishes or, if you've got a bit more time, the excellent DIY Korean-style barbecue.

DRINKING & NIGHTLIFE

★WTF   BAR

Map p282 (www.wtfbangkok.com; 7 Soi 51, Th Sukhumvit; ⊘6pm-1am Tue-Sun; ☎; Ⓢ Thong Lo exit 3) Wonderful Thai Friendship (what did you think it stood for?) is a funky and friendly neighbourhood bar that also packs in a gallery space. Arty locals and resident foreigners come for the old-school cocktails, live music and DJ events, poetry readings, art exhibitions and tasty bar snacks. And we, like them, give WTF our vote for Bangkok's best bar.

★Q&A BAR   BAR

Map p282 (www.qnabar.com; 235/13 Soi 21/Asoke, Th Sukhumvit; ⊘7pm-2am Mon-Sat) Imagine a mid-century modern dining car or airport lounge, and you're close to picturing the interior of Q&A. The short list of featured cocktails can appear to be a divergence from the classic vibe, but an old-world dress code and manners are encouraged.

★STUDIO LAM   BAR, CLUB

Map p282 (www.facebook.com/studiolambangkok; 3/1 Soi 51, Th Sukhumvit; ⊘6pm-1am Tue-Sun; Ⓢ Thong Lo exit 3) Studio Lam is an extension of uberhip record label ZudRangMa, and boasts a Jamaican-style sound system custom-built for world and retro-Thai DJ sets and the occasional live show. For a night of dancing in Bangkok that doesn't revolve around Top 40 cheese, this is the place.

★TUBA   BAR

Map p282 (www.facebook.com/tubabkk; 34 Room 11-12 A, Soi Thong Lor 20/Soi Ekamai 21; ⊘11am-2am; Ⓢ Ekkamai exit 1 & taxi) Part storage room for over-the-top vintage furniture, part restaurant and part friendly local boozer; this quirky bar certainly doesn't lack in diversity – nor fun. Indulge in a whole bottle (they'll hold onto it for your next visit if you don't finish it) and don't miss the moreish chicken wings or the delicious deep-fried *lâhp* (a tart/spicy salad of minced meat).

MIKKELLER   BAR

Map p282 (www.mikkellerbangkok.com; 26 Yaek 2, Soi Ekamai 10; ⊘5pm-midnight; Ⓢ Ekkamai exit 1 & taxi) These buzz-generating Danish 'gypsy' brewers have set up shop in Bangkok, granting us more than 30 beers on tap. Expect brews ranging from the local (Sukhumvit Brown Ale) to the insane (Beer Geek, a 13% alcohol oatmeal stout), as well as an inviting atmosphere and good bar snacks.

WAON   KARAOKE

Map p282 (10/11 Soi 26, Th Sukhumvit; ⊘8pm-1am Mon-Sat) Is the canned soundtrack the only thing that's preventing you from obtaining karaoke superstardom? At Waon, muzak is replaced by a real live piano player. The music and clientele are predominantly Japanese, but the friendly owner is happy to play Western standards. And even if you can't sing, you can pitch in via maracas, bongos or acoustic guitar.

A R SUTTON & CO ENGINEERS SIAM   BAR

Map p282 (Parklane, Soi 63/Ekamai, Th Sukhumvit; ⊘6pm-midnight; Ⓢ Ekkamai exit 2) Skeins of copper tubing, haphazardly placed one-of-a-kind antiques, zinc ceiling panels, and rows of glass vials and baubles culminate in one of the most unique and beautifully fantastical bars in Bangkok – if not anywhere. An adjacent distillery provides fuel for the bar's largely gin-based cocktails.

A SUKHUMVIT NIGHTLIFE CHEAT SHEET

Th Sukhumvit is home to many of Bangkok's best bars, clubs and live-music venues. So many, in fact, that it can be hard to decide. So based on the type of night you'd like to have (or avoid), we've put together a handy cheat sheet.

For a uniquely Thai night out: Lam Sing (p152), Nung-Len (p152), Badmotel (p150)

For cocktails: Sugar Ray (p150), Q&A Bar (p149), J Boroski Mixology (p150)

For beer: Mikkeller (p149), **Taproom** (Map p282; ☎087 460 2626; www.taproombkk.com; 51 Soi 26, Th Sukhumvit; 🕐5pm-midnight; [S]Phrom Phong), **Beer Belly** (Map p282; ☎02 392 7770; www.facebook.com/beerbellybkk; 72 Soi 55/Thong Lor, Th Sukhumvit; 🕐5pm-2am; [S]Thong Lo)

For a unique soundtrack: Studio Lam (p149), Glow (p150), WTF (p149)

For live music: Titanium (p152), Parking Toys' Watt (p152), **Apoteka** (Map p282; www.apotekasoi11.com; Soi 11, Th Sukhumvit; 🕐5pm-1am Mon-Thu, to 2am Fri & Sat, 3pm-1am Sun; [S]Nana exit 3)

For good bar snacks: Tuba (p149), Walden (p150), Above 11 (p151)

For a sophisticated night out: A R Sutton & Co Engineers Siam (p149), Living Room (p152), Black Amber Social Club (p151)

For a late night out: Levels (p151), Club Insanity (p152), Scratch Dog (p152)

SUGAR RAY BAR

Map p282 (www.facebook.com/sugarraybkk; off Soi Ekamai 21; 🕐8pm-2am Wed, Fri & Sat; [S]Ekkamai exit 1 & taxi) Run by a team of fun and funky Thai dudes who make flavoured syrups, Sugar Ray is a fun, funky hidden bar serving fun, funky cocktails; think an Old Fashioned made with aged rum, orange and cardamom syrup, and garnished with a piece of caramelised bacon.

WALDEN BAR

Map p282 (7/1 Soi 31, Th Sukhumvit; 🕐6.30pm-1am Mon-Sat; [S]Phrom Phong exit 5) Get past the hyper-minimalist *Kinfolk* vibe, and the thoughtful Japanese touches of this bar make it one of the more welcoming places in town. The brief menu of drinks spans Japanese-style 'highballs', craft beers from the USA, and simple, delicious bar snacks.

BEAM CLUB

Map p282 (www.beamclub.com; 72 Courtyard, 72 Soi 55/Thong Lor, Th Sukhumvit; 🕐9pm-late Wed-Sat; [S]Thong Lo exit 3 & taxi) High-profile guest DJs spinning deep house and techno, a diverse crowd and a dance floor that literally vibrates have combined to make Beam Bangkok's club of the moment. Check the website for special events.

J BOROSKI MIXOLOGY BAR

Map p282 (www.josephboroski.com; off Soi 55/Thong Lor, Th Sukhumvit; 🕐7pm-2am; 📶; [S]Thong Lo exit 3 & taxi) The eponymous mixologist here has done away with both addresses and cocktail menus to arrive at the modern equivalent of the speakeasy. Tell the boys behind the bar what flavours you fancy, and using top-shelf liquor and unique ingredients they'll create something memorable. Located in an unmarked street near Soi Thong Lor 7; refer to the website for the exact location.

BADMOTEL BAR

Map p282 (www.facebook.com/badmotel; 331/4-5 Soi 55/Thong Lor, Th Sukhumvit; 🕐5pm-1am; [S]Thong Lo exit 3 & taxi) Badmotel blends the modern and the kitschy, the cosmopolitan and the Thai, in a way that has struck a nerve among Bangkok hipsters. This is manifested in drinks that combine rum with Hale's Blue Boy, a Thai childhood drink staple, and bar snacks such as *naam prik ong* (a northern Thai-style dip), here served with papadums.

GLOW CLUB

Map p282 (www.facebook.com/GlowBkk; 96/415 Soi Prasanmit; from 350B; 🕐9pm-3am Wed-Sat, to midnight Sun; [M]Sukhumvit exit 2, [S]Asok exit 3) Pocket-sized, and boasting a world-class sound system and legit underground cred, Glow is a veteran of Bangkok's dance scene. Check the Facebook page for visiting DJs and upcoming events.

HAVANA SOCIAL CLUB CLUB

Map p282 (www.facebook.com/pg/havanasocial-bkk; Soi 11, Th Sukhumvit; 🕐6pm-2am) Locate the phone booth, dial the secret code (the doorman will help you out here) and cross the threshold to pre-revolution Havana. Part bar, part dance club, Havana combines live music, great drinks and an expat-heavy crowd who all seem to know the right dance steps. A great place to escape the cheesiness and Top 40 soundtrack that dominate most Bangkok clubs.

DEMO CLUB

Map p282 (www.facebook.com/demobangkok; Arena 10, Soi Thong Lor 10/Soi Ekamai 5; ⏲9pm-2am; [S]Ekkamai exit 2 & taxi) Demo combines blasting beats and a NYC warehouse vibe. Fridays and Saturdays see a 400B entrance fee for foreigners, and ID is necessary to gain entry.

BLACK AMBER SOCIAL CLUB BAR

Map p282 (www.facebook.com/blackambersocial club; Soi 55/Thong Lor 6; ⏲6.30pm-midnight; [S]Thong Lo exit 3 & taxi) We're happy to tell you about Black Amber if you promise to keep it to yourself. A dark, sumptuous ambience (furnishings include an entire ostrich skeleton), moustached and/or coiffed staff (Black Amber is linked to a barber shop of the same name), and a drinks list that doesn't stray far from scotch give Black Amber an authentically retro, in-the-know, speakeasy vibe.

ABOVE 11 BAR

Map p282 (www.aboveeleven.com; 33rd fl, Fraser Suites Sukhumvit, Soi 11, Th Sukhumvit; ⏲6pm-2am; [S]Nana exit 3) This sophisticated rooftopper combines downward glances of Bangkok's most cosmopolitan neighbourhood with DJ sets and Peruvian/Japanese bar snacks.

SHADES OF RETRO BAR

Map p282 (www.facebook.com/shadesofretrobar; Soi Thararom 2, Soi 55/Thong Lor, Th Sukhumvit; ⏲5pm-2am; [S]Thong Lo exit 3 & taxi) As the name suggests, this eclectic place takes Bangkok's vintage fetish to the max. You'll have to wind around Vespas and Naugahyde sofas to reach your seat, but you'll be rewarded with friendly service, free popcorn and a varied domestic soundtrack (the people behind Shades also run the domestic indie label Small Room).

SING SING THEATER BAR

Map p282 (www.singsingbangkok.com; Soi 45, Th Sukhumvit; ⏲9pm-2am Tue-Sun; [S]Thong Lo exit 1) Dancers dressed in cheongsams or neon spacesuits (depending on the night) float through secret rooms, across towering platforms and onto the tiny dance floor at this wonderfully surreal bar-slash-nightclub. The strong drinks only help to heighten the feeling that you've fallen into a Chinese opium den. Check Facebook (www.facebook.com/SingSingTheater) for a list of the bar's theme nights.

LEVELS CLUB

Map p282 (www.levelsclub.com; 6th fl, Aloft, 35 Soi 11, Th Sukhumvit; 500B; ⏲9pm-late; [S]Nana exit 3) Come 1am, when most Soi 11 bars are beginning to close up, folks begin to file into this popular hotel nightclub. See the website for guest DJs and other promotions.

[i] BANGKOK TAXI ALTERNATIVES

Getting burnt by taxi drivers who refuse to use the meter or take you where you want to go? Rest assured that there are alternatives to traditional taxis in Bangkok – sort of.

Uber (www.uber.com/cities/bangkok), undoubtedly the most well-known – and controversial – ride service in the world, was introduced to Thailand in 2014. It quickly gained popularity among those looking to avoid the usual Bangkok taxi headaches: communication issues, perpetual lack of change and reckless drivers. Yet in late 2014, Thailand's Department of Land Transport deemed the app-based outfit illegal, declaring that its vehicles weren't properly registered, its fares unregulated and its drivers unlicensed. At the time of research, the situation seemed to have reached a stalemate, with Uber still operating in Bangkok, albeit less conspicuously.

The good news is that other outfits such as **GrabTaxi** (www.grabtaxi.com/bangkok-thailand) and **Easy Taxi** (www.easytaxi.com/th), both of which operate via taxis that are already registered, haven't been affected by the ruling. And in 2015, a domestic alternative, **All Thai Taxi** (www.allthaitaxi.com), was introduced.

However, if you insist on keeping it old school, here's a Bangkok taxi tip: avoid taxis parked in front of hotels or tourist zones, who inevitably never use the meter and who tend to be selective about where they go. Instead, walk a block or so away and flag a moving taxi.

NUNG-LEN · CLUB

Map p282 (www.facebook.com/nunglen.escobar; 217 Soi 63/Ekamai, Th Sukhumvit; ⏱7pm-1am Mon-Sat; ⓢEkkamai exit 1 & taxi) Young, loud and Thai, Nung-Len (literally 'sit and chill') is a ridiculously popular den of live music and uni students on buzzy Th Ekamai. Get there before 10pm or you won't get in at all.

IRON FAIRIES · BAR

Map p282 (www.facebook.com/ironfairiesbkk; 394 Soi 55/Thong Lor, Th Sukhumvit; ⏱6pm-2am; ⓢThong Lo exit 3 & taxi) Imagine, if you can, an abandoned fairy factory in Paris c 1912, and you'll begin to get an idea of the vibe at this popular pub/wine bar. If you manage to wrangle one of the handful of seats, you can test their claim of serving Bangkok's best burgers. There's live music after 9.30pm.

LONG TABLE · BAR

Map p282 (www.longtablebangkok.com; 25th fl, Column Bldg, 48 Soi 16, Th Sukhumvit; ⏱5pm-2am; ⓜSukhumvit exit 2, ⓢAsok exit 6) Come to this slick, 25th-floor balcony to sip fruity cocktails and gloat at the poor sods stuck in traffic below. In addition to views, there's a menu of Thai-inspired dishes and generous happy-hour specials. It's located about 200m down Soi 16, which is accessible via Th Ratchadaphisek.

CLUB INSANITY · CLUB

Map p282 (www.clubinsanitybangkok.com; 32/2 Soi 11, Th Sukhumvit; 200B; ⏱8pm-late; ⓜSukhumvit exit 3, ⓢAsok exit 2) This late-night staple has moved into new digs on Soi 11. It's not the most sophisticated place in town, but beyond 2am the options are few.

NARZ · CLUB

Map p282 (www.narzclubbangkok.net; 112 Soi 23, Th Sukhumvit; from 400B; ⏱9pm-2am; ⓜSukhumvit exit 2, ⓢAsok exit 3) Like a small clubbing neighbourhood, Narz consists of three vast zones boasting an equal variety of music. It's largely a domestic scene, but the odd guest DJ can pull a large crowd. Open later than most.

SCRATCH DOG · CLUB

Map p282 (basement, Windsor Suites Hotel, 8-10 Soi 20, Th Sukhumvit; 400B; ⏱midnight-late; ⓜSukhumvit exit 2, ⓢAsok exit 4) Scratch Dog is as cheesy as the name and the bulldog-as-DJ logo suggest, but it manages to pull a (relatively) mixed crowd and is probably the least dodgy of Bangkok's late-late nightclubs. Don't bother showing up before 2am.

☆ ENTERTAINMENT

★ THE LIVING ROOM · LIVE MUSIC

Map p282 (☏02 649 8888; www.thelivingroomatbangkok.com; level 1, Sheraton Grande Sukhumvit, 250 Th Sukhumvit; ⏱6pm-midnight; ⓜSukhumvit exit 3, ⓢAsok exit 2) Don't let looks deceive you: every night this bland hotel lounge transforms into the city's best venue for live jazz. True to the name, there's comfy, sofa-based seating, all of it within earshot of the music. Enquire ahead of time to see which sax master or hide-hitter is in town. An entry fee of 300B is charged after 8.30pm.

LAM SING · LIVE MUSIC

(อีสานลำซิ่ง; www.facebook.com/isanlamsing; 57/5 Th Phet Phra Ram; ⏱9.30pm-4am; ⓢEkkamai exit 1 & taxi) Even Ziggy Stardust–era David Bowie has nothing on this dark, decadent, rhinestone-encrusted den, one of Bangkok's best venues for *mŏr lam* and *lôok tûng*, music with roots in Thailand's rural northeast. Come for raucous live-music performances accompanied by tightly choreographed, flagrantly costumed back-up dancers. There's no English-language sign here, but most taxi drivers are familiar with the place.

PARKING TOYS' WATT · LIVE MUSIC

Map p287 (www.facebook.com/Wattparkingtoys; 164 Soi Sun Wichai 14; ⏱4pm-2am; ⓢEkkamai exit 4 & taxi) Resembling a Moroccan souk stuffed with kitschy Thai furniture, this is one of Bangkok's quirkier options for a night of live music. And like its mother venue, Parking Toys (p165), it's also a great place to eat; don't miss tasty Thai-style drinking snacks such as 'larb pork balls'.

TITANIUM · LIVE MUSIC

Map p282 (www.titaniumbangkok.com; 2/30 Soi 22, Th Sukhumvit; ⏱8pm-1am; ⓢPhrom Phong exit 6) Many come to this cheesy 'ice bar' for the chill, the skimpily dressed working girls and the flavoured vodka, but we come for Unicorn, the all-female house band, who rock the house from Monday to Saturday.

FRIESE-GREENE CLUB · CINEMA

Map p282 (FGC; ☏087 000 0795; www.fgc.in.th; 259/6 Soi 22, Th Sukhumvit; ⓢPhrom Phong exit 6) You couldn't find a bigger contrast with Bangkok's huge, mall-bound cinemas than this private theatre with just nine seats. Check the website for a schedule of upcoming films.

SOI COWBOY
RED-LIGHT DISTRICT

Map p282 (Soi Cowboy; ☺4pm-2am; ⓂSukhumvit exit 2, ⓈAsok exit 3) This single-lane strip of raunchy bars claims direct lineage to the post–Vietnam War R&R era. A real flesh trade functions amid the flashing neon.

NANA ENTERTAINMENT
PLAZA
RED-LIGHT DISTRICT

Map p282 (Soi 4, Th Sukhumvit; ☺4pm-2am; ⓈNana exit 2) Nana is a three-storey go-go bar complex where the sexpats are separated from the gawking tourists. It's also home to a few *gà·teu·i* (cross-dresser or transgender; also spelt *kàthoey*) bars.

🛍 SHOPPING

QUARTOR
FASHION & ACCESSORIES

Map p282 (2nd fl, Bldg C Emquartier, 695 Th Sukhumvit; ☺10am-10pm; ⓈPhrom Phong exit 1) Taking up nearly an entire floor is this zone dedicated entirely to the works of Thai designers. Almost exclusively a female affair, the looks range from conservative to outrageous, and span all the top Thai labels.

ANOTHER STORY
HOMEWARES

Map p282 (4th fl, Emquartier, Th Sukhumvit; ☺10am-10pm; ⓈPhrom Phong exit 1) A self-proclaimed 'lifestyle concept store', Another Story is probably more accurately described as an engaging assemblage of cool stuff. Even if you're not planning to buy, it's fun to flip through the unique, domestically made items such as ceramics from Prempacha in Chiang Mai, leather goods from brands like labrador, and fragrant soaps, oils and candles from BsaB.

DULY
CLOTHING

Map p282 (☎02 662 6647; www.laladuly.co.th; Soi 49, Th Sukhumvit; ☺10am-7pm; ⓈPhrom Phong exit1) High-quality Italian fabrics and experienced tailors make Duly one of the best places in Bangkok to commission a sharp shirt.

ZUDRANGMA RECORDS
MUSIC

Map p282 (www.zudrangmarecords.com; 7/1 Soi 51, Th Sukhumvit; ☺2-9pm Tue-Sun; ⓈThong Lo exit 1) The headquarters of this retro/world label is a chance to finally combine the university-era pastimes of record-browsing and drinking. Come to snicker at corny old Thai vinyl covers or invest in some of the label's highly regarded compilations of classic *mŏr lam* and *lôok tûng* (Thai-style country music).

THAICRAFT FAIR
ARTS & CRAFTS

Map p282 (www.thaicraft.org; L fl, Jasmine City Bldg, cnr Soi 23 & Th Sukhumvit; ⓂSukhumvit exit 2, ⓈAsok exit 3) This twice-monthly event

---

BANGKOK'S SAVILE ROW

The strip of Th Sukhumvit between BTS stops at Nana and Asok is home to tonnes of tailors – both reputable and otherwise. Some of the former:

Tailor on Ten (Map p282; ☎084 877 1543; www.tailoronten.com; 93 Soi 8, Th Sukhumvit; ☺9.30am-7pm Mon-Sat) It's not the cheapest in town, but set prices and good tailoring have earned this outfit heaps of praise and repeat customers.

Raja's Fashions (Map p282; ☎02 253 8379; www.rajasfashions.com; 160/1 Th Sukhumvit; ☺10.30am-8pm Mon-Sat; ⓈNana exit 4) With his photographic memory for names, Bobby will make you feel as important as the long list of ambassadors, foreign politicians and officers he's fitted over his family's decades in the business.

Rajawongse (Map p282; ☎02 255 3714; www.dress-for-success.com; 130 Th Sukhumvit; ☺10.30am-8pm Mon-Sat; ⓈNana exit 2) Another legendary and long-standing Bangkok tailor; Jesse's and Victor's creations are particularly renowned among American visitors and residents.

Ricky's Fashion House (Map p282; ☎02 254 6887; www.rickysfashionhouse.com; 73/5 Th Sukhumvit; ☺11am-10pm Mon-Sat & 1-5.30pm Sun; ⓈNana exit 1) Ricky gets positive reviews from locals and resident foreigners alike for his more casual styles of custom-made trousers and shirts.

Nickermann's (Map p282; ☎02 252 6682; basement, Landmark Hotel, 138 Th Sukhumvit; ☺10am-8pm Mon-Sat; ⓈNana exit 2) Corporate ladies rave about Nickermann's tailor-made power suits. Formal ball gowns are another area of expertise.

SPA CENTRAL

Th Sukhumvit is home to many of Bangkok's recommended and reputable massage studios, including the following spots:

Health Land (Map p282; ☑02 261 1110; www.healthlandspa.com; 55/5 Soi 21/Asoke, Th Sukhumvit; Thai massage 2hr 550B; ⊙9am-11pm; ⓂSukhumvit exit 1, ⓈAsok exit 5) A winning formula of affordable prices, expert treatments and pleasant facilities has created a small empire of Health Land centres, including branches on **Soi Ekamai 10** (Map p282; ☑02 392 2233; 96/1 Soi Ekamai 10; ⊙9am-11pm; ⓈEkkamai exit 2 & taxi) and Th Sathon Neua (p140).

Asia Herb Association (Map p282; ☑02 261 2201; www.asiaherbassociation.com; 20/1 Soi 31, Th Sukhumvit; Thai massage 1hr 500B, with herbal compress 1½hr 1100B; ⊙9am-midnight; ⓈPhrom Phong exit 5) This Japanese-owned chain specialises in massage using *prà-kóp* (traditional Thai herbal compresses) filled with 18 different herbs. There are multiple branches along Th Sukhumvit, including on **Soi 55/Thong Lor** (Map p282; ☑02 392 3631; 58/19-25 Soi 55/Thong Lor, Th Sukhumvit; ⊙9am-midnight; ⓈThong Lo exit 3).

Divana Massage & Spa (Map p282; ☑02 261 6784; www.divanaspa.com; 7 Soi 25, Th Sukhumvit; massage from 1200B, spa packages from 2650B; ⊙11am-11pm Mon-Fri, 10am-11pm Sat & Sun; ⓂSukhumvit exit 2, ⓈAsok exit 6) Divana retains a unique Thai touch with a private and soothing setting in a garden house.

Coran (Map p282; ☑02 726 9978; www.coranbangkok.com; 94-96/1 Soi Ekamai 10, Soi 63/Ekamai, Th Sukhumvit; Thai massage per hour from 600B; ⊙11am-10pm; ⓈEkkamai exit 4 & taxi) A classy, low-key spa housed in a Thai villa. Aroma and Thai-style massage are also available.

Lavana (Map p282; ☑02 229 4510; www.lavanabangkok.com; 4 Soi 12, Th Sukhumvit; Thai massage per hour 550B; ⊙9am-midnight; ⓂSukhumvit exit 3, ⓈAsok exit 2) Another spa with an emphasis on traditional Thai healing using *prà-kóp*. Oil massage is also available.

Rakuten (Map p282; ☑02 258 9433; www.rakutenspa.com; 94 Soi 33, Th Sukhumvit; Thai massage per hour 250B; ⊙noon-midnight; ⓈPhrom Phong exit 5) A Japanese-themed spa that gets good reports for its Thai-style massage.

Baan Dalah (Map p282; ☑02 653 3358; www.baandalahmindbodyspa.com; 2 Soi 8, Th Sukhumvit; Thai massage per hour 350B; ⊙10am-midnight; ⓈNana exit 4) A small, conveniently located spa with services ranging from foot massage to full-body Thai massage.

(held from 10am to 3pm) is a great chance to browse through the products of more than 60 community groups. For 20 years, ThaiCraft has marketed quality handicrafts made by artisans from across Thailand, and recent fairs have seen products such as handmade baskets and mulberry-bark notebooks. Check the website to see if one is scheduled during your visit.

SOP MOEI ARTS
ARTS & CRAFTS

Map p282 (www.sopmoeiarts.com; Soi 49/9, Th Sukhumvit; ⊙9.30am-5pm Tue-Sat; ⓈPhrom Phong exit 3 & taxi) The Bangkok showroom of this non-profit organisation features the vibrant cloth creations of Karen weavers from Mae Hong Son, in northern Thailand. It's located at the end of Soi 49/9, in the Racquet Club complex.

EMQUARTIER
SHOPPING CENTRE

Map p282 (www.theemdistrict.com; 693-695 Th Sukhumvit; ⊙10am-10pm; ⓈPhrom Phong exit 1) One of Bangkok's newest malls and arguably its flashiest. Come for brands you're not likely to find elsewhere, or get lost in the Helix, a seemingly never-ending spiral of more than 50 restaurants.

TERMINAL 21
SHOPPING CENTRE

Map p282 (www.terminal21.co.th; cnr Th Sukhumvit & Soi 21/Asoke; ⊙10am-10pm; ⓂSukhumvit exit 3, ⓈAsok exit 3) Catering to an innate Thai need for wacky objects to be photographed in front of, this huge mall is worth a visit for the spectacle as much as the shopping. Start at the basement-level 'airport' and proceed upwards through 'Paris', 'Tokyo' and other city-themed floors.

THANON SUKHUMVIT MARKET
GIFTS & SOUVENIRS

Map p282 (btwn Soi 3 & Soi 15, Th Sukhumvit; ⏰11am-11pm Tue-Sun; [S]Nana exits 1 & 3) Knock-off clothes and watches, stacks of skin-flick DVDs, Chinese throwing stars and other questionable gifts perfect for your teenage brother dominate this market catering to package and sex tourists.

SPORTS & ACTIVITIES

★COOKING WITH POO & FRIENDS
COOKING

(☎080 434 8686; www.cookingwithpoo.com; classes 1500B; ⏰8.30am-1pm; 👪) This popular cooking course was started by a native of Khlong Toey's slums and is held in her neighbourhood. Courses, which must be booked in advance, span three dishes and include a visit to Khlong Toey Market and transport to and from Emporium Shopping Centre.

YUNOMORI ONSEN & SPA
ONSEN

Map p282 (www.yunomorionsen.com; 120/5 Soi 26, Th Sukhumvit; onsen 450B, massage 1hr 350B; ⏰10.30am-11pm; [S]Phrom Phong exit 3 & taxi) Bangkok as a whole can often seem like a sauna, but for a more refined approach to sweating, consider this *onsen* (Japanese-style hot-spring bath). The thermal water is trucked up from southern Thailand and employed in the gender-divided, open pools. In addition to sauna, steam bath and soak pools, massage and other spa treatments are also available.

EIGHT LIMBS
MARTIAL ARTS

Map p282 (☎090 987 9590; www.facebook.com/8limbsluaythaigym; Soi 24, Th Sukhumvit; lessons from 580B; ⏰10am-8.30pm Tue-Sun; [S]Phrom Phong exit 2) This small gym in downtown Bangkok offers 1½-hour walk-in lessons in *moo·ay tai* (Thai boxing; also spelt *muay Thai*) for all skill levels. See the Facebook page for times.

PHUSSAPA THAI MASSAGE SCHOOL
HEALTH & WELLBEING

Map p282 (☎02 204 2922; www.facebook.com/phussapa; 25/8 Soi 26, Th Sukhumvit; tuition from 6000B, Thai massage per hour 250B; ⏰lessons 9am-4pm, massage 11am-11pm; [S]Phrom Phong exit 4) Run by a long-time Japanese resident of Bangkok, the basic course in Thai massage here spans 30 hours over five days; there are shorter courses in foot massage and self massage.

BANGKOK BIKE RIDES
CYCLING

(☎02 381 7490; www.bangkokbikerides.com; tours from 1250B; 👪) A division of tour company Spice Roads, this outfit offers a variety of cycling tours, both urban and rural, including a night tour of Bangkok. Pick-up is available.

ABC AMAZING BANGKOK CYCLISTS
CYCLING

Map p282 (☎081 812 9641; www.realasia.net; 10/5-7 Soi Aree, Soi 26, Th Sukhumvit; tours from 1300B; ⏰daily tours at 8am, 10am, 1pm & 6pm; 👪; [S]Phrom Phong exit 4) A long-running operation offering morning, afternoon and all-day bike tours of Bangkok and its suburbs.

YOGA ELEMENTS STUDIO
YOGA

Map p282 (☎02 255 9552; www.yogaelements.com; 7th fl, 185 Dhammalert Bldg, Th Sukhumvit; classes from 600B; [S]Chit Lom exit 5) Run by American Adrian Cox, who trained at Om in New York and who teaches primarily *vinyasa* and *ashtanga*, this is the most respected yoga studio in town. The high-rise location helps you rise above it all, too.

Northern Bangkok

Neighbourhood Top Five

❶ Chatuchak Weekend Market (p158) Getting lost in the one of the world's largest markets, a must-do Bangkok experience.

❷ Chang Chui (p161) Following Bangkok's hipsters to this eccentric, art-themed market place.

❸ Ko Kret (p162) Ditching the smog and traffic of the big city and heading to this rural-feeling island in Mae Nam Chao Phraya.

❹ Route 66 (p163) Partying at the bars and clubs of RCA/Royal City Ave, for

locals one of the city's most famous nightlife strips.

❺ Nonthaburi Market (p161) Experiencing the charms of provincial Thailand at this market, one of the area's most old-school-style places of commerce.

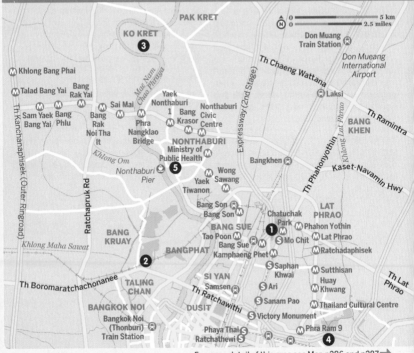

For more detail of this area see Map p286 and p287 ➡

Explore Northern Bangkok

There are several reasons to visit Northern Bangkok, but most people come for the markets: the northern suburbs are home to some of the city's best. Chatuchak Weekend Market draws tens of thousands of shoppers and is a hectic but must-do Bangkok experience. The Nonthaburi Market is an expansive wet market that shows the area's provincial side, while the new Chang Chui art park is a Bangkok-hipster magnet. Other reasons to visit Bangkok's suburbs include nightlife, with the RCA/Royal City Ave entertainment strip drawing thousands of weekend partiers.

For the day markets you'll want to arrive as early as possible. Set aside at least half a day for Chatuchak. Getting to Nonthaburi Market by boat takes at least an hour; keep in mind that the market has pretty much packed up by 9am. Most clubs and live-music venues don't get going until 11pm and close at 2am.

Most of the markets are located within easy access of the northern extents of the BTS (Skytrain) and/or MRT (Metro). Reaching other destinations in Bangkok's burbs often involves a taxi ride from BTS or MRT terminal stations and a bit of luck. A smartphone with a mapping function is an invaluable tool for helping you arrive at the right place and on time.

Local Life

➜ **Chatuchak Weekend Market** (also known as JJ) may be a huge draw for tourists, but it's still very much a local affair, with thousands of Thais shuffling between stalls and eating snacks.

➜ **RCA** For decades, the dance clubs, live-music venues and bars along Royal City Ave have been the first nightlife choice for most young Thais. In recent years the clientele has grown up – slightly, at least – and RCA now hosts locals and visitors of just about every age.

➜ **Local Style** Ditch your central Bangkok comfort zone and head to Chang Chui, an art-themed market that's also a great place to witness the various cliques of modern Thai youth.

➜ **Full-Flavoured Eats** Although a bit of a schlep, an excursion to Bangkok's suburbs can be a profoundly tasty experience, with heaps of restaurants that don't tone down their flavours for foreigners. The city's outskirts are also a great place to sample regional Thai cuisine.

Getting There & Away

➜ **BTS** Ari and Mo Chit.

➜ **MRT** Chatuchak Park, Huay Khwang, Kamphaeng Phet, Lat Phrao, Phra Ram 9, Sutthisan, Thailand Cultural Centre.

➜ **River ferry** Nonthaburi Pier.

➜ **Klorng Boat** Asoke-Phetchaburi Pier.

Lonely Planet's Top Tip

Make a point of arriving at Chatuchak Weekend Market as early as possible – around 10am is a good bet – as the crowds are much thinner and the temperatures slightly lower.

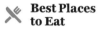 Best Places to Eat

➜ Chatuchak Weekend Market (p158)

➜ Yusup (p162)

➜ Khua Kling Pak Sod (p163)

➜ Puritan (p163)

➜ Or Tor Kor Market (p161)

➜ Baan Pueng Chom (p163)

For reviews, see p162 ➜

Best Drinking & Nightlife

➜ Parking Toys (p165)

➜ Route 66 (p163)

For reviews, see p164 ➜

Best Places to Shop

➜ Chatuchak Weekend Market (p158)

➜ Chang Chui (p161)

➜ Or Tor Kor Market (p161)

➜ Nonthaburi Market (p161)

For reviews, see p165 ➜

NORTHERN BANGKOK

CHATUCHAK WEEKEND MARKET

Imagine all of Bangkok's markets fused together in a seemingly never-ending commerce-themed barrio. Now add a little artistic flair, a sauna-like climate and bargaining crowds and you've got a rough sketch of Chatuchak (also spelled 'Jatujak' or nicknamed 'JJ'). Once you're deep in its bowels, it will seem like there is no order and no escape, but Chatuchak is actually arranged into relatively coherent sections.

Antiques, Handicrafts & Souvenirs

Section 1 is the place to go for Buddha statues, old LPs and random antiques.

More secular arts and crafts, like musical instruments and hill-tribe items, can be found in Sections 25 and 26. **Meng** (Section 26, Stall 195, Soi 8) features a mish-mash of quirky antiques from Thailand and Myanmar.

Baan Sin Thai (Section 24, Stall 130, Soi 1) sells *kŏhn* masks and old-school Thai toys, while **Kitcharoen Dountri** (Section 8, Stall 464) specialises in Thai musical instruments, including flutes, whistles and drums, and CDs of classical Thai music.

Golden Shop (Section 17, Stall 36) is a one-stop souvenir shop, and boasts an equal blend of tacky and worthwhile items, ranging from traditionally dressed dolls to commemorative plates. For something quirkier, consider the lifelike plastic Thai fruit and vegetables at **Marché** (Section 17, Stall 254, Soi 1) or their scaled-down miniature counterparts nearby at **Papachu** (Section 17, Stall 23).

Section 7 is a virtual open-air art gallery; we particularly like the Bangkok-themed murals at **Pariwat A-nantachina** (Section 7, Stall 117, Soi 63/3).

Several shops in Section 10, including **Tuptim Shop** (Section 10, Stall 261, Soi 19), sell Burmese lacquerware.

DON'T MISS

➡ Cheap clothes
➡ One-of-a-kind souvenirs
➡ A market meal

PRACTICALITIES

➡ ตลาดนัดจตุจักร, Talat Nat Jatujak
➡ Map p286, C1
➡ www.chatuchakmarket.org
➡ 587/10 Th Phahonyothin
➡ ⏰7am-6pm Wed & Thu plants only, 6pm-midnight Fri wholesale only, 9am-6pm Sat & Sun
➡ ⓂChatuchak Park exit 1, Kamphaeng Phet exits 1 & 2, Ⓢ Mo Chit exit 1

Clothing & Accessories

Clothing dominates much of Chatuchak, starting in Section 8 and continuing through the even-numbered sections to 24. Sections 5 and 6 deal in used clothing for every Thai youth subculture, from punks to cowboys; Soi 7, where it transects Sections 12 and 14, is heavy on hip-hop and skate fashions. Tourist-sized clothes and textiles are found in sections 8 and 10.

Sections 2 and 3, particularly the tree-lined Soi 2 of the former, is the Siam Sq of Chatuchak, and is home to heaps of trendy independent labels. Moving north, Soi 4 in Section 4 boasts several shops selling locally designed T-shirts. In fact, Chatuchak as a whole is a particularly good place to pick up quirky T-shirts of all types.

For something more rustic, **Khaki-Nang** (Section 8, Stall 267-268, Soi 17) sells canvas clothing and tote bags, many featuring old-school Thai themes. And if you can't make it up to Chiang Mai, **Roi** (Section 25, Stall 268, Soi 4) and similar shops nearby are where you'll find hand-woven cotton scarves, clothes and other accessories from Thailand's north.

For accessories, several shops in Sections 24 and 26, such as **Orange Karen Silver** (Section 26, Stall 229, Soi 34/8), specialise in chunky silver jewellery and uncut semiprecious stones.

Housewares & Decor

The western edge of the market, particularly sections 8 to 26, features all manner of housewares, from cheap plastic buckets to expensive brass woks. This area is a particularly good place to stock up on inexpensive Thai ceramics, ranging from celadon to the traditional rooster-themed bowls from Lampang. **PL Bronze** (Section 25, Stall 185, Soi 4) has a huge variety of stainless-steel flatware, and **Ton-Tan** (Section 8, Stall 460, Soi 15/1) deals in coconut- and sugar-palm-derived plates, bowls and other utensils.

Those looking to spice up the house should stop by **Spice Boom** (Section 26, Stall 246, Soi 8), where you can find dried herbs and spices for both consumption and decoration. Other notable olfactory indulgences include the handmade soaps, lotions, salts and scrubs at **D-narn** (Section 19, Stall 203, Soi 1) and the fragrant perfumes and essential oils at **AnyaDharu Scent Library** (Section 3, Stall 3, Soi 43/2).

Plants & Gardening

The interior perimeter of sections 2 to 4 features a huge variety of potted plants, flowers, herbs and fruits, and the accessories needed to maintain them. Some of these shops are open on weekday afternoons.

IMPORTANT STUFF

There is an information centre and several banks with ATMs and foreign-exchange booths at the **Chatuchak Park office**, near the northern end of the market's Soi 1, Soi 2 and Soi 3. Pay toilets are located sporadically throughout the market.

DID YOU KNOW?

Several vendors – largely those selling clothing, accessories and food – open up shop on Friday nights from around 8pm to midnight.

TAKE A BREAK

If you need to escape the crowds, cross Th Kamphaengphet 1 to the food court at Or Tor Kor Market (p161). If you're in the heart of the market and need a cold beer, consider a pit stop at **Viva's** (Map p286; Section 26, Stall 161).

NORTHERN BANGKOK CHATUCHAK WEEKEND MARKET

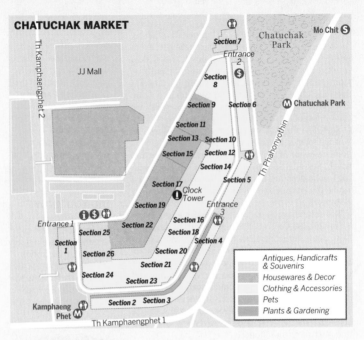

CHATUCHAK MARKET

Th Kamphaengphet 2

JJ Mall

Section 7

Entrance 2

Chatuchak Park

Mo Chit S

Section 8

Section 9   Section 6

Chatuchak Park

Section 11

Section 13   Section 10

Section 15   Section 12

Section 14

Section 17   Clock Tower

Section 5

Th Phahonyothin

Section 19

Entrance 3

Entrance 1

Section 22   Section 16

Section 25   Section 18

Section 1   Section 26   Section 20   Section 4

Section 21

Section 24   Section 23

Kamphaeng Phet

Section 2   Section 3

Th Kamphaengphet 1

Antiques, Handicrafts & Souvenirs

Housewares & Decor

Clothing & Accessories

Pets

Plants & Gardening

Eating & Drinking

Lots of Thai-style eating and snacking will stave off Chatuchak rage (cranky behaviour brought on by dehydration or hunger), and numerous food stalls are set up throughout the market, particularly between Sections 6 and 8. Long-standing standouts include **Foontalop** (Section 26, Stall 319, no Roman-script sign; mains 20-70B; ⊘10am-6pm Sat & Sun), an incredibly popular Isan restaurant; **Café Ice** (Section 7, Stall 267, mains 250-490B; ⊘10am-6pm Sat & Sun), a Western-Thai fusion joint that does good, if overpriced, *pàt tai* (fried noodles) and tasty fruit shakes; **Saman Islam** (Section 16, Stall 34, Soi 24, mains 40-100B; ⊘10am-6pm Sat & Sun), a restaurant that serves a tasty chicken biriani, in addition to other Thai-Muslim dishes; and **Toh-Plue** (opposite Section 17, mains 150-400B; ⊘noon-8pm Sat & Sun) for all the Thai standards.

Viva 8 (www.facebook.com/Viva8JJ; Section 8, Stall 371, mains 150-300B; ⊘9am-10pm Sat & Sun) features a bar, a DJ and, when we stopped by, a Spanish chef making huge platters of paella. As evening draws near, down a beer at Viva's (p159), a cafe-bar that features live music and stays open late.

Top Tips

➡ Schematic maps are located throughout Chatuchak; if you need more detail (not to mention insider tips), consider purchasing **Nancy Chandler's Map of Bangkok** (www.nancychandler.net), available at most Bangkok bookstores.

➡ Arrive at Chatuchak early – ideally around 9am or 10am – to beat the crowds and heat.

◉ SIGHTS

The main sights in Bangkok's northern suburbs are its markets.

CHATUCHAK WEEKEND MARKET   MARKET
See p158.

CHANG CHUI   MARKET
(ช่างชุ่ย; www.en.changchuibangkok.com; 460/8 Th Sirindhorn; 20-40B; ⊙11am-11pm Tue-Sun) An abandoned areoplane, craft-beer bars, a hipster barber shop, performance spaces, a skull-shaped florist, an insect-themed restaurant... This tough-to-pin-down marketplace is one of the most eclectic and exciting openings Bangkok has seen in years. Spanning 18 different structures (all of which are made from discarded objects), a handful of the outlets are open during the day, but the best time to go is during weekend evenings, when the place has the vibe of an artsy, more sophisticated Chatuchak Weekend Market.

MUSEUM OF CONTEMPORARY ART   GALLERY
(MOCA; www.mocabangkok.com; 3 Th Viphawadee Rangsit; 250B; ⊙10am-5pm Tue-Fri, 11am-6pm Sat & Sun; ⓂChatuchak Park exit 2 and taxi, ⓈMo Chit exit 1 & taxi) The city's largest space dedicated to Thai contemporary art. It's probably the best place in the country to familiarise oneself with the genre, but don't expect New York City's MOMA.

NUMTHONG GALLERY   GALLERY
Map p286 (www.gallerynumthong.com; 72/3 Soi Ari 5; ⊙11am-6pm Mon-Sat; ⓈAri exit 3) This long-standing Bangkok gallery has found a new home in the increasingly hip Ari hood. Exhibitions, which change approximately monthly, centre largely around both up-and-coming and established Thai artists.

NONTHABURI MARKET   MARKET
(ตลาดนนทบุรี; Tha Nam Nonthaburi, Nonthaburi; ⊙5-9am; 🚢Nonthaburi Pier) Exotic fruits, towers of dried chillies, smoky grills and the city's few remaining rickshaws form a very un-Bangkok backdrop at this, one of the most expansive and atmospheric produce markets in the area. Come early though, as most vendors are gone by 9am.

To get to the market, take the Chao Phraya Express Boat to Nonthaburi Pier, the northernmost stop for most lines. The market is a two-minute walk east along the main road from the pier.

OR TOR KOR MARKET   MARKET
Map p286 (องค์กรตลาดเพื่อเกษตรกร; Th Kamphaengphet 1; ⊙8am-6pm; ⓂKamphaeng Phet exit 3) Or Tor Kor is Bangkok's highest-quality fruit and agricultural market, taking in the toddler-sized mangoes and dozens of pots full of curries amounts to culinary trainspotting. The vast majority of vendors' goods are takeaway only, but a small food court and a few informal restaurants can also be found.

ⓘ A LITTLE BIG TIME

The suburbs north of Bangkok are home to a handful of kid-oriented museums and theme parks. All of the following are accessible via taxi from Mo Chit BTS station or Chatuchak Park MRT station.

Children's Discovery Museum (พิพิธภัณฑ์เด็ก; Map p286; Th Kamphaengphet 4, Queen Sirikit Park; ⊙9am-5pm Tue-Fri, 10am-6pm Sat & Sun; 👶; ⓂChatuchak Park exit 1, ⓈMo Chit exit 1) FREE Learning is well-disguised as fun at this museum, open again after a lengthy renovation. The interactive exhibits range in topic from construction to culture, although we suspect most will be drawn to the Dino Detective Zone, where kids can dig in sand to find and reassemble dinosaur bones.

Siam Park City (☏02 919 7200; www.siamparkcity.com; 203 Th Suansiam; adult/child US$30/25; ⊙10am-6pm; ⓂChatuchak Park exit 2 & taxi, ⓈMo Chit exit 1 & taxi) Features more than 30 rides and a water park with the largest wave pool in the world.

Dream World (☏02 577 8666; www.dreamworld.co.th; 62 Mu 1, Th Rangsit-Nakornnayok, Pathum Thani; from 1200B; ⊙10am-5pm Mon-Fri, to 7pm Sat & Sun; ⓂChatuchak Park exit 2 & taxi, ⓈMo Chit exit 1 & taxi) Expansive amusement park that boasts a snow room.

WORTH A DETOUR

KO KRET

An easy rural getaway from Bangkok, Ko Kret is an artificial 'island', the result of a canal having been dug nearly 300 years ago to shorten an oxbow bend in Mae Nam Chao Phraya. The area is one of Thailand's oldest settlements of Mon, who were a dominant people of central Thailand between the 6th and 10th centuries AD. Today, Ko Kret is a popular weekend escape, known for its hand-thrown terracotta pots and its busy weekend market.

A 6km paved path circles the island, and can be easily completed on foot or by bicycle, the latter available for hire from Ko Kret's main pier (40B per day). Alternatively, it's possible to charter a long-tail boat for up to 10 people for 500B; the typical island tour stops at a batik workshop, a sweets factory and, on weekends, a floating market.

Ko Kret's most identifiable landmark is the curiously leaning stupa at **Wat Poramai Yikawat** (วัดปรมัยยิกาวาส; Ko Kret, Nonthaburi; ⏰9am-5pm; 🚌166 & river-crossing ferry from Wat Sanam Neua). The temple is also home to an interesting Mon-style marble Buddha statue and a simple **museum** (Wat Poramai Yikawat, Ko Kret; ⏰1-4pm Mon-Fri, 9am-5pm Sat & Sun; 🚌166 & cross-river ferry from Wat Sanam Neua) **FREE**. From here, go in either direction to find both abandoned kilns and working pottery centres on the island's east and north coasts. Yet even more prevalent than temples or pottery is food. On weekends, droves of Thais flock to Ko Kret to eat deep-fried savoury snacks and Thai-style sweets. One dish to look for is *khâw châa*, an unusual but delicious Mon concoction of savoury titbits served with chilled, fragrant rice. **Pa Ka Lung** (Restaurant River Side; Ko Kret; mains 30-60B; ⏰8am-4pm Mon-Fri, to 6pm Sat & Sun; 🚌166 & river-crossing ferry from Wat Sanam Neua), an open-air food court with an English-language menu and sign, serves *khâw châa* and other dishes. Arrive on a weekday and the eating options are much fewer, but you'll have the island to yourself.

Ko Kret is in Nonthaburi, about 15km north of central Bangkok. To get there, take bus 166 from the Victory Monument or a taxi to Pak Kret, before boarding the cross-river ferry (2B, from 5am to 9pm) that leaves from Wat Sanam Neua.

To get here, take the MRT to Kamphaeng Phet station and exit on the side opposite Chatuchak (the exit says 'Marketing Organization for Farmers').

✖ EATING

Although a bit of a trek, an excursion to Bangkok's suburbs can be a profoundly tasty experience, with heaps of restaurants that don't tone down their flavours for foreigners. The city's outskirts are also a great place to sample regional Thai cuisine.

YUSUP   THAI **$**

(531/12 Kaset-Navamin Hwy; mains 50-120B; ⏰8.30am-3pm; 🚇Mo Chit exit 3 & taxi) The Thai-language sign in front of this restaurant boldly says *rah·chah kôw mòk* (King of Biryani) and Yusup indeed backs it up with

flawless biryani, not to mention sour oxtail soup and decadent *gaang mát·sà·màn* ('Muslim curry'). For dessert try *roh·dee wǎn,* a paratha-like crispy pancake with sweetened condensed milk and sugar – a dish that will send most carb-fearing Westerners running away screaming.

To get here, take a taxi heading north from BTS Mo Chit and tell the driver to take you to the Kaset intersection and turn right on Th Kaset-Navamin. Yusup is on the left-hand side, about 1km past the first stoplight.

KAOBAHN   THAI **$**

Map p286 (www.facebook.com/kaobahn; Aran Bicicletta, 128/10 Soi, Th Phahonyothin; mains 50-120B; ⏰11am-9pm Fri-Wed; 🚇Ari exit 2) Kaobahn means, roughly, home cooking, which is an accurate description of the no-frills-yet-full-flavoured central Thai dishes here. There's no English-language menu, but there's an iPad with images of the dishes, which range from a rich, spicy red curry with pork and pumpkin to a dip of grilled mackerel. Nor will you find an English-language sign, but the restaurant is located behind Aran Bicicletta cafe.

KHUA KLING PAK SOD THAI $$

Map p286 (☎02 617 2553; www.khuaklingpaksod.com; 24 Soi 5, Th Phahonyothin; mains 150-380B; ⏰11am-2.30pm & 5.30-9.30pm; ❄; [S]Ari exit 1) Southern Thai is probably the country's spiciest regional cuisine, so if you're going to sweat over dinner, why not do so in white-tablecloth comfort. Recommended dishes include the eponymous *khua kling*, minced meat fried in an incendiary curry paste, or *moo hong*, fragrant, almost candy-like braised pork belly, a Chinese-Thai speciality of Phuket.

BAAN PUENG CHOM THAI $$

Map p286 (Soi Chua Chit, off Soi 7/Ari, Th Phahonyothin; mains 90-250B; ⏰11am-2pm & 4-10pm Mon-Sat; ❄; [S]Ari exit 1) These days, it takes venturing to the burbs to find an old-school Thai restaurant like this. Ensconced in a watery jungle of a garden, Baan Pueng Chom has a fat, illustrated menu of typically full-flavoured, fragrant Thai dishes you're unlikely to find elsewhere. Call ahead if you wish to sit indoors.

PURITAN DESSERTS $$

Map p286 (46/1 Soi Ari 5, Th Phahonyothin; cakes & pastries from 120B; ⏰1-10pm Tue-Fri, 11am-10pm Sat & Sun; ❄; [S]Ari exit 1) In an attempt to describe the vibe of this uniquely bizarre dessert cafe, our source uttered the words 'a knight wearing a tiara'. Oddly enough this is a pretty accurate summary of Puritan, although the 16-plus chandeliers, taxidermied animals, cherubs and other antiquated, Europhile touches need to be seen in person. Most importantly, however, there are excellent and authentic cakes and pies.

YANG GAO GORN THAI $$

Map p286 (☎081 930 5260; www.facebook.com/YangGaoGorn; 3/2 Soi 14, Th Phahonyothin; mains 70-320B; ⏰11.30am-10pm; ❄; [S]Ari exit 3 & taxi)

RCA

By day a bland-looking strip of offices, come Friday and Saturday nights, Royal City Ave – known by everybody as RCA – transforms into one of Bangkok's most popular nightlife zones. Although some of the bigger clubs can draw thousands, keep in mind that they often require an ID check and also maintain a dress code (no shorts or sandals).

The easiest way to approach RCA is via taxi from the MRT stop at Phra Ram 9; taxis generally can't enter RCA itself, so you'll have to U-turn or cross busy Th Phet Uthai on foot. Approaching the strip from Th Phet Uthai, you'll find the following venues:

Onyx (Map p287; www.facebook.com/onyxbkk; RCA/Royal City Ave; 500B; ⏰8pm-2am; [M]Phra Ram 9 exit 3 & taxi) Probably the most sophisticated club along RCA – evidenced by the hefty entry fee and the coiffed and coddled clientele. Check the Facebook page for upcoming DJ events.

Route 66 (Map p287; www.route66club.com; 29/33-48 RCA/Royal City Ave; 300B; ⏰8pm-2am; [M]Phra Ram 9 exit 3 & taxi) This vast club has been around just about as long as RCA has, but frequent facelifts and expansions have kept it relevant. Top 40 hip hop rules the main space here, although there are several different themed 'levels', featuring anything from Thai pop to live music.

Vesbar (Map p287; www.facebook.com/GoVesBar; 29/68 RCA/Royal City Ave; ⏰11am-midnight Mon-Sat; [M]Phra Ram 9 exit 3 & taxi) This Vespa-themed bar-restaurant serves up international dishes, import beers and jazzy live music (Wednesday, Friday and Saturday).

Taksura (Map p287 ; 9 RCA/Royal City Avenue; ⏰6pm-2am; [M]Phra Ram 9 exit 3 & taxi) Existing somewhere between restaurant and pub is retro-themed Taksura. If you're fuelling up for the clubs, the spicy *gàp glâam* (Thai drinking snacks) won't disappoint.

LOCAL KNOWLEDGE

DRINKING IN ARI

Ari has been touted as one of Bangkok's up-and-coming hoods for years now, and we think its time has finally arrived. Yet unlike most of Bangkok's nightlife areas, which tend to draw a clear line between eateries and bars, Ari seems to excel at places that blend the two genres – here's some of our favourites.

Fatbird (Map p286; ☎02 619 6609; www.facebook.com/fatbird; Soi 7/Ari, Th Phahonyothin; mains 160-300B; ⏲5.30pm-midnight Tue-Sun; ❄; [S]Ari exit 3) The dishes here, which range from tater tots to 'tom-yum-kung fried rice', don't quite cut it for dinner. But approach them as bar snacks, especially when combined with Fatbird's great drinks, eclectic shophouse atmosphere and fun soundtrack, and you have yourself a winner.

Casa Azul (Map p286; www.facebook.com/casaazulbkk; 2/23 Soi 7/Ari, Th Phahonyothin; dishes 150-250B; ⏲11am-midnight; ❄; [S]Ari exit 3) A short menu of Tex-Mex staples, a huge list of imported microbrews and a fun atmosphere (check the Facebook page for theme nights) make up this place that can't seem to decide if it's a restaurant or bar.

Salt (Map p286; ☎02 619 6886; www.saltbangkok.com; Soi 7/Ari, Th Phahonyothin; mains 220-1350B; ⏲5pm-midnight Mon-Sat; ❄; [S]Ari exit 1) Flashing a strategically placed copy of *Larousse Gastronomique*, and serving dishes ranging from sushi to wood-fired pizza, Salt is the epitome of the type of contemporary, eclectic restaurant/bar that has come to define Ari. Be sure to book ahead if dining or drinking on a weekend.

The Yard (Map p286; 51 Soi 5, Th Phahonyothin; ⏲5pm-midnight; [S]Ari exit 1) The open-air lawn of this hostel functions as a fun, informal bar, while **Paper Butter & the Burger** (Map p286: www.facebook.com/PaperButter; The Yard, 51 Soi 5, Th Phahonyothin; mains 120-190B; ⏲11am-2pm & 5-10pm Mon-Sat; ❄; [S]Ari exit 1), an on-site burger shack, is its restaurant.

Located in cosy home in a suburban-feeling street, Yang Gao Gorn does appropriately homestyle Thai dishes; think sweet/savoury salads, rich curries and spicy stir-fries. The offerings definitely aren't those of your typical Thai place, but there's an English-language menu and the friendly, English-speaking owners can assist in the ordering process.

ANOTAI — VEGETARIAN $$

Map p287 (www.facebook.com/anotaigo; 976/17 Soi Rama 9 Hospital, Rama IX; mains 150-300B; ⏲10am-9.30pm Thu-Tue; ❄✎; [M]Phra Ram 9 exit 3 & taxi) Upscale-ish Thai- and Italian-style vegie eats can be found at this long-standing restaurant, which also has its own vegetable market and organic farm.

🍷 DRINKING & NIGHTLIFE

Northern Bangkok spans a lot of real estate, but for years, the epicentre of entertainment has been the strip known as Royal City Ave. The area broadly known as Ari is also home to an increasingly sophisticated spread of restaurants that function equally well as bars.

O'GLEE — BAR

Map p286 (www.facebook.com/ogleearil; Soi Ari 1, Soi 7/Ari, Th Phahonyothin; ⏲5.30pm-midnight; [S]Ari exit 3) The name and decor of this bar vaguely call to mind an Irish pub. But rather than shamrocks and clichés, you get an astonishing selection of imported microbrews – both in bottles and draught – served by a charming Thai family.

AREE — BAR

Map p286 (cnr Soi Ari 4/Nua & Soi 7/Ari, Th Phahonyothin; ⏲6pm-1am; [S]Ari exit 3) Exposed brick, chunky carpets and warm lighting give Aree a cosier feel than your average Bangkok bar. It also offers live music (from 8pm Tuesday to Sunday), contemporary Thai drinking snacks, and a relatively sophisticated drinks list.

FAKE CLUB THE NEXT GEN — CLUB, GAY

(www.facebook.com/fakeclubthenextgen; 222/32 Th Ratchadaphisek; ⏲9pm-3am; [M]Sutthisan exit 3) In new digs is this long-standing, popular gay staple. Expect live music, cheesy choreography and lots of lasers.

⭐ ENTERTAINMENT

★PARKING TOYS   LIVE MUSIC

(📞02 907 2228; 17/22 Soi Mayalap, off Kaset-Navamin Hwy; ⊘4pm-2am; Ⓜ️Chatuchak Park exit 2 & taxi, Ⓢ️Mo Chit exit 3 & taxi) One of Bangkok's best venues for live music, Parking Toys hosts an eclectic revolving cast of fun bands ranging in genre from rockabilly to electro-funk jam acts.

To get here, take a taxi heading north from BTS Mo Chit (or the MRT Chatuchak Park) and tell the driver to take you to the Kaset intersection and turn right on Th Kaset-Navamin; Parking Toys is just past the second stoplight on this road.

LUMPINEE
BOXING STADIUM   SPECTATOR SPORT

(📞02 282 3141; www.muaythailumpinee.net; 6 Th Ramintra; tickets 3rd class/2nd class/ringside 1000/1500/2500B; Ⓜ️Chatuchak Park exit 2 & taxi, Ⓢ️Mo Chit exit 3 & taxi) The other of Bangkok's two premier Thai boxing rings is located in a modern venue far north of town. Matches occur on Tuesdays and Fridays from 6.30pm to 11pm, and on Saturdays from 2pm to 8.30pm.

It's located well north of central Bangkok; the best way to get here is via taxi from BTS Mo Chit or MRT Chatuchak Park.

PLAYHOUSE
MAGICAL CABARET   CABARET

(📞02 024 5522; www.playhousethailand.com; 5 Th Ratchadapisek, Chompol Sub-District, Chatuchak; 960B; ⊘show times 8pm & 9.30pm; Ⓢ️Lat Phrao exit 1) Watching *gà·teu·i* (also spelt *kàthoey*) – Thai cross-dressers or transgender people – perform show tunes has, not surprisingly, become a staple on the Bangkok tourist circuit. Playhouse caters to the trend, with choreographed stage shows featuring Broadway high kicks and lip-synched pop performances.

HOUSE   CINEMA

Map p287 (www.houserama.com; 3rd fl, RCA Plaza, RCA/Royal City Ave; Ⓜ️Phetchaburi exit 1 & taxi) Bangkok's first and biggest art-house cinema, House shows lots of foreign flicks of the non-Hollywood type.

HOLLYWOOD AWARDS   LIVE MUSIC

Map p287 (72/1 Soi 4, Th Ratchadaphisek; ⊘8pm-2am; Ⓜ️Phra Ram 9 exit 3) Like taking a time machine back to the previous century, Hollywood is a holdover from the days when a night out in Bangkok meant corny live stage shows, wiggling around the whisky-set table and neon, neon, neon. As is the case with many of its counterparts, you'll need to purchase a bottle of whisky at the door to gain entry.

SIAM NIRAMIT   THEATRE

Map p287 (📞02 649 9222; www.siamniramit. com; 19 Th Thiam Ruammit; tickets 1500-2850B; ⊘shows 8pm; Ⓜ️Thailand Cultural Centre exit 1 & access by shuttle bus) A cultural theme park, this enchanted kingdom transports visitors to a Disneyfied version of ancient Siam with a brightly coloured stage show of traditional performance depicting the Lanna Kingdom, Buddhist heaven and Thai festivals.

A free shuttle-bus service is available at Thailand Cultural Centre MRT station, running every 15 minutes from 6pm to 7.45pm.

🛍 SHOPPING

Commerce is what draws most visitors to Bangkok's northern suburbs. And even if you're not buying, it's possible to treat the area's markets like sights, offering, as they do, a colourful and hectic taste of the many diverse facets of Thai life – from stacks of produce and hill-tribe wares through to fancy pet outfits and cut-rate clothes.

TALAT ROT FAI 2   MARKET

Map p287 (Esplanade Complex, 99 Th Ratchadaphisek; ⊘5pm-1am Thu-Sun; Ⓢ️Thailand Cultural Centre exit 4) A small and conveniently located vintage market. To get here, take the MRT to Thailand Cultural Centre and walk through the Esplanade mall.

FORTUNE TOWN   ELECTRONICS

Map p287 (Th Ratchadaphisek; ⊘10am-9pm; Ⓜ️Phra Ram 9 exit 1) If you need to supplement your digital life with cheap software, a camera or computer peripherals, this multistorey mall is a much saner alternative to Pantip Plaza (p123).

IS BANGKOK SINKING?

Anybody who has been to Bangkok during the rainy season has probably witnessed it firsthand: floods that make the city's streets seem more like rivers than roads. While traditionally these occurrences were seasonal, some predict that a perfect storm of factors means that in the future the city will be encountering such scenarios – and potentially much worse – on a more frequent basis.

Much of Bangkok was built on soft clay, and scientists suspect that the weight of all those tall buildings is effectively compressing the soil. Some estimate that the city is sinking at a rate of between 10mm and 20mm per year, a phenomenon exacerbated by unregulated use of ground water. And located only 2m above sea level and a scant 50km from the Gulf of Thailand, Bangkok is also threatened by rising sea levels. Indeed, the head of Thailand's National Disaster Warning Center has predicted that by the year 2030, the city will be under 1.5m of water, and by 2100, a virtual Atlantis.

Solutions posed include building a massive sea wall in the Gulf of Thailand, but at an estimated cost of nearly US$3 billion, it's a hard sell. Some have even proposed moving the capital to another location altogether. For the time being, it's most likely that Bangkok will forget about its likely fate until the next rainy season, when the floods will serve as a watery reminder.

🏃 SPORTS & ACTIVITIES

BAIPAI THAI
COOKING SCHOOL   COOKING

(☑02 561 1404; www.baipai.com; 8/91 Soi 54, Th Ngam Wong Wan; classes 2200B; ⊙9.30am-1.30pm & 1.30-5.30pm) Housed in an attractive suburban villa, with classes taught by a small army of staff, Baipai offers two daily lessons of four dishes each. Transport there is provided.

MUAYTHAI INSTITUTE   MARTIAL ARTS

(☑082 985 1115; www.muaythai-institute. net; Rangsit Stadium, 336/932 Th Prachatipat, Pathum Thani; weeklong course from 6900B; Ⓜ Chatuchak Park exit 2 & taxi, Ⓢ Mo Chit exit 3 & taxi) Associated with the respected World Muay Thai Council, the institute offers a fundamental course in Thai boxing (consisting of three levels of expertise), as well as courses for instructors, referees and judges.

FAIRTEX MUAY THAI   MARTIAL ARTS

(☑086 776 0488; www.fairtexbangplee.com; 99/5 Mu 3, Soi Buthamanuson, Th Thaeparak, Samut Prakan; tuition & accommodation per day from 1450B; Ⓢ Chong Nonsi exit 2 & taxi) A popular, long-running Thai boxing camp south of Bangkok.

HOUSE OF DHAMMA   MEDITATION

(☑02 511 0439; www.houseofdhamma.com; 26/9 Soi 15, Th Lat Phrao; fee by donation; Ⓜ Lat Phrao exit 3) Helen Jandamit has opened her suburban Bangkok home to meditation retreats and two-day classes in *vipassana* (insight meditation). Check the website to see what workshops are on offer and be sure to reserve a spot at least a week in advance.

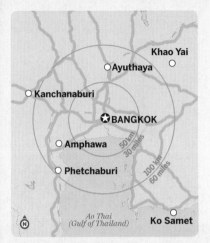

Excursions from Bangkok

Ayuthaya Historical Park p168

Thailand's heroic former capital, Ayuthaya is a Unesco World Heritage site and a major pilgrimage site for anyone interested in ancient history.

Ko Samet p172

This island, only a few hours from Bangkok, has famously squeaky sand beaches and accommodation to fit any budget.

Amphawa p175

Amphawa's canal-side setting and ancient wooden houses look like they are straight out of a movie; its homestays provide an up-close experience of this unique community.

Phetchaburi (Phetburi) p178

Phetchaburi's temples and peak-roofed wooden houses combine to form the epitome of central Thai life.

Kanchanaburi p182

Recent history is only a train ride away in Kanchanaburi, where vivid museums and touching monuments bring home the area's history as a WWII labour camp.

Khao Yai p187

Home to Khao Yai National Park, one of Thailand's biggest and best reserves, where mountainous monsoon forests boast hundreds of resident species.

 TOP SIGHT
AYUTHAYA HISTORICAL PARK

Ancient ruins, a rural Thai vibe, tasty food, good-value accommodation – and all this only 70km from Bangkok: Ayuthaya is the easiest and most worthwhile escape from the Big Mango.

The riverside city served as the seat of one of ancient Thailand's most powerful kingdoms until 1767, when it was destroyed in warfare by the Burmese. Today the ruins of the former capital, **Ayuthaya Historical Park**, are one of Thailand's biggest tourist sites. They're separated into two distinct districts: the ruins 'on the island', in the central part of town west of Th Chee Kun, are most easily visited on bicycle (40B to 50B per day) or motorbike (250B to 300B per day); those 'off the island', opposite the river from the centre, are best visited by evening boat tour (250B per person). For more detailed descriptions of the ruins, pick up the Ayuthaya booklet from the Ayutthaya Tourist Center.

On the Island

Ayutthaya Tourist Center

This **museum** (ศูนย์ท่องเที่ยวอยุธยา; ☑035 246076; off Th Si Sanphet; ☉8.30am-4.30pm) `FREE` should be your first stop in Ayuthaya, as the excellent upstairs exhibition hall puts everything in context and describes the city's erstwhile glories, while the ground-floor TAT office has lots of maps and good advice.

Wat Phra Si Sanphet

At this captivating ruined **temple** (วัดพระศรีสรรเพชญ์; 50B; ☉8am-6pm), three wonderfully intact stupas form one of Ayuthaya's most iconic views; unlike at many other ruins, it's possible to clamber up the stairs for a lofty vantage point (and epic selfie). Built in the late 15th century, this was a royal temple inside palace grounds; these were the model for

Bangkok's Wat Phra Kaew and Royal Palace. This temple once contained a 16m-high standing Buddha (Phra Si Sanphet) covered with at least 143kg of gold.

Wihan Phra Mongkhon Bophit

This **sanctuary hall** (วิหารพระมงคลบพิตร; ⊗8am-5pm) **FREE** houses one of Thailand's largest bronze Buddha images, dating to 1538. Coated in gold, the 12.5m-high figure (17m with the base) was badly damaged by a lightning-induced fire around 1700, and again when the Burmese sacked the city. The Buddha and the building were repaired in the 20th century.

Wat Phra Ram

Though it isn't in the best state of preservation, the tall main *prang* (Hindu/Khmer-style stupa) of this **temple** (วัดพระราม; off Th Naresuan; 50B; ⊗8am-6pm; [P]) is worth a visit. The temple is thought to have been constructed in 1369 on the cremation site of King U Thong (the Ayuthaya kingdom's first sovereign), though details of its history are unclear.

Wat Ratchaburana

The *prang* in this sprawling **temple complex** (วัดราชบูรณะ; off Th Naresuan; 50B; ⊗8am-6pm) is one of the best extant versions in the city, with detailed carvings of lotus flowers and mythical creatures; it's surrounded by another four stupas. If you aren't afraid of heights, small spaces or bats, you can climb inside the *prang* to visit the crypt (the largest in Thailand), decorated with faint murals of the Buddha from the early Ayuthaya period.

Wat Mahathat

Ayuthaya's most photographed attraction is in these **temple grounds** (วัดมหาธาตุ; Th Chee Kun; 50B; ⊗8am-6.30pm; [P]): a sandstone Buddha head tangled within a bodhi tree's entwined roots. Founded in 1374, during the reign of King Borom Rachathirat I, Wat Mahathat was the seat of the supreme patriarch and the kingdom's most important temple. The central *prang* once stood 43m high and it collapsed on its own long before the Burmese sacked the city. It was rebuilt in more recent times, but collapsed again in 1911.

Wat Lokayasutharam

This **temple ruin** (วัดโลกยสุธาราม; off Th Khlong Thaw; ⊗daylight hours; [P]) **FREE** in the island's northwest features an impressive 42m-long reclining Buddha, ostensibly dating back to the early Ayuthaya period. A visit is worth the short bike trip it takes to reach it.

GETTING THERE & AWAY

Ayuthaya is 70km north of Bangkok. Minivans depart from Bangkok's Northern & Northeastern station (Mo Chit; 55B to 70B, one to 1½ hours, frequent from 6am to 9pm). Northbound trains leave Bangkok's Hualamphong Station (20B to 65B, 1½ to 2½ hours) every 30 minutes from 6.20am to 9pm (less frequently from 9.30am to 4pm). A taxi to Ayuthaya costs between 1500B and 2000B.

Most visitors are on a big bus and a tight schedule. Instead, explore by túk-túk (pronounced *đúk đúk*), boat or bicycle.

INFORMATION

The Tourism Authority of Thailand **office** (TAT; ☎035 246076; tatyutya@tat.or.th; Th Si Sanphet; ⊗8.30am-4.30pm) is in an art deco building west of the park.

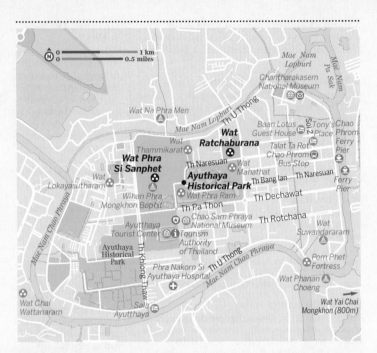

Wat Suwandararam

Although there was a **temple** (วัดสุวรรณดาราราม; ⊙daylight hours) FREE here in the Ayuthaya era, the present buildings are from the current reign, with the *bòht* (ordination hall) built by King Rama I and the adjacent *wí·hăhn* (sanctuary) by King Rama IV. Both have fascinating murals inside that show, among other things, scenes of daily life and stories from the life of King Naresuan.

Chao Sam Phraya National Museum

The most impressive treasure of Ayuthaya's largest **museum** (พิพิธภัณฑสถานแห่ง ชาติเจ้าสามพระยา; ☑035 244570; cnr Th Rotchana & Th Si Sanphet; adult/child 150B/free; ⊙9am-4pm Wed-Sun; P) is the haul of royal gold (jewellery, utensils, gourds, spittoons) unearthed from the crypts of Wat Mahathat and Wat Ratchaburana. Beautifully carved teak friezes, some flecked with gold leaf, and numerous Buddha statues (some sculpted in the 7th century) are also on display.

Chantharakasem National Museum

The **museum** (พิพิธภัณฑสถานแห่งชาติจันทรเกษม; ☑035 251586; Th U Thong; 100B; ⊙9am-4pm Wed-Sun) is within the grounds of Wang Chan Kasem (Chan Kasem Palace), built for King Rama IV at the site of a palace used by King Naresuan and seven subsequent Ayuthaya kings. The museum is large, but the collection (Buddhist art, pottery, ancient weapons, lacquered cabinets and original furnishings) isn't – the highly decorated buildings themselves are the main attraction.

Wat Thammikarat

This is both an active **temple** (วัดธรรมิกราช; off Th U Thong; 20B; ⊙8am-7pm; P) and a pleasant place to sit among the ruins. The most prominent feature is a central *chedi* (Buddhist stupa) surrounded by 13 *singha* (guardian lion) sculptures.

Off the Island

Wat Chai Wattanaram

Glorious at sunset, this **temple** (วัดไชยวัฒนาราม ; Ban Pom; 50B; 8am-6pm) is Ayuthaya's most impressive off-island site thanks to its 35m-high Khmer-style central *prang* and fine state of preservation. Relief panels are heavily eroded, but you can make out carved scenes from the Buddha's life.

Wat Phanan Choeng

This lively **temple** (วัดพนัญเชิง; Khlong Suan Plu; 20B; ⊘daylight hours), believed to date to 1324, is a fascinating place to observe merit-making ceremonies, which unfold beneath the gaze of the 19m-high Phra Phanan Choeng Buddha. This enormous statue, a guardian for seafarers, is the focus of most visits. He sits within a soaring *wí·hǎhn* (shrine hall; open 8am to 5pm) surrounded by 84,000 small Buddha images lining the walls.

Wat Yai Chai Mongkhon

Visitors to this photogenic **ruin** (วัดใหญ่ชัยมงคล; 20B; ⊘6am-6pm) can climb stairs up the bell-shaped *che·di* (Buddhist stupa) for a view of sculpted gardens and dozens of stone Buddhas. There's a 7m-long reclining Buddha near the entrance and the local belief is that if you can get a coin to stick to the Buddha's feet, good luck will come your way.

Wat Na Phra Men

Housing a gorgeous 6m-high Buddha flanked by maroon columns, this **temple** (วัดหน้าพระเมรุ; Lum Phli; 20B; ⊘daylight hours; P) was one of the few to escape the wrath of Burma's invading army in 1767; it survived by serving as the army's main base and weapons storehouse. The *bòht* is massive, larger than most modern ones, and the Buddha image wears 'royal attire', which was very common in the late Ayuthaya era. Despite what the English sign inside says, it's made of bronze, not gold.

Baan Hollanda

This bright and beautifully curated **museum** (บ้าน ฮอลันดา; ☎035 245683; www.baanhollanda.org; Soi Khan Rua, Mu 4; 50B; ⊘9am-5pm Wed-Sun; P) features an excellent exhibition of Thai-Dutch history alongside the excavated foundations of centuries-old Dutch buildings. The Dutch East India Company (Verenigde Oost-Indische Compagnie; VOC) arrived in Ayuthaya in 1604 and set up a trading post here, hoping to use Thailand (then Siam) as a gateway to China.

EXCURSIONS FROM BANGKOK AYUTHAYA HISTORICAL PARK

TEMPLE ETIQUETTE

Ayuthaya's ruins are symbols of both royalty and religion, two fundamental elements of Thai society, so visit respectfully. That means no posing for photos with your head positioned above Buddhas or taking the place of the statues' missing heads. Unless it's abundantly clear that you are permitted to ascend a stupa, do not climb on the ruins.

Guided elephant rides are frequently offered to tourists as a way to tour Ayuthaya's temples but we strongly advise against partaking in this cruel activity.

COMBINED TEMPLES TICKET

A pass for six major ruins costs 220B, lasts 30 days and can be bought at each site. It covers Wat Ratchaburana, Wat Phra Si Sanphet, Wat Phra Ram, Wat Mahathat, Wat Maheyong and Wat Chai Wattanaram.

SLEEPING IN AYUTHAYA

Ayothaya Riverside House (☎081 644 5328; www.facebook.com/ayothayariverside house; 17/2 Mu 7, Tambon Banpom; d without bathroom 400B, d on boat 1500B; ❄️🛜) Across the Mae Nam Chao Phraya on the west side of Ayuthaya, this wonderful guesthouse offers a choice between pleasant rooms with fans and mosquito nets or satin-and-wood-decorated rooms on a boat (with air-con).

Promtong Mansion (☎089 165 6297; www.promtong.com; off 23 Th Pa Thon; d 1100B; ❄️🛜) Extending the warmest welcome in Ayuthaya, Promtong Mansion is filled with fabulous wood-carved sculptures. Large, comfortable rooms are decked with elephant-shaped bedside lamps and other local trimmings. The owner is a fount of local knowledge, complimentary fruit platters are offered throughout guests' stays, and the location is quiet but convenient.

Baan Thai House (☎080 437 4555; www.baanthaihouse.com; Pai Ling; villas 1900-2800B, d/f all incl breakfast 2500/3800B; 🅿️❄️🛜🏊) Stone walkways threading through lush grounds, complete with lagoon and fountain, set the tone for this tranquil resort. Thai-style villas are awash in golden yellow and have fridges and TVs. Spacious double and family rooms are wood-lined, snug and similarly well equipped.

Ko Samet   เกาะเสม็ด

Explore

It takes at least five hours to reach Ko Samet from Bangkok, so schedule in at least two nights if you really want to experience the island's famously fine sands. Long weekends can be particularly busy, with thousands of Bangkokians beelining for the island; arrive on a weekday and you'll probably have Ko Samet to yourself.

The Best...

➡ **Place to Eat** Jep's Restaurant
➡ **Place to Drink** Audi Bar
➡ **Beach** Ao Wong Deuan

Top Tip

Ko Samet is a relatively dry island, making it an excellent place to visit during the rainy season (approximately June to October).

Getting There & Away

➡ **Minivan** Minivans to Ban Phe (the pier for ferries to Ko Samet) depart from Bangkok's Eastern Bus Terminal (250B, three hours, hourly from 6am to 8pm).
➡ **Bus** Buses to Ban Phe leave from Bangkok's Eastern Bus Terminal (166B, four hours, every two hours from 7am to 6pm).
➡ **Boat** Boats to Ko Samet leave from Ban Phe's many piers. Most boats go to Na

Dan Pier (return 100B, 40 minutes, hourly from 8am to 5pm). You can also charter a speedboat (about 1500B depending on demand) for up to 10 people.

Need to Know

➡ **Location** 200km southeast of Bangkok
➡ **National Parks Main Office** (Map p174; www.dnp.go.th; Hat Sai Kaew; ⊘8.30am-8pm) There's another office at Ao Wong Deuan.

🔘 SIGHTS

KHAO LAEM YA/MU KO SAMET
NATIONAL PARK   NATIONAL PARK

Map p174 (อุทยานแห่งชาติเขาแหลมหญ้า-หมู่เกาะเสม็ด; ☎038 653034; www.dnp.go.th; adult/child 200/100B) **Ko Man Klang**, **Ko Kudee** and **Ko Man Nok**, along with **Ko Man Nai** to the west, are part of **Khao Laem Ya/Mu Ko Samet National Park**. This official status hasn't kept away all development, only moderated it. Ko Kudee has a small, pretty sandy stretch, clear water for decent snorkelling and a nice little hiking trail.

The best way to visit is to join a boat tour from Ko Samet.

Beaches

Ko Samet is shaped like a golf tee, with the wide part in the north tapering away along a narrow strip to the south. Most boats from the mainland arrive at Na Dan Pier in the north, which is little more than a transit point for most visitors. Starting just south of Na Dan Pier and moving clockwise, the island's most noteworthy beaches include:

Hat Sai Kaew (หาดทรายแก้ว; Map p174) On the northeastern coast is the most developed stretch of beaches and the best place for nightlife. Wealthy Bangkokians with their designer sunglasses and designer dogs file straight into Hat Sai Kaew's air-con bungalows.

Ao Hin Khok & Ao Phai (อ่าวหินโคก/อ่าวไผ่; Map p174) Scattered south along the eastern shore are a scruffier set of beaches that were once populated solely by backpackers but are increasingly catering to flashpackers and Bangkok expats.

Ao Phutsa (อ่าวพุทรา/อ่าวทับทิม, Ao Tub Tim; Map p174) This wide and sandy beach is a favourite for solitude seekers, families and gay men who need access to 'civilisation' but not a lot of other stimulation.

Ao Wong Deuan (อ่าววงเดือน; Map p174) Immediately to the south is the prom queen of the bunch, with a graceful stretch of sand that is home to an entourage of sardine-packed sun-worshippers, package tourists, screaming jet-skis and honky-tonk bars.

Ao Thian (อ่าวเทียน, Candlelight Beach; Map p174) This beach is punctuated by big boulders that shelter small sandy spots, creating a castaway feel. Thai college kids claim these for all-night guitar jam sessions and if you're also on a tight budget, this beach is your best bet.

Ao Wai (อ่าวหวาย; Map p174) A lovely beach far removed from everything else (though in reality it is 2km from Ao Thian).

Ao Prao (อ่าวพร้าว, Coconut Beach; Map p174) The only developed beach on the steeper western side of the island, it hosts three up-market resorts and moonlights as 'Paradise Beach' to those escaping winter climates.

 **EATING & DRINKING**

Every hotel and guesthouse has a restaurant, and choosing one can be as difficult as a walk along the beach inspecting menus along the way. There are several food stalls along the main drag between Na Dan Pier and Hat Sai Kaew, and it's worth looking out for the nightly beach barbecues, particularly along Ao Hin Khok and Ao Phai. Likewise, every hotel has a beachside bar, and there are plenty of stand-alone bar-restaurants that occupy the beachfront at Hat Sai Kaew and Ao Wong Deuan.

JEP'S RESTAURANT INTERNATIONAL $

Map p174 (☏038 644 112; www.jepsbungalows. com; Ao Hin Khok; mains 70-200B; ☻7am-11pm; ☏) Canopied by the branches of an arching tree decorated with pendant lights, this pretty place right on the sand does a wide range of international, and some Thai, dishes. Leave room for dessert.

KITT & FOOD SEAFOOD, THAI $$

Map p174 (☏038 644087; Hat Sai Kaew; mains 120-400B; ☻11am-10.30pm) Better than most of the beachfront restaurants, this is a romantic place for dinner, with tables almost lapped by the waves. Don't plough too deep into the phonebook of a menu – seafood is the speciality here. Various fresh fish (mostly farmed) are arrayed; pick one and decide how you want it done. Baked in salt takes a while but is great.

RED GINGER INTERNATIONAL, THAI $$

Map p174 (☏084 383 4917; www.redgingersamed. com; Na Dan; mains 120-565B; ☻11am-10pm; ☏☏) An atmospheric main-street eatery that feels like an extension of this Canadian-Thai family's lounge room: expect cheery informality, quirks and chatting over a drink with the personable owner. The menu is short but tasty, with authentic, flavoursome Thai dishes complemented by a handful of international offerings. Excellent oven-baked ribs slathered in barbecue sauce are the highlight.

AUDI BAR BAR

Map p174 (☏084 418 8213; Na Dan; ☻4pm-4am; ☏) Sharing an upstairs main-street space with a gym, this bar offers good people-watching from its high vantage point, the Samet-standard Day-Glo graffiti and a couple of pool tables. It's notably welcoming – staff want you to enjoy yourself – and serves as a one-last-drink venue for those straggling back from the beach dance floors.

TALAY BAR BAR

Map p174 (☏083 887 1588; Hat Sai Kaew; ☻2pm-midnight; ☏) Cheerily fronted by burning torches and Thai flags, this is at the eastern end of the island's busiest beach, away from the most crowded parts. It's an upbeat, enthusiastic spot with space to lounge on the sand and kick back with a cocktail or beer bomb from the unfeasibly large menu.

Ko Samet

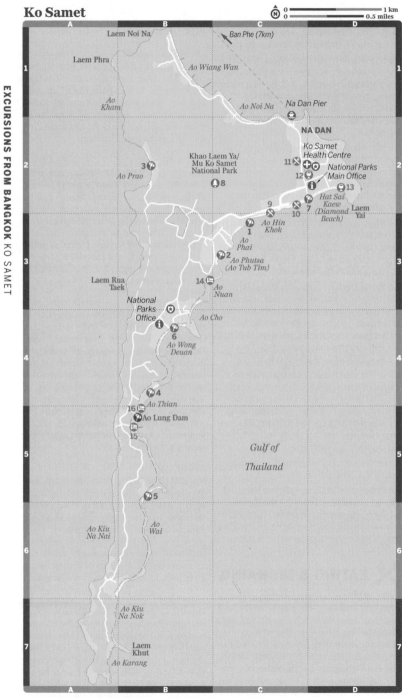

0 —————— 1 km
0 —————— 0.5 miles

Laem Noi Na

Laem Phra

Ao Wiang Wan

Ban Phe (7km)

Ao Kham

Ao Noi Na

Na Dan Pier

NA DAN

Ao Prao

3

Khao Laem Ya/
Mu Ko Samet
National Park

8

Ko Samet
Health Centre

11

National Parks
Main Office

12

13

*Hat Sai
Kaew
(Diamond
Beach)*

9

7

10

Laem
Yai

1

*Ao Hin
Khok*

*Ao
Phai*

2

*Ao Phutsa
(Ao Tub Tim)*

Laem Rua
Taek

14

*Ao
Nuan*

National
Parks
Office

Ao Cho

6

*Ao Wong
Deuan*

4

Ao Thian

16

Ao Lung Dam

7

15

Gulf of

Thailand

5

*Ao Kiu
Na Nai*

*Ao
Wai*

*Ao Kiu
Na Nok*

Laem
Khut

Ao Karang

Ko Samet

🛏 SLEEPING

Due to the high demand, Ko Samet's prices can seem elevated compared with the amenities on offer, especially on weekends. A ramshackle hut starts at about 700B and with air-con this can climb to 1000B. Reservations aren't always honoured, so at peak times (most weekends and especially public-holiday weekends) it is advisable to arrive early, poised for the hunt.

APACHÉ BUNGALOW $
Map p174 (☏081 452 9472; Ao Thian; r 800-1500B; ❋⊛) Apaché's eclectic, quirky decorations and cheerfully random colour scheme add character to this super-chilled spot at the southern end of a tranquil strip. Bungalows are basic but adequate. The on-site restaurant on stilts is well worthwhile.

★VIKING HOLIDAYS RESORT BUNGALOW $$
Map p174 (☏038 644354; www.vikingholidays resort.com; Ao Thian; r incl breakfast 1500-1800B; ❒❋⊛⊗) One of a line of casual bungalow complexes on this tranquil beachside, Viking is well run and has pretty, compact rooms with carpet and strings of seashells for decoration. Staff are particularly helpful and friendly and good English is spoken. Unlike many Ko Samet bungalows, you can book online (and pick your bungalow location).

★AO NUAN BUNGALOWS BUNGALOW $$
Map p174 (☏081 781 4875; Ao Nuan; bungalows with fan 800-1200B, with air-con 1500-3000B; ❋⊛) Samet's one remaining bohemian bay is tucked off the main road down a dirt track. Running down a jungle hillside to the sea are cute wooden bungalows ranging from simple fan-cooled affairs with shared cold-water bathroom to romantic air-conditioned retreats with elegant deck furniture. There's a bar and simple restaurant; if you need more action, Tubtim beach is a few minutes' stroll.

Amphawa อัมพวา

Explore

Amphawa is located within day-trip distance from Bangkok, but is probably best approached as an overnighter. The trip is easy enough by bus or minivan or via a more circuitous route (p177), and after you've seen the town, Amphawa is a good jumping-off point for other floating markets such as Damnoen Saduak and Tha Kha.

The Best...
➡ **Sight** Amphawa
➡ **Place to Eat** Amphawa Floating Market (p176)
➡ **Place to Stay** ChababaanCham Resort (p177)

Top Tip

Amphawa is mobbed with tourists from Bangkok every weekend. For cheaper accommodation and a calmer environment, make a point of hitting the town during the week.

Getting There & Away
➡ **Bus** From Bangkok's Southern Bus Terminal in Thonburi, board any bus bound for Damnoen Saduak and ask to get off at Amphawa (80B, two hours, frequent 6am to 9pm).
➡ **Minivan** From Bangkok's Southern Bus Terminal there are frequent minivans to Samut Songkhram (also known as Mae Klong; 70B, 1½ hours, frequent from 6am

to 9pm). From there, you can hop in a *sŏrng·tăa·ou* (passenger pick-up truck; 8B) near the market for the 10-minute ride to Amphawa.

Need to Know

➡ **Location** 80km southwest of Bangkok

➡ **Tourist Office** (☎034 752 847; 71 Th Prachasret; ⊙8.30am-4.30pm)

◉ SIGHTS

AMPHAWA   VILLAGE

(Samut Songkhram) This canalside village has become a popular destination among city folk who seek out what many consider its quintessentially 'Thai' setting. This urban influx has sparked quite a few signs of gentrification, but the canals, old wooden buildings, atmospheric cafes and quaint water-borne traffic still retain heaps of charm. At weekends, Amphawa puts on a fun floating market (p184).

FIREFLIES GUIDED TOURS   BOATING

(Amphawa; per person Fri-Sun 60B, 2hr charter Mon-Thu 500B; ⊙5-10pm) At night, long-tail boats zip through Amphawa's sleepy canals and rivers to watch the Christmas-tree-like light dance of the *hìng hôy* (fireflies), most populous during the wet season (from approximately July to October). From Friday to Sunday, a number of operators from several piers lead tours; outside of these days, a two-hour charter is available.

WAT AMPHAWAN
CHETIYARAM   BUDDHIST TEMPLE

(วัดอัมพวันเจติยาราม; off Rte 6006, Amphawa, Samut Songkhram; ⊙daylight hours) Steps from Amphawa's central footbridge is this graceful temple thought to be located at the place of the family home of Rama II (King Phraphutthaloetla Naphalai; r 1809–24), and which features accomplished murals.

DON HOI LOT   BEACH

(ดอนหอยหลอด; Samut Songkhram) The Amphawa area's second-most-famous tourist attraction is a bank of fossilised shells at the mouth of Mae Nam Mae Klong, not far from Samut Songkhram. These shells come from *hŏy lòrt* (clams with a tube-like shell). The shell bank is best seen during April and May when the river surface has receded to its lowest level.

To get there hop into a *sŏrng·tăa·ou* in front of Samut Songkhram's Somdet Phra Phuttalertla Hospital at the intersection of Th Prasitpattana and Th Tamnimit (10B, about 15 minutes). Or charter a boat from Mae Klong Market pier (*tâh dà·làht mâa glorng*), a scenic journey of around 45 minutes (about 1000B).

KING BUDDHALERTLA
(PHUTTHA LOET LA)
NAPHALAI MEMORIAL PARK   MUSEUM

(อุทยานพระบรมราชานุสรณ์ พระบาทสมเด็จ พระพุทธเลิศหล้านภาลัย/อุทยาน ร. ๒; off Rte 6006, Amphawa, Samut Songkhram; 20B; ⊙8.30am-5pm) This park is a museum housed in a collection of traditional central Thai–style houses set on four landscaped acres. Dedicated to Rama II, who was born in the area, the museum contains rare Thai books and antiques from early-19th-century Siam.

✕ EATING

In addition to suggestions here, there are several basic Thai restaurants in Amphawa; many more are open on weekends.

SEAFOOD RESTAURANTS   SEAFOOD $

(Don Hoi Lot, Samut Songkhram; mains 70-200B; ⊙10am-10pm) The road leading to Don Hoi Lot is lined with seafood restaurants, nearly all serving dishes made with *hŏy lòrt*, the area's eponymous shellfish.

AMPHAWA FLOATING MARKET   MARKET $

(ตลาดน้ำอัมพวา; Amphawa; dishes 20-40B; ⊙4-9pm Fri-Sun) If you're in Amphawa on a weekend, plan your meals around this fun market where grilled seafood and other dishes are served directly from boats.

🛏 SLEEPING

Amphawa is popular with Bangkok's weekend warriors and virtually every other house has opened its door to tourists in the form of homestays. These can range from little more than a mattress and a mosquito net to upmarket guesthouse-style accommodation. Fan rooms start at about 250B while air-con rooms, many of which share bathrooms, begin at about 1000B. Prices are half this on weekdays. If you prefer something a bit more private, consider one of the following.

THE LONG WAY TO AMPHAWA

Amphawa is only 80km from Bangkok, but if you play your cards right, you can reach the town via a long journey involving trains, boats, a motorcycle ride and a short jaunt in the back of a truck. Why? Because sometimes the journey is just as interesting as the destination.

The adventure begins at Thonburi's **Wong Wian Yai** (☑02 465 2017, call centre 1690; www.railway.co.th; off Th Phra Jao Taksin; [S]Wongwian Yai exit 4 & taxi) train station. Just past the Wong Wian Yai traffic circle is a fairly ordinary food market that camouflages the unspectacular terminus of this commuter line. Hop on one of the hourly trains (10B, one hour, 5.30am to 8.10pm) to Samut Sakhon.

After 15 minutes on the rattling train, the city density yields to squat villages. From the window you can peek into homes, temples and shops built a carefully considered arm's length from the passing trains. Further on, palm trees, patchwork rice fields and marshes filled with giant elephant ears and canna lilies line the route, punctuated by whistle-stop stations.

The backwater farms evaporate quickly as you enter **Samut Sakhon**, popularly known as Mahachai because it straddles the confluence of Mae Nam Tha Chin and Khlong Mahachai. This is a bustling port town, several kilometres upriver from the Gulf of Thailand, and the end of the first rail segment. Before the 17th century it was called Tha Jiin (Chinese Pier) because of the large number of Chinese junks that called here.

After working your way through one of the most hectic fresh markets in the country, you'll come to a vast harbour clogged with water hyacinths and wooden fishing boats. A few rusty cannons pointing towards the river testify to the existence of the town's crumbling fort, built to protect the kingdom from sea invaders.

Take the ferry across to **Baan Laem** (3B to 5B), where you'll jockey for space with school teachers riding motorcycles and people running errands. If the infrequent 5B ferry hasn't already deposited you there, take a motorcycle taxi (10B) for the 2km ride to **Wat Chawng Lom** (วัดช่องลม; Ban Laem, Samut Sakhon; ⏲daylight hours) **FREE**, home to the **Jao Mae Kuan Im Shrine**, a 9m-high fountain in the shape of the Mahayana Buddhist Goddess of Mercy that is popular with regional tour groups. Beside the shrine is Tha Chalong, a train stop with three daily departures for Samut Songkhram at 8.10am, 12.05pm and 4.40pm (10B, one hour). The train rambles out of the city on tracks that the surrounding forest threatens to engulf, and this little stretch of line genuinely feels a world away from the big smoke of Bangkok.

The jungle doesn't last long, and any illusion that you've entered a parallel universe free of concrete is shattered as you enter **Samut Songkhram**. And to complete the seismic shift, you'll emerge directly into a hubbub of hectic market stalls. Between train arrivals and departures these stalls are set up directly on the tracks and must be hurriedly cleared away when the train arrives – it's quite an amazing scene.

Commonly known as Mae Klong, Samut Songkhram is a tidier version of Samut Sakhon and offers a great deal more as a destination. Owing to flat topography and abundant water sources, the area surrounding the provincial capital is well suited to the steady irrigation needed to grow guava, lychee and grapes. From Mae Klong Market pier (*tâh dà·làht mâa glorng*), you can charter a boat (1000B) or hop in a *sŏrng·tăa·ou* (passenger pick-up truck; 8B) near the market for the 10-minute ride to Amphawa.

CHABABAANCHAM RESORT　　HOTEL $$$
(☑081 984 1000; www.chababaancham.com; Th Rim Khlong; r incl breakfast 1900-2400B; ❉🅟) Located just off the canal, this place has attractive, modern and spacious duplex-style rooms, the more expensive of which come equipped with a rooftop lounge area.

BAAN KU PU　　HOTEL $$$
(☑081 941 1249; Th Rim Khlong; bungalows incl breakfast 1600-2000B; ❉🅟) A Thai-style 'resort' featuring wooden bungalows in a relatively peaceful, canalside enclave.

PLOEN AMPHAWA RESORT　　HOTEL $$$
(☑081 458 9411; www.facebook.com/ploen amphawa; Th Rim Khlong; r incl breakfast 1400-3000B; ❉🅟) Not a resort at all, but rather a handful of rooms in a refurbished wooden home in the thick of the canal area.

Phetchaburi (Phetburi) เพชรบุรี

Explore

Phetchaburi (colloquially known as Phetburi) is only about two hours from Bangkok. It is probably best approached as an overnighter, although it's worth noting that the town's hotels are a dreary lot. Regardless, despite the number of worthwhile sights, very few foreign tourists make it to Phetchaburi, and you'll likely have the town to yourself.

If you have time, consider extending your stay to take in the jungle at Kaeng Krachan National Park.

The Best

➜ **Sight** Phra Nakhon Khiri Historical Park

➜ **Place to Eat** Rabieng Rimnam (p181)

➜ **Place to Stay** White Monkey Guesthouse (p181)

Top Tip

The train is the slowest but arguably the most scenic way to reach Phetchaburi.

Getting There & Away

➜ **Minivan** Minivans depart from both Bangkok's Southern and Mo Chit terminals (100B, two hours, frequent from 3.30am to 7.30pm).

➜ **Train** There are frequent services from Bangkok's Hualamphong Train Station; fares vary depending on the train and class (34B to 388B, three to 3½ hours, 12 daily).

Need to Know

➜ **Location** 166km south of Bangkok

⊙ SIGHTS

★PHRA NAKHON KHIRI HISTORICAL PARK   HISTORIC SITE

Map p179 (อุทยานประวัติศาสตร์พระนครคีรี; ☑032 401006; 150B, cable car return 50B; ☺park 8.30am-4.30pm, museum 9am-4pm) This national historical park sits regally atop Khao Wang (Palace Hill), surveying the city with subdued opulence. Rama IV (King Mongkut) built the palace and dozens of surrounding structures in 1859 as a retreat from Bangkok. The hilltop location allowed the king to pursue his interest in astronomy. Parts of the palace, made in a mix of European, Thai and Chinese styles, are now a **museum** furnished with royal belongings.

Rolling cobblestone paths lead from the palace through the forested hill to three summits, each topped by a stupa. The 40m-tall white spire of **Phra That Chom Phet** skewers the sky from the central peak. You can climb up through the interior to its waist. The western peak features **Wat Phra Kaew Noi** (Little Wat Phra Kaew), a small building slightly resembling one from Bangkok's most important temples, and **Phra Prang Daeng** stupa with a Khmer-influenced design.

There are two entrances to the site. The **east** (ทางเข้าทิศตะวันออก; Map p179; Th Khiriataya) (front) entrance is across from Th Ratwithi and involves a not-too-strenuous footpath. The **west** (ทางเข้าทิศตะวันตก; Map p179; Th Rim Khao Wang) entrance on the opposite side of the hill has a **cable car** (closed for 15 days each June for regular maintenance and a few other days during the year to change the cable) that glides up and down to the summit. At both, keep a leery eye on the troops of unpredictable monkeys (p180). This place is a popular school-group outing and you'll be as much of a photo op as the historic buildings.

★WAT MAHATHAT WORAWIHAN   BUDDHIST TEMPLE

Map p179 (วัดมหาธาตุวรวิหาร; Th Damnoen Kasem; ☺daylight hours) **FREE** Centrally located, gleaming white Wat Mahathat is one impressive temple. The showpiece is a 42m-tall five-tiered Ayuthaya-style *prang* (corn-cob shaped stupa) decorated in stucco relief, a speciality of Phetchaburi's local artisans you'll see all over town, while inside the *wí·hăhn* (sanctuary) that fronts it are important, though highly damaged, early 20th-century murals.

When leaving or arriving at the temple follow **Th Suwanmunee** through the old teak house district, now filled with lottery vendors, for a picture-postcard view of the *prang* from the bridge. There are historical signs in front of some of the notable buildings on this street and Th Klongkrachang.

Phetchaburi (Phetburi)

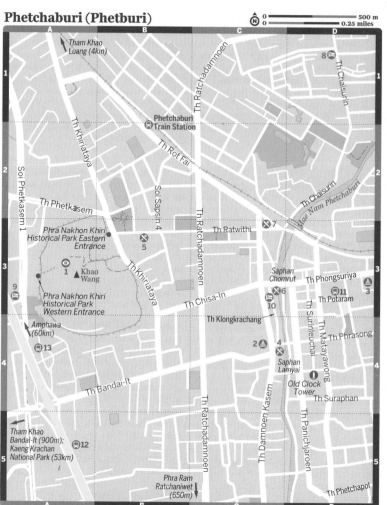

Phetchaburi (Phetburi)

THAM KHAO LUANG   CAVE

(ถ้ำเขาหลวง; ☉8am-4pm Mon-Fri, 8am-5pm Sat & Sun) **FREE** About 4km north of town is Khao Luang Cave, a dramatic stalactite-stuffed cavern that's one of Thailand's most impressive cave shrines, and a favourite of King Rama IV when he was a monk. Accessed via steep stairs, it's lit by a heavenly glow every morning (clouds permitting) when sunbeams filter in through the natural skylight.

Things change throughout the year, but the sun shower generally happens between 9am and noon; earlier is better. And note that you have to be standing in the right spot to see it. From February to April the light illuminates the main Buddha image.

Deeper in the cave there are more chambers and shrines, although the back exit is no longer in use. The story is that Rama IV built the stone gate that separates the main chamber from the others as a security measure for a couple who once lived in the cave.

You can walk up the steep hill to the entrance, or ride in a truck for 15B. You'll meet many brazen monkeys (p180) looking for handouts here, though they don't go inside the cave. There are also sometimes guides asking to join you. They're not necessary, and a tip will be expected.

WAT YAI SUWANNARAM   BUDDHIST TEMPLE

Map p179 (วัดใหญ่สุวรรณาราม; Th Phongsuriya; ☉bòht 7am-6pm, sǎh·lah 8am-5pm) **FREE** This expansive temple, founded in the late Ayuthaya era, holds quite a bit of history. Foremost are the faded murals inside the beautiful *bòht* (ordination hall), which date back to about 1700, making them some of the oldest Thai-temple murals still in existence. Mostly they're rows of various deities though the entrance wall vividly shows the demon Mara and his army trying to stop the Buddha from reaching enlightenment.

Next door is a large, elaborate teak *sǎh·lah* (often spelt sala; an open pavilion) built in Ayuthaya during the 17th century and later moved to Phetchaburi by boat. Legend has it that the gash in the ornately carved wooden back door dates to the Burmese attack; however, this is highly unlikely. Finally there are also two *hǒr đrai* (sacred manuscript libraries) on stilts to guard against termites, a petite one in a pond and a tall one on land next to the monks' quarters.

PHRA RAM RATCHANIWET   HISTORIC SITE

(พระรามราชนิเวศน์, Ban Peun Palace; Th Damnoen Kasem; 50B; ☉8.30am-4pm Mon-Fri, 8.30am-4.30pm Sat & Sun) Construction of this elegant summer palace, an incredible art nouveau creation, began in 1910 at the behest of Rama V (who died just after the project was started) and finished in 1916. It was designed by German architects who indulged the royal family's passion for all things European with a Poseidon statue, badminton court, ceramic cherubs lining the double spiral staircase and a state-of-the-art, for the time, adjustable shower in the king's bathroom.

The lack of furnishings and, usually, other visitors makes a visit feel quite odd. It's on a military base and normally no identification is required, but it's best to bring your passport in case things change.

◉ Around Phetchaburi

KAENG KRACHAN
NATIONAL PARK   NATIONAL PARK

(อุทยานแห่งชาติแก่งกระจาน; ☎032 772311; Open Nov-Jul; adult/child 300/200B, car 30B; ☉visitors centre 8.30am-4.30pm) Wake to an eerie symphony of gibbon calls as the early-morning mist floats through the forest canopy, and then hike through lush forests in search of elephant herds and other wildlife. Thailand's largest (2915 sq km) national park is surprisingly close to civilisation but shelters an intense tangle of wilderness that sees relatively few tourists.

Despite the park having a poaching problem, animal life includes wild elephants, tigers, leopards, tapir, gaur (wild cattle), white-handed gibbons, dusky langurs and black giant squirrels. This park also occupies an interesting, overlapping biozone for birds as the southernmost spot for northern species and the northernmost for southern species. The result is a bird list that exceeds 400 species.

EATING

Phetchaburi is especially famous for its desserts, many of which can claim a royal pedigree. The desserts get their sweetness from the fruit of the sugar palms that dot the countryside around here. Two of the most famous sweets on offer include *môr gaang* (an egg-and-coconut-milk custard) and *kà·nŏm đahn* (bright yellow steamed buns sweetened with sugar-palm kernels).

RABIENG RIMNAM   THAI, INTERNATIONAL $
Map p179 (☏032 425707; rabieng@gmail.com; 1 Th Chisa-In; mains 50-120B; ⊙8am-midnight; �) This riverside restaurant serves up a real bygone-days atmosphere from an 1897 wooden home perched over the river and usually some good food, too – try the sugar palm tree fruit curry with prawn. English-speaking owners Nid and Tom will often join you for a chat about Thailand and share their decades of travel advice.

There are a few fan-cooled shared-bath guest rooms here, too, but the owners are gradually easing into retirement and at this point the rooms are not what they once were – have a look before planning a stay.

CUCINA   THAI $
Map p179 (Th Suwanmunee; mains 50-390B; ⊙10.30am-9pm; 糝♨) Hidden down a little passageway in front of Wat Mahathat (p178), this small restaurant has a big menu ranging from green curry fried rice to chicken teriyaki to waffle sandwiches. There's a few fun fusion foods like the *đôm yam* fish salad and 'cucina pizza', which is pizza with instant noodles as the crust.

On the beverage side you can order a macchiato, matcha tea, smoothie or mojito.

TALAT TAA ROT TUA   MARKET $
Map p179 (Th Ratwithi; ⊙4-9pm) Big and bustling from the late afternoon, head to this covered night market for all the standard Thai favourites plus Phetchaburi's famous *kà·nŏm jeen tôrt man* (fresh rice noodles with curried deep-fried fishcake). There's lots of seating available.

JEK MENG   THAI $
Map p179 (JM Cuisine; www.jm-cuisine.com; 85 Th Ratwithi; mains 50-100B; ⊙7am-5pm) A cut above your average hole-in-the-wall joint, you can get some really good soups and stir-fries here. It's signed in English as JM Cuisine and has a second branch at the Phra Nakhon Khiri west entrance (p178).

🛏 SLEEPING

Once bereft of guesthouses, Phetchaburi's accommodation options have improved significantly in recent years. But there aren't many places, so it's worth booking ahead, especially in high season.

★2N GUESTHOUSE   GUESTHOUSE $
Map p179 (☏085 366 2451; two_nguesthouse@hotmail.com; 98/3 Mu 2, Tambol Bankoom; d & tw/q incl breakfast 580/850B; ❉❉糝) In a generally quiet neighbourhood 1.5km north of the city centre, the six rooms here are big and bright, and great for the price. The English-speaking owners do everything themselves and are really dedicated to pleasing their guests. They have free bicycles and can help with travel planning.

★WHITE MONKEY GUESTHOUSE   GUESTHOUSE $$
Map p179 (☏092 840 1633; whitemonkey.guesthouse@gmail.com; 78/7 Th Klongkrachang; tw/d/f 500-650/900/1500; ❉❉@糝) Excellent guesthouse with bright, spacious, spick-and-span rooms (the cheapest with shared bathrooms and no air-con) and a great location. There's views of Phra Nakhon Khiri Historical Park (p178) and Wat Mahathat Worawihan (p178) from the rooftop terrace and helpful English-speaking staff who can organise trips in the area.

SUN HOTEL   HOTEL $$
Map p179 (☏032 401000; www.sunhotelthailand.com; Th Rim Khao Wang; r incl breakfast 850-950B; ❉❉@糝) Sitting opposite the cable car entrance to Phra Nakhon Khiri

Historical Park (p178), the Sun Hotel has helpful staff and large, uninspiring rooms that are fine, but should be a little cheaper. There's a pleasant cafe downstairs and bikes are free.

While the location might sound good, it's actually pretty isolated from everything except the historical park.

Kanchanaburi

กาญจนบุรี

Explore

There are multiple ways to approach Kanchanaburi's sights. Many choose to charter a boat, which for 800B will take up to six people on a 1½-hour tour of the area's big sights. With a bit more time, bike (50B per day) and motorcycle (200B per day) are cheaper overall, and still viable ways to get around. And if you also have the time for this option, there are tourist trains that (slowly) whisk visitors over the Death Railway Bridge to the Hellfire Pass Memorial. In fact, it's worth staying overnight in Kanchanaburi, as there's good-value accommodation, and after the sun sets, the river boom-booms its way through the night with disco and karaoke barges packed with Bangkokians letting their hair down, especially at weekends

The Best

→ **Sight** Death Railway Bridge
→ **Place to Eat** Blue Rice (p185)
→ **Place to Drink** 10 O'Clock (p186)

Top Tip

Try as you might, you will find very few Thais who have ever heard of the River Kwai. The river over which the Death Railway trundled is pronounced like 'quack' without the '-ck'.

Getting There & Away

→ **Minivan** Frequent minivans depart from Bangkok's Northern & Northeastern (Mo Chit) and Southern terminals (100B to 120B, 2½ hours) during the day.
→ **Train** Trains depart from the Bangkok

Noi station in Thonburi at 7.45am and 1.35pm (100B, two hours).

Need to Know

→ **Location** 130km west of Bangkok
→ **Tourism Authority of Thailand** (TAT; Map p183; ☑034 511200; www.tourismthailand.org/Kanchanaburi; Th Saengchuto; ☺8.30am-4.30pm)

◉ SIGHTS

★**DEATH RAILWAY BRIDGE**   HISTORIC SITE
Map p183 (สะพานข้ามแม่น้ำแคว, Bridge Over the River Kwai; ☺24hr) **FREE** This 300m-long bridge is heavy with the history of the Thailand–Burma Railway, the construction of which cost thousands of imprisoned labourers their lives. Its centre was destroyed by Allied bombs in 1945; only the outer curved spans are original. You're free to roam over the bridge; stand in a safety point if a train appears. Food and souvenir hawkers surround the bridge, so the site can have a jarring, funfair-like atmosphere; come early or late to avoid the scrum.

The three old trains in the **park** near the station were used during WWII. Across the river, pop in to the **Chinese temple** on the right and view the bridge from its tranquil garden. Nothing remains of a second (wooden) bridge the Japanese built 100m downstream.

During the last weekend of November and first weekend of December, an informative **sound and light show** (Death Railway Bridge; ☺late Nov/early Dec) tells the history of the Death Railway.

★**THAILAND–BURMA RAILWAY CENTRE**   MUSEUM
Map p183 (ศูนย์รถไฟไทย-พม่า; ☑034 512721; www.tbrconline.com; 73 Th Jaokannun; adult/child 140/60B; ☺9am-5pm) This excellent museum balances statistics and historical context with personal accounts of the conditions endured by POWs and other imprisoned labourers forced to build the Thailand–Burma Railway. Kanchanaburi's role in WWII is thoroughly explained, but most of the museum traces the journey of railway workers from transport in cramped boxcars to disease-ridden labour camps in the jungle, as well as survivors' fates after the war. Allow time for the poignant video with testimony from both POWs and Japanese soldiers.

Kanchanaburi

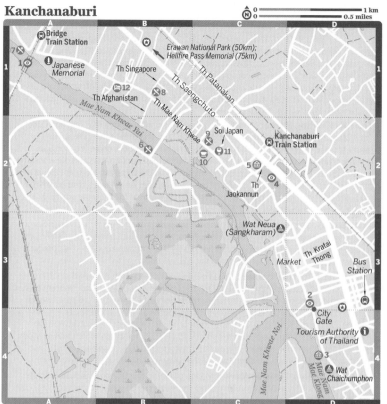

Erawan National Park (50km);
Hellfire Pass Memorial (75km)

Kanchanaburi

◎ Sights

1	Death Railway Bridge	A1
2	Heritage Walking Street	D3
3	JEATH War Museum	D4
4	Kanchanaburi War Cemetery	C2
5	Thailand–Burma Railway Centre	C2

⊗ Eating

6	Blue Rice	B2

7	Keeree Tara	A1
8	Library Cafe	B1
9	On's Thai-Issan	C2

⊜ Drinking & Nightlife

10	10 O'Clock	C2
11	Sugar Member	C2

⊜ Sleeping

12	Sabai@Kan	B1

Galleries upstairs display wartime artefacts, and there's a 3m-deep diorama showing how Hellfire Pass got its name. Allow at least an hour for your visit.

For in-depth wartime and railway history, the centre can organise half-day to week-long tours in and around Kanchanaburi; enquire via their website (under 'Railway Pilgrimages').

★ **KANCHANABURI WAR CEMETERY**   CEMETERY

Map p183 (สุสานทหารพันธมิตรดอนรัก, Allied War Cemetery; Th Saengchuto; ⊙24hr) Immaculately maintained by the Commonwealth War Graves Commission, this, the largest of Kanchanaburi's two war cemeteries, is right in town. Of the 6982 soldiers buried here, nearly half were British; the rest came

FLOATING MARKETS

Pictures of *đà·làht nám* (floating markets) jammed full of wooden canoes pregnant with colourful exotic fruits have defined the official tourist profile of Thailand for decades. The idyllic scenes are as iconic as the Grand Palace or the Reclining Buddha, but they are also almost completely contrived for, and dependent upon, foreign and domestic tourists – roads and motorcycles moved Thais' daily errands onto dry ground long ago. That said, if you can see them for what they are, a few of Thailand's floating markets are worth a visit.

Tha Kha Floating Market (ตลาดน้ำท่าคา; Tha Kha, Samut Songkhram; ⏲7am-noon, 2nd, 7th & 12th day of waxing & waning moons plus Sat & Sun) The most real-feeling floating market is also the most difficult to reach. A handful of vendors coalesce along an open rural *klorng* (canal; also spelt *Khlang*) lined with coconut palms and old wooden houses. Boat rides (20B per person, 45 minutes) can be arranged along the canal and there are lots of tasty snacks and fruits for sale. Contact Amphawa's **tourist office** (p176) to see when the next one is. To get here, take one of the morning *sŏrng·tăa·ou* (passenger pick-up trucks; 20B, 45 minutes) from Samut Songkhram's market area.

Amphawa Floating Market (p176) The Amphawa Floating Market, located in Samut Songkhram Province, convenes near Wat Amphawa. The emphasis is on edibles and tourist knick-knacks; because the market is only there on weekends and is popular with tourists from Bangkok, things can get pretty hectic.

Taling Chan Floating Market (p76) Located just outside Bangkok on the access road to Khlong Bangkok Noi, Taling Chan looks like any other fresh-food market busy with produce vendors from nearby farms. But the twist emerges at the canal where several floating docks serve as informal dining rooms and the kitchens are canoes tethered to the docks. Taling Chan is in Thonburi and can be reached via taxi from Wongwian Yai BTS station or via air-con bus 79 (16B, 25 minutes), which makes stops on Th Ratchadamnoen Klang. Long-tail boats from any large Bangkok pier can also be hired for a trip to Taling Chan and the nearby Khlong Chak Phra.

Damnoen Saduak Floating Market (ตลาดน้ำดำเนินสะดวก; Damnoen Saduak, Ratchaburi; ⏲7am-noon) This 100-year-old floating market – the country's most famous – is now essentially a floating souvenir stand filled with package tourists. This in itself can be a fascinating insight into Thai culture, as the vast majority of tourists here are Thais and watching the approach to this cultural 'theme park' is instructive. But beyond the market, the residential canals are quite peaceful and can be explored by hiring a boat (100B per person) for a longer duration. Trips stop at small family businesses, including a Thai candy maker, a pomelo farm and a knife crafter. Minivans from the Southern Bus Terminal in Thonburi can link you with Damnoen Saduak (80B, two hours, frequent from 6am to 9pm).

Don Wai Market (ตลาดดอนหวาย; Don Wai, Nakhon Pathom; ⏲6am-6pm) Not technically a swimmer, this market claims a river bank location in Nakhon Pathom Province, having originally started out in the early 20th century as a floating market for pomelo and jackfruit growers and traders. As with many tourist attractions geared towards Thais, the main draw is food, including fruit, traditional sweets and *bèt pah·lóh* (five-spice stewed duck), which can be consumed aboard large boats that cruise Mae Nam Nakhorn Chaisi (60B, one hour). The easiest way to reach Don Wai Market is to take a minibus (45B, 35 minutes) from beside **Central Pinklao** (Th Somdet Phra Pin Klao; ⏲10am-10pm; [S]Talat Phlu exit 3 & taxi or Victory Monument exit 3 & taxi) in Thonburi.

mainly from Australia and the Netherlands. As you stand at the cemetery entrance, the entire right-hand side contains British victims, the front-left area contains Australian graves, the rear left honours Dutch and unknown soldiers, and those who were cremated lie at the furthest spot to the left.

All remains of American POWs were returned to the USA. If you're looking for the resting place of a loved one, a register is kept at the entrance.

HERITAGE WALKING STREET AREA

Map p183 (ถนนปากแพรก; Th Pakprak) A stroll along this enchanting street offers a glimpse of a bygone Kanchanaburi. Many buildings date to the interwar period. Though worn by the passage of time, their Sino-Portuguese, Thai, Vietnamese and Chinese styles have been preserved; yellow signs reveal their history, architecture and current owners. The walk begins at the restored **City Gate** (ประตู เมือง; Map p183; Th Lak Meuang).

Highlights include the elegant parapets of **Sirichumsang Shophouse** (1932), the gold-flecked former jewellery shop **Chansiri House** (1927) and the Chinese-style **Kanchanaburi Hotel** (1937), which retains its original coloured glass.

JEATH WAR MUSEUM MUSEUM

Map p183 (พิพิธภัณฑ์สงคราม; cnr Th Wisuttharangsi & Th Pak Phraek; 50B; ⊗8.30am-4.30pm) This small, open-air museum displays correspondence and artwork from former POWs involved in the building of the Death Railway. Their harsh living conditions are evident in the many photos on display alongside personal effects and war relics, including an unexploded Allied bomb dropped to destroy the bridge. One of the three galleries is built from bamboo in the style of the shelters (called *attap*) the POWs lived in; another has a 10-minute video presentation.

◉ Around Kanchanaburi

★ ERAWAN NATIONAL PARK NATIONAL PARK

(อุทยานแห่งชาติเอราวัณ; ☎034 574222; adult/ child 300/200B, car/motorbike 30/20B; ⊗8am-4.30pm; P) Splashing in cerulean pools under **Erawan Falls** is the highlight of this 550-sq-km park. Seven tiers of waterfall tumble through the forest, and bathing beneath these crystalline cascades is equally popular with locals and visitors. Reaching the first three tiers is easy; beyond here, walking shoes and some endurance are needed to complete the steep 2km hike (it's worth it to avoid the crowds in the first two pools). There are hourly buses from Kanchanaburi (50B, 1½ hours).

★ HELLFIRE PASS MEMORIAL MUSEUM

(พิพิธภัณฑ์ช่องเขาขาด; ☎034 919605; Hwy 323; ⊗museum 9am-4pm, grounds 7.30am-6pm; P) **FREE** A poignant museum and memorial trail pay tribute to those who died building the Thailand–Burma Railway in WWII. Begin at the museum and ask for the free audio guide, which provides historical detail and fascinating first-person accounts from survivors. Then descend behind the museum to a trail following the original rail bed. The infamous cutting known as Hellfire Pass was the largest along the railway's length and the most deadly for the labourers forced to construct it.

✕ EATING & DRINKING

Kanchanaburi is not a culinary destination, and guesthouse-style and tourist-oriented restaurants serving bland Thai standards seem to dominate. It is, however, something of a nightlife town, and bars extend nearly the entire length of Th Mae Nam Khwae. Of these, tacky hostess bars dominate the southern end, backpacker-friendly pubs define the middle, and open-air bar-restaurants for the Thai crowd can be found at the street's northern end.

★ BLUE RICE THAI $

Map p183 (www.applenoikanchanaburi.com; 153/4 Mu 4, Ban Tamakahm; mains from 135B; ⊗noon-2pm & 6-10pm; P🔊🖉) Masterful spice blends, a creative menu and peaceful river views make this one of the most irresistible restaurants in Kanchanaburi. The signature massaman curry is perfectly balanced, and the menu is packed with reinvented Thai classics such as *yam sôm oh* (pomelo salad) and chicken-coconut soup with banana plant. The eponymous rice is stained with pea-flower petals, if you're wondering.

★ ON'S THAI-ISSAN VEGETARIAN $

Map p183 (☎087 364 2264; www.onsthaiissan.com; Th Mae Nam Khwae; mains from 70B; ⊗noon-10pm; ❄🖉) At this casual restaurant, vegetarian and vegan recipes borrow Isan flavours and reinvent classic Thai dishes from entirely plant-based ingredients, with other healthy flourishes such as brown rice. Banana flower salad, ginger tofu and 'morning glory' (pan-seared greens) are cooked before your eyes on fryers outside and served in generous portions.

Friendly On will even teach you how to make your favourite dishes. A two-hour, three-dish **cookery course** costs 600B (book a few days ahead).

TIGER SANCTUARY OR TOURIST TRAP?

The Tiger Temple near Kanchanaburi was arguably Thailand's most controversial attraction. It started in 1999 as a rescue shelter for orphaned tiger cubs, but it later became a very profitable tourist draw, with a breeding program that increased the tiger population to almost 150.

Despite persistent rumours of breaking the law, providing substandard care for tigers, not following even the most basic conservation protocol and accusations of selling tigers to overseas buyers as pets and for their body parts, the Tiger Temple continued to attract throngs of tourists. (It's worth noting that many travel insurance companies do not cover visits to this kind of attraction.)

In June 2016, the Thailand Wildlife Conservation Office began to relocate the temple's 137 tigers and made the grisly discovery of 40 frozen cubs. Dozens more animal remains were found in a subsequent raid, adding weight to long-standing rumours of illegal trading of animal body parts; 22 people were subsequently charged with animal trafficking offences. In early 2017, plans to open a new tiger attraction – ostensibly a zoo – under the name Golden Tiger (Thailand) Co Ltd were met with concern, with animal rights activists fearing a repeat of the Tiger Temple travesty.

★ **KEEREE TARA** THAI $$
Map p183 (☎034 513855; www.facebook.com/keereeTara; 431/1 Th Mae Nam Khwae; mains 150-400B; ☉11am-11pm) This refined riverside eatery is ever so slightly upriver from the melee around the bridge. It serves upmarket Thai dishes from duck stuffed with lily to succulent catfish heaped with red curry. Still hungry? Choose from Thai desserts including *đa·go peu·ak* (taro pearls in coconut milk) and French-inspired gateaux and white chocolate mousse.

LIBRARY CAFE DESSERTS $$
Map p183 (☎034 514300; Soi Singapore, Th Mae Nam Khwae; sweets from 170B; ☉9am-10.30pm; ❋🛜) It's eye-wateringly expensive if you compare it to Kanchanaburi's markets, but a platter of *bingsu* (a Korean-style shaved ice dessert) served in Library Cafe's sultry surrounds is a guilty pleasure. The *bingsu* arrives big, adorned with mango, chocolate brownies, red beans and all manner of treats.

★ **10 O'CLOCK** CAFE
Map p183 (off Th Mae Nam Khwae; ☉10am-10pm; 🛜) Flanked by a fountain that wouldn't look out of place in a Viennese palace, 10 O'Clock (guess the opening hours) has outdoor tables under shady trees. Within the clock-bedecked cafe, passionfruit frappés and good coffee are served to the clickety-clack of patrons using the free wi-fi.

The cafe also serves pan-Asian meals including smoked fish and teriyaki pork burgers in rice buns (mains 90B to 175B).

SUGAR MEMBER BAR
Map p183 (Th Mae Nam Khwae; ☉6pm-late) 'Drink! Drunk! Dance!' urges the sign above Sugar Member, and punters happily comply. This is a classic Kanchanaburi backpacker bar, with a vague reggae theme and friendly staff who will sip whisky buckets with you all night.

🛏 SLEEPING

Travellers tend to navigate towards a 1km stretch of Th Mae Nam Khwae, where budget guesthouses offer riverfront views on raft houses. In contrast, there are several new boutique midrange spots on this strip and just out of town.

★ **BAN SABAI SABAI** GUESTHOUSE $$
(☎089 040 5268; www.bansabaisabai.com; 102/3 Mu 4, Nong Bua; d 400-800B, f from 1650B; 🅿❋🛜) Out in the countryside, 7km or so west of town along Hwy 323, this friendly place lives up to its name: 'Relaxation House'. Tile-floored rooms arranged around the florid garden are simple but very well maintained, and hosts can arrange anything from cooking classes to onward transport.

You can ask ahead for a free pick-up from town, but it's best to have your own wheels if staying here for a few days.

★ **SABAI@KAN** RESORT $$
Map p183 (☎034 521559; www.sabaiatkan.com; 317/4 Th Mae Nam Khwae; d incl breakfast 1400-1700B, tr 2100B; 🅿❋🛜🏊) Hospitable and

impeccably managed, this boutique resort has modern cream-and-mahogany rooms arranged around a swimming pool. Rooms have huge windows overlooking the pretty poolside garden, and it has the feel of a haven despite being close to Kanchanaburi's main tourist drag.

★ **ORIENTAL KWAI RESORT**   RESORT **$$$**
(☎616 730670; www.orientalkwai.com; 194/5 Mu 1, Tambon Lat Ya; cottages incl breakfast 2800-4900B; ❀ 🐕 🏊) This Thai-Dutch-run spot has an exclusive feel. Set in a semi-wild garden, all four cottages are sumptuously decorated with Thai sculpture and fabrics and brooding oxblood walls. Amenities include fridges and flat-screen TVs. Two are designed for families and sleep up to six people. It's 13km northwest of town, almost 2km off the road to Erawan National Park (p185).

Khao Yai   เขาใหญ่

Explore

Khao Yai is only about 200km from Bangkok, but the area is best approached as an overnight trip. There are two strategies for doing this, depending on your interests. If you've come for the nature, the logical option is to sleep at the park (or at a guesthouse that provides tours to the park), which can be reached via public transport. If you're looking for a more leisurely weekend getaway to take in the restaurants, resorts, wineries and other attractions that surround the actual park, you'll need to hire a car.

The Best
➡ **Sight** Khao Yai National Park
➡ **Place to Eat** Khrua Khao Yai (p188)
➡ **Place to Stay** Hotel Des Artists (p188)

Top Tip
The best time to visit the park is in the dry season (December to June), but during the rainy season river rafting and waterfall-spotting will be more dramatic.

Getting There & Away
➡ **Bus** First-class buses link Bangkok and Pak Chong (133B, three hours). From Pak Chong, *sŏrng·tǎa·ou* (passenger pick-up trucks) travel the 30km to the park's northern gate every 30 minutes from 6am to 5pm (40B, one hour).

➡ **Minivan** Frequent minivans depart from Bangkok's Northern & Northeastern (Mo Chit) Terminal to Pak Chong (160B, three hours, every 30 minutes).

➡ **Train** Ten daily trains link Bangkok and Pak Chong (23B to 363B, two to three hours).

➡ **Hire Car** For more freedom, hire a car and drive.

Need to Know
➡ **Location** 196km northeast of Bangkok
➡ **Visitor Centre** (☎086 092 6529; Khao Yai National Park; ☺6am-9pm, staffed from 8am)

◉ SIGHTS

★ **KHAO YAI**
NATIONAL PARK   NATIONAL PARK
(อุทยานแห่งชาติเขาใหญ่; ☎086 092 6529; 400B, car/motorcycle 50/30B; ☺entrance 6am-6pm) Cool and lush, Khao Yai National Park is an easy escape into the primordial jungle. The 2168-sq-km park, part of a Unesco World Heritage site, spans five forest types teeming with wildlife. There are good hiking trails and some fantastic waterfalls including **Nam Tok Haew Suwat** (น้ำตกเหวสุวัด; ☺7am-5pm) and **Nam Tok Haew Narok** (น้ำตกเหวนรก; ☺7am-5pm) that put on thundering shows in the rainy season.

KHAO YAI ART MUSEUM   GALLERY
(เขาใหญ่ อาร์ต มิวเซียม; ☎044 756060; www.khaoyaiartmuseum.com; ☺10am-5.30pm) `FREE` This excellent private gallery has three rooms of modern art from some of Thailand's top artists, including Anupong Chantorn and Lampu Kansanoh, and a sculpture garden. It's 3km east of Th Thanarat turn at the bus shelter near Km 16 and follow the signs.

✗ EATING

In recent years, the area surrounding Khao Yai National Park has become a minor culinary destination, with restaurants featuring cuisines ranging from upmarket Italian to Muslim-Thai. The towns that surround

THAILAND'S NAPA VALLEY

Thailand is the pioneer of 'New Latitude Wines' and, with over a dozen wineries in the region, the Khao Yai area is now the epicentre of this increasingly respected industry. Two of the leaders – **PB Valley,** (พีบีวัลเล่ย์ เขาใหญ่ไวน์เนอรี่; ☎081 733 8783; www.khaoyaiwinery.com; tastings from 150B, tours 300B; ⏲tours 9am, 10.30am, noon, 1.30pm & 3.30pm) which corked its first bottle in 1998, and **GranMonte** (กราน-มอนเต้; ☎044 009543; www.granmonte.com; tastings/tours250/300B; ⏲tours 10am, 11.30am, 1.30pm, 3pm & 4.30pm Sat, Sun & holidays, 10.30am, 11.30am, 1.30pm & 3pm weekdays), which got into the game three years later and is under the watch of Thailand's first female oenologist – lie along Muak Lek-Khao Yai road (exit Hwy 2 at Km 144), the direct route from Bangkok to the national park. Both are scenically set and offer tours (book in advance), tastings, gourmet gift shops, luxury lodging and classy restaurants for lunch and dinner. They're 22.5km and 16km respectively from the national park gate.

the park have lively night markets; but if you don't have a car, you'll find restaurants within the park.

ROMA SAUSAGE THAI, INTERNATIONAL **$$**

(Km 18, Th Thanarat; mains 80-850B; ⏲10.30am-9.30pm Sun-Tue & Thur, 10.30am-11pm Fri-Sat; P 📶) This casual alfresco spot on one of the busiest stretches of Th Thanarat manages to succeed at both Thai (yellow curry with mackerel and crispy tofu *lâhp*) and European (smoked chicken wings, duck confit and ultra-thin pizzas) food.

YAEK KUT KHA NIGHT MARKET THAI

(แยกกุดคล้า; Km 20, Th Thanarat; ⏲3.30-7.30pm) A bustling night market serving take-home food to the local community. A few street carts in this area are open during the morning hours, too.

KHRUA KHAO YAI THAI **$$**

(Km 13.5, Th Thanarat; mains 60-430B; ⏲9am-8pm, to 9pm if busy; P 📶 🖉) This open-air hut is hugely popular with visiting Bangkokians because of both the quality of the food and the emphasis on healthy eating, with choices such as mushroom *đôm yam* and stir-fried sunflower sprouts. The English-language menu is limited, so if you don't see what you want it's worth asking if it's available.

SLEEPING

Th Thanarat, the road that links Pak Chong and the park, is home to several midrange to upmarket resorts targeted at Thai tourists.

SAN KHAO YAI GUESTHOUSE GUESTHOUSE **$$**

(☎098 210 5098; www.sankhaoyaitour.com; Th Thanarat; bungalows 800B; P ❄ 📶) These colourful cottages just 100m from the park entrance are basic but very clean and a step up from most other budget lodging in the area. And there's no better place to be if you want to stay outside the park but get an early start on your wildlife-watching. It also hires motorcycles, arranges tours and serves food.

★HOTEL DES ARTISTS HOTEL **$$$**

(☎044 297444; hoteldesartists@gmail.com; Th Thanarat, Km 22; incl breakfast r/villa 4600/7500B; P ❄ @ 📶) This tasteful hotel goes for French-colonial chic rather than a nature theme, though with its mountain views out the back you won't forget where you are. The rooms are gorgeous, though small, and the villas sit right by the large swimming pool.

★KHAO YAI NATIONAL PARK – ZONE 2 BUNGALOW **$$$**

(Thio That; ☎086 092 6529; http://nps.dnp.go.th/reservation.php; Khao Yai National Park; bungalows 2000-2400B; P) The smallest zone, Thio That is a pleasant place on a shady hillside 2.5km from the visitor centre. There are five two-bedroom, two-bathroom bungalows with beds for either six or eight people. There's no restaurant. It's along a seldom-travelled dead-end road, so don't stay here if you don't have your own vehicle.

Sleeping

If your idea of the typical Bangkok hotel was influenced by The Hangover Part II, you'll be relieved to learn that the city is home to a variety of modern hostels, guesthouses and hotels. To further improve matters, much of Bangkok's accommodation offers excellent value and competition is so intense that fat discounts are almost always available.

Hostels

Those counting every baht can get a dorm bed (or a closet-like room) with a shared bathroom for as little as 250B. The latest trend is slick 'flashpacker' hostels that blur the line between budget and midrange. A bed at these will cost between around 400B and 800B.

Guesthouses

In Bangkok, this designation usually refers to any sort of budget accommodation rather than a room in a family home, although we use it to describe the latter. Guesthouses and similar budget hotels are generally found in somewhat inconveniently located corners of old Bangkok (Banglamphu, Chinatown and Thewet), which means that the money you're saving in rent will probably go on taxi fares. Rates begin at about 500B.

Hotels

The widest part of the accommodation spectrum, the term 'hotel' can mean a variety of things. Bangkok's midrange hotels often have all the appearance of a Western-style hotel, but without the predictability. If you're on a lower-midrange budget, and don't care much about aesthetics, some very acceptable rooms can be had for between 1200B and 2000B. If your budget is higher, it really pays to book ahead, as online discounts here can be substantial. You'll find several midrange hotels along lower Th Sukhumvit, near Siam Sq and in Banglamphu.

Luxury, Business & Boutique Hotels

Bangkok is home to a huge number of top-end hotels ranging from boutique (small but cosy) to luxury (big and brash). Most hotels of this type are located on Th Sukhumvit and Th Silom, or along Mae Nam Chao Phraya. Rooms generally start between 5000B and 9000B before hefty online discounts.

Amenities

BUDGET

The cheapest hostels and guesthouses often share bathrooms and may not even supply a towel. Some remain fan-cooled or, in the case of dorms, will only run the air-con between certain hours. Wi-fi, if available, is typically free at budget places. If on offer, breakfast at most Bangkok hostels and budget hotels is little more than instant coffee and toast.

MIDRANGE

Increasingly, midrange has come to mean a private room with air-con, a fridge, hot water, TV and free wi-fi. It's not uncommon for a room to boast all of these but lack a view or even windows. Breakfast can range from 'buffets' based around toast and oily fried eggs to healthier meals with yoghurt or tropical fruit.

TOP END

Top-end hotels in Bangkok supply all the facilities you'd expect at this level. The more thoughtful places have amenities such as en suite, computers and free wi-fi; in other places, it's not uncommon to have to pay a premium for the last of these. In sweaty Bangkok, pools are almost standard, not to mention fitness and business centres, restaurants and bars. Breakfast is often buffet-style.

NEED TO KNOW

Price Ranges

Accommodation is broken down into three categories. We've listed high-season walk-in rates, excluding the 'plus-plus' that most top-end places charge, which in Thailand is made up of 10% service and 7% government tax.

$	less than 1000B
$$	1000B to 4000B
$$$	more than 4000B

Websites

➡ **Agoda** (www.agoda.com/city/bangkok-th.html) Asia-based hotel booking site that offers a lowest-price guarantee.

➡ **Travelfish** (www.travelfish.org/country/thailand) Independent reviews with lots of reader feedback.

➡ **Lonely Planet** (www.lonelyplanet.com/thailand/bangkok/hotels) Find reviews and make bookings.

Lonely Planet's Top Choices

AriyasomVilla (p115) Sumptuous refurbished villa with a classy B&B vibe.

Phra-Nakorn Norn-Len (p108) A unique, fun and thoughtful hotel in a refreshingly untouristed hood.

Siam Heritage (p112) Homey touches and warm service make this the closest you may come to sleeping in a Thai home.

Loy La Long (p111) Rustic, retro, charming boutique on the river.

Lamphu Treehouse (p105) Handsome, spotless midranger.

Sukhothai Hotel (p113) A near-perfect convergence of class, service and design.

Best by Budget

$

Lub*d (p106) Youthful-feeling hostel with two convenient locations in central Bangkok.

Chern (p106) Surprisingly sophisticated dorms and rooms for the price.

S-Box (p115) Contemporary-feeling budget accommodation.

$$

Smile Society (p112) A homey haven in the middle of Bangkok's financial district.

Feung Nakorn Balcony (p109) Former school turned cute midranger.

Tints of Blue (p114) Heavy on the charm, easy on the wallet.

$$$

Metropolitan by COMO (p113) Urban sophistication and excellent dining.

Mandarin Oriental (p113) Bangkok's oldest hotel remains one of its best.

Peninsula Hotel (p113) Sky-high standards of service.

Best Affordable Luxury

Hansar (p110) Spacious, good-value, apartment-like rooms.

S31 (p114) Conveniently located, contemporary accommodation at a fair price.

Trinity Silom Hotel (p112) Top-end style and service for rates that are just above midrange.

Best Artsy Stays

Beat Hotel (p114) One-of-a-kind, wall-sized murals and bright colours shape the vibe here.

Mystic Place (p116) No two rooms are the same at this eccentric hotel.

Hotel Indigo (p110) Local history and culture are reinterpreted as design at this hotel.

Shanghai Mansion (p109) Let this hotel take you back to 1930s-era China.

Best Contemporary Cool

W Bangkok (p113) Almost too cool for school.

Lit Bangkok Hotel & Residence (p110) With an emphasis on edgy architecture.

S31 (p114) Clean urban living.

Okura Prestige (p110) Japanese minimalism.

Best Romantics

Old Capital Bike Inn (p107) Refurbished shophouse with a secluded, seductive vibe.

Eugenia (p115) Sumptuous, retro-themed accommodation.

Bhuthorn (p111) A handful of retro-themed rooms in an ancient shophouse.

Praya Palazzo (p107) A former palace on Mae Nam Chao Phraya.

Where to Stay

Neighbourhood	For	Against
Ko Ratanakosin & Thonburi	Bangkok's most famous sights at your door; river views; (relatively) fresh air; old-school Bangkok feel.	Difficult to reach; few budget options; touts.
Banglamphu	Close to main sights; proximity to classic Bangkok hood; numerous good-value budget beds; melting-pot feel; virtually interminable dining options; one of the city's best nightlife areas.	Getting to and from the area can be troublesome; Th Khao San can be noisy; budget places can have low standards; relentless touts.
Thewet & Dusit	Good budget options; riverside village feel; fresh air; close to a handful of visit-worthy sights.	Few midrange and upscale options; not very convenient access to rest of Bangkok; relatively few dining and drinking options; comatose at night.
Chinatown	Some interesting budget and midrange options; off the beaten track; easy access to worthwhile sights and some of the city's best food; close to Bangkok's main train station.	Noisy; polluted; hectic.
Siam Square, Pratunam, Phloen Chit & Ratchathewi	Wide spread of accommodation alternatives; megaconvenient access to shopping; steps away from BTS (Skytrain).	Touts; unpristine environment; relative lack of dining and entertainment options in immediate area; lacks character.
Riverside, Silom & Lumphini	Some of the city's best upscale accommodation; river boats and river views; superconvenient access to BTS and MRT (Metro); lots of dining and nightlife options; gay-friendly.	Can be noisy and polluted; budget options can be pretty dire; hyperurban feel away from the river.
Sukhumvit	Some of the city's most sophisticated hotels; lots of midrange options; easy access to BTS and MRT; international dining; easy access to some of the city's best bars; home to several reputable spas and massage parlours.	Annoying street vendors and sexpat vibe; noisy; hypertouristy.
Northern Bangkok	Less hectic setting; good value; convenient airport access.	Transport can be inconvenient; lack of drinking and entertainment options.

Ko Ratanakosin & Thonburi

ROYAL THA TIEN VILLAGE · HOTEL $$

Map p265 (095 151 5545; www.facebook.com/theroyalthatienvillage; 392/29 Soi Phen Phat; r 1200B; ✳@☎; ⛴Tien Pier) These 12 rooms spread over two converted shophouses are relatively unassuming, but TV, fridge, air-con, lots of space and shiny wood floors, not to mention a cosy homestay atmosphere, edge this place into the recommendable category. It's popular, so be sure to book ahead.

★ INN A DAY · HOTEL $$$

Map p265 (02 221 0577; www.innaday.com; 57-61 Th Maha Rat; incl breakfast r 3500-4200B, ste 7500-9000B; ✳@☎; ⛴Tien Pier) Inn a Day wows with its hyper-cool retro/industrial theme (the hotel is in a former sugar factory) and its location (it towers over the river and Wat Arun). The 11 rooms aren't huge, but they include unique touches such as clear neon shower stalls, while the top-floor suites have two levels and huge claw-foot tubs.

CHAKRABONGSE VILLAS · HOTEL $$$

Map p265 (02 622 1900; www.chakrabongsevillas.com; 396/1 Th Maha Rat; incl breakfast r 5000B, ste 10,000-25,000B; ✳@☎☀; ⛴Tien Pier) This almost fairy-tale-like compound incorporates three sumptuous but cramped rooms and four larger suites and villas, some with great river views, all surrounding a still-functioning royal palace dating back to 1908. There's a pool, jungle-like gardens and an elevated deck for romantic riverside dining. No walk-ins.

SALA RATANAKOSIN · HOTEL $$$

Map p265 (02 622 1388; www.salaresorts.com/rattanakosin; Soi Tha Tian; incl breakfast r 3230-5270B, ste 8590B; ✳@☎; ⛴Tien Pier) Sala boasts a sleek, modernist feel – a somewhat jarring contrast with the former warehouse it's located in. The 15 rooms are decked out in black and white, and boast open-plan bathrooms and big windows looking out on the river and Wat Arun. They can't be described as vast, but will satisfy the fashion-conscious.

AURUM: THE RIVER PLACE · HOTEL $$$

Map p265 (02 622 2248; www.aurum-bangkok.com; 394/27-29 Soi Pansuk; r incl breakfast 3700-4600B; ✳@☎; ⛴Tien Pier) The 12 rooms here don't necessarily reflect the grand European exterior of this refurbished shophouse. Nonetheless they're comfortable, modern and well appointed, and most offer fleeting views of Mae Nam Chao Phraya.

Banglamphu

SUNETA HOSTEL KHAOSAN · HOSTEL $

Map p268 (02 629 0150; www.sunetahostel.com; 209-211 Th Kraisi; incl breakfast dm 470-570B, r 1180B; ✳@☎; ⛴Phra Athit/Banglamphu Pier) A pleasant, low-key atmosphere, a unique, retro-themed design (some of the dorm rooms resemble sleeping-car carriages), a location just off the main drag and friendly service are what make Suneta stand out.

KHAOSAN IMMJAI · HOSTEL $

Map p268 (02 629 3088; www.khaosanimmjai.com; 240 Soi 1, Th Samsen; dm incl breakfast 300-350B; ✳@☎; ⛴Phra Athit/Banglamphu Pier) There's nothing flashy or particularly exceptional about this hostel. But a homey feel and positive feedback edge it into the recommendable column. Dorms, which range from four to 14 beds, are clean, done out in pastel tones and have ample natural light. There's access to lots of convenient amenities (washing machines, computers etc), although none of these are free.

VIVIT HOSTEL · HOSTEL $

Map p268 (02 224 5888; www.vivithostel.com; 510 Th Tanao; dm/r incl breakfast 475/965B; ✳☎; ⛴klorng boat to Phanfa Leelard Pier) Flower-patterned curtains, framed portraits of flowers and grandfather clocks provide this hostel with an overwhelmingly mature feel, despite it having opened in 2017. Nonetheless the dorms represent excellent – if slightly bland – value.

FORTVILLE GUESTHOUSE · HOTEL $

Map p268 (02 282 3932; www.fortvilleguesthouse.com; 9 Th Phra Sumen; r 820-1190B; ✳@☎; ⛴Phra Athit/Banglamphu Pier) With an exterior that combines elements of a modern church and/or castle, and an interior that relies on mirrors and industrial themes, the design concept of this hotel is tough to pin down. The rooms themselves are stylishly minimalist, and the more expensive ones include perks such as a fridge and balcony.

BANGKOK'S BEST HOSTELS

If you're on a shoestring budget, Bangkok has heaps of options for you, ranging from high-tech, pod-like dorm beds in a brand-new hostel to cosy bunk beds in a refurbished Chinatown shophouse. (And if you decide that you need a bit more privacy, nearly all of Bangkok's hostels also offer private rooms.) And best of all, at the places listed here, we found the bathrooms to be clean and convenient – sharing will hardly feel like a compromise. Some of our picks:

Lub*d (Map p274; ☑02 612 4999; www.siamsquare.lubd.com; Rama I; dm 550B, r 1900-2500B; ❄ @ 🛜; ⓢNational Stadium exit 1) The title is a play on the Thai *làp dee,* meaning 'sleep well', but the fun atmosphere at this modern-feeling hostel might make you want to stay up all night. Diversions include an inviting communal area stocked with games and a bar, and thoughtful facilities range from washing machines to a theatre room.

Chern (Map p268; ☑02 621 1133; www.chernbangkok.com; 17 Soi Ratchasak; dm 400B, r 1400-1900B; ❄ @ 🛜; 🚤klorng boat to Phanfa Leelard Pier) The vast, open spaces and white, overexposed tones of this hostel converge in an almost afterlife-like feel.

Niras Bangkoc (Map p268; ☑02 221 4442; www.nirasbankoc.com; 204-206 Th Mahachai; dm 450-500B, r 1300-1500B; ❄🛜; 🚤klorng boat to Phanfa Leelard Pier) Niras takes advantage of its location in an antique shophouse to arrive at a charmingly old-school feel. Both the four- and six-bed dorms here feature dark woods and vintage furniture, with access to friendly staff, a cosy ground-floor cafe and a location in an atmospheric corner of the city.

Silom Art Hostel (Map p278; ☑02 635 8070; www.silomarthostel.com; 198/19-22 Soi 14, Th Silom; dm 300-350B, r 1300-1500B; ❄ @ 🛜; ⓢChong Nonsi exit 3) Quirky, artsy, bright and fun, Silom Art Hostel combines recycled materials, unconventional furnishings and colourful wall paintings to culminate in a hostel that's quite unlike anywhere else in town. It's not all about style though: beds are functional and comfortable, with lots of appealing communal areas.

Loftel 22 (Map p272; www.loftel22bangkok.com; 952 Soi 22, Th Charoen Krung; dm 250-300B, r with shared bathroom 850-1300B; ❄ @ 🛜; 🚤Marine Department Pier, ⓜHua Lamphong exit 1) Stylish, inviting dorms have been coaxed out of these two adjoining shophouses. Friendly service and a location in one of Chinatown's most atmospheric corners round out the package.

NapPark Hostel (Map p268; ☑02 282 2324; www.nappark.com; 5 Th Tani; dm 440-600B; ❄ @ 🛜; 🚤Phra Athit/Banglamphu Pier) This popular hostel features dorm rooms of various sizes, the smallest and most expensive of which boasts six pod-like beds outfitted with powerpoints, mini-TV, reading lamp and wi-fi.

Chao Hostel (Map p274; ☑02 217 3083; www.chaohostel.com; 8th fl, 865 Rama I; incl breakfast dm 550B, r 1600-1800B; ❄ @ 🛜; ⓢNational Stadium exit 1) Blending modern minimalist and Thai design elements, not to mention tonnes of open space, the new Chao is one of the most sophisticated hostels we've encountered in Bangkok.

Pause Hostel (Map p282; ☑02 108 8855; www.onedaybkk.com; Oneday, 51 Soi 26, Th Sukhumvit; incl breakfast dm 450-600B, r 1300-1500B; ❄ @ 🛜; ⓢPhrom Phong exit 4) Attached to a cafe/coworking space is this modern, open-feeling hostel. Dorms span four to eight beds and are united by a handsome industrial-design theme and inviting, sun-soaked communal areas.

S1 Hostel (p198) A huge new hostel with dorm beds decked out in a simple yet attractive primary-colour scheme. A host of facilities (laundry, kitchen, rooftop garden) and a convenient location within walking distance of the MRT make it great value.

Bed Station Hostel (Map p271; ☑02 019 5477; www.bedstationhostel.com; 486/149-150 Soi 16, Th Phetchaburi; incl breakfast dm 500-650B, r 1350-1550B; ❄ @ 🛜; ⓢRatchathewi exit 3) A handsome industrial-chic theme unites the dorms at this modern-feeling hostel. They range from four to eight beds and include access to tidy toilet facilities and a laundry room.

★ LAMPHU TREEHOUSE
HOTEL $$

Map p268 (☑02 282 0991; www.lamphutreehotel.
com; 155 Wanchat Bridge, off Th Prachathipatai;
incl breakfast r 1650-2500B; ste 3500-4500B;
❋@♠☒; ☻klorng boat to Phanfa Leelard Pier)
Despite the name, this attractive midranger
has its feet firmly on land, and as such rep-
resents brilliant value. The wood-panelled
rooms are inviting and well maintained,
and the rooftop sun lounge, pool, internet
cafe, restaurant and quiet canalside location
ensure that you may never feel the need to
leave. An annexe a few blocks away increases
the odds of snagging an elusive reservation.

SOURIRE
HOTEL $$

Map p268 (☑02 280 2180; www.sourirebangkok.
com; Soi Chao Phraya Si Phiphat; r incl breakfast
1500-3500B; ❋@♠; ☻klorng boat to Phanfa
Leelard Pier) More home than hotel, the 38
rooms here exude a calming, matronly vibe.
Soft lighting, comfortable and sturdy wood
furniture, and the friendly, aged owners
complete the package. To reach the hotel,
follow Soi Chao Phraya Si Phiphat to the
end and knock on the tall brown wooden
door immediately on your left.

BAAN DINSO
HOSTEL $$

Map p268 (☑02 621 2808; www.baandinso.com;
113 Trok Sin; r incl breakfast 900-2500B; ❋@♠;
☻klorng boat to Phanfa Leelard Pier) This an-
tique wooden villa may not represent the
best value in Bangkok, but for accommoda-
tion with a nostalgic feel and palpable sense
of place, it's almost impossible to beat. Of the
10 small yet spotless rooms, only five have
en suite bathrooms, while all have access to
functional and inviting communal areas.

THE WAREHOUSE
HOTEL $$

Map p268 (☑02 622 2935; www.thewarehouse
bangkok.com; 120 Th Bunsiri; r incl breakfast
2280-2580B; ❋@♠; ☻klorng boat to Phanfa
Leelard Pier) Wooden pallets as furniture, yel-
low-and-black wall art, and exposed fittings
and other industrial elements contribute to
the factory theme here. Against all odds, the
Warehouse pulls it off, and what you get are
36 rooms that are fun, functional and relatively spacious, if not stupendous value.

VILLA PHRA SUMEN
HOTEL $$

Map p268 (☑080 085 0085; www.villaphra
sumen.com; 457 Th Phra Sumen; r incl breakfast
2500-3700B; ❋@♠; ☻klorng boat to Phanfa
Leelard Pier) Surrounding a garden and edg-
ing the canal, Villa Phra Sumen boasts a se-

cluded, secret feel. Gain access to the com-
pound and inside you'll find 24 somewhat
tight (and likewise overpriced) rooms, all of
which come equipped with balconies and
contemporary amenities, and are looked
after by service-minded staff.

BAN THUNGDAENG
GUESTHOUSE $$

Map p268 (☑02 622 3225; 117 Trok Sin; r 1300B;
❋♠; ☻klorng boat to Phanfa Leelard Pier) Eight
rooms in a whitewashed wooden house
tucked away in a classic Bangkok alleyway.
Rooms aren't huge, but are attractive and
well furnished.

NANDA HERITAGE
HOTEL $$

Map p268 (☑02 282 2900; www.nandaheritage.
com; 632 Th Wisut Kasat; incl breakfast r 2500-
4000B, ste 6000B; ❋♠; ☻klorng boat to Phanfa
Leelard Pier) Taking cues from the teak home
that used to reside here and the wooden build-
ings that still surround it is this new, design-
forward hotel. Rooms are well-equipped, and
come decked out in subtle, earthy colours,
with spacious en suite bathrooms. A clever
choice for the sophisticated but still-want-to-
be-near-Th-Khao-San crowd.

PRAYA PALAZZO
HOTEL $$$

Map p268 (☑02 883 2998; www.prayapalazzo.
com; 757/1 Somdej Prapinklao Soi 2; incl breakfast r 6900-8900B; ste 11,900-18,900B; ❋♠☒;
☻hotel shuttle boat from Phra Athit/Banglam-
phu Pier) After lying dormant for nearly 30
years, this elegant 19th-century mansion
in Thonburi has been reborn as an attractive riverside boutique hotel. The 17 rooms
can seem rather tight, and river views can
be elusive, but the meticulous renovation,
handsome antique furnishings and bucolic
atmosphere convene in a boutique hotel
with authentic old-world charm.

OLD CAPITAL BIKE INN
HOTEL $$$

Map p268 (☑02 629 1787; www.oldcapitalbkk.com;
609 Th Phra Sumen; r incl breakfast 3200-7800B;
❋@♠; ☻klorng boat to Phanfa Leelard Pier) The
dictionary definition of a honeymoon hotel,
this antique shophouse has 10 rooms that
are decadent and sumptuous, blending rich
colours and heavy wood furnishings. True to
its name, the bicycle theme runs throughout,
and bikes can be borrowed free.

RIVA SURYA
HOTEL $$$

Map p268 (☑02 633 5000; www.rivasuryabang
kok.com; 23 Th Phra Athit; r incl breakfast 3500-
5500B; ❋@☒; ☻Phra Athit/Banglamphu Pier)

A former condo has been transformed into one of the more design-conscious hotels in this part of town. The 68 rooms are decked out in greys and blacks, with contemporary furnishings, and in the case of the Deluxe and Riva rooms, great river views, although not always tonnes of space.

PANNEE RESIDENCE
HOTEL **$$**

Map p268 (02 629 4560; www.panneelodge. com; 117 Th Din So; r incl breakfast 1100-1700B; ❄@🛜; 🚤klorng boat to Phanfa Leelard Pier) Pannee is a multistorey hotel offering tidy, if somewhat character-anaemic, rooms. The cheapest rooms are small, but like all the others include a safe, TV and fridge. An upper-floor patio with outdoor rain showers and daybeds for sunbathing provides a bit more room to stretch, and proximity to Bangkok's big sights makes the decision easy.

🛏 Thewet & Dusit

★PHRA-NAKORN NORN-LEN
HOTEL **$$**

Map p270 (02 628 8188; www.phranakorn-norn len.com; 46 Soi Thewet 1; r incl breakfast 2200-4200B; ❄@🛜; 🚤Thewet Pier) Set in an enclosed garden compound decorated like a Bangkok neighbourhood of yesteryear, this bright and cheery hotel is a fun and atmospheric, if not necessarily stupendous-value, place to stay. Although the 31 rooms are attractively furnished, it's worth noting that they don't include TV, a fact made up for by daily activities, massage and endless opportunities for peaceful relaxing.

★SAM SEN SAM PLACE
GUESTHOUSE **$$**

Map p270 (02 628 7067; https://samsensam. com; 48 Soi 3, Th Samsen; r incl breakfast 600-2400B; ❄@🛜; 🚤Thewet Pier) One of the homiest places in this area, if not Bangkok, this colourful, refurbished antique villa gets glowing reports about its friendly service and quiet location. All the 18 rooms here are extremely tidy, and the cheapest are fan-cooled and share a bathroom.

BAAN MANUSARN
GUESTHOUSE **$$**

Map p270 (02 281 2976; www.facebook.com/ baanmanusarn; Th Krung Kasem; r incl breakfast 1400B; ❄@🛜; 🚤Thewet Pier) Steps from Thewet Pier is this inviting vintage shophouse with four rooms. All feature beautiful wood floors and lots of space – with the two family rooms being the most generous – and half boast balconies and en suite bathrooms.

SSIP BOUTIQUE
HOTEL **$$**

Map p270 (02 282 6489; www.ssiphotelthai land.com; 42 Th Phitsanulok; r incl breakfast 2200-3500B; ❄@🛜; 🚤Thewet Pier) Handsome tiles, heavy wood furniture, antique furnishings: the 20 rooms here have been meticulously styled to emulate an old-school Bangkok feel. But modern amenities (TV, fridge, safe) and thoughtful staff ensure a thoroughly contemporary stay.

THE SIAM
HOTEL **$$$**

Map p270 (02 206 6999; www.thesiamhotel. com; 3/2 Th Khao; incl breakfast r 16,100-22,400B, villa 26,300-37,000B; ❄@🛜🏊; 🚤Thewet Pier, or hotel shuttle boat from Sathon/Central Pier) Zoom back to the 1930s in this contemporary riverside hotel, where art deco influences, copious marble and beautiful antiques define the look. Rooms are spacious and well appointed, while villas up the ante with rooftop balcony and plunge pool. Yet it's not just about self-indulging, with activities ranging from Thai boxing lessons to a private theatre to keep you busy.

🛏 Chinatown

WANDERLUST
HOSTEL **$**

Map p272 (083 046 8647; www.facebook. com/onederlust; 149-151 Rama IV; dm 450B, r 1300-1800B; ❄🛜; 🚇, Ⓜ Hua Lamphong exit 1) An almost clinical-feeling industrial vibe rules at this new hostel. The dorms span four to eight beds, and the private rooms are on the tight side, with the cheapest sharing bathrooms. These are united by a hyper-chic ground-floor cafe-restaurant. Not the greatest value accommodation in Chinatown, but quite possibly the most image-conscious.

CHIC HOSTEL
HOSTEL **$**

Map p272 (02 237 9989; www.chicth.com; 23/48-51 Th Traimit; incl breakfast dm 390B, r 800-1100B; ❄@🛜🏊; Ⓜ Hua Lamphong exit 1) This new hostel packs dorms ranging from two to 14 beds and a handful of private rooms. The latter have few amenities (only the 'deluxe' rooms have en suite bathrooms), but this is made up for via a bright, colourful vibe and a swimming pool.

@HUA LAMPHONG
HOSTEL **$**

Map p272 (02 639 1925; www.hualamphong hostel.com; 326/1 Rama IV; dm 400-450B, r 750-1400B; ❄@🛜; 🚤Ratchawong Pier, Ⓜ Hua

BANGKOK'S BEST SMALL HOTELS

Although the big chains dominate the skyline, Bangkok is also home to several attractive hotels and guesthouses with fewer than 10 rooms. Some of our favourites:

Arun Residence (Map p265; ☑02 221 9158; www.arunresidence.com; 36-38 Soi Pratu Nokyung; incl breakfast r 3500-4200B, ste/villa 5800/12,000B; ❋@☎; ⛴Tien Pier) Although strategically located on the river directly across from Wat Arun, this multilevel wooden house boasts much more than just great views. The six rooms here manage to feel both homey and stylish, some being tall and loftlike, while others cojoin two rooms (the best are the top-floor, balcony-equipped suites).

Loy La Long (Map p272; ☑02 639 1390; www.loylalong.com; 1620/2 Th Songwat; r incl breakfast 2700-4900B; ❋@☎; ⛴Ratchawong Pier, ⓂHua Lamphong exit 1 & taxi) Rustic, retro, charming – the six rooms in this 100-year-old wooden house can lay claim to more than their fair share of personality. United by a unique location elevated over Mae Nam Chao Phraya complete with breezy, inviting nooks and crannies, the whole place is also privy to a hidden, almost secret, feel. The only hitch is in finding it: to get here, proceed to Th Songwat and cut directly through Wat Patumkongka Rachaworawiharn to the river.

W Home (☑02 291 5622; www.whomebangkok.com; Yaek 8, Soi 79, Th Charoen Krung; r incl breakfast 1200-1500B; ❋@☎; ⓈSaphan Taksin exit 2 & taxi) It's admittedly off the grid, but that's part of the charm at this 60-year-old renovated house. Welcoming hosts, four small but attractive and thoughtfully furnished rooms (although only one has en suite bathroom), inviting communal areas and an authentic homestay atmosphere round out the package. Soi 79 branches off Th Charoen Krung about 1km south of Saphan Taksin; W Home is about 250m east of the main road.

Bhuthorn (Map p268; ☑02 622 2270; www.thebhuthorn.com; 96-98 Th Phraeng Phuthon; r incl breakfast 5000-6300B; ❋@☎; ⛴Saphan Phut/Memorial Bridge Pier, Pak Klong Taladd Pier) Travel a century back in time by booking one of the three rooms in this beautiful antique shophouse located in a classic Bangkok neighbourhood. They're not particularly huge, but are big on atmosphere and come equipped with both antique furnishings and modern amenities. The sister hotel, **Asadang** (Map p272; ☑085 180 7100; 94-94/1 Th Atsadang; r incl breakfast 3900-6000B; ❋@☎; ⛴Saphan Phut/Memorial Bridge Pier, Pak Klong Taladd Pier), a couple of blocks away, offers a similar package.

Café Ice Residence (Map p278; ☑02 636 7831; cafeiceresidences@gmail.com; 44/4 Soi Phiphat 2; r incl breakfast 2310-3600B; ❋@☎; ⓈChong Nonsi exit 2) This spotless villa is more home than hotel, with nine inviting, spacious and comfortable rooms. Outfitted with subtle yet attractive furnishings, they also share a location with a Thai restaurant and a quiet street.

Loog Choob Homestay (Map p270; ☑085 328 2475; www.loogchoob.com; 463/5-8 Th Luk Luang; incl breakfast r 2100B, ste 3800-4400B; ❋@☎; ⛴Thewet Pier, ⓈPhaya Thai exit 3 & taxi) Staying in a former gem factory outside the tourist zone might sound iffy, but the five rooms here are stylish and inviting, and are supplemented with a huge array of thoughtful amenities and friendly, heartfelt service.

Baan Noppawong (Map p268; ☑02 224 1047; www.facebook.com/baannoppawong; 112-114 Soi Damnoen Klang Tai; incl breakfast r 2500-3400B, ste 4400-5100B; ❋☎; ⛴klorng boat to Phanfa Leelard Pier) If your nana ran a hotel in Bangkok, it might resemble the seven rooms in this fastidiously tidy antique house. Rooms don't have much space, but are light-filled, comfortable and homey, and attractively decorated with antique furnishings. A secluded location augments the homestay vibe.

Lamphong) Not only does this hostel provide the most convenient access to Bangkok's main train terminal, it's clean and well run. The private rooms, some of which are huge, are particularly good value.

OLDTOWN HOSTEL **$**
Map p272 (☑02 639 4879; www.oldtownhostelbkk.com; 1048-1054 Soi 28, Th Charoen Krung; dm 230-270B; r shared bathroom 800-1250B; ❋@☎; ⛴Marine Department Pier, ⓂHua Lamphong exit

1) The dorms and rooms at this shophouse-bound hostel all share bathrooms and are relatively plain, but this is made up for by lots of communal space, including a vast lobby with a pool table, kitchen, computers and comfy chairs, and an adjoining cafe.

FEUNG NAKORN BALCONY　　　　HOTEL **$$**

Map p272 (☎02 622 1100; www.feungnakorn.com; 125 Th Fuang Nakhon; incl breakfast r 2200-4400B, ste 4300-4800B; ❈@🛜; 🚇Saphan Phut/Memorial Bridge Pier, Pak Klong Taladd Pier) Located in a former school, the 42 rooms here surround an inviting garden courtyard and are generally large, bright and cheery. Amenities such as a free minibar, safe and flat-screen TV are standard, and the hotel has a quiet and secluded location away from the strip, with capable staff. A charming and inviting (if not exceedingly great-value) place to stay.

SHANGHAI MANSION　　　　HOTEL **$$$**

Map p272 (☎02 221 2121; www.shanghaimansion. com; 479-481 Th Yaowarat; incl breakfast r 2500-4500B, ste 4500B; ❈@🛜; 🚇Ratchawong Pier, Ⓜ Hua Lamphong exit 1 & taxi) Easily the most consciously stylish place to stay in Chinatown, if not in all of Bangkok; this award-winning boutique hotel screams Shanghai c1935 with stained glass, an abundance of lamps, bold colours and cheeky Chinatown kitsch. If you're willing to splurge, ask for one of the bigger streetside rooms with tall windows that allow more natural light.

🛏 Siam Square, Pratunam, Phloen Chit & Ratchathewi

BOXPACKERS HOSTEL　　　　HOSTEL **$**

Map p271 (☎02 656 2828; www.boxpackershostel. com; 39/3 Soi 15, Th Phetchaburi; incl breakfast dm 390-570B, r 1360-2000B; ❈🛜; 🚇Ratchathewi exit 1 & taxi) A contemporary, sparse hostel with dorms ranging in size from four to 12 double-decker pods – some of which are double beds. Communal areas are inviting, and include a ground-floor cafe and a lounge with pool table. A linked hotel also offers 14 small but similarly attractive private rooms.

BANGKOKIANS GARDEN HOME　HOMESTAY **$**

Map p271 (☎081 809 0623; www.thebangkokians. com; 335/1 Soi 12, Th Ratchaprarop; r 900-1300B; ❈🛜) Weary of the standard hotel experience? Then consider a stay at this residential-feeling, homestay-like hotel. Housed in four bungalows dotting an inviting garden, the rooms offer space, lots of natural light and old-school Thai charm. Check-in is at the nearby Hotel de Bangkok.

K MAISON　　　　BOUTIQUE HOTEL **$$**

Map p271 (☎02 245 1953; www.kmaisonboutique. com; Soi Ruam Chit; incl breakfast r 2200-3500B, ste 6500B; ❈🛜; 🚇Victory Monument exit 4) The lobby, with its virginal white, swirling marble and streaks of blue, sets the tone of this boutique hotel. The 21 rooms follow suit, and are handsome in a delicate and attractively sparse way. Lest you think it's all about image, fear not: K Maison is also functional and comfortable.

BIZOTEL　　　　HOTEL **$$**

Map p271 (☎02 245 2424; www.bizotelbkk.com; 104/40 Th Rang Nam; r incl breakfast 1900-2100B; ❈@🛜; 🚇Victory Monument exit 4) Attractive, bright and stuffed with useful amenities: you could be fooled into believing that the rooms at this hotel cost twice this much. A location in a relatively quiet part of town is another bonus, and helpful, friendly staff seal the deal.

CACHA HOTEL　　　　HOTEL **$$**

(☎02 216 8950; www.cachahotel.com; 156/5-9 Th Phetchaburi; r incl breakfast 1200-2000B; ❈🛜; 🚇Ratchatewi exit 3) The ubiquitous industrial chic look is given a breath of fresh air via Thai/elephant touches at this charming, if somewhat inconveniently located small hotel. The 35 rooms are decked out in stylish, functional furniture and colourful wall paintings, although some of the cheapest lack windows. Thoughtful amenities, including a laundry room and a ground-floor cafe, are pluses.

RENO HOTEL　　　　HOTEL **$$**

Map p274 (☎02 644 5744; www.renohotel.co.th; 40 Soi Kasem San 1; incl breakfast r 1420B, ste 1700-2390B; ❈@🛜🏊; 🚇National Stadium exit 3) Rooms here are large and light-filled, and reflect the renovations evident in the lobby and exterior. But the cafe and pool of this Vietnam War vet still cling to the past. Nonetheless, a good-value option.

HANSAR　　　　HOTEL **$$$**

Map p274 (☎02 209 1234; www.hansarbangkok. com; 3 Soi Mahadlekluang 2; ste incl breakfast 5800-24,000B; ❈@🛜🏊; 🚇Ratchadamri exit 4) The Hansar can claim that elusive amalgam of style and value. All 94 rooms here are handsome and feature huge bathrooms and giant desks, but the smallest (and cheapest) studios are probably the best deal, as they have a kitchenette, washing machine, standalone tub, free wi-fi and in most, a balcony.

★SIAM@SIAM HOTEL $$$

Map p274 (☎02 217 3000; www.siamatsiam.com; 865 Rama I; r incl breakfast 4500-7800B; ❄@📶🏊; [S]National Stadium exit 1) A seemingly random mishmash of colours and industrial/recycled materials in the lobby here result in a style one could only describe as 'junkyard chic' – but in a good way, of course. The rooms, which largely continue the theme, are found between the 14th and 24th floors, and offer terrific city views. There's a rooftop restaurant and an 11th-floor pool, and a recent renovation has it looking better than ever.

OKURA PRESTIGE HOTEL $$$

Map p274 (☎02 687 9000; www.okurabangkok.com; 57 Th Witthayu/Wireless Rd; incl breakfast r 6300-8500B, ste 29,000-110,000B; [P]❄@📶🏊; [S]Phloen Chit exit 5) The Bangkok venture of this Japanese chain – the first branch outside of its homeland – is, unlike other recent, big-name openings in Bangkok, distinctly unflashy. But we like the minimalist, almost contemplative feel of the lobby and the 240 rooms, and the subtle but thoughtful, often distinctly Japanese touches. Significant online discounts are available.

HOTEL INDIGO HOTEL $$$

Map p274 (☎02 207 4999; www.ihg.com; 81 Th Witthayu/Wireless Rd; incl breakfast r 3300-4200B, ste 13,600B; ❄@📶🏊; [S]Phloen Chit exit 5) An international chain with local flavour, the Indigo has borrowed from the history and culture of this corner of Bangkok to arrive at a hotel that is retro, modern, Thai and artsy all at the same time. Many of the 192 rooms overlook some of the greener areas of Bangkok's embassy district, and all are decked out with colourful furnishings and functional amenities.

LIT BANGKOK HOTEL & RESIDENCE HOTEL $$$

Map p274 (☎02 612 3456; www.litbangkok.com; 36/1 Soi Kasem San 1; incl breakfast r 4250-4625B, ste 6895-7480B; ❄@📶🏊; [S]National Stadium exit 1) This modern, architecturally striking hotel has a variety of room styles united by a light theme. Check out a few, as they vary significantly, and some features, such as a shower that can be seen from the living room, aren't necessarily for everybody.

Riverside, Silom & Lumphini

S1 HOSTEL HOSTEL $

Map p277 (☎02 679 7777; www.facebook.com/s1hostelbangkok; 35/1-4 Soi Ngam Du Phli; dm 330-380B, r 700-1300B; ❄@📶; [M]Lumphini exit 1) A huge hostel with dorm beds (and private rooms) decked out in a simple yet attractive primary-colour scheme. A host of facilities (laundry, kitchen, rooftop garden) and a convenient location within walking distance of the MRT make it great value.

GLUR BANGKOK HOSTEL $

Map p280 (☎02 630 5595; www.glurbangkok.com; 45 Soi 50, Th Charoen Krung; incl breakfast dm 285-720B, r 1300-1600B; ❄📶; ⛴Sathon/Central Pier, [S]Saphan Taksin exit 1) A narrow shophouse with three attractive and comfy eight-bed dorms. Space is limited, but Glur makes the most of it with fun and functional communal areas, including a ground-floor cafe.

MILE MAP HOSTEL HOSTEL $

Map p278 (☎02 635 1212; 36/4 Th Pan; dm 250-285B, r 600-900B; ❄@📶; [S]Chong Nonsi exit 3) Despite the quasi-industrial theme, this hostel feels inviting, warm and fun. The 10-bed dorms are one of the best deals in town, and the private rooms have a funky, minimalist feel, although not much natural light.

HQ HOSTEL HOSTEL $

Map p278 (☎02 233 1598; www.hqhostel.com; 5/3-4 Soi 3, Th Silom; incl breakfast dm 380-490B, r 1090-1490B; ❄@📶; [M]Si Lom exit 2, [S]Sala Daeng exit 2) HQ is a flashpacker hostel in the polished-concrete-and-industrial-style mould. It includes four- to 10-bed dorms, a few private rooms (some with en suite bathroom) and inviting communal areas in a narrow multistorey building in the middle of Bangkok's financial district.

★SMILE SOCIETY HOTEL $$

Map p278 (☎081 442 5800, 081 444 1596; www.smilesocietyhostel.com; 30/3-4 Soi 6, Th Silom; incl breakfast dm 450-600B, r 1100-2200B; ❄@📶; [M]Si Lom exit 2, [S]Sala Daeng exit 1) Part boutique hotel, part hostel, this four-storey shophouse combines small but comfortable

HOTEL ALTERNATIVES IN BANGKOK

If you're planning on staying longer than a few days, or don't need housekeeping, there are ample alternatives to the traditional hotel in Bangkok.

Airbnb (www.airbnb.com/s/Bangkok--Thailand) has heaps of listings in the city, ranging from condos and apartments to small hotels masquerading as condos and apartments. For something a bit more established there's **House by the Pond** (Map p282; ☎02 259 3543; www.housebythepond.com; 230/3 Soi Sainumthip 2; r 1400-2500B; ❄@📶🏊; [S]Phrom Phong exit 6 & taxi), an old-school-style Bangkok apartment that offers nightly, weekly and monthly stays.

On the other hand, if you've got a bit more money and don't want to forgo the perks of staying at a hotel, a clever route is the ubiquitous serviced apartment. Bangkok is loaded with apartments that offer long-stay options with the benefits of a hotel (door attendants, cleaning, room service, laundry). But what few people realise is that most serviced apartments are happy to take short-term guests as well as longer stayers – and that by booking ahead you can get a luxury apartment with a lot more space and facilities (kitchen, washing machine, etc) than a hotel room for the same or less money. It's really a great way to stay in town, especially if you're a family who needs more space than two hotel rooms. Recommended outfits include:

Siri Sathorn (Map p278; ☎02 266 2345; www.sirisathorn.com; 27 Soi Sala Daeng 1; ste 2900-23,540B; ❄@📶🏊; [M]Si Lom exit 2, [S]Sala Daeng exit 2) Chic modern apartments starting at 60 sq metres; also includes shuttle bus, spa and professional service.

Centrepoint (☎02 630 6345; www.centrepoint.com; incl breakfast r & ste 6970-16,750B; ❄📶🏊) One of Bangkok's biggest managers of serviced apartments, with five properties across the city.

Urbana (☎02 227 9999; www.urbanahospitality.com; ste 3000-9000B; ❄📶🏊) Reputable serviced-apartment provider with two properties in Bangkok.

and well-equipped rooms, and dorms with spotless shared bathrooms. A central location, overwhelmingly positive guest feedback, and helpful, English-speaking staff are other perks. And a virtually identical annexe next door helps with spillover as Smile Society gains more fans.

★KOKOTEL — HOTEL $$

Map p278 (☎02 235 7555; www.kokotel.com; 181/1-5 Th Surawong; r 1400-3400B; ❄@📶; [S]Chong Nonsi exit 3) Quite possibly the city's family-friendliest accommodation, kokotel unites big, sun-filled rooms with puffy beds, an expansive children's play area and a downstairs cafe (with, appropriately, a slide). Friendly rates also make it great value.

AMBER — HOTEL $$

Map p278 (☎02 635 7272; www.amberboutique-silom.com; 200 Soi 14, Th Silom; r incl breakfast 1900-2400B; ❄@📶; [S]Chong Nonsi exit 3) Spanning design themes such as Moroccan, Sino-Portuguese and Modern, it's easy to assume that Amber might emphasise style over comfort. But nothing here is flashy or overwrought, and what you'll get are 19 excellent-value, spacious rooms with lots of amenities and natural light in a quiet location. Frequent promotions bring the rates down even lower than this, making it terrific value.

SILOM ONE — HOTEL $$

Map p278 (☎02 635 5130; www.silomone.com; 281/15 Soi 1, Th Silom; r incl breakfast 2500-3500B; ❄📶; [M]Si Lom exit 2, [S]Sala Daeng exit 2) Barely squeezing into the midrange bracket is this hotel with 10 rooms that boast an almost Japanese minimalism. You can't beat its convenient location in a dead-end alley, steps away from public transport and heaps of street food.

LUXX — HOTEL $$

Map p278 (☎02 635 8844; www.staywithluxx.com; 6/11 Th Decho; r 1060-1445B, ste 1570B; ❄@📶; [S]Chong Nongsi exit 3) LUXX, the Th Decho branch of **LUXX XL** (Map p277; ☎02 684 1111; 82/8 Th Lang Suan; incl breakfast r 1500-2400B, ste 3700-7700B; ❄@📶🏊; [S]Ratchadamri exit 2), flaunts the same hip minimalist vibe of its big sibling, and though rooms here can be a bit tight, and some lack natural light, they are all decked out with appropriately stylish furnishings.

FROM LITERATI TO GLITTERATI

Now a famous grande dame, the Mandarin Oriental (p201) started its career as the seafarers' version of a Th Khao San guesthouse. The original owners, two Danish sea captains, traded the nest to Hans Niels Andersen, the founder of the formidable East Asiatic Company. Andersen transformed the hotel into a civilised palace of grand architecture and luxurious standards. He hired an Italian architect, S Cardu, to design what is now the Authors' Wing, which was the city's most fantastic building not commissioned by the king.

The rest of the hotel's history relies on its famous guests. A Polish-born sailor named Joseph Conrad stayed here in 1888. The hotel brought him good luck: he got his first command on the ship *Otago*, from Bangkok to Port Adelaide, Australia, which in turn gave him ideas for several early stories. W Somerset Maugham stumbled into the hotel with an advanced case of malaria. In his feverish state, he heard the German manager arguing with the doctor about how a death in the hotel would hurt business. Maugham's overland Southeast Asian journey is recorded in *The Gentleman in the Parlour: A Record of a Journey from Rangoon to Haiphong,* which gave literary appeal to the hotel. Other notable guests have included Noël Coward, Graham Greene, John le Carré, James Michener, Gore Vidal and Barbara Cartland. Some modern-day writers claim that a stay here will help overcome writer's block – though we suspect any writer booking in these days would need a very generous advance indeed.

SWAN HOTEL   HOTEL $$
Map p280 (☑02 235 9271; www.swanhotelbkk.com; 31 Soi 36/Rue de Brest, Th Charoen Krung; r incl breakfast 1200-2000B; ☀@🛜🏊; ☸Oriental Pier) The 1960s-era furnishings date this classic Bangkok hotel, despite renovations. But the rooms are airy and virtually spotless, and the antiquated vibe provides the Swan, particularly its pool area, with a fun, groovy vibe.

TRINITY SILOM HOTEL   HOTEL $$
Map p278 (☑02 231 5050; www.glowbyzinc.com/trinity-silom; 150 Soi Phiphat 2; r incl breakfast 1900-3300B; ☀@🛜🏊; ⓢChong Nonsi exit 2) A sophisticated hotel with rates that weigh in at just below midrange, Glow has spacious, modern-feeling rooms, professional service, and a pool and fitness facilities just next door.

URBAN HOUSE   HOTEL $$
Map p278 (☑081 492 7778; www.urbanh.com; 35/13 Soi Yommarat; incl breakfast r 800-2300B, ste 1580B; ☀🛜; ⓜSi Lom exit 2, ⓢSala Daeng exit 4) There's nothing showy about this shophouse with six rooms, but that's exactly what we like about it. Rooms are subtle, comfortable and relatively spacious, and the place boasts a peaceful, homey atmosphere, largely due to the kind host and the quiet residential street it's located on.

ROSE HOTEL   HOTEL $$
Map p278 (☑02 266 8268; www.rosehotelbkk.com; 118 Th Surawong; incl breakfast r 1900-2300B, ste 3300-3800B; ☀@🛜🏊; ⓜSi Lom exit 2, ⓢSala Daeng exit 3) Don't let the unremarkable exterior fool you: the convenient location, modern rooms, pool, gym and sauna make this Vietnam War–era vet a pretty solid deal.

★ SIAM HERITAGE   HOTEL $$$
Map p278 (☑02 353 6101; www.thesiamheritage.com; 115/1 Th Surawong; incl breakfast r 3500-3800B, ste 5000-6500B; ☀@🛜🏊; ⓜSi Lom exit 2, ⓢSala Daeng exit 1) Tucked off busy Th Surawong, this hotel overflows with homey Thai charm – probably because the owners also live in the same building. The 73 rooms are decked out in silk and dark woods with classy design touches and thoughtful amenities. There's an inviting rooftop garden/pool/spa, and it's all cared for by a team of professional, accommodating staff. Highly recommended.

★ METROPOLITAN BY COMO   HOTEL $$$
Map p277 (☑02 625 3333; www.comohotels.com; 27 Th Sathon Tai/South; incl breakfast r 3500-5300B, ste 6200-27,000B; ☀@🛜🏊; ⓜLumphini exit 2) The exterior of Bangkok's former YMCA has changed relatively little, but a peek inside reveals one of the city's sleekest, sexiest hotels. The 171 rooms come in striking tones of black, white and yellow, though it's worth noting that the City rooms tend to feel a bit tight, while in contrast the two-storey penthouse suites are like small homes.

SUKHOTHAI HOTEL
HOTEL $$$

Map p277 (☑02 344 8888; www.sukhothai.com; 13/3 Th Sathon Tai/South; incl breakfast r 4000-5200B, ste 6000-80,000B; ✳@☎☂; MLumphini exit 2) This is one of Bangkok's classiest luxury options, and, as the name suggests, the Sukhothai employs brick stupas, court-yards and antique sculptures to create a peaceful, almost temple-like atmosphere. The rooms contrast this with high-tech TVs, phones and; in some cases, high-tech toilets.

MANDARIN ORIENTAL
HOTEL $$$

Map p280 (☑02 659 9000; www.mandarinorien tal.com; 48 Soi 40/Oriental, Th Charoen Krung; incl breakfast r 14,000-30,000B, ste 26,700-160,000B; ✳@☎☂; Oriental Pier, or hotel shuttle boat from Sathon/Central Pier) For the true Bangkok experience, a stay at this grand old riverside hotel is a must. The majority of rooms are in the modern and recently refurbished New Wing, but we prefer the old-world ambience of the Garden and Authors' Wings. The ho-tel is also home to one of the region's most acclaimed spas, a legendary fine-dining res-taurant and a cooking school.

MILLENNIUM HILTON
HOTEL $$$

Map p280 (☑02 442 2000; www.bangkok.hilton. com; 123 Th Charoen Nakhon; incl breakfast r 4000-5900B, ste 6500-7000B; ✳@☎☂; ho-tel shuttle boat from Sathon/Central Pier) As soon as you enter the dramatic lobby, it's ob-vious that this is among Bangkok's young-est, most modern riverside hotels. Rooms, all of which boast widescreen river views, carry on the theme and are decked out with funky furniture and Thai-themed photos. A glass elevator and an artificial beach are just some of the fun touches.

PENINSULA HOTEL
HOTEL $$$

Map p280 (☑02 861 2888; www.peninsula.com; 333 Th Charoen Nakhon; incl breakfast r 7500-8100B, ste 10,600-130,000B; ✳@☎☂; hotel shuttle boat from Sathon/Central Pier) At the age of 20, the Pen still seems to have it all: the lo-cation (towering over the river), the rep (it's consistently one of the top-ranking luxury hotels in the world) and one of the highest levels of service in town. If money is no ob-stacle, stay on one of the upper floors where you literally have all of Bangkok at your feet.

W BANGKOK
HOTEL $$$

Map p278 (☑02 344 4000; www.whotels. com/bangkok; 106 Th Sathon Neua/North; incl breakfast r 5770-7095B, ste 7840-154,350B;

✳@☎☂; SChong Nonsi exit 1) A bold, brash, big-chain, the W has correspondingly youngish rooms with cheeky touches (think Thai-boxing-themed furnishings) and high-tech amenities. Glitter and glass, a lobby bar and a pool that glows are some of the other touches that make this a front runner for Bangkok's clubbiest hotel.

SOFITEL SO
HOTEL $$$

Map p277 (☑02 624 0000; www.sofitel.com; 2 Th Sathon Neua/North; incl breakfast r 8100-9100B, ste 13,000-48,000B; ✳@☎☂; MLumphini exit 2) Taking inspiration from (and featur-ing amazing views of) adjacent Lumphini Park, this is one of a handful of large-yet-hip brand-name hotels to open in Bangkok over the last few years. The four-elements-inspired design theme has no two rooms looking quite the same, but all are spacious and stylish, contemporary and young.

🛏 Sukhumvit

FU HOUSE HOSTEL
HOSTEL $

Map p282 (☑098 654 5505; www.facebook.com/ fuhouseghostel; 77 Soi 8, Th Sukhumvit; dm/r incl breakfast 500/1650B; ✳☎; SNana exit 4) Great for a quiet, low-key stay is this two-storey wooden villa on a residential street. Choose between attractive bunk beds in one of two spacious, private-feeling dorms, or rooms with en suite bathrooms.

ATLANTA
HOTEL $

Map p282 (☑02 252 1650; www.theatlantahotel bangkok.com; 78 Soi 2, Th Sukhumvit; incl breakfast r 750-1050B, ste 950-1950B; ✳@☎☂; SNana exit 2) Defiantly antiquated and equal parts frumpy and grumpy, this crumbling gem has changed very little since its 1952 construction. The opulent lobby stands in stark contrast to the simple rooms, and the anti-sex-tourist warnings are frantic in tone, but the inviting pool (allegedly the country's first hotel pool) and delightful restaurant (for guests only) are just enough incentive to get past these.

★TINTS OF BLUE
HOTEL $$

Map p282 (☑099 289 7744; www.tintsofblue. com; 47 Soi 27, Th Sukhumvit; r incl breakfast 1800-2000B; ✳☎☂; MSukhumvit exit 2, SAsok exit 6) The location in a leafy, quiet street is reflected in the rooms here, which manage to feel se-cluded, homey and warm. Equipped with kitchenettes, lots of space and natural light, and balconies, they're also a steal at this price.

RETROASIS
HOTEL $$

Map p282 (☑02 665 2922; www.retroasishotel.
com; 503 Th Sukhumvit; r incl breakfast 1400-
2300B; ❄ @ � ☎; ⓜSukhumvit exit 2, ⓢAsok exit
6) This former tryst hotel dating back to the
'60s has been converted to a fun midranger.
Bright paint and an inviting central pool
give the hotel a young, fresh vibe, while
vintage furniture and architecture serve as
reminders of its real age.

BEAT HOTEL
HOTEL $$

(☑02 178 0077; www.beathotelbangkok.com;
69/1 Th Sukhumvit; r incl breakfast 2000-2500B;
❄ @ ☎ ☎; ⓢPhra Khanong exit 3) This art-
themed hotel has a vibrant, youthful vibe
that kicks off in the lobby. The 54 rooms
continue this feeling, ranging in design
from those with colourful floor-to-ceiling
wall art to others painted in a monochro-
matic bold hue. It's worth shelling out for
the super-huge Deluxe rooms.

NAPA PLACE
HOTEL $$

Map p282 (☑02 661 5525; www.napaplace.com;
11/3 Soi Napha Sap 2; incl breakfast r 2200-2600B,
ste 3400-4600B; ❄ @ ☎; ⓢThong Lo exit 2) Hid-
den in the confines of a typical Bangkok
urban compound is what must be the city's
homeliest accommodation. The 12 expan-
sive rooms have been decorated with dark
woods from the family's former lumber busi-
ness and light-brown cloths from the hands
of Thai weavers, while the cosy communal
areas might not be much different from the
suburban living room you grew up in.

S31
HOTEL $$

Map p282 (☑02 260 1111; www.s31hotel.com;
545 Soi 31, Th Sukhumvit; incl breakfast r 3700B,
ste 4200-25,000B; ❄ ☎ ☎; ⓢPhrom Phong exit
5) The bold patterns and graphics of its
interior and exterior make the S31 a fun,
youthful choice. Thoughtful touches like
kitchenettes with large fridge, super-huge
beds and courses (Thai boxing and yoga)
prove that the style also has substance. Significant discounts can be found online, and
additional branches are located on Soi 15
and Soi 33.

S-BOX
HOTEL $$

Map p282 (☑02 262 0991; www.sboxhotel.com; 4
Soi 31, Th Sukhumvit; r incl breakfast 1100-2200B;
❄ @ ☎; ⓢPhrom Phong exit 5) The name says
it all: the rooms here are little more than
boxes – albeit attractive, modern boxes with
stylish furniture and practical amenities.

The cheapest are pod-like and lack natural
light, while the more expensive have floor-
to-ceiling windows.

HOTEL CLOVER
HOTEL $$

Map p282 (☑02 258 8555; www.hotelclover-th.
com; 9 Soi 16, Th Ratchadaphisek; r incl breakfast 2500-2800B; ❄ @ ☎ ☎; ⓜSukhumvit exit
3, ⓢAsok exit 6) The rooms here aren't vast,
but splashes of colour, a contemporary and
comfortable vibe, and a location steps from
both the BTS and MRT make the Clover a
clever midrange option.

STABLE LODGE
HOTEL $$

Map p282 (☑02 653 0017; www.stablelodge.com;
39 Soi 8, Th Sukhumvit; r 2200-2800B; ❄ ☎ ☎;
ⓢNana exit 4) To be honest, we were slightly
disappointed that the faux-Tudor theme of
the downstairs restaurant didn't carry on
into the rooms, but could find few other
faults. Rooms are plain, but are also rela-
tively spacious, conveniently located and
offer access to an inviting pool.

U SUKHUMVIT
HOTEL $$

Map p282 (☑02 651 3355; 81 Soi 15, Th Sukhumvit; r incl breakfast 2600-3200B; ❄ ☎ ☎;
ⓜSukhumvit exit 3, ⓢAsok exit 5) A modern
hotel featuring the Thai regions as a design
theme. Rooms are colourful, with lively
rustic touches, not to mention spacious and
well equipped. A midrange keeper.

FUSION SUITES
HOTEL $$

Map p282 (☑02 665 2778; www.fusionbangkok.
com; 143/61-62 Soi 21/Asoke, Th Sukhumvit; r incl
breakfast 1700-2400B; ❄ @ ☎; ⓜSukhumvit exit
1, ⓢAsok exit 1) A disproportionately funky
hotel for this price range. The unconven-
tional furnishings provide the rooms here
with heaps of style, although the cheapest
can be a bit dark.

BAAN SUKHUMVIT
HOTEL $$

Map p282 (☑02 258 5630; www.baansukhumvit.
com; 392/38-39 Soi 20, Th Sukhumvit; r incl
breakfast 1540-1650B; ❄ @ ☎; ⓜSukhumvit exit
1, ⓢAsok exit 1) With only 12 rooms, this hotel
exudes an approachable, cosy feel. Rooms
lack bells and whistles, but are subtly attractive; the more expensive include a bit
more space, a bathtub and a safe. There's
another branch nearby on Soi 18.

★ARIYASOMVILLA
HOTEL $$$

Map p282 (☑02 254 8880; www.ariyasom.com;
65 Soi 1, Th Sukhumvit; r incl breakfast 6900-

AIRPORT ACCOMMODATION

The vast majority of visitors to Bangkok need not consider the airport hotel rigmarole as taxis are cheap and plentiful, and early-morning traffic means the trip shouldn't take too long. That said, those worried about a super-early departure or late arrival may consider a stay at one of the following:

Novotel Suvarnabhumi Airport Hotel (☑02 131 1111; www.novotelairportbkk.com; Suvarnabhumi International Airport; incl breakfast r 4500-7300B, ste 9500-10,400B; ❄ @ ⓢ; ⓢPhra Khanong exit 3 & taxi, ⓡSuvarnabhumi Airport & hotel shuttle bus) Has 600-plus luxurious rooms; located within the Suvarnabhumi International Airport compound.

The Cottage (☑02 727 5858; www.thecottagebangkokairport.com; 888/8 Th Lad Krabang; r incl breakfast 880-1379B; ❄ @ ⓢ ▨; ⓢPhra Khanong exit 3 & taxi, ⓡSuvarnabhumi Airport & hotel shuttle bus) This solid midranger is near the Suvarnabhumi International Airport compound and within walking distance of food and shopping; has an airport shuttle.

Sleep Box (☑02 535 7555; Terminal 2, Don Mueang International Airport; r 1800B; ❄ ⓢ) Finally, an alternative to snoozing on the chairs at Don Mueang International Airport. Rooms may induce claustrophobia, but include en suite bathrooms, water, wi-fi and even food coupons. Short stays (1000B for three hours) and showers (300B) are also available.

Amari Airport Hotel (☑02 566 1020; www.amari.com/donmuang; 333 Th Choet Wut-thakat; r 1845-2205B, ste 2205-3105B; ❄ @ ⓢ ▨; ⓜChatuchak Park exit 2 & taxi, ⓢMo Chit exit 3 & taxi) International-standard hotel located directly opposite Don Mueang International Airport.

10,500B; ❄ @ ⓢ ▨; ⓢPhloen Chit exit 3) Located at the end of Soi 1 behind a wall of tropical greenery, this beautifully renovated 1940s-era villa is one of the worst-kept accommodation secrets in Bangkok. The 24 rooms are spacious and meticulously outfitted with thoughtful Thai design touches and sumptuous, beautiful antique furniture. There's also a spa and an inviting tropical pool. Book well in advance.

Breakfast is vegetarian and served in the villa's stunning glass-encased dining room.

SHERATON GRANDE SUKHUMVIT
HOTEL $$$

Map p282 (☑02 649 8888; www.sheratongrande sukhumvit.com; 250 Th Sukhumvit; incl breakfast r 11,000-13,800B, ste 19,000-56,000B; ❄ @ ⓢ; ⓜSukhumvit exit 3, ⓢAsok exit 2) This conveniently located, business-oriented hotel offers some of the biggest rooms in town and fills them with a generous spread of amenities. Guest feedback is overwhelmingly positive, and by the time you read this, ongoing renovations will be making what was already a very good hotel an excellent one.

EUGENIA
HOTEL $$$

Map p282 (☑02 205 0111; www.theeugeniahotel. wordpress.com; 267 Soi 31, Th Sukhumvit; r incl breakfast 6000-11,000B; ❄ @ ⓢ ▨; ⓢPhrom Phong exit 6 & taxi) Art deco prints, worn wooden floors and antique furniture spur the retro vibe at this boutique choice. You won't find tonnes of modern amenities, but the hotel has an inviting pool and is linked to one of Bangkok's best spa chains.

MA DU ZI
HOTEL $$$

Map p282 (☑02 615 6400; www.maduzihotel. com; cnr Th Ratchadaphisek & Soi 16, Th Sukhumvit; incl breakfast r 5100-5500B, ste 7700-11,700B; ❄ @ ⓢ; ⓜSukhumvit exit 3, ⓢAsok exit 6) The name is Thai for 'come take a look', somewhat of a misnomer for this reservations-only, no-walk-ins hotel. If you've gained access, behind the gate you'll find a modern, sophisticated midsized hotel steeped in dark, chic tones and designs. We particularly like the immense bathrooms, equipped with a walk-in tub and minimalist shower.

🛏 Northern Bangkok

THE YARD
HOSTEL $

Map p286 (☑089 677 4050; www.theyardhostel. com; 51 Soi 5, Th Phahonyothin; incl breakfast dm 550-650B, r 1200-1900B; ❄ ⓢ; ⓢAri exit 1) This fun hostel is comprised of 10 converted shipping containers. Predictably, neither the dorm nor private rooms are huge (nor great value), but are attractive and cosy, and have access to inviting communal areas ranging from the eponymous lawn (which also functions as a bar) to a kitchen.

YIM HUAI KHWANG HOSTEL   HOSTEL $

Map p286 (☑02 118 6038; www.yimhuaikhwang. com; 70 Th Pracha Rat Bamphen; incl breakfast dm 450-550B, r 1550-3000B; ❄@⚗; Ⓜ Huay Khwang exit 1) A new suburban hostel decked out in an eclectic, colourful fashion, with dorm rooms ranging in size from four to six comfortable, hi-tech bunk beds. Yes, it's far from any sights, but it is very close to the MRT.

SIAMAZE   HOSTEL $

(☑02 693 6336; www.siamaze.com; Soi 17, Th Ratchadaphisek; incl breakfast dm 390-490B, r 1200-2000B; ❄@⚗; Ⓜ Sutthisan exit 4) Siamaze is an unflashy, casual budget hotel with spacious private rooms and tech-outfitted bunk-bed dorms. The latter share big, clean bathrooms and access to thoughtful, convenient facilities. If you're OK with staying away from the main tourist drag, it's an excellent deal.

MYSTIC PLACE   HOTEL $$

Map p286 (☑02 270 3344; www.mysticplacebkk. com; 224/5-9 Th Pradiphat; r incl breakfast 2200-2650B; ❄@⚗; Ⓢ Saphan Khwai exit 2 & taxi) This hotel unites 36 rooms, each of which is individually and playfully designed. One we checked out combined a chair upholstered with stuffed animals and walls covered with graffiti, while another was swathed in eye-contorting op art. Heaps of fun and perpetually popular, so be sure to book ahead.

BE MY GUEST BED & BREAKFAST   GUESTHOUSE $$

Map p286 (☑02 692 4037; 212/4 Soi 1, Soi 7, Th Ratchadaphisek; r incl breakfast 900-1400B; ❄@⚗; Ⓜ Thailand Cultural Centre exit 4 & taxi) With only four rooms and the owner living upstairs, you really are the eponymous guest at this friendly, tidy guesthouse. Rooms are neat but simple, and supplemented by user-friendly communal areas, personal service and a genuinely homey vibe. Contact in advance, both to ensure vacancy and to ask for detailed instructions on locating the place.

★ BANGKOK TREE HOUSE   HOTEL $$$

(☑082 995 1150; www.bangkoktreehouse. com/cozy-nests.html; near Wat Bang Na Nork, Phrapradaeng; bungalow incl breakfast 6000-10,000B; ❄@⚗⊠; Ⓢ Bang Na exit 2 & taxi) Located in the lush green zone known as the Phrapradaeng Peninsula, the Bangkok Tree House's 12 multilevel bungalows are stylishly sculpted from sustainable and recycled materials, giving it the feel of a sophisticated, ecofriendly summer camp. Thoughtful amenities include private computers equipped with movies, free mobilephone and bicycle use and free ice cream. Significant online discounts are available.

To get here, take the BTS to Bang Na and then a taxi for the short ride to the pier at Wat Bang Na Nork. From there, take the river-crossing ferry (4B, 5am to 9.30pm) and continue by motorcycle taxi (10B) or on foot (call ahead for directions).

Understand Bangkok

Bangkok Today

Bangkok is nothing if not resilient. Recent years have brought explosive protests, army curfews and actual explosions to Thailand's capital, but the city keeps grinding onwards. Thailand's seat of power since the era of direct palace rule has taken on added prominence now that the staunchly royalist and Bangkok-centric military rules the country outright. But intimately familiar with junta rule after 12 previous coups d'état, the city's inhabitants tend to to be concerned with everyday woes, such as money, traffic and flooding.

Best on Film

Monrak Transistor (directed by Pen-Ek Ratanaruang; 2001) An aspiring loôk tûng (Thai country music) singer trades his bucolic life for one of struggle in the big city.

Nang Nak (directed by Nonzee Nimibutr; 1999) This classic Thai tale is a fascinating peek at Thai beliefs, as well as the provincial village that existed before Bangkok was taken over by concrete.

Best in Print

Sightseeing (Rattawut Lapcharoensap; 2004) Written by an American-born Thai who later moved to Bangkok, the short stories in this book provide a look at the lives of normal Thais who live in the type of suburbs and towns most visitors will never see.

Four Reigns (Kukrit Pramoj; Thai 1953, English 1981) This novel follows the fictional life of Phloi, a minor courtier during the Bangkok palace's last days of absolute monarchy.

Return to Authoritarian Rule

Thailand's ruler, former army general Prayut Chan-o-cha, has quipped that the country is '99 percent democratic' now that his junta reigns supreme, but that's not remotely true. Since the coup d'état in 2014 that landed him in power, Thailand is still most accurately described as a military dictatorship.

The junta's darker side was previously only felt by the political class: deposed officials, academics, activists and dissidents. The military government has rounded up critics for 'attitude adjustment', which translates to confinement on an army base. Prayut tends to equate dissent with sedition and once joked about 'executing' critical journalists.

But the military's policies are starting to have an impact on average Thais. Beginning in 2016, the junta put pressure on the Bangkok Metropolitan Authority (BMA) to shut down street vendors in a handful of neighbourhoods. The next year, the BMA was ordered to shut down all of Bangkok's street stalls, though at press time it remains to be seen if these orders will be enforced or if the vendors will obey them.

The junta's vow to eliminate corruption and 'return happiness' to all Thais remains largely unfulfilled: the economy is stagnant, the currency has weakened (good news for tourists, perhaps) and the bombing of a heavily touristed shrine in 2015 indicates that Bangkok is not immune to the threat of international terrorism.

The military has promised elections in 2018, but a new constitution (the country's 20th charter – only two nations in the world have had more) ensconces military power indefinitely while also assuring that the junta can't be found guilty of having committed any human rights violations.

A Changing Urban Landscape

In recent years the military junta has embarked on several policies and projects that have had a huge impact on Bangkok's skyline.

At ground level, a ban on street vendors in certain neighbourhoods has already altered the city's footpaths. Yes, it's now possible to walk along Th Thong Lo without having to wind through a virtual gamut of stalls and vendors, but this comes at the expense of the street food that is both a cheap eating option for locals and a massive draw for tourists.

Above and below the streets, Bangkok is furiously expanding its public transport network. By 2020, Bangkok's MRT (metro) is set to reach Ko Ratanakosin, making getting to some of the city's most famous tourist destinations a breeze. It is also being expanded to regions west of the city centre. At the same time, the city's commuter train network is being expanded north, eventually linking Don Mueang International Airport with the city centre.

Yet the most significant impact these changes are having is on 'old' Bangkok. In 2016 the BMA ordered all of the vendors at Bangkok's long-standing night-time flower market to relocate indoors. A plan to build a 14km promenade along Mae Nam Chao Praya has already resulted in the demolition of nearly 300 riverside structures, many of which were decades old. And the BMA seems intent on going through with long-held plans to demolish the 18th-century Mahakan Fort and the centuries-old community that flanks it, replacing both with a 'tourism park'. These forces, coupled with commercial interests, mean that Bangkok is changing at an astonishing rate, and some fear its transformation will result in a sterile, Singapore-like city.

Sinking into the Earth

All of Bangkok's glitz and grime, its glowing mall districts and drab cement slums sit on squishy ground. Centuries ago this area was a marshland. Today, it's the foundation upon which Bangkok rests and the city is literally sinking.

Thailand's disaster specialists have long predicted this sinking problem. Rising sea levels are partially to blame, as are factories on the city's outskirts that suck up groundwater and hasten the massive city's descent into the ground. Experts warn that by 2100 much of Bangkok may be flooded and unlivable.

But far-off doomsday scenarios are overshadowed by more immediate concerns: the annual ritual of panicking over floods. Monsoons can transform streets into streams, and the city is vulnerable to the occasional megadeluge that brings large-scale flooding. A 2011 tropical storm was among the worst in recent memory, leaving millions homeless, killing around 800 people and causing more than US$45 billion in damages. Wracked by political turmoil, Thailand's leaders have done little to prepare for the next flooding calamity. A proposed solution to the long-term sinking problem, a sea wall in the Gulf of Thailand that would cost billions, remains laughably far-fetched, and come the next monsoon, it's likely that the rains will, yet again, catch Bangkok off guard.

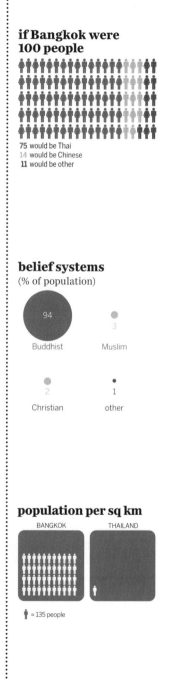

if Bangkok were 100 people

75 would be Thai
14 would be Chinese
11 would be other

belief systems
(% of population)

94 Buddhist

3 Muslim

2 Christian

1 other

population per sq km

BANGKOK   THAILAND

♦ ≈ 135 people

History

Since the late 18th century, the history of Bangkok has essentially been the history of Thailand. Many of the country's defining events have unfolded here, and today the language and culture of the city have come to represent those of the entire country. This situation may once have seemed impossible, given the city's origins as little more than an obscure Chinese trading port, but, today boasting a population of almost 10 million, Bangkok will continue to shape Thailand's history.

From the Beginning

Ayuthaya & Thonburi

Before it became the capital of Siam – as Thailand was then known – in 1782, the tiny settlement known as Bang Makok was merely a backwater village opposite the larger Thonburi Si Mahasamut on the banks of Mae Nam Chao Phraya, not far from the Gulf of Siam.

Thonburi had been founded by a group of wealthy Siamese during the reign of King Chakkraphat (r 1548–68) as an important relay point for sea- and river-borne trade between the Gulf of Siam and Ayuthaya, 86km upriver. Ayuthaya served as the royal capital of Siam from 1350 to 1767, and throughout this time European powers tried without success to colonise the kingdom.

Eventually an Asian power subdued the capital when the Burmese sacked Ayuthaya in 1767. Many Siamese were marched off to Pegu (Bago, Myanmar today), where they were forced to serve the Burmese court. However, the remaining Siamese regrouped under Phraya Taksin, a half-Chinese, half-Thai general who decided to move the capital further south along Mae Nam Chao Phraya, closer to the Gulf of Siam. Thonburi was a logical choice for the new capital.

The Chakri Dynasty & the Birth of Bangkok

Taksin eventually succumbed to mental illness and was executed, and one of his key generals, Phraya Chakri, came to power and was crowned in 1782 as Phraphutthayotfa. Fearing Thonburi to be vulnerable to Burmese

King Taksin's execution was in the custom reserved for royalty – he was sealed inside a velvet sack to ensure no royal blood touched the ground before being beaten to death with a scented sandalwood club.

TIMELINE	1548–68	1768	1779
	Thonburi Si Mahasamut, at the time little more than a Chinese trading post on the west bank of Mae Nam Chao Phraya, is founded.	King Taksin the Great moves the Thai capital from Ayuthaya to Thonburi Si Mahasamut, a location he regarded as beneficial for both trade and defence.	After a brutal war of territorial expansion, the Emerald Buddha, Thailand's most sacred Buddha image, is brought to Bangkok from Laos, along with hundreds of Laotian slaves.

attack from the west, Chakri moved the Siamese capital across the river to Bang Makok (Olive Plum riverbank), named for the trees that grew there in abundance. As the first monarch of the new Chakri royal dynasty – which continues to this day – Phraya Chakri was posthumously dubbed Rama I.

The first task set before the planners of the new city was to create hallowed ground for royal palaces and Buddhist monasteries. Astrologers divined that construction of the new royal palace should begin on 6 May 1782, and ceremonies consecrated King Phraphutthayotfa's transfer to a temporary new residence a month later.

In time, Ayuthaya's control of tribute states in Laos and western Cambodia was transferred to Bangkok and thousands of prisoners of war were brought to the capital to work. Bangkok also had ample access to free Thai labour via the *prâi lŏoang* (commoner/noble) system, under which all commoners were required to provide labour to the state in lieu of taxes.

Using this immense pool of labour, Rama I augmented Bangkok's natural canal and river system with hundreds of artificial waterways feeding into Thailand's hydraulic lifeline, the broad Mae Nam Chao Phraya. He also ordered the construction of 10km of city walls and *klorng rôrp grung* (canals around the city) to create a royal 'island' – Ko Ratanakosin – between Mae Nam Chao Phraya and the canal loop.

Temple and canal construction remained the highlight of early development in Bangkok until the reign of Rama III (King Phranangklao; r 1824–51), when attention turned to upgrading the port for international sea trade. The city soon became a regional centre for Chinese trading ships, slowly surpassing in importance even the British port at Singapore.

The Age of Politics
European Influence & the 1932 Revolution

Facing increasing pressure from British colonies in neighbouring Burma and Malaya, in 1855 Rama IV (King Mongkut; r 1851–68) signed the Bowring Treaty with Britain. This agreement marked Siam's break from exclusive economic involvement with China, a relationship that had dominated the previous century.

The signing of this document, and the subsequent ascension of Rama V (King Chulalongkorn; r 1868–1910), led to the largest period of European influence on Siam. Wishing to head off any potential invasion plans, Rama V ceded Laos and Cambodia to the French and northern Malaya to the British between 1893 and 1910. The two European powers,

Rama IV was the first monarch to show his face to the Thai public; Rama IX continued this tradition by making numerous visits to remote parts of the country.

1782	1783	1785	1821
Rama I re-establishes the Siamese court across the river from Thonburi, resulting in the creation of both the current Thai capital and the Chakri dynasty.	Chinese residents of the present-day Ko Ratanakosin area are relocated upriver along Mae Nam Chao Phraya to today's Yaowarat district, resulting in the city's Chinatown.	The majority of the construction of Ko Ratanakosin, Bangkok's royal district, including famous landmarks such as the Grand Palace and Wat Phra Kaew, is finished.	A boatload of opium marks the visit of the first Western trader to Bangkok; the trade of this substance is eventually banned nearly 20 years later.

EXTENDED FAMILIES INDEED...

Until polygamy was outlawed by Rama VI (King Vajiravudh; r 1910–25), it was expected of Thai monarchs to maintain a harem consisting of numerous 'major' and 'minor' wives and the children of these relationships. This led to some truly vast families: Rama I (King Phraphutthayotfa; r 1782–1809) had 42 children by 28 mothers; Rama II (King Phraphutthaloetla Naphalai; r 1809–24), 73 children by 40 mothers; Rama III (King Phranangklao; r 1824–51), 51 children by 37 mothers (he would eventually accumulate a total of 242 wives and consorts); Rama IV (King Mongkut; r 1851–68), 82 children by 35 mothers; and Rama V (King Chulalongkorn; r 1868–1910), 77 children by 40 mothers. In the case of Rama V, his seven 'major' wives were all half-sisters or first cousins, a conscious effort to maintain the purity of the bloodline of the Chakri dynasty. Other consorts or 'minor' wives were often the daughters of families wishing to gain greater ties with the royal family.

In contrast to the precedent set by his predecessors, Rama VI had one wife and one child, a girl born only a few hours before his death. As a result, his brother, Prajadhipok, was appointed as his successor. Rama VII also had only one wife and failed to produce any heirs. After abdicating in 1935 he did not exercise his right to appoint a successor, so lines were drawn back to Rama V, and the grandson of one of his remaining 'major' wives, nine-year-old Ananda Mahidol, was chosen to be the next king (Rama VIII; r 1935–46).

for their part, were happy to use Siam as a buffer state between their respective colonial domains.

Rama V gave Bangkok 120 new roads during his reign, inspired by street plans from Batavia (the Dutch colonial centre now known as Jakarta), Calcutta, Penang and Singapore. Germans were hired to design and build railways emanating from the capital, while the Dutch contributed the design of Bangkok's Hualamphong train station, today considered a minor masterpiece of civic art deco.

In 1893 Bangkok opened its first railway line, extending 22km from Bangkok to Pak Nam, where Mae Nam Chao Phraya enters the Gulf of Siam. A 20km electric tramway opened the following year, paralleling the left bank of Mae Nam Chao Phraya.

Americans established Siam's first printing press along with the kingdom's first newspaper in 1864. The first Siamese-language newspaper, *Darunovadha*, came along in 1874 and by 1900 Bangkok boasted three daily English-language newspapers: the *Bangkok Times, Siam Observer* and *Siam Free Press.*

As Bangkok prospered, many wealthy merchant families sent their children to study in Europe. Students of humbler socioeconomic

In 1861 Bangkok's European diplomats and merchants delivered a petition to Rama IV requesting roadways so they could enjoy horse riding for physical fitness and pleasure. The royal government acquiesced and established a handful of roads suitable for horse-drawn carriages and rickshaws.

1851	1855	1868	1893
Rama IV, the fourth king of the Chakri dynasty, comes to power, courts relations with the West and encourages the study of modern science in Siam.	Bangkok, now Siam's major trading centre, begins to feel pressure from colonial influences; Rama IV signs the Bowring Treaty, which liberalises foreign trade in Siam.	At the age of 15, Chulalongkorn, the oldest son of Rama IV, becomes the fifth king of the Chakri dynasty upon the death of his father.	After a territorial dispute, France sends gunboats to threaten Bangkok, forcing Siam to give up most of its territory east of the Mekong River; Siam gains its modern boundaries.

status who excelled at school had access to government scholarships for overseas study as well. In 1924 a handful of Siamese students in Paris formed the Promoters of Political Change, a group that met to discuss ideas for a future Siamese government modelled on Western democracy.

A bloodless revolution in 1932, initiated by the Promoters of Political Change and a willing Rama VII (King Prajadhipok; r 1925–35), transformed Siam from an absolute monarchy into a constitutional one. Bangkok thus found itself the nerve centre of a vast new civil service, which, coupled with its growing success as a world port, transformed the city into a mecca for Siamese seeking economic opportunities.

WWII & the Struggle for Democracy

Phibun Songkhram, appointed prime minister by the People's Party in December 1938, changed the country's name from Siam to Thailand and introduced the Western solar calendar. Phibun, who in 1941 allowed Japanese regiments access to the Gulf of Thailand, resigned in 1944 under pressure from the Thai underground resistance and was eventually exiled to Japan. Bangkok resumed its pace towards modernisation, even after Phibun returned to Thailand in 1948 and took over the leadership again via a military coup. Over the next 15 years, bridges were built over Mae Nam Chao Phraya, canals were filled in to provide space for new roads, and multistorey buildings began crowding out traditional teak structures.

In 1957 Phibun's successor General Sarit Thanarat subjected the country to a true military dictatorship: abolishing the constitution, dissolving the parliament and banning all political parties. In the 1950s the US partnered with Sarit and subsequent military dictators, Thanom Kittikachorn and Praphat Charusathien (who controlled the country from 1964 to 1973), to allow the US military to develop bases in Thailand during the war in Vietnam in exchange for economic incentives. During this time Bangkok gained notoriety as a 'rest and recreation' (R&R) spot for foreign troops stationed in Southeast Asia.

By 1973 an opposition group of left-wing activists, mainly intellectuals and students, organised political rallies demanding a constitution from the military government. On 14 October that year the military brutally suppressed a large demonstration in Bangkok, killing 77 people and wounding more than 800. The event is commemorated by a monument on Th Ratchadamnoen Klang in Bangkok, near the Democracy Monument. King Bhumibol stepped in and refused to support further bloodshed, forcing Thanom and Praphat to leave Thailand.

HISTORY THE AGE OF POLITICS

Water-borne traffic, supplemented by a meagre network of footpaths, dominated Bangkok for well into the middle of the 19th century.

Since becoming a constitutional monarchy in 1932, Thailand has had a whopping 20 constitutions; only Venezuela and Ecuador have had more.

1910	1914	1917	1932
Vajiravudh becomes the sixth king of the Chakri dynasty after the death of his older brother; he fails to produce a male heir during his reign.	Official opening of Don Mueang, Thailand's first international airport, which remained the country's main domestic and international airport until the opening of Suvarnabhumi in 2006.	Bangkok's first Western-style institute of higher education, Chulalongkorn University, is founded; it's still regarded as the country's most prestigious.	A bloodless coup transforms Siam from an absolute to a constitutional monarchy; deposed king Rama VII remains on the throne until he resigns three years later.

The Crisis & the People's Constitution

In 1988 Prem was replaced in elections by Chatichai Choonhavan, leader of the Chat Thai Party, who created a government dominated by well-connected provincial business people. His government shifted power away from the bureaucrats and set about transforming Thailand into an 'Asian Tiger' economy. But the business of politics was often bought and sold like a commodity and Chatichai was overthrown by the military on grounds of extreme corruption. This coup demarcated an emerging trend in Thai politics: the Bangkok business community and educated classes siding with the military against provincial business-politicians and their money politics.

In May 1992 several huge demonstrations demanding the resignation of the next in a long line of military dictators, General Suchinda Kraprayoon, rocked Bangkok and the large provincial capitals. Charismatic Bangkok governor Chamlong Srimuang, winner of the 1992 Magsaysay Award (a humanitarian service award issued in the Philippines) for his role in galvanising the public to reject Suchinda, led the protests. After confrontations between the protesters and the military near the Democracy Monument resulted in nearly 50 deaths and hundreds of injuries, Rama IX summoned both Suchinda and Chamlong for a rare public scolding. Suchinda resigned, having been in power for less than six weeks.

Bangkok approached the new millennium riding a tide of events that set new ways of governing and living in the capital. The most defining moment occurred in July 1997 when – after several months of warning signs that nearly everyone in Thailand and the international community ignored – the Thai currency fell into a deflationary tailspin and the national economy screeched to a virtual halt. The country's economy was plagued by foreign-debt burdens, an overextension in the real-estate sector and a devalued currency. Within months of the crisis, the Thai currency plunged from 25B to 56B per US$1. Bangkok, which rode at the forefront of the 1980s double-digit economic boom, suffered more than elsewhere in the country in terms of job losses and massive income erosion. The International Monetary Fund (IMF) stepped in to impose financial and legal reforms and economic liberalisation programs in exchange for more than US$17 billion to stabilise the Thai currency.

In the following years, the left-oriented student movement grew more radical, creating fears among working-class and middle-class Thais of home-grown communism. In 1976 Thanom returned to Thailand (ostensibly to become a monk) and was received warmly by the royal family. In response, protesters organised demonstrations

> Although it was forced to cede land to both England and France, Thailand is the only country in Southeast Asia that escaped colonisation by a European power.

1935–46	1939	1946	1951–63
Ananda Mahidol, grandson of one of Rama V's 'major' wives, is appointed king; his reign ends abruptly when he is shot dead in his room in mysterious circumstances.	The country's name is changed from Siam to Thailand.	Pridi Phanomyong becomes Thailand's first democratically elected prime minister; after a military coup, Pridi is forced to flee Thailand, returning only briefly one more time.	Field marshal Sarit Thanarat wrests power from Phibun Songkhram, abolishes the constitution and embarks on one of the most authoritarian regimes in modern Thai history.

at Thammasat University against the perceived perpetrator of the 14 October massacre. Right-wing, anticommunist civilian groups clashed with the students, resulting in bloody violence. In the aftermath, many students and intellectuals were forced underground and joined armed communist insurgents – known as the People's Liberation Army of Thailand (PLAT) – based in the jungles of northern and southern Thailand.

Military control of the country continued through the 1980s. The government of the 'political soldier', General Prem Tinsulanonda, enjoyed a period of political and economic stability. Prem dismantled the communist insurgency through military action and amnesty programs. But the country's new economic success presented a challenging rival: prominent business leaders who criticised the military's role in government and their now-dated Cold War mentality.

The Recent Past

Thaksin Shinawatra: CEO Prime Minister

In January 2001 billionaire and former police colonel Thaksin Shinawatra became prime minister after winning a landslide victory in nationwide elections – the first in Thailand under the strict guidelines established in the 1997 constitution. Thaksin's new party, called Thai Rak Thai (TRT; Thais Love Thailand), swept into power on a populist agenda that seemed at odds with the man's enormous wealth and influence. Self-styled as a CEO-politician, Thaksin swiftly delivered on his campaign promises for rural development, including agrarian debt relief, village capital funds and cheap health care.

Despite numerous controversies, during the February 2005 general elections Thaksin became the first Thai leader in history to be re-elected to a consecutive second term. His popularity among the working class and rural voters was immense.

However, time was running short for Thaksin and his party. In 2006 Thaksin was accused of abusing his powers and of conflicts of interest, most notably in his family's sale of their Shin Corporation to the Singaporean government for 73 billion baht (US$1.88 billion), a tax-free gain thanks to legislation he helped craft. Demonstrations in Bangkok called for his ousting and many of the PM's most highly placed supporters also turned against him.

Historical Reads

....

Thailand: A Short History (David K Wyatt; 1984; updated 2003)

....

A History of Thailand (Chris Baker & Pasuk Phongpaichit; 2005)

....

Chronicle of Thailand (William Warren & Nicholas Grossman, Editions Didier Millet; 2010)

The Coup and the Red & Yellow Divide

On the evening of 19 September 2006, while Thaksin was attending a UN conference in New York City, the Thai military took power in a

1962	1973	1981	1985
US involvement in the Indochina War leads to economic and infrastructural expansion of Bangkok; dissatisfaction with the Thai government leads to communist insurgency.	Student protests lead to violent military suppression; 1971 coup leader Thanom Kittikachorn is exiled by Rama IX; Kukrit Pramoj's civilian government takes charge.	General Prem Tinsulanonda is appointed prime minister after a military coup and is largely able to stabilise Thai politics over the next eight years.	Chamlong Srimuang is elected mayor of Bangkok; three years later, after forming his own largely Buddhist-based political group, the Palang Dharma Party, he is re-elected as mayor.

bloodless coup. Calling themselves the Council for Democratic Reform under the Constitutional Monarch, the junta cited the TRT government's alleged violations of lèse-majesté laws (royal treason), corruption, interference with state agencies and creation of social divisions as justification for the coup. Thaksin quickly flew to London, where he remained in exile until his UK visa was revoked in 2008.

In a nationwide referendum held on 19 August 2007, Thais approved a military-drafted constitution. Under the new constitution, elections were finally held in late 2007. After forming a loose coalition with several other parties, parliament chose veteran politician and close Thaksin ally Samak Sundaravej as prime minister. This was an unsatisfactory outcome for the military and the anti-Thaksin group known as the People's Alliance for Democracy (PAD), comprised of mainly urban elites nicknamed 'Yellow Shirts' because they wore yellow (the then-king's birthday colour). It was popularly believed that Thaksin was consolidating power during his tenure so that he could interrupt royal succession.

In September 2008 Samak Sundaravej was unseated by the Constitutional Court on a technicality: while in office, he hosted a TV cooking show deemed to be a conflict of interest. Concerned that another election would yield another Thaksin win, on 25 November, hundreds of armed PAD protesters stormed Bangkok's Suvarnabhumi and Don Mueang airports, entering the passenger terminals and taking over the control towers. Thousands of additional PAD sympathisers eventually flooded Suvarnabhumi, leading to the cancellation of all flights and leaving as many as 230,000 domestic and international passengers stranded. The stand-off lasted until 2 December, when the Supreme Court wielded its power yet again in order to ban Samak's successor, Prime Minister Somchai Wongsawat, from politics and ordered his political party and two coalition parties dissolved.

In December 2008 a tenuous new coalition was formed, led by Oxford-educated Abhisit Vejjajiva, leader of the Democrat Party. Despite Abhisit being young, photogenic, articulate and allegedly untainted by corruption, his perceived association with the PAD did little to placate the United Front for Democracy against Dictatorship (UDD), a loose association of red-shirted Thaksin supporters, who by 2010 were holding large-scale protests in central Bangkok to demand that he stand down. Thailand, which had mostly experienced a relatively high level of domestic stability and harmony throughout its modern history, was now effectively polarised between the predominantly middle- and upper-class, urban-based PAD and the largely working-class, rural UDD.

A mere 13 sq km in 1900, today, the Bangkok Metropolitan Region (which includes Nakhon Pathom, Non-thaburi, Pathum Thani, Samut Prakan, Samut Sakhon and Thonburi) spans an astounding 7762 sq km.

1992	1997	1999	2001
Protests led by Chamlong Srimuang against 1991 coup leader Suchinda Kraprayoon lead to violent confrontations; Suchinda resigns following a public scolding by Rama IX.	Thailand devalues the baht, triggering the Asian economic crisis; massive unemployment and personal debt, and a crash of the Thai stock market follow.	The BTS (Skytrain), Bangkok's first expansive public transport system, opens in commemoration of Rama IX's 6th cycle (72nd) birthday.	Thaksin Shinawatra, Thailand's richest man, is elected prime minister on a populist platform in what some have called the most open, corruption-free election in Thai history.

THAILAND'S CONSTITUTIONAL CRISES

Since transitioning to a constitutional monarchy in 1932, Thailand has seen a staggering 18 constitutions (20 by some counts) – on average a new charter every four years, thought to be the most constitutionally unstable of any country.

The most lauded of Thailand's charters is undoubtedly the 1997 constitution. Often called the 'people's constitution', the charter fostered great hope in a population left emotionally battered by the 1997 economic crisis by guaranteeing – at least on paper – more human and civil rights than had ever been granted in Thailand. The document, which was drafted largely by elected officials and subject to public scrutiny, called for the upper and lower chambers of parliament to be fully elected by popular vote, essentially strengthening the influence of voters and the role of prime minister. It was this power to the people that paved the way for Thaksin and his well-loved Thai Rak Thai party to win just short of half of the seats in parliament in 2001, and nearly complete control of parliament in 2005.

Subsequent constitutions, largely drafted under the gaze of military regimes, have grown notably thicker (the draft constitution proposed in 2015 spanned a whopping 194 pages and 315 articles) and have moved in the opposite direction of the spirit of the 1997 charter, essentially weakening the executive branch while increasing the influence and power of the judiciary. The most recent constitution, drafted by the National Council for Peace and Order (NCPO) – the military junta – and signed by the king in 2017, includes controversial provisions that allow for an unelected prime minister, grants the military sweeping powers and enshrines its amnesty from past and future actions. The document is thought to pave the way for elections in 2018.

In April 2010 violent clashes between police and protesters (numbering in the tens of thousands) resulted in 25 deaths. Red-shirted protesters barricaded themselves into an area stretching from Lumphini Park to the shopping district near Siam Sq, effectively shutting down parts of central Bangkok. In May the protesters were eventually dispersed by force, but not before at least 36 buildings were set alight and at least 15 people killed. Crackdown-related arson damage was estimated at US$1.5 billion and the death toll from the 2010 conflicts amounted to nearly 100 people, making it Thailand's most deadly and costly political unrest in 20 years.

Yingluck Shinawatra & a Return to Military Rule

Parliamentary elections in 2011 saw the election of Yingluck Shinawatra, the younger sister of the still-exiled Thaksin. A former businesswoman, Yingluck had no prior political experience and was described by her older brother as his 'clone'. Yingluck's leadership was tested almost

2004	9 June 2006	19 September 2006	August 2007
The MRT (Metro), Bangkok's first underground public transport system, is opened; an accident the next year injures 140 and causes the system to shut down for two weeks.	Thailand celebrates the 60th anniversary of Rama IX's ascension to the throne; the Thai king continues to be the longest-serving monarch in the world.	A bloodless coup sees the Thai military take power from Thaksin while he is at a UN meeting in New York; at the time of research he remains in exile.	In a nationwide referendum, voters agree to approve a military-drafted constitution, Thailand's 17th since becoming a constitutional monarchy in 1932.

IN MEMORY OF KING BHUMIBOL

King Bhumibol Adulyadej (Rama IX; 1927–2016) was born in the USA, where his father Prince Mahidol was studying medicine at Harvard University. He was fluent in English, French, German and Thai and ascended the throne in 1946. An ardent jazz composer and saxophonist, Rama IX hosted jam sessions with the likes of jazz greats Woody Herman and Benny Goodman. The king was also a sailor and a painter. He is credited for his extensive development projects, particularly in rural areas of Thailand. *King Bhumibol Adulyadej: A Life's Work* (Nicholas Grossman & Dominic Faulder eds; 2011) is the official biography of the king.

King Bhumibol and Queen Sirikit had four children: Princess Ubol Ratana (b 1951), King Maha Vajiralongkorn (b 1952), Princess Mahachakri Sirindhorn (b 1955) and Princess Chulabhorn (b 1957).

Along with nation and religion, the monarchy is very highly regarded in Thai society – negative comments about the king or any member of the royal family is a social as well as legal taboo.

immediately, when in mid-2011 the outskirts of Bangkok were hit by the most devastating floods in decades. Although nearly all of central Bangkok was spared from flooding, it was largely perceived that this was done at the expense of upcountry regions.

Yingluck's tenure progressed relatively uneventfully until 2013, when she had to deal with the fallout from both a botched rice scheme and a proposed bill that would have granted amnesty to her brother, potentially allowing Thaksin to return to Thailand without facing trial for previous corruption convictions. The bill was rejected, but Yingluck's intentions were made clear. Within weeks, antigovernment protesters were staging frequent rallies, eventually taking over sections of central Bangkok in early 2014. After violent clashes that led to dozens of deaths and a nullified election, in May 2014, Thailand's Constitutional Court found Yingluck and nine members of her cabinet guilty of abuse of power, forcing them to stand down.

In 2011 Yingluck Shinawatra became the first female prime minister in Thai history; at only 43 years old, she was also the country's youngest leader in 60 years.

The military quickly filled the vacuum after Yingluck's ousting, declaring martial law on 20 May and, two days later, officially announcing that it had seized power of the country, carrying out Thailand's 12th successful military coup since 1932. Yingluck was subsequently impeached (thus banning her from participating in politics for five years) and at the time of writing is facing criminal charges.

In August 2014 former Commander in Chief of the Royal Thai Army Prayut Chan-o-cha shed his uniform to become Thailand's prime minister – the country's 29th since 1932. To date, Prayut's rule has been

November 2008	April 2010	July 2011	5 August 2011
Thousands of yellow-shirted anti-Thaksin protesters – the People's Alliance for Democracy (PAD) – take over Bangkok's airports; tourist numbers drop.	Pro-Thaksin supporters clash with troops in central Bangkok, leading to 25 deaths, several hundred injuries and the torching of several buildings.	Heavy monsoon rains lead to floods covering much of central Thailand, including parts of Bangkok, although protective measures spare nearly all the city's central districts.	Thai parliament approves the election of Yingluck Shinawatra, younger sister of deposed former prime minister Thaksin Shinawatra and the country's first female prime minister.

heavy-handed, quickly squashing protests and incarcerating political opponents in the name of 'attitude adjustment'. Press freedom in Thailand is highly restricted and lèse-majesté-related convictions have spiked.

On 17 August 2015, a bomb planted at Bangkok's Erawan Shrine exploded, killing 20 people, mostly Chinese tourists. At the time of writing, two suspects had been arrested and the incident was thought to be tied to Uighur militants, ostensibly in revenge for Thailand's forced repatriation of 109 Uighurs to China earlier in the year.

On 13 October 2016, at the age of 89, King Bhumibol, Thailand's – and the world's – longest-serving monarch, passed away. The occasion was marked by a year of mourning culminating in a funeral at Bangkok's Grand Palace that cost US$90 million. Power was passed to his son, Maha Vajiralongkorn, who had assumed many of the royal duties during his father's illness.

Although royal transition was smooth, the junta, at press time in power for more than four years, has failed to address Thailand's slumping economy. Foreign investment, exports and GDP all contracted after the coup. In 2016 a much-needed infrastructure investment plan was announced to help bolster the downturn. Tourism continues to be the bright spot in the economy.

October 2013– February 2014	22 May 2014	17 August 2015	3 October 2016
Antigoverment protesters seize key sections of Bangkok; violent incidents lead to 825 injuries and 28 deaths.	The Thai military seizes control of the country in what is Thailand's 12th coup d'état since abolishing absolute monarchy in 1932.	A terrorist bomb is set off at Erawan Shrine, killing 20.	King Bhumibol Adulyadej, Thailand's longest-serving monarch, passes away. His extravagant royal cremation ceremony is held following a year of mourning, in October 2017.

People & Culture

Bangkok is both utterly Thai and totally foreign. Old and new ways clash and mingle, constantly redrawing the lines of what it means to be 'Thai'. Despite the international veneer, a Thai value system – built primarily on religious and monarchical devotion – guides every aspect of life. Almost all Thais are dedicated Buddhists aiming to be reborn into a better life by making merit (giving donations to temples or feeding monks), regarding this as the key to their earthly success.

People of Bangkok

Bangkok accommodates every rung of the economic ladder, from the aristocrat to the slum dweller. It is the new start for the economic hopefuls and the last chance for the economic refugees. The lucky ones from the bottom rung – taxi drivers, food vendors, maids, nannies and even prostitutes – form the working-class backbone of the city. Many hail from the northeastern provinces and send hard-earned baht back to their families in small rural villages. At the very bottom are the dispossessed, who live in squatter communities on marginal, often polluted land. While the Thai economy has surged, a truly comprehensive social net has yet to be constructed. Meanwhile, Bangkok is also the great incubator for Thailand's new generation of young creatives, from designers to architects, and has long nurtured the archetype of the country's middle class.

The city has also represented economic opportunity for foreign immigrants. Approximately half of its population claims some Chinese ancestry, be it Cantonese, Hainanese, Hokkien or Teochew. Although the first Chinese labourers faced discrimination from the Thais, their descendants' success in business, finance and public affairs helped to elevate the status of Chinese and Thai-Chinese families.

Immigrants from South Asia also migrated to Bangkok and comprise the second-largest Asian minority. Sikhs from northern India typically make their living in tailoring, while Sinhalese, Bangladeshis, Nepalis and Pakistanis can be found in the import-export or retail trade.

Thailand Demographics

Population: 68.4 million

Fertility Rate: 1.5

Percentage of people over 65: 10.5%

Urban population: 52.7%

Life expectancy: 74 years

The Thai Character

Much of Thailand's cultural value system is hinged upon respect for family, religion and the monarchy. Within that system each person knows their place and Thai children are strictly instructed in the importance of group conformity, respecting elders and suppressing confrontational views. In most social situations, establishing harmony often takes a leading role and Thais take personal pride in making others feel at ease.

Other notable cultural characteristics include a strong belief in the concept of saving face and an equally strong regard for *sà·nùk*, Thai-style fun.

Religion

Religion plays a sigificant role in the life of most Bangkokians. Indeed, the people of Bangkok could be said to literally wear their religion on their sleeves, as clothing, amulets and other talismans are often clear indicators of one's faith. Around 90% are Buddhists, who believe that individuals compound merit through a combination of good works, meditation and study of the dharma (Buddhist philosophy). Other belief systems that feature prominently in Bangkok include Islam and animism.

Theravada Buddhism

The social and administrative centre for Thai Buddhism is the wát (temple or monastery), a walled compound containing several buildings constructed in the traditional Thai style with steep, swooping roof lines and colourful interior murals; the most important structures contain solemn Buddha statues cast in bronze.

Walk the streets of Bangkok early in the morning and you'll catch the flash of shaved heads bobbing above bright ochre robes, as monks all over the city engage in *bìn·tá·bàht*, the daily house-to-house alms-food gathering. Thai men are expected to shave their heads and don monastic robes temporarily at least once in their lives.

Guardian Spirits

Animism predates the arrival of all other religions in Bangkok, and it still plays an important role in the everyday life of most city residents. Believing that *prá poom* (guardian spirits) inhabit rivers, canals, trees and other natural features, and that these spirits must be placated whenever humans trespass upon or make use of these features, the Thais build spirit shrines to house the displaced spirits. These dollhouse-like structures perch on wood or cement pillars next to their homes and receive daily offerings of rice, fruit, flowers and, frequently, bottles of Fanta.

Cultural Readings

....

Being Dharma: The Essence of the Buddha's Teachings (Ajahn Chah; 2001)

....

Very Thai (Philip Cornwel-Smith; 2013)

....

Sacred Tattoos of Thailand (Joe Cummings; 2011)

PEOPLE & CULTURE RELIGION

THE CHINESE INFLUENCE

In many ways Bangkok is a Chinese, as much as a Thai, city. The presence of the Chinese in Bangkok dates back to before the founding of the city, when Thonburi Si Mahasamut was little more than a Chinese trading outpost on Mae Nam Chao Phraya. In the 1780s, during the construction of the new capital under Rama I (King Phraphutthayotfa; r 1782–1809), Hokkien, Teochew and Hakka Chinese were hired as labourers. The Chinese already living in the area were relocated to the districts of Yaowarat and Sampeng, today known as Bangkok's Chinatown.

During the reign of Rama I, many Chinese began to move up in status and wealth. They controlled many of Bangkok's shops and businesses, and because of increased trading ties with China, were responsible for an immense expansion in Thailand's market economy. Visiting Europeans during the 1820s were astonished by the number of Chinese trading ships on Mae Nam Chao Phraya and some assumed that the Chinese formed the majority of Bangkok's population.

The newfound wealth of certain Chinese trading families created one of Thailand's first elite classes that was not directly related to royalty. Known as *jôw sŏo·a*, these 'merchant lords' eventually obtained additional status by accepting official posts and royal titles, as well as offering their daughters to the royal family.

During the reign of Rama III (King Phranangklao; r 1824–51), the Thai capital began to absorb many elements of Chinese food, design, fashion and literature. This growing ubiquity of Chinese culture, coupled with the tendency of Chinese men to marry Thai women and assimilate into Thai culture, had, by the beginning of the 20th century, resulted in relatively little difference between the Chinese and their Siamese counterparts. By the turn of the 21st century, approximately half the people in Bangkok were able to lay claim to some Chinese ancestry.

WHAT'S A WÁT?

Bangkok is home to hundreds of wáts, temple compounds that have traditionally been at the centre of community life.

Buddha Images

Elongated earlobes, no evidence of bone or muscle, arms that reach to the knees, a third eye: these are some of the 32 characteristics, originating from 3rd-century India, that govern the depiction of the Buddha in sculpture and denote his divine nature. Other symbols to be aware of are the various hand positions and 'postures', which depict periods in the life of the Buddha.

Sitting Teaching or meditating. If the right hand is pointed towards the earth, the Buddha is subduing the demons of desire. If the hands are folded in the lap, the Buddha is meditating.

Reclining The exact moment of the Buddha's passing into *parinibbana* (post-death nirvana).

Standing Bestowing blessings or taming evil forces.

Walking The Buddha after his return to earth from heaven.

Buildings & Structures

Even the smallest *wát* will usually have a *bòht, wí·hǎhn* and monks' living quarters.

Bòht The ordination hall, the most sacred prayer room at a wát. Aside from the fact it does not house the main Buddha image, you'll know the *bòht* because it is usually more ornately decorated and has eight cornerstones to mark its boundary.

Chedi (stupa) A large bell-shaped tower usually containing five structural elements symbolising (from bottom to top) earth, water, fire, wind and void; depending on the wát, relics of the Buddha, a Thai king or some other notable are typically housed inside.

Drum Tower Elevates the ceremonial drum beaten by novices.

Gù·đì Monks' living quarters.

Hŏr đrai The manuscript library: a structure for holding Buddhist scriptures. As these texts were previously made from palm leaves, *hŏr đrai* were typically elevated or built over water to protect them from flooding and/or termites.

Mon·dòp An open-sided, square building with four arches and a pyramidal roof, used to worship religious objects or texts.

Săh·lah (sala) A pavilion, often open-sided, for relaxation, lessons or miscellaneous activities.

Wí·hǎhn (vihara) The sanctuary for the temple's main Buddha image and where lay-people come to make their offerings. Classic architecture typically has a three-tiered roof representing the triple gems: the Buddha (the teacher), dharma (the teaching) and sangha (the followers).

þrahng A towering phallic spire of Khmer origin serving the same religious purpose as a chedi .

Other Religions

Thai royal ceremony remains almost exclusively the domain of one of the most ancient religious traditions still functioning in the kingdom, Brahmanism. White-robed, topknotted priests of Indian descent keep alive an arcane collection of rituals that, it is generally believed, must be performed at regular intervals to sustain the three pillars of Thai nationhood: sovereignty, religion and the monarchy.

Green-hued onion domes looming over rooftops belong to mosques and mark the immediate neighbourhood as Muslim, while brightly painted and ornately carved cement spires indicate a Hindu temple.

Wander down congested Th Chakkaraphet in Bangkok's Phahurat district to find Gurdwara Siri Guru Singh Sabha, a Sikh temple where visitors are very welcome. A handful of steepled Christian churches, including a few historic ones, have been built over the centuries and can be found near the banks of Mae Nam Chao Phraya. In Chinatown, large round doorways topped with heavily inscribed Chinese characters and flanked by red paper lanterns mark the location of *săhn jôw,* Chinese temples dedicated to the worship of Buddhist, Taoist and Confucian deities.

Monarchy

The Thais' relationship with their king is deeply spiritual and intensely personal. All Thai kings are referred to as 'Rama', one of the incarnations of the Hindu god Vishnu, and are seen as a father figure (the previous king's birthday is also the national celebration of Father's Day). Thailand's previous monarch, King Bhumibol Adulyadej, also known as Rama IX, was the longest-serving in Thailand and the world until he passed away in late 2016. He has been succeeded by his son, Maha Vajiralongkorn, Rama X.

It's worth mentioning that, in Thai society, not only is criticising the monarchy an extreme social faux pas, it's also illegal.

Visual Arts

Buddha sculptures and murals communicate a continuous visual language of the religion and are arguably Thailand's highest art form. Adapting traditional themes to the secular canvas didn't begin until around the turn of the 20th century, when Western influence surged in the region.

Much of Bangkok's best ancient art is on display inside its temples, while the city's museums curate more contemporary collections.

Divine Inspiration

The wát served as a locus for the highest expressions of Thai art for roughly 800 years, from the Lanna to Ratanakosin eras. Accordingly, Bangkok's 400-plus Buddhist temples are brimming with the figuratively imaginative, if thematically formulaic, art of Thailand's foremost muralists. Always instructional in intent, such painted images range from the depiction of the *Jataka* (stories of the Buddha's past lives) and scenes from the *Ramakian,* the Thai version of the Indian Hindu epic *Ramayana,* to elaborate scenes detailing daily life in Thailand.

The development of Thai religious art and architecture is broken into different periods defined by the patronage of the ruling capital. The best examples of a period's characteristics are seen in the variations of the *chedi* shape and in the features of the Buddhist sculpture, including facial features, the top flourish on the head, the dress and the position of the feet in meditation.

The Modern Era

In general, early contemporary Thai painting favoured abstraction over realism, and often preserves the one-dimensional perspective of traditional mural paintings. In the 1970s Thai artists tackled the modernisation of Buddhist themes through abstract expressionism. In the 1990s there was a push to move art out of museums and into public spaces. Today, there are two major trends in contemporary Thai art: the updating of religious themes and tongue-in-cheek social commentary. In particular, Thai sculpture is often considered to be the strongest of the contemporary arts.

PEOPLE & CULTURE MONARCHY

Arts Readings

....

Flavours: Thai Contemporary Art (Steven Pettifor; 2003)

....

The Thai House: History and Evolution (Ruethai Chaichongrak et al; 2002)

....

The Arts of Thailand (Steve Van Beek; 1991)

Music

Throughout Thailand you'll encounter a rich diversity of musical genres and styles, from the serene court music that accompanies classical dance-drama to the bass-heavy house music shaking dance clubs in the bigger cities.

Bangkok, not surprisingly, is the epicentre of the country's music scene, home to its biggest record labels and studios, although immigrants from upcountry have introduced a thriving culture of *lôok tûng* and *mŏr lam*, roughly analgous to country-and-western music in the US.

A handy English-language resource for contemporary Thai music is Deungdutjai (www.deungdu tjai.com), which also has English-language translations of popular Thai songs.

Classical Thai

Classical central-Thai music *(pleng tai deum)* features a dazzling array of textures and subtleties, hair-raising tempos and pastoral melodies. The classical orchestra *(pèe-pâht)* can include as few as five players or might have more than 20. Leading the band is *pèe,* a straight-lined woodwind instrument with a reed mouthpiece and an oboe-like tone; you'll hear it most at *moo·ay tai* (Thai boxing; also spelt *muay Thai)* matches. The four-stringed *phin,* plucked like a guitar, lends subtle counterpoint, while *rá·nâht èhk,* a bamboo-keyed percussion instrument resembling the xylophone, carries the main melodies. The slender *sor,* a bowed instrument with a coconut-shell soundbox, provides soaring embellishments, as does the *klòo·i,* a wooden Thai flute.

Lôok Tûng & Mŏr Lam

Popular Thai music has borrowed much from Western music, particularly in instruments, but retains a distinct flavour of its own. The best selling of all modern musical genres in Thailand remains *lôok tûng.* Literally 'children of the fields', *lôok tûng* dates back to the 1940s, is comparable to country-and-western in the USA and is a genre that tends to appeal most to working-class Thais. Subject matter almost always concerns tales of lost love, tragic early death and the dire circumstances of farmers who work day in and day out and, at the end of the year, still owe money to the bank.

Another genre more firmly rooted in northeastern Thailand, and nearly as popular in Bangkok, is *mŏr lam.* Based on the songs played on the Lao-Isan *kaan,* a wind instrument devised of a double row of bamboo-like reeds fitted into a hardwood soundbox, *mŏr lam* features a simple but insistent bass beat and plaintive vocal melodies.

In recent years*lôok tûng* and *mŏr lam* from the 1960s and '70s have seen a resurgence of popularity in Thailand and have also garnered a cult following abroad, largely aided by successful retro compilations.

Thai Playlist

Bird Hits for Fan: Love Hits (Bird Thongchai; 2011)

Moderndog-Soem Sukhaphap (Moderndog; 1994)

Mint (Silly Fools; 2000)

Palmy (Palmy; 2001)

Romantic Comedy (Apartment Khunpa; 2006)

Begins (Big Ass; 2006)

Songs for Life

The 1970s ushered in a new music style inspired by the politically conscious folk rock of the US and Europe, which the Thais dubbed *pleng pêu·a chee·wít* (literally 'music for life') after Marxist Jit Phumisak's earlier Art for Life movement. Closely identified with the Thai band Caravan – who still perform – the introduction of this style was the most significant musical shift in Thailand since *lôok tûng* arose in the 1940s.

Pleng pêu·a chee·wít has political and environmental topics rather than the usual love themes. During the authoritarian dictatorships of the '70s many of Caravan's songs were banned. Following the massacre of student demonstrators in 1976, some members of the band fled to the hills to take up with armed communist groups.

T-Pop & Indie

For more than three decades now, Thailand has had a thriving teen-pop industry – sometimes referred to as T-Pop – centred on artists who have been chosen for their good looks and then matched with syrupy song arrangements. Thongchai 'Bird' McIntyre, who released his first album in 1986, is arguably the king of this genre. In the 1990s labels such as GMM Grammy and RS Productions released a flood of T-pop copycat acts, often emulating Western-style boy bands or Japanese and Taiwanese musical trends. The current crop of Thai pop stars can be seen imitating the signature dance moves of Korean pop stars (Japan pop, or J-pop, is out).

In the 1990s an alternative pop scene – known as *glorng sĕh·ree* (free drum), also *pleng dâi din* (underground music) – grew in Bangkok. Moderndog, a Britpop-inspired band of four Chulalongkorn University graduates, is generally credited with bringing independent Thai music into the mainstream and their success prompted an explosion of similar bands and indie recording labels. Although some of the influential indie labels have been bought out by bigger conglomerates, today the alt scene lives on in a variety of other forms – lounge pop, garage rock and electronica.

Cinema

Bangkok Film launched Thailand's film industry with the first Thai-directed silent movie, *Chok Sorng Chan,* in 1927. Perhaps partially influenced by India's famed masala movies – which enjoyed a strong following in post-WWII Bangkok – early Thai films blended romance, comedy, melodrama and adventure to give audiences a little bit of everything. Popular Thai cinema ballooned in the 1960s and '70s, especially when the government levied a tax on Hollywood imports, which spawned a home-grown industry.

However, the Thai movie industry almost died during the '80s and '90s, swamped by Hollywood extravaganzas and the boom era's taste for anything imported. From a 1970s peak of about 200 releases per year, by 1997 the Thai output shrank to an average of only 10 films a year. The Southeast Asian economic crisis that year threatened to further bludgeon the ailing industry, but the lack of funding coupled with foreign competition brought about a new emphasis on quality rather than quantity.

Thai cinema graduated into international film circles in the late 1990s and early 2000s, with directors like Apichatpong Weerasethakul earning accolades from critics, including at Cannes. Film-fest fare has been bolstered by independent film clubs and self-promotion through social media. This is how low-budget filmmakers are bypassing the big studios, the censors (who are ever-vigilant) and the skittish, controversy-averse movie theatres. At the same time, Thailand's big studios continue to put out ghost stories, horror flicks, sappy love stories and camp comedies. Popular and elaborate historical movies serve a dual purpose: making money and promoting national identity.

Traditional Theatre & Dance

Bangkok's high arts have declined since the palace transitioned from a cloistered community, although some endangered art forms have been salvaged and revived for a growing tourist community. The most famous example of this is *kŏhn,* a dance-drama that depicts the *Ramakian,* the Thai version of India's *Ramayana.*

Kŏhn

Scenes performed in traditional *kŏhn* (and *lá·kon*) come from the 'epic journey' tale of the *Ramakian*, with parallels in the Greek *Odyssey* and

---

Thai Movies

Ong Bak; Muay Thai Warrior (directed by Prachya Pinkaew; 2003)

Uncle Boonmee Who Can Recall His Past Lives (directed by Apichatpong Weerasethakul; 2010)

How to Win at Checkers (Every Time) (directed by Josh Kim; 2015)

the myth of Jason and the Argonauts. In all *kŏhn* performances, four types of characters are represented – male humans, female humans, monkeys and demons. Monkey and demon figures are always masked with the elaborate head coverings often seen in tourist promo material. Behind the masks and make-up, all actors are male. Traditional *kŏhn* is very expensive to produce – Ravana's retinue alone (Ravana is the *Ramakian's* principal villain) consists of more than 100 demons, each with a distinctive mask.

Lá·kon

The more formal *lá·kon nai* (inner *lá·kon*, which means that it is performed inside the palace) was originally performed for lower nobility by all-female ensembles. Today it's a dying art, even more so than royal *kŏhn*. In addition to scenes from the *Ramakian*, *lá·kon nai* performances may include traditional Thai folk tales; whatever the story, text is always sung. *Lá·kon nôrk* (outer *lá·kon*, performed outside the palace) deals exclusively with folk tales and features a mix of sung and spoken text, sometimes with improvisation. Male and female performers are permitted. Like *kŏhn* and *lá·kon nai*, performances of *lá·kon nôrk* are increasingly rare.

A variation on *lá·kon* that has evolved specifically for shrine worship, *lá·kon gâa bon* involves an ensemble of about 20, including musicians. At an important shrine such as Bangkok's Lak Meuang, four troupes may perform in rotation, each for a week at a time, as each performance lasts from 9am to 3pm and there is usually a long list of worshippers waiting to hire them.

English-language versions of Thai literature are hard to come by, but translations of several Thai short stories and novels can be downloaded as e-books at www. thaifiction.com.

Lí·gair

In outlying working-class neighbourhoods of Bangkok you may be lucky enough to come across the gaudy, raucous *lí·gair*. This theatrical art form is thought to have descended from drama-rituals brought to southern Thailand by Arab and Malay traders. The first native public performance in central Thailand came about when a group of Thai Muslims staged *lí·gair* for Rama V in Bangkok during the funeral commemoration of Queen Sunantha. *Lí·gair* grew very popular under Rama VI, peaked in the early 20th century and has been fading slowly since the 1960s.

Lá·kon Lék

Lá·kon lék (little theatre; also known as *hùn lŏo·ang,* or royal puppets), like *kŏhn*, was once reserved for court performances. Metre-high marionettes made of *kòi* paper and wire, wearing elaborate costumes modelled on those of the *kŏhn*, were used to convey similar themes, music and dance movements.

Two or three puppet masters were required to manipulate each *hùn lŏo·ang* – including arms, legs, hands, even fingers and eyes – by means of wires attached to long poles. Stories were drawn from Thai folk tales, particularly *Phra Aphaimani* (a classical Thai literary work), and occasionally from the *Ramakian*. Surviving examples of a smaller, 30cm court version called *hùn lék* (little puppets) are occasionally used in live performances; only one puppeteer is required for each marionette in *hùn lék*.

Food & Drink

For many visitors, food is one of the main reasons for choosing Thailand as a destination. Even more remarkable, however, is the locals' own love for food: Thais get just as excited as tourists when presented with a bowl of perfectly prepared noodles, or when seated at a renowned hawker stall. This unabashed enthusiasm for eating, as well as an abundance of fascinating ingredients and influences, has generated one of the most fun and diverse food scenes anywhere on the planet

How Thais Eat

Aside from the occasional indulgence in deep-fried savouries, most Thais sustain themselves on a varied and relatively healthy diet of fruits, rice and vegetables mixed with smaller amounts of animal protein and fat. Satisfaction seems to come not from eating large amounts of food at any one meal, but rather from nibbling at a variety of dishes with as many different flavours as possible throughout the day.

Nor are certain kinds of food restricted to certain times of day. Practically anything can be eaten first thing in the morning, whether it's sweet, salty or chilli-ridden. *Kôw gaang* (curry over rice) is a very popular breakfast, as are *kôw něe·o mŏo tôrt* (deep-fried pork with sticky rice) and *kôw man gài* (sliced chicken served over rice cooked in chicken broth). Lighter morning choices, especially for Thais of Chinese descent, include *pah·tôrng·gŏh* (deep-fried fingers of dough) dipped in warm *nám đow·hôo* (soy milk). Thais also eat noodles, whether fried or in soup, with great gusto in the morning, or as a substantial snack at any time of the day or night.

As the staple with which almost all Thai dishes are eaten (noodles are still seen as a Chinese import), *kôw* (rice) is considered an indispensable part of the daily diet. Most Bangkok families will put on a pot of rice, or start the rice cooker, just after rising in the morning to prepare a base for the day's menu.

Finding its way into almost every meal is *plah* (fish), even if it's only in the form of *nám plah* (a thin amber sauce made from fermented anchovies), which is used to salt Thai dishes, much as soy sauce is used in east Asia. Pork is undoubtedly the preferred protein, with chicken in second place. Beef is seldom eaten in Bangkok, particularly by Thais of Chinese descent who subscribe to a Buddhist teaching that forbids eating 'large' animals.

Thais are prodigious consumers of fruit. Vendors push glass-and-wood carts filled with a rainbow of fresh sliced papaya, pineapple, watermelon and mango, and a more muted palette of salt-pickled or candied seasonal fruits. These are usually served in a small plastic bag with a thin bamboo stick to use as an eating utensil.

Because many restaurants in Thailand are able to serve dishes at an only slightly higher price than they would cost to make at home, Thais dine out far more often than their Western counterparts.

Appon's Thai Food (www.khiewchanta.com) features nearly 1000 authentic and well-organised Thai recipes written by a Thai. Many of the recipes have helpful audio recordings of their Thai names.

SOMETHING'S FISHY

Westerners might scoff at the all-too-literal name of this condiment, but for much of Thai cooking, fish sauce is more than just another ingredient, it is *the* ingredient.

Essentially the liquid extracted from salted fish, fish sauce is one of the most common seasonings in the Thai kitchen, and takes various guises depending on the region. In northeastern Thailand, discerning diners prefer a thick, pasty mash of fermented freshwater fish and sometimes rice. Elsewhere, where people have access to the sea, fish sauce takes the form of a thin, amber liquid extracted from salted anchovies – much like with olive oil, the first extraction is considered the finest. In both cases the result has an admittedly pungent nose, but is generally salty, rather than fishy, in taste. Indeed, *prík nám plah,* a tiny bowl of fish sauce, supplemented with thinly sliced chillies and garlic – an item found on just about every restaurant table in Thailand – can be considered the Thai equivalent of the salt shaker.

Dining with others is always preferred because it means everyone has a chance to sample several dishes. When forced to fly solo by circumstances – such as during lunch breaks at work – a single diner usually sticks to one-plate dishes such as fried rice or curry over rice.

The Four Flavours

Simply put, sweet, sour, salty and spicy are the parameters that define Thai food, and although many associate the cuisine with fiery heat, virtually every dish is an exercise in balancing these four tastes. This balance might be obtained by a squeeze of lime juice, a spoonful of sugar and a glug of fish sauce, or a tablespoon of fermented soybeans and a strategic splash of vinegar. Bitter also factors into many Thai dishes, and often comes from the addition of a vegetable or herb. Regardless of the source, the goal is the same: a favourable balance of four clear, vibrant flavours.

Staples & Specialities

Rice & Noodles

In Thailand, to eat is to eat rice, and for most of the country, a meal is not acceptable without this staple. Thailand maintains the world's fifth-largest amount of land dedicated to growing rice, an industry that employs more than half the country's arable land and a significant portion of its population. Rice is so central to Thai food culture that the most common term for 'eat' is *gin kôw* (literally, 'consume rice') and one of the most common greetings is *Gin kôw rěu yang?* (Have you consumed rice yet?).

There are many varieties of rice in Thailand and the country has been among the world leaders in rice exports since the 1960s. The highest grade is *kôw hŏrm má·lí* (jasmine rice), a fragrant long grain that is so coveted by neighbouring countries that there is allegedly a steady underground business in smuggling out fresh supplies. The grain is customarily served alongside main dishes such as curries, stir-fries or soups, which are lumped together as *gàp kôw* (with rice). When you order plain rice in a restaurant you use the term *kôw plòw* ('plain rice') or *kôw sŏo·ay* ('beautiful rice'). Residents of Thailand's north and northeast eat *kôw něe·o* ('sticky rice'), a glutinous short-grained rice that is cooked by steaming, not boiling. And in Chinese-style eateries, *kôw đôm,* 'boiled rice', a watery porridge sometimes employing brown or purple rice, is a common carb.

Thailand is the world's second-largest exporter of rice – in 2016 it exported approximately 9.5 million tonnes of the grain.

Curries & Soups

In Thai, *gaang* (it sounds somewhat similar to the English 'gang') is often translated as 'curry', but it actually describes any dish with a lot of liquid and can thus refer to soups (such as *gaang jèut*) as well as the classic chilli-paste-based curries for which Thai cuisine is famous. The preparation of the latter begins with a *krêu·ang gaang,* created by mashing, pounding and grinding an array of fresh ingredients with a stone mortar and pestle to form an aromatic, extremely pungent-tasting and rather thick paste. Typical ingredients in a *krêu·ang gaang* include chilli, galangal, lemongrass, kaffir lime zest, shallots, garlic, shrimp paste and salt.

Another food celebrity that falls into the soupy category is *đôm yam,* the famous Thai spicy-and-sour soup. Fuelling the fire beneath *đôm yam's* often velvety surface are fresh *prík kêe nŏo* (tiny chillies) or, alternatively, half a teaspoonful of *nám prík pŏw* (roasted chilli paste). Lemongrass, kaffir lime leaf and lime juice give *đôm yam* its characteristic tang.

Lonely Planet's *From the Source: Thailand* features authentic recipes straight from the Thai kitchens where they were perfected.

Stir-Fries & Deep-Fries

The simplest dishes in the Thai culinary repertoire are the various *pàt* (stir-fries), introduced to Thailand by the Chinese, who are famed for being able to stir-fry a whole banquet in a single wok.

The list of *pàt* dishes seems endless. Many cling to their Chinese roots, such as the ubiquitous *pàt pàk bûng fai daang* (morning glory flash-fried with garlic and chilli), while some are Thai-Chinese hybrids, such as *pàt pèt* (literally 'spicy stir-fry'), in which the main ingredients, typically meat or fish, are quickly stir-fried with red curry paste.

Tôrt (deep-frying in oil) is mainly reserved for snacks such as *glôo·ay tôrt* (deep-fried bananas) or *pò·pée·a* (egg rolls). An exception is *plah tôrt* (deep-fried fish), which is a common way to prepare fish.

Hot & Tangy Salads

Standing right alongside curries in terms of Thai-ness is the ubiquitous *yam,* a hot and tangy 'salad' typically based around seafood, meat or vegetables. Lime juice provides the tang, while the abundant use of chilli generates the heat. Most *yam* are served at room temperature, or just slightly warmed by any cooked ingredients. The dish functions equally well as part of a meal or on its own as *gàp glâam,* snack food to accompany a night of boozing.

Nám Prík

Although more home than restaurant food, *nám prík* are spicy chilli-based dips. Typically eaten with rice and vegetables and herbs, they're also among the most regional of Thai dishes – you could probably pinpoint the province you're in by simply looking at the *nám prík* on offer.

Thai Food by David Thompson (2002) is widely considered the most authoritative English-language book on Thai cooking. Thompson's follow-up, *Thai Street Food* (2013), focuses on more casual street cuisine.

Fruits

Being a tropical country, Thailand excels in the fruit department. *Má·môo·ang* (mangoes) alone come in a dozen varieties that are eaten at different stages of ripeness. Other common fruit include *sàp·pà·rót* (pineapple), *má·lá·gor* (papaya) and *đaang moh* (watermelon), all of which are sold from ubiquitous vendor carts and accompanied by a dipping mix of salt, sugar and ground chilli. A highlight of visiting

Thailand is sampling the huge variety of indigenous fruits of which you've probably never heard. Many are available year-round nowadays, but April and May is peak season for several of the most beloved varieties, including durian, mangoes and mangosteen.

Here is a list of other lesser-known tropical fruits:

Custard apple Known in Thai as *nóy nàh,* the knobbly green skin of this fruit conceals hard black seeds and sweet, gloopy flesh with a granular texture.

Durian Known in Thai as *tú·ree·an,* the king of fruit is also Thailand's most infamous, due to its intense flavour and odour, which can suggest everything from custard to onions.

Guava A native of South America, *fa·ràng* – the same as the word for Westerner – is a green, apple-like ball containing pink or white flesh that's sweet and crispy.

Jackfruit The gigantic green pod of *kà·nǔn* – it's considered the world's largest fruit – conceals dozens of waxy yellow sections that taste like a blend of pineapple and bananas (it reminds us of Juicy Fruit chewing gum).

Langsat Strip away the yellowish peel of this fruit, known in Thai as *long·gong,* to find a segmented, perfumed pearlescent flesh with a lychee-like flavour.

Longan *Lam yai* takes the form of a tiny hard ball; it's like a mini lychee with sweet, perfumed flesh. Peel it, eat the flesh and spit out the hard seed.

Lychee The pink skin of *lín·jèe* conceals an addictive translucent flesh similar in flavour to a grape. It's generally only available between April and June.

Mangosteen The hard purple shell of *mang·kút,* the queen of Thai fruit, conceals delightfully fragrant white segments, some containing a hard seed.

Pomelo Like a grapefruit on steroids, *sôm oh* takes the form of a thick pithy green skin hiding sweet, tangy segments. Cut into the skin, peel off the pith and then break open the segments and munch on the flesh inside.

Rambutan People have different theories about what *ngó* look like, not all repeatable in polite company. Regardless, the hairy shell contains sweet translucent flesh that you scrape off the seed with your teeth.

Rose apple Known in Thai as *chom·pôo,* rose apple is an elongated pink or red fruit with a smooth, shiny skin and pale, watery flesh. It's a good thirst-quencher on a hot day.

Salak Also known as snake fruit because of its scaly skin. The exterior of *sàlà* looks like a mutant strawberry and the soft flesh tastes like unripe bananas.

Starfruit The star-shaped cross-section of *má·feu·ang* is the giveaway. The yellow flesh is sweet and tangy and believed by many to lower blood pressure.

Sweets

English-language Thai menus often have a section called 'Desserts', but Thai-style sweets are generally consumed as breakfast or as a sweet snack, not directly following a meal. Sweets also take two slightly different forms in Thailand. *Kŏrng wăhn,* which translates as 'sweet things', are small, rich sweets that often boast a slightly salty flavour. Prime ingredients for *kŏrng wăhn* include grated coconut, coconut milk, rice flour (from white rice or sticky rice), cooked sticky rice, tapioca, mung-bean starch, boiled taro and various fruits. Egg yolks are a popular ingredient for many *kŏrng wăhn,* including the ubiquitous *fŏy torng* (literally 'golden threads'), probably influenced by Portuguese desserts and pastries introduced during the early Ayuthaya era.

Thai sweets roughly similar to the European concept of pastries are called *kà·nŏm.* Probably the most popular type of *kà·nŏm* in Thailand are the bite-sized items wrapped in banana leaves, especially *kôw đôm gà·tí* and *kôw đôm mát.* Both consist of sticky rice grains steamed with *gà·tí* (coconut milk) inside a banana-leaf wrapper to form a solid, almost taffy-like mass.

Maintained by a Thai woman living in the US, She Simmers (www. shesimmers.com) is a good resource for those wanting to make Thai food outside when they return home.

Bangkok's Top 50 Street Food Stalls by Chawadee Nualkhair also functions well as a general introduction and guide to Thai-style informal dining.

(CON)FUSION CUISINE

A popular dish at restaurants across Thailand is *kôw pàt à·me·rí·gan,* 'American fried rice'. Taking the form of rice fried with ketchup, raisins and peas, sides of ham and deep-fried hot dogs, and topped with a fried egg, the dish is, well, every bit as revolting as it sounds. But at least there's an interesting history behind it: American fried rice allegedly dates back to the Vietnam War era, when thousands of US troops were based in northeastern Thailand. A local cook is said to have taken the 'American Breakfast' (also known as ABF; fried eggs with ham and/or hot dogs, and white bread, typically eaten with ketchup) and made it 'Thai' by frying the various elements with rice.

This culinary cross-pollination is only one example of the tendency of Thai cooks to pick and choose from the variety of cuisines at their disposal. Other (significantly more palatable) examples include *gaang mát·sà·màn,* 'Muslim curry', a classic blend of Thai and Middle Eastern cooking styles, and the famous *pàt tai,* essentially a blend of Chinese cooking methods and ingredients (frying, rice noodles) with Thai seasonings (fish sauce, chilli, tamarind).

Drinks

Coffee, Tea & Fruit Drinks

Thais are big coffee drinkers, and good-quality arabica and robusta are cultivated in the hilly areas of northern and southern Thailand. The traditional filtering system is nothing more than a narrow cloth bag attached to a steel handle. This type of coffee is served in a glass, mixed with sugar and sweetened with condensed milk – if you don't want either, be sure to specify *gah·faa dam* (black coffee) followed with *mâi sài nám·đahn* (without sugar).

Black tea, both local and imported, is available at the same places that serve real coffee. *Chah tai,* Thai-style tea, derives its characteristic orange-red colour from ground tamarind seed added after curing.

Fruit drinks appear all over Thailand and are an excellent way to rehydrate after water becomes unpalatable. Most *nám pŏn·lá·mái* (fruit juices) are served with a touch of sugar and salt and a whole lot of ice. Many foreigners object to the salt, but it serves a metabolic role in helping the body to cope with tropical temperatures.

Beer & Spirits

There are several brands of beer in Thailand, ranging from domestic brands (Singha, Chang, Leo) to foreign-licensed labels (Heineken, Asahi, San Miguel). They are all largely indistinguishable in terms of taste and quality.

Domestic rice whisky and rum are favourites of the working class, struggling students and at family gatherings as they're more affordable than beer. Once spending money becomes a priority, Thais often upgrade to imported whiskies. These are usually drunk with lots of ice, soda water and a splash of Coke. On a night out, buying a whole bottle is the norm in most of Thailand. If you don't finish it, it will simply be kept at the bar for your next visit.

Pok Pok by Andy Ricker with JJ Goode (2013) features recipes of the rustic, regional Thai dishes served at Ricker's eponymous Portland, Oregon and New York City restaurants.

Vegetarians & Vegans

Vegetarianism isn't a widespread trend in Thailand, but many tourist-oriented restaurants cater to vegetarians, and there are also a handful of *ráhn ah·hăhn mang·sà·wí·rát* (vegetarian restaurants) where the food is served buffet-style and is very inexpensive. Dishes are almost always 100% vegan (ie no meat, poultry, fish or fish sauce, dairy or egg products).

During the Vegetarian Festival, celebrated by Chinese Buddhists in September/October, many restaurants and street stalls in Bangkok go meatless for one month.

The phrase 'I'm vegetarian' in Thai is *pŏm gin jair* (for men) or *dì·chăn gin jair* (for women). Loosely translated this means 'I eat only vegetarian food', which includes no eggs and no dairy products – in other words, total vegan.

Habits & Customs

Like most of Thai culture, eating conventions appear relaxed and informal but are orchestrated by many implied rules.

Whether at home or in a restaurant, Thai meals are always served 'family style' – that is, from common serving platters, with the plates appearing in whatever order the kitchen can prepare them. When serving yourself from a common platter, put no more than one spoonful onto your plate at a time. Heaping your plate with all 'your' portions at once will look greedy to Thais unfamiliar with Western conventions. Another important factor in a Thai meal is achieving a balance of flavours and textures. Traditionally the party orders a curry, a steamed or fried fish, a stir-fried vegetable dish and a soup, taking great care to balance cool and hot, sour and sweet, salty and plain.

Originally Thai food was eaten with the fingers, and it still is in certain regions of the kingdom. In the early 20th century Thais began setting their tables with fork and spoon to affect a 'royal' setting, and it wasn't long before fork-and-spoon dining became the norm in Bangkok and later spread throughout the kingdom. To use these tools the Thai way, use a serving spoon, or alternatively your own, to take a single mouthful of food from a central dish and ladle it over a portion of your rice. The fork is then used to push the now-food-soaked portion of rice back onto the spoon before entering the mouth.

If you're not offered chopsticks, don't ask for them. Chopsticks are reserved for eating Chinese-style food from bowls, or for eating in all-Chinese restaurants. In either case you will be supplied with chopsticks without having to ask. Unlike their counterparts in many Western countries, restaurateurs in Thailand won't assume you don't know how to use them.

The download-able Vegetarian Thai Food Guide (www.eating thaifood.com/ vegetarian-thai-food-guide) is a handy resource for vegetarians visiting Thailand.

The Sex Industry in Thailand

Thailand has had a long and complex relationship with prostitution that persists today. It is also an international sex tourism destination, a designation that began around the time of the Vietnam War. The industry targeted to foreigners is very visible, with multiple red-light districts in Bangkok alone, but there is also a more clandestine domestic sex industry and myriad informal channels of sex-for-hire.

An Illegal & Vast Industry

Prostitution is technically illegal in Thailand. However, anti-prostitution laws are often ambiguous and unenforced. Some analysts have argued that the high demand for sexual services in Thailand limits the likelihood of the industry being curtailed; however, limiting abusive practices within the industry is the goal of many activists and government agencies.

It is difficult to determine the number of sex workers in Thailand, the demographics of the industry or its economic significance. This is because there are many indirect forms of prostitution, the illegality of the industry makes research difficult and different organisations use varying approaches to collect data. In 2003 measures to legalise prostitution cited the Thai sex industry as being worth US$4.3 billion (about 3% of GDP) and employing roughly 200,000 sex workers. A study conducted in 2003 by Thailand's Chulalongkorn University estimated 2.8 million sex workers, of which 1.98 million were adult women, 20,000 were adult men and 800,000 were children, defined as any person under the age of 18. A 2007 report compiled by the Institute for Population and Social Research at Mahidol University estimated that there are between 200,000 and 300,000 active female sex workers in Thailand at any given time.

The Coalition Against Trafficking in Women (CATW; www.catwinternational.org) is an NGO that works internationally to combat prostitution and trafficking in women and children.

History & Cultural Attitudes

Prostitution has been widespread in Thailand since long before the country gained a reputation among international sex tourists. Throughout Thai history the practice was accepted and common among many sectors of society, though it has not always been respected by society as a whole.

Due to international pressure from the UN, prostitution was declared illegal in 1960, though venues (go-go bars, beer bars, massage parlours, karaoke bars and bathhouses) are governed by a separate law passed in 1966. These establishments are licensed and can legally provide nonsexual services (such as dancing, massage or a drinking buddy); sexual services occur through these venues but they are not technically the businesses' primary purpose.

With the arrival of the US military in Southeast Asia during the Vietnam War era, enterprising forces adapted the existing framework to

PROS & CONS

Women's rights groups take oppositional approaches to the issue of prostitution. Abolitionists see prostitution as exploitation and an infraction of basic human rights. Meanwhile, mitigators recognise that there is demand and supply, and try to reduce the risks associated with the activity through HIV/AIDS prevention and education programs (especially for economic migrants). Sex-worker organisations argue that prostitution is a legitimate job and the best way to help women is to treat the issue from a workers' rights perspective, demanding fair pay and compensation, legal redress and mandatory sick and holiday time. Also, according to pro-sex-worker unions, the country's quasi-legal commercial sex establishments provide service-industry jobs (dishwashers, cooks, cleaners) to non-sex-worker staff, who would otherwise qualify for employment protection if the employer were a restaurant or a hotel.

suit foreigners, in turn creating an international sex tourism industry that persists today. Indeed, this foreigner-oriented sex industry is still a prominent part of Thailand's tourist economy.

In 1998 the International Labour Organization, a UN agency, advised Southeast Asian countries, including Thailand, to recognise prostitution as an economic sector and income generator. It is estimated that one third of the entertainment establishments are registered with the government and the majority pay an informal tax in the form of police bribes.

Economic Motivations

Regardless of their background, most women in the sex industry are there for financial reasons: many find that sex work is one of the highest-paying jobs for their level of education and/or they have financial obligations (be it dependants or debts). The most comprehensive data on the economics of sex workers comes from a 1993 survey by Dr Kritaya Archavanitkul, a demographer from Mahidol University. The report found that sex workers made a mean income of 17,000B per month (US$18 per day), the equivalent of a midlevel civil-servant job, a position acquired with advanced education and family connections. At the time of the study, most sex workers did not have a high-school degree.

These economic factors provide a strong incentive for rural, unskilled women (and, to a lesser extent, men) to engage in sex work.

As with many in Thai society, a large percentage of sex workers' wages are remitted back to their home villages to support their families (parents, siblings and children). Kritaya's 1993 report found that between 1800B and 6100B per month was sent back home to rural communities. The remittance-receiving households typically bought durable goods (TVs and washing machines), bigger houses and motorcycles or automobiles. Their wealth displayed their daughters' success in the industry and acted as a free advertisement for the next generation of sex workers.

Help stop child-sex tourism by reporting suspicious behaviour on a dedicated hotline (☑1300) or by reporting perpetrators directly to the embassy of their home country.

Working Conditions

The unintended consequence of prostitution prohibition is the lawless working environment it creates for women who enter the industry. Sex work becomes the domain of criminal networks that are often involved in other illicit activities that circumvent the laws through bribes and violence.

Sex workers are not afforded the rights of other workers: there is no minimum wage; no required holiday pay, sick leave or break time; no deductions for social security or employee-sponsored health insurance; and no legal redress.

Bars can set their own punitive rules that fine a worker if she doesn't smile enough, arrives late or doesn't meet the drink quota. Empower, an NGO that fights for safe and fair standards in the sex industry, reported that most sex workers will owe money to the bar at the end of the month through these deductions. In effect, the women have to pay to be prostitutes and the fines disguise a pimp relationship.

Through lobbying efforts, groups such as Empower hope that lawmakers will recognise all workers at entertainment places (including dishwashers and cooks as well as 'working girls') as employees subject to labour and safety protections.

Other commentators, such as the Coalition Against Trafficking in Women (CATW), argue that legalising prostitution is not the answer, because such a move would legitimise a practice that is always going to be dangerous and exploitative for the women involved. Instead,

DR WIWAT, MR CONDOM & THE PREVENTION OF AIDS

In Thailand in 1990, there were approximately 100,000 new cases of HIV. In the three years that followed, that number leapt to an estimated one million. A progressive-minded regional bureaucrat, Dr Wiwat Rojanapithayakorn, noted that the vast majority of these cases were among sex workers and kick-started a local campaign to encourage the use of condoms. This was a herculean task, as not only did most Thai men at the time eschew condoms, but the central government essentially did not acknowledge the existence of Thailand's sex industry. By collaborating with local authorities and venue owners, Dr Wiwat distributed free condoms and established a 'no condom, no sex' policy among sex venues that, within months, caused transmission rates to plummet dramatically.

Given his success and the immense threat that HIV/AIDS posed to Thailand in the early 1990s, Dr Wiwat proposed implementing his initiative on a national scale. The government enlisted the help of a charismatic family-planning advocate known colloquially as Mr Condom, Mechai Viravaidya. By 1993, the government budget for anti-AIDS programs was increased nearly 20-fold and a massive anti-AIDS public awareness campaign was launched, with frequent messages broadcast on TV and radio and free condoms distributed nationwide. In less than three years, condoms were essentially destigmatised in Thailand and their use among sex workers went from an estimated 25% to more than 90%; indeed, for a while, condoms were known as *mechai* in Thai. Between 1991 and 2001 new transmissions of HIV in Thailand dropped from 143,000 per year to fewer than 14,000, and Thailand's methods in tackling the problem became a model for other countries, both in the region and elsewhere.

Thailand's campaign continues to be successful today. According to the UN program on AIDS/HIV (UNAIDS), in 2000 there were an estimated 683,841 people in Thailand living with HIV; by 2014 this number had dropped to an estimated 445,504 and, during the same period, new transmissions of HIV plummeted by approximately 75%. Likewise, during the same period, the rates of HIV infection among female sex workers in Thailand continued to drop, and in 2014 was at an estimated 1.1%.

Indeed, some feel that Thailand's anti-HIV/AIDS campaign has been too successful, in effect leading Thais to believe that the disease no longer poses a risk and that they don't need to protect themselves. A UNAIDS report from 2010 estimates that only 50% of venue-based sex workers had undergone an HIV test in the last year, and after an alarming spike around 2005, Thailand's rate of HIV infection among men who have sex with men remains relatively high at an estimated 9.2%, according to a 2014 report compiled by the same agency.

these groups focus on how to enable the women to leave prostitution and make their way into different types of work.

Child Prostitution & Human Trafficking

Urban job centres such as Bangkok have large populations of displaced and marginalised people (immigrants from Myanmar, ethnic hill-tribe members and impoverished rural Thais). Children of these fractured families often turn to street begging, which is a pathway to prostitution, often through low-level criminal gangs. According to a number of reports conducted by different research bodies, there are an estimated 60,000 to 800,000 children involved in prostitution in Thailand.

In 1996 Thailand passed a reform law to address the issue of child prostitution (defined by two tiers: 15 to 18 years old and under 15 years old). Fines and jail time are imposed on customers, establishment owners and even parents involved in child prostitution (under the old law only prostitutes were culpable). Many countries also have extraterritorial legislation that allows nationals to be prosecuted in their own country for such crimes committed in Thailand.

Thailand is also a conduit and destination for people-trafficking (including child-trafficking) from Myanmar, Laos, Cambodia and China. As stated by the UN, human trafficking is a crime against humanity and involves recruiting, transporting, harbouring and receiving a person through force, fraud or coercion for purposes of exploitation. In 2015 the US State Department labelled Thailand as a Tier 3 country, meaning that it does not comply with the minimum standards for prevention of human-trafficking and is not making significant efforts to do so.

Organisations working across borders to stop child prostitution include Ecpat (End Child Prostitution & Trafficking; www.ecpat.org) and its Australian affiliate Child Wise (www.childwise.org.au).

Survival Guide

Transport

ARRIVING IN BANGKOK

Most travellers will arrive in Bangkok via air, but for those entering the city on ground transport, or who have plans to move onward, following is a summary of the city's major transport hubs.

Flights, cars and tours can be booked online at lonely planet.com/bookings.

Suvarnabhumi International Airport

Located 30km east of central Bangkok, **Suvarnabhumi International Airport** (☏02 132 1888; www.suvarnabhumiairport. com) began commercial international and domestic service in 2006. The airport's name is pronounced *sù·wan·ná·poom*, and it inherited the airport code

(BKK) previously held by the old airport at Don Mueang. The airport website has real-time details of arrivals and departures.

Train

The **Airport Rail Link** (☏call centre 1690; www.srtet. co.th) connects Suvarnabhumi International Airport with the BTS (Skytrain) stop at Phaya Thai (45B, 30 minutes, from 6am to midnight) and the MRT (Metro) stop at Phetchaburi (45B, 25 minutes, from 6am to midnight).

Taxi

→ Metered taxis are available kerbside at Floor 1 – ignore the 'official airport taxi' touts who approach you inside the terminal.

→ Typical metered fares from Suvarnabhumi include 200B to 250B to Th Sukhumvit; 250B to 300B to Th Khao San; and

400B to Mo Chit. Toll charges (paid by passengers) vary between 25B and 70B. Note that there's a 50B surcharge added to all fares departing from the airport, payable directly to the driver.

Bus

→ There is a public transport centre 3km from the airport that includes a bus terminal with buses to a handful of provinces and inner-city-bound buses and minivans. A free airport shuttle connects the transport centre with the passenger terminals.

→ Bus lines that city-bound tourists are likely to use include line 551 to BTS Victory Monument station (40B, frequent from 5am to 10pm) and 552 to BTS On Nut (20B, frequent from 5am to 10pm). From these points, you can continue by public transport or taxi to your hotel.

CLIMATE CHANGE & TRAVEL

Every form of transport that relies on carbon-based fuel generates CO_2, the main cause of human-induced climate change. Modern travel is dependent on aeroplanes, which might use less fuel per kilometre per person than most cars but travel much greater distances. The altitude at which aircraft emit gases (including CO_2) and particles also contributes to their climate change impact. Many websites offer 'carbon calculators' that allow people to estimate the carbon emissions generated by their journey and, for those who wish to do so, to offset the impact of the greenhouse gases emitted with contributions to portfolios of climate-friendly initiatives throughout the world. Lonely Planet offsets the carbon footprint of all staff and author travel.

Don Mueang International Airport

Bangkok's other airport, **Don Mueang International Airport** (☑02 535 2111; www.donmueangairport thai.com), 25km north of central Bangkok, was retired from service in 2006 only to reopen later as the city's de facto budget hub. Terminal 1 handles international flights, while Terminal 2 is for domestic destinations.

Train

The walkway that crosses from the airport to the Amari Airport Hotel also provides access to Don Muang Train Station, which has trains to Hualamphong Train Station every one to 1½ hours from 4am to 11.30pm and then roughly hourly from 2pm to 9.30pm (from 5B to 10B).

Taxi

As at Suvarnabhumi, public taxis leave from outside both arrival halls and there is a 50B airport charge added to the meter fare.

Bus

➡ From outside the arrivals hall, there are four bus lines: bus A1 stops at BTS Mo Chit (50B, frequent from 7.30am to 11.30pm); A2 stops at BTS Mo Chit and BTS Victory Monument (50B, every 30 minutes from 7.30am to 11.30pm); A3 stops at Pratunam and Lumphini Park (50B, every 30 minutes from 7.30am to 11.30pm); and A4 stops at Th Khao San and Sanam Luang (50B, every 30 minutes from 7.30am to 11.30pm).

➡ Public buses stop on the highway in front of the airport. Useful lines include 29, with a stop at Victory Monument BTS station, before terminating at Hualamphong Train Station (24 hours); line 59, with a stop near Th Khao San (24 hours); and line 538, stopping at Victory Monument BTS station (4am to 10pm); fares are approximately 20B.

Northern & Northeastern Bus Terminal

The **Northern & Northeastern Bus Terminal** (Mo Chit; ☑northeastern routes 02 936 2852, ext 602/605, northern routes 02 936 2841, ext 325/614; Th Kamphaengphet; M Kamphaeng Phet exit 1 & taxi, S Mo Chit exit 3 & taxi) is located just north of Chatuchak Park. This hectic bus station is also commonly called *kŏn sòng mŏr chít* (Mo Chit station) – not to be confused with Mo Chit BTS station. Buses depart from here for all northern and northeastern destinations, as well as regional international destinations including Pakse (Laos), Phnom Penh (Cambodia), Siem Reap (Cambodia) and Vientiane (Laos). To reach the bus station, take BTS to Mo Chit or MRT to Kamphaeng Phet and transfer onto city bus

3, 77 or 509, or get a taxi or motorcycle taxi.

Southern Bus Terminal

The **Southern Bus Terminal** (Sai Tai Mai; ☑02 422 4444, call centre 1490; Th Boromaratchachonanee), commonly called *săi đâi mài*, lies a long way west of the centre of Bangkok. Besides serving as the departure point for all buses to destinations south of Bangkok, transport to Kanchanaburi and western Thailand also departs from here. The easiest way to reach the station is by taxi, or you can take bus 79, 159, 201 or 516 from Th Ratchadamnoen Klang.

Eastern Bus Terminal

The **Eastern Bus Terminal** (Map p282; ☑02 391 2504; Soi 40, Th Sukhumvit; S Ekkamai exit 2) is the departure point for buses to Pattaya, Rayong, Chanthaburi and other points east, except for the border crossing at Aranya Prathet. Most people call it *sà·tăh·nee èk·gà·mai* (Ekamai station). It's near the Ekkamai BTS station.

Hualamphong Train Station

The city's main train terminus is known as **Hualamphong** (⏱02 220 4334, call centre 1690; www.railway.co.th; off Rama IV; MHua Lamphong exit 2). It's advisable to ignore all touts here and avoid the travel agencies. To check timetables and prices for destinations, check out the website of the State Railway of Thailand (www.railway.co.th/main/index_en.html).

GETTING AROUND BANGKOK

Bangkok may seem chaotic and impenetrable at first, but its transport system is gradually improving, and although you'll almost certainly find yourself stuck in traffic at some point, the jams aren't as legendary as they used to be.

BTS & MRT

➡ The elevated **BTS** (Skytrain; ⏱02 617 6000, tourist information 02 617 7341; www.bts.co.th), also known as the Skytrain (rót fai fáa), whisks you through 'new' Bangkok (Silom, Sukhumvit and Siam Sq). The interchange between the two lines is at Siam station and trains run frequently from 6am to midnight. Fares range from 16B to 44B or 140B for a one-day pass. Most ticket machines only accept coins, but change is available at the information booths.

➡ Bangkok's Metro, the **MRT** (⏱02 354 2000; www.bangkokmetro.co.th) is most helpful for people staying in the Sukhumvit or Silom area to reach the train station at Hualamphong. Fares cost from 16B to 42B or 120B for a one-day pass. The trains run frequently from 6am to midnight.

Taxi

➡ Although many first-time visitors are hesitant to use them, in general Bangkok's taxis are new and comfortable and the drivers are courteous and helpful, making them an excellent way to get around.

➡ All taxis are required to use their meters, which start at 35B, and fares to most places within central Bangkok cost 60B to 90B. Freeway tolls – 25B to 70B depending on where you start – must be paid by the passenger.

➡ **Taxi Radio** (⏱1681; www.taxiradio.co.th) and other 24-hour 'phone-a-cab' services are available for 20B above the metered fare.

➡ If you leave something in a taxi your best chance of getting it back (still pretty slim) is to call ⏱1644.

Taxi Alternatives

App-based alternatives to the traditional taxis that operate in Bangkok:

All Thai Taxi (www.allthaitaxi.com)

GrabTaxi (www.grab.com/th)

Uber (www.uber.com/cities/bangkok)

Boat

A fleet of boats, both those that run along Mae Nam Chao Phraya and along the city's canals, serve Bangkok's commuters.

River Ferries

➡ The **Chao Phraya Express Boat** (⏱02 623 6001; www.chaophrayaexpressboat.com) operates the main ferry service along Mae Nam Chao Phraya. The central pier is known as Tha Sathon, Saphan Taksin or sometimes Sathon/Central Pier, and connects to the BTS at Saphan Taksin station.

➡ Boats run from 6am to 8pm. You can buy tickets (10B to 40B) at the pier or on board; hold on to your ticket as proof of purchase (an occasional formality).

➡ The most common boats are the orange-flagged express

BANGKOK TAXI TIPS

➡ Never agree to take a taxi that won't use the meter; usually these drivers park outside hotels and in tourist areas. Simply get one that's passing by instead.

➡ Bangkok taxi drivers will generally not try to 'take you for a ride' as happens in some other countries; they make more money from passenger turnover.

➡ It's worth keeping in mind that many Bangkok taxi drivers are in fact seasonal labourers fresh from the countryside and may not know their way around.

➡ If a driver refuses to take you somewhere, it's probably because they need to return the hired cab before a certain time, not because they don't like how you look.

➡ Very few Bangkok taxi drivers speak much English, so an address written in Thai can help immensely.

➡ Older cabs may be less comfortable but typically have more experienced drivers because they are driver-owned, as opposed to the new cabs, which are usually hired.

EXTENDING BANGKOK'S PUBLIC TRANSPORT

Weighing in at less than a paltry 50km of track, Bangkok's public transport network (the MRT and BTS) is admittedly a lightweight. Yes, it has much of 'downtown' Bangkok covered, but other than two relatively new BTS extensions east and west, it doesn't provide much help to those bound for the city's suburbs. However, at the time of research, work was well underway on some significant extensions to both the MRT and BTS systems.

The MRT's 'blue line' and 'purple line' extensions will see the system pierce far-western Bangkok, east of Mae Nam Chao Phraya in Thonburi and northwest to Nonthaburi. Perhaps most beneficially, for tourists at least, the extensions will include much-needed stops in Ko Ratanakosin. The 'purple line' extension from Bang Sue northwest to Bang Yai was the first to open in 2017. When finished, both extensions will essentially double the length of the current network, ultimately making it into a loop.

Similarly, the BTS is being extended in an easterly direction, from Bearing to Samut Prakan, set to be finished around 2018, as well as north from Mo Chit, set to be completed by 2019.

boats. These run between Wat Rajsingkorn, south of Bangkok, to Nonthaburi, north, stopping at most major piers (15B, frequent from 6am to 7pm).

➡ A blue-flagged tourist boat (40B, every 30 minutes from 9.30am to 5pm) runs from Sathon/Central Pier to Phra Athit/Banglamphu Pier, with stops at eight major sightseeing piers and a barely comprehensible English-language commentary. Vendors at Sathon/Central Pier tout a 150B all-day pass, but unless you plan on doing a lot of boat travel, it's not great value.

➡ There are also dozens of cross-river ferries, which charge 3B and run every few minutes until late at night.Private long-tail boats can be hired for sightseeing trips at Phra Athit/Banglamphu Pier, Chang Pier, Tien Pier and Oriental Pier.

Klorng (Khlong) Boats

Canal taxi boats run along Khlong Saen Saep (Banglamphu to Ramkhamhaeng) and are an easy way to get between Banglamphu and Jim Thompson House, the Siam Sq shopping centres (get off at Sapan Hua Chang Pier for both) and other points further east along Th Sukhumvit – after a

mandatory change of boat at Pratunam Pier.

➡ These boats are mostly used by daily commuters and pull into the piers for just a few seconds – jump straight on or you'll be left behind.

➡ Fares range from 9B to 19B and boats run from 5.30am to 7.15pm from Monday to Friday, from 6am to 6.30pm on Saturday and from 6am to 6pm on Sunday.

Motorcycle Taxis

➡ Motorcycle taxis (known as *motorsai*) serve two purposes in Bangkok.

➡ Most commonly and popularly they form an integral part of the public transport network, running from the corner of a main thoroughfare, such as Th Sukhumvit, to the far ends of sois (lanes) that run off that thoroughfare. Riders wear coloured, numbered vests and gather at either end of their soi, usually charging 10B to 20B for the trip (without a helmet unless you ask).

➡ Their other purpose is as a means of beating the traffic. You tell your rider where you want to go, negotiate a price (from 20B for a short trip up to about 150B going across town), strap on the helmet (they will

insist for longer trips) and say a prayer to any god you're into.

Túk-Túk

➡ Bangkok's iconic túk-túk (pronounced *đúk đúk;* a type of motorised rickshaw) are used by Thais for short hops not worth paying the taxi flagfall for. For foreigners, however, these emphysema-inducing machines are part of the Bangkok experience, so despite the fact that they overcharge outrageously and you can't see anything due to the low roof, pretty much everyone takes a túk-túk at least once.

➡ Túk-túk are notorious for taking little 'detours' to commission-paying gem and silk shops and massage parlours. En route to 'special' temples, you'll meet 'helpful' locals who will steer you to even more rip-off opportunities. Ignore anyone offering too-good-to-be-true 20B trips.

➡ The vast majority of túk-túk drivers ask too much from tourists (expat *fa-ràng* never use them). Expect to be quoted a 100B fare, if not more, for even the shortest trip. Try bargaining them down to about 60B for a short trip, preferably at night when the pollution (hopefully) won't be quite so bad. Once you've done it, you'll find taxis are cheaper, cleaner, cooler and quieter.

Car

For short-term visitors, you will find parking and driving a car in Bangkok more trouble than it is worth. If you need private transport, consider hiring a car and driver through your hotel or hire a taxi driver that you find trustworthy. One reputable operator is **Julie Taxi** (☑082 664 4789, 081 846 2014; www.facebook.com/tourwithjulietaxi), which offers a variety of vehicles and excellent service.

But if you still want to give it a go, all the big car-hire companies have offices in Bangkok, as well as counters at Suvarnabhumi and Don Mueang International airports. Rates start at around 1000B per day for a small car. A passport plus a valid licence from your home country (with English translation if necessary) or an International Driving Permit are required for all rentals.

Bus

Bangkok's public buses are run by the **Bangkok Mass Transit Authority** (☑02 246 0973, call centre 1348; www.bmta.co.th).

➡ As the routes are not always clear, and with Bangkok taxis being such a good deal, you'd really have to be pinching pennies to rely on buses as a way to get around Bangkok.

➡ Air-con bus fares range from 10B to 23B and fares for fan-cooled buses start at 6.50B.

➡ Most of the bus lines run between 5am and 10pm or 11pm, except for the 'all-night' buses, which run from 3am or 4am to mid-morning.

➡ You'll most likely require the help of thinknet's *Bangkok Bus Guide*. Alternatively, you can download Transit Bangkok's guide to all the city's public transport including bus, MRT, BTS and boats at www.transitbangkok.com.

Bicycle

See p50 for details on getting around Bangkok by bicycle.

Walking

You'll notice very few Thais walking around in Bangkok, and it doesn't take long to see why: hot weather, pollution, uneven or nonexistent footpaths, footpaths clogged with vendors and motorcycles and the sheer expanse of the city make walking one of the least convenient ways to get around.

TOURS

Bangkok is a big, intimidating place and some visitors might appreciate a bit of hand-holding in the form of a guided tour. But even if you already know your way around, themed tours led by a private guide or bicycle tours are great ways to see another side of the city.

See p49 for Bangkok's walking, biking, guided and river tours.

Directory A–Z

Customs Regulations

➡ White-uniformed customs officers prohibit the import or export of the usual array of goods – porn, weapons, drugs. If you're caught with drugs in particular, expect life never to be the same again. The usual 200 cigarettes or 250g of tobacco are allowed in without duty, along with up to 1L of wine or spirits.

➡ For customs details, check out www.customs.go.th.

➡ Licences are required for exporting religious images and other antiquities.

Electricity

Type A
220V/50Hz

Type C
220V/50Hz

Embassies & Consulates

Australian Embassy (Map p277; ☑02 344 6300; www. thailand.embassy.gov.au; 181 Th Witthayu/Wireless Rd, Bangkok; ⊗8.30am-4.30pm Mon-Fri; Ⓜ Lumphini exit 2)

Cambodian Embassy (Map p287; ☑02 957 5851; 518/4 Soi Ramkhamhaeng 39, Th Pra-cha Uthit, Bangkok; ⊗8.30am-noon & 2-5pm Mon-Fri; Ⓜ Phra Ram 9 exit 3 & taxi)

Canadian Embassy (Map p277; ☑02 646 4300; www.thailand. gc.ca; 15th fl, Abdulrahim Pl,

990 Rama IV, Bangkok; ⊗9am-noon Mon-Fri; Ⓜ Si Lom exit 2, Ⓢ Sala Daeng exit 4)

French Embassy (Map p280; ☑02 657 5100; www.amba france-th.org; 35 Soi 36/Rue de Brest, Th Charoen Krung, Bangkok; ⊗8.30am-noon Mon-Fri; ⚓ Oriental Pier)

German Embassy (Map p277; ☑02 287 9000; www.bangkok. diplo.de; 9 Th Sathon Tai/South, Bangkok; ⊗7.30-11.30am Mon-Fri; Ⓜ Lumphini exit 2)

Irish Embassy (Map p275; ☑02 016 1360; www.dfa.ie/ irish-embassy/thailand; 12th fl, 208 Th Witthayu/Wireless Rd, Bangkok; ⊗9.30am-12.30pm & 2.30-3.30pm Mon-Thu, 9.30am-noon Fri; Ⓢ Phloen Chit exit 1)

Laotian Embassy (Map p287; ☑02 539 6667; 502/1-3 Soi Sahakarnpramoon, Th Pracha Uthit/Soi Ramkhamhaeng 39, Bangkok; ⊗8am-noon & 1-4pm Mon-Fri; Ⓜ Phra Ram 9 exit 3 & taxi)

Malaysian Embassy (Map p277; ☑02 629 6800; www. kln.gov.my/web/tha_bangkok/ home; 33-35 Th Sathon Tai/ South, Bangkok; ⊗8am-4pm Mon-Fri; Ⓜ Lumphini exit 2)

Myanmar Embassy (Map p287; ☑02 233 7250; www. myanmarembassybkk.com; 132 Th Sathon Neua/North, Bangkok; ⊗9am-noon & 1-3pm Mon-Fri; Ⓢ Surasak exit 3)

Netherlands Embassy (Map p274; ☎02 309 5200; www.netherlandsworldwide.nl/countries/thailand; 15 Soi Ton Son; ⏰8.30am-noon & 1.30-4.30pm Mon-Thu, 8.30-11.30am Fri; [S]Chit Lom exit 4)

New Zealand Embassy (Map p274; ☎02 254 2530; www.nzembassy.com/thailand; 14th fl, M Thai Tower, All Seasons Pl, 87 Th Witthayu/Wireless Rd, Bangkok; ⏰8am-noon & 1-2.30pm Mon-Fri; [S]Phloen Chit exit 5)

UK Embassy (Map p274; ☎02 305 8333; www.gov.uk/government/world/organisations/british-embassy-bangkok; 14 Th Witthayu/Wireless Rd, Bangkok; ⏰8am-4.30pm Mon-Thu, to 1pm Fri; [S]Phloen Chit exit 5)

US Embassy (Map p274; ☎02 205 4000; https://th.usembassy.gov; 95 Th Witthayu/Wireless Rd, Bangkok; ⏰8am-4pm Mon-Fri; [S]Phloen Chit exit 5)

Emergencies & Important Numbers

The police contact number functions as the de facto universal emergency number in Thailand and can also be used to call an ambulance or report a fire.

Bangkok area code	☎02
Country code	☎66
Directory assistance (free)	☎1133
International access code	☎001, ☎007
Operator-assisted international calls	☎100
Police, amulance, fire	☎191
Tourist Police	☎1155

Health

While urban horror stories can make a trip to Bangkok seem frighteningly dangerous, few travellers experience anything more than an upset stomach and the resulting clenched-cheek waddles to the bathroom. If you do have a problem, Bangkok has some very good hospitals.

Air Pollution

Bangkok has a reputation for air pollution, and on bad days the combination of heat, dust and motor fumes can be a powerful brew of potentially toxic air.

The good news is that more efficient vehicles (and fewer of them thanks to the BTS/Skytrain and MRT/Metro) and less industrial pollution mean Bangkok's skies are much cleaner than they used to be.

Flu

Present year-round in the tropics, influenza (flu) symptoms include high fever, muscle aches, runny nose, cough and sore throat. Flu is the most common vaccine-preventable disease contracted by travellers and everyone should consider vaccination. There is no specific treatment, just rest and paracetamol. Complications such as bronchitis or middle-ear infection may require antibiotic treatment.

Food

Eating in restaurants is the biggest risk factor for contracting traveller's diarrhoea. Ways to avoid it include eating only freshly cooked food and avoiding food that has been sitting around in buffets. Peel all fruit and cook vegetables. Eat in busy restaurants with a high turnover of customers.

Heat

For most people it takes at least two weeks to adapt to the hot climate. Prevent swelling of the feet and ankles as well as muscle cramps caused by excessive sweating by avoiding dehydration and excessive activity in the heat of the day.

Heat stroke requires immediate medical treatment. Symptoms come on suddenly and include weakness, nausea, a hot dry body with a body temperature of more than 41°C, dizziness, confusion, loss of coordination, fits and eventually collapse and loss of consciousness.

HIV & AIDS

HIV is now one of the most common causes of death in people under the age of 50 in Thailand. Always practise safe sex and avoid getting tattoos, piercings or using unclean syringes.

Water & Ice

Although it's deemed potable by the authorities, Thais don't drink tap water and neither should you. Stick to bottled or filtered water during your stay.

Insurance

A travel-insurance policy to cover theft, loss and medical problems is a good idea. There is a wide variety of policies available offering differing medical-expense options, so check the small print. Be sure that the policy covers ambulances or an emergency flight home. A locally acquired motorcycle licence is not valid under some policies. You may prefer a policy that pays doctors or hospitals directly rather than you having to pay on the spot and claim later. If you have to claim later, make sure you keep all documentation.

Worldwide travel insurance is available at www.lonelyplanet.com/travel-insurance. You can buy, extend and claim online any time – even if you're already on the road.

Internet Access

Wi-fi is standard in guesthouses and cafes. Signal strength deteriorates in the upper floors of multistorey buildings; you can always request a room near a router. Cellular data networks continue to expand and increase in capability.

Legal Matters

➡ Thailand's police don't enjoy a squeaky clean reputation, but as a foreigner, and especially a tourist, you probably won't have much to do with them. While some expats will talk of being targeted for fines while driving, most anecdotal evidence suggests Thai police will usually go out of their way not to arrest a foreigner breaking minor laws.

➡ Most Thai police view drugtakers as a social scourge and consequently see it as their duty to enforce the letter of the law; for others it's an opportunity to make untaxed income via bribes. Which direction they'll go often depends on drug quantities: small-time offenders are sometimes offered the chance to pay their way out of an arrest, while traffickers usually go to jail.

➡ Smoking is banned in all indoor spaces, including bars and pubs. The ban extends to open-air public spaces, which means lighting up outside a shopping centre, in particular, might earn you a polite request to butt out. If you throw your cigarette butt on the ground, however, you could then be hit with a hefty littering fine.

➡ If you are arrested for any offence, police will allow you to make a phone call to your embassy or consulate, if you have one, or to a friend or relative. There's a whole set of legal codes governing the length of time and manner in which you can be detained before being charged or put on trial. Police have a lot of discretion and are more likely to bend these codes in your favour than the reverse. However, as with police worldwide, if you don't show respect you will only make matters worse, so keep a cool head.

LGBT Travellers

Thai culture is relatively tolerant of both male and female homosexuality. There is a fairly prominent LGBT scene in Bangkok, Pattaya and Phuket. With regard to dress or mannerism, the LGBT community are generally accepted without comment. However, public displays of affection – whether heterosexual or homosexual – are frowned upon.

Medical Services

More than Thailand's main health-care hub, Bangkok has become a major destination for medical tourism, with patients flying in for treatment from all over the world.

Hospitals

The following hospitals have English-speaking doctors:

Bangkok Christian Hospital (☎02 625 9000; www.bch.in.th; 124 Th Silom; Ⓜ Si Lom exit 2, Ⓢ Sala Daeng exit 1) Modern hospital in central Bangkok.

BNH (☎02 686 2700; www.bnhhospital.com; 9 Th Convent; Ⓜ Si Lom exit 2, Ⓢ Sala Daeng exit 2) Modern, centrally located hospital.

Bumrungrad International Hospital (Map p282; ☎02 667 1000; www.bumrungrad.com; 33 Soi 3, Th Sukhumvit; ⊙24hr; Ⓢ Phloen Chit exit 3) An internationally accredited hospital.

Samitivej Hospital (Map p282; ☎02 022 2222; www.samitivejhospitals.com; 133 Soi 49, Th Sukhumvit; Ⓢ Phrom Phong exit 3 & taxi) Modern hospital.

Dentists

Business is good in the teeth game, partly because so many *fa·ràng* (Westerners) are combining their holiday with a spot of cheap root-canal work or some 'personal outlook' care – a teeth-whitening treatment by any other name. Prices are a bargain compared with Western countries and the quality of dentistry is generally high.

Bangkok Dental Spa (Map p282; ☎02 651 0807; www.bangkokdentalspa.com; 2nd fl, Methawattana Bldg, 27 Soi 19, Th Sukhumvit; ⊙by appointment only; Ⓜ Sukhumvit exit 3, Ⓢ Asok exit 1) Dental-care in a spa-like environment.

DC-One the Dental Clinic (Map p277; ☎02 240 2800; 31 Th Yen Akat; ⊙by appointment only; Ⓜ Lumphini exit 2 & taxi) Dental clinic with reputation for excellent work and relatively high prices; popular with UN staff and diplomats.

Dental Hospital (Map p282; ☎02 260 5000; www.dentalhospitalbangkok.com; 88/88 Soi 49, Th Sukhumvit; ⊙9am-8pm Mon-Sat, to 4.30pm Sun; Ⓢ Phrom Phong exit 3 & taxi) A private dental clinic with fluent English-speaking dentists.

Siam Family Dental Clinic (Map p274; ☎081 987 7700; www.siamfamilydental.com; 209 Th Phayathai; ⊙11am-8pm Mon-Fri, 10am-7pm Sat & Sun; Ⓢ Siam exit 2) Private dental clinic in central Bangkok.

Pharmacies

Pharmacies are plentiful, and in central areas most pharmacists will speak English. If you don't find what you need in a Boots, Watsons or a local pharmacy, try one of the hospitals.

Money

ATMs

Debit and ATM cards issued by a bank in your own country can be used at ATMs around Thailand to withdraw cash (in Thai baht only) directly from your account back home. ATMs are widespread throughout the country and can be relied on for the bulk of your spending cash. Most ATMs allow a maximum of 20,000B in withdrawals per day.

The downside is that Thai ATMs charge a 200B foreign-transaction fee on top of whatever currency conversion and out-of-network fees your home bank charges. Before leaving home, shop around for a bank account that has free international ATM usage and reimburses fees incurred at other institutions' ATMs.

Changing Money

Banks or private money changers offer the best foreign-exchange rates. When buying baht, US dollars is the most accepted currency, followed by British pounds and euros. Most banks charge a commission and duty for each travellers cheque cashed. Current exchange rates are posted at exchange counters.

Credit & Debit Cards

Credit cards as well as debit cards can be used for purchases at some shops, hotels and restaurants. The most commonly accepted cards are Visa and MasterCard. American Express is typically only accepted at high-end hotels and restaurants.

Contact your bank and your credit-card provider before you leave home and notify them of your upcoming trip so that your accounts aren't suspended due to suspicious overseas activity.

To report a lost or stolen credit/debit card, call the following hotlines in Bangkok:

American Express
(☏02 273 5544)

MasterCard
(☏001 800 11887 0663)

Visa
(☏001 800 11 535 0660)

Exchange Rates

Australia	A$1	25B
Canada	C$1	24B
China	Y10	50B
Euro Zone	€1	39B
Japan	¥100	30B
New Zealand	NZ$1	23B
South Korea	1000W	29B
UK	£1	44B
US	US$1	31B

For current exchange rates, see www.xe.com.

Currency

The basic unit of Thai currency is the baht. There are 100 satang in one baht – though the only place you'll be able to spend them is in the ubiquitous 7-Elevens. Coins come in denominations of 25 satang, 50 satang, 1B, 2B, 5B and 10B. Paper currency comes in denominations of 20B (green), 50B (blue), 100B (red), 500B (purple) and 1000B (beige).

Tipping

Tipping is not a traditional part of Thai life and, except in big hotels and posh restaurants, tips are appreciated but not expected.

Opening Hours

Banks and government offices close for national holidays. Some bars and clubs close during elections and certain holidays when alcohol sales are banned. Shopping centres have banks that open late.

Banks 8.30am-3.30pm; 24hr ATMs

Bars 6pm-midnight or 1am

Clubs 8pm-2am

Government Offices 8.30am-4.30pm Monday to Friday; some close for lunch

Restaurants 8am-10pm

Shops 10am-7pm

Post

Thailand has a very efficient postal service and local postage is inexpensive. Post offices open from 8.30am to 4.30pm weekdays and 9am to noon on Saturday. Larger main post offices may also be open for a half-day on Sunday.

Most post offices will sell do-it-yourself packing boxes. Don't send cash or other valuables through the mail.

Thailand's poste restante service is generally very reliable, though these days few tourists use it. When you receive mail, you must show your passport and fill out some paperwork.

Public Holidays

Government offices and banks close their doors on the following public holidays. For the precise dates of lunar holidays, see the Events & Festivals page of the Tourism Authority of Thailand's website (www.tourismthailand.org/Events-and-Festivals).

1 January New Year's Day

February (date varies) Makha Bucha Day, Buddhist holy day

6 April Chakri Day, commemorating the founder of the Chakri dynasty, Rama I

13–15 April Songkran Festival, traditional Thai New Year and water festival

1 May Labour Day

5 May Coronation Day

May/June (date varies) Visakha Bucha, Buddhist holy day

July/August (date varies) Asanha Bucha, Buddhist holy day

28 July Maha Vajiralongkorn's Birthday

12 August Queen Sirikit's Birthday/Mother's Day

23 October Chulalongkorn Day

5 December Commemoration of Late King Bhumiphol/Father's Day

10 December Constitution Day

31 December New Year's Eve

Safe Travel

As Thailand has in the past been the site of both violent political protest and military coups, it's wise to check the situation before planning your trip. The following government websites offer travel advisories and information on current hot spots:

Australian Department of Foreign Affairs (http://smarttraveller.gov.au)

British Foreign Office (www.gov.uk/foreign-travel-advice)

Canadian Department of Foreign Affairs (www.dfait-maeci.gc.ca)

Ministry of Foreign Affairs Japan (www.mofa.go.jp/announce/announce/2002/4/0425.html)

New Zealand Foreign Affairs & Trade (www.safetravel.govt.nz)

US State Department (https://travel.state.gov/content/passports/en/alertswarnings.html)

Scams

Generally, Bangkok is a safe city but it's good to keep the following in mind to avoid joining the list of tourists sucked in by Bangkok's numerous scam artists:

Flat-fare taxi rides Walk away from the tourist strip to hail a taxi that will actually use the meter. Flat fares will usually be about three times more expensive than the reasonable meter rate. Tell the driver 'meter'. If the driver refuses to put the meter on, get out.

Túk-túk rides for 50B Skip the 50B túk-túk ride unless you have the time and willpower to resist a heavy sales pitch in a tailor or gem shop. Good jewellery, gems and tailor shops aren't found through a túk-túk driver.

Friendly strangers Ignore 'helpful', often well-dressed, English-speaking locals who tell you that tourist attractions and public transport are closed for a holiday or cleaning; it's the beginning of a con, most likely a gem scam.

Taxes & Refunds

Thailand has a 7% value-added tax (VAT) on many goods and services. Mid-range and top-end hotels and restaurants might also add a 10% service tax. When the two are combined this becomes the 17% hit known as 'plus plus' or '++'.

You can get a refund on VAT paid on shopping, though not on food or hotels, as you leave the country. For how-to info, go to www.rd.go.th/vrt/engindex.html.

Telephone

The telephone country code for Thailand is 66 and

Media

➡ Bangkok's predominant English-language newspapers are the *Bangkok Post* (www.bangkokpost.com) and the business-heavy *Nation* (www.nationmultimedia.com).

➡ Weeklies such as the *Economist* and *Time* are sold at numerous news-stands.

➡ *Bangkok 101* (www.bangkok101.com) is a tourist-friendly listings magazine; *BK* (www.bk.asia-city.com) is a slightly more in-depth listings mag.

Weights & Measures

➡ The metric system is used.

Smoking

➡ Smoking is banned in all indoor places, including restaurants and bars, and all open-air public spaces.

Discount Cards

➡ Unfortunately, discount cards are virtually unknown in Bangkok.

---

is used when calling the country from abroad. All Thai telephone numbers are preceded by a '0' if you're dialling domestically (the '0' is omitted when calling from overseas). After the initial '0', the next three numbers represent the provincial area code, which is now integral to the telephone number. If the initial '0' is followed by a '6', an '8' or a '9', then you're dialling a mobile phone.

Domestic Calls

Inside Thailand all telephone numbers include an initial 0 plus the area code and the subscriber number. The only time you drop the initial 0 is when you're calling from outside Thailand.

➡ **Bangkok area code** ☏02

➡ **Operator-assisted international calls** ☏100

➡ **Free local directory assistance** ☏1133

International Calls

If you want to call an international number from a telephone in Thailand, you must first dial an international access code plus the country code followed by the subscriber number.

In Thailand there are various international access codes charging different rates per minute. The standard direct-dial prefix is 001; it is operated by CAT and is considered to have the best sound quality. It connects to the largest number of countries, but is also the most expensive. The next best is 007, a prefix operated by TOT with reliable quality and slightly cheaper rates. Economy rates are available through different carriers – do an internet search to determine promotion codes.

International country codes include:

➡ Australia ☑61

➡ UK ☑44

➡ US ☑1

Dial 100 for operator-assisted international calls or reverse-charge (collect) calls.

Mobile Phones

The easiest phone option in Thailand is to acquire a mobile (cell) phone equipped with a local SIM card. Buying a prepaid SIM is as simple as finding a 7-Eleven. SIM cards include talk and data packages and you can add more funds with a prepaid reload card.

Thailand is on the GSM network and mobile phone providers include AIS (1 2 Call), DTAC and True Move, all of which operate on a 4G network. Coverage and quality of the different carriers varies from year to year based on network upgrades and capacity. Carriers usually sell talk-data packages based on usage amounts.

The main networks:

AIS (1 2 Call; www.ais.co.th /12call/th)

DTAC (www.dtac.co.th)

TrueMove (www.truemove.com)

Time

➡ Thailand is seven hours ahead of GMT/UTC. Thus, noon in Bangkok is 9pm the previous night in Los Angeles, midnight the same day in New York, 5am in London, 6am in Paris, 1pm in Perth and 3pm in Sydney. Times are an hour later in countries or regions that are on Daylight Saving Time (DST). Thailand does not use daylight saving.

➡ The official year in Thailand is reckoned from the Western calendar year 543 BC, the beginning of the Buddhist Era (BE), so that AD 2016 is 2559 BE, AD 2017 is 2560 BE, etc.

Toilets

Increasingly, the Asian-style squat toilet is less of the norm in Thailand. There are still specimens in rural places, provincial bus stations, older homes and modest restaurants, but the Western-style toilet is becoming more prevalent and appears wherever foreign tourists can be found.

If you encounter a squat, here's what you should know. You should straddle the two foot pads and face the door. To flush use the plastic bowl to scoop water out of the adjacent basin and pour into the toilet bowl. Some places supply a small pack of toilet paper at the entrance (5B), otherwise bring your own stash or wipe the old-fashioned way with water.

Even in places where sit-down toilets are installed, the septic system may not be designed to take toilet paper. In such cases there will be a waste basket where you're supposed to place used toilet paper and feminine hygiene products. Some toilets also come with a small spray hose – Thailand's version of the bidet.

Tourist Information

Bangkok Information Center (Map p265; ☎02 225 7612-4; www.bangkoktourist.com; 17/1 Th Phra Athit; ⊗8am-7pm Mon-Fri, 9am-5pm Sat & Sun; ⊕Phra Athit/Banglamphu Pier) Handles city-specific tourism information.

Tourism Authority of Thailand (TAT; Map p282; ☎02 250 5500, nationwide 1672; www.tourismthailand.org; 1600 Th Phetchaburi; ⊗8.30am-4.30pm; Ⓜ Phetchaburi exit 2) Government-operated tourist information and promotion service founded in 1960. Produces excellent pamphlets on sightseeing; check the website for contact information.

Travellers with Disabilities

Thailand presents one large, ongoing obstacle course for the mobility impaired. With its high kerbs, uneven footpaths and nonstop traffic, Thai cities can be particularly difficult. In Bangkok many streets must be crossed on pedestrian bridges flanked with steep stairways, while buses and boats don't stop long enough even for the fully abled. Rarely are there any ramps or other access points for wheelchairs.

A number of more expensive top-end hotels make consistent design efforts to provide disabled access to their properties. Other deluxe hotels with high employee-to-guest ratios are better equipped to accommodate the mobility impaired by providing staff help where building design fails. For the rest, you're pretty much left to your own resources.

Download Lonely Planet's free Accessible Travel guide

from http://lptravel.to/ AccessibleTravel. Alternatively, some organisations and publications that offer tips on international travel include the following:

Accessible Journeys (www.disabilitytravel.com)

Asia Pacific Development Centre on Disability (www.apcdfoundation.org)

Mobility International USA (www.miusa.org)

Society for Accessible Travel & Hospitality (www.sath.org)

Wheelchair Holidays @ Thailand (www.wheelchairtours.com)

Visas

Most nationalities can receive a 30-day visa exemption on arrival at international airports or a 15-day visa at land borders; a 60-day tourist visa is available through Thai consulates.

➡ Thailand's **Ministry of Foreign Affairs** (☑02 203 5000; www.mfa.go.th) oversees immigration and visa issues. In the past several years there have been new rules almost annually regarding visas and extensions; the best online monitor is Thaivisa (www.thaivisa.com).

➡ Citizens of 62 countries (including most European countries, Australia, New Zealand and the USA) can enter Thailand at no charge. Depending on nationality, these citizens are issued a 14- to 90-day visa exemption if they arrive by air (most nationalities receive 30 days) or for 15 to 30 days by land.

➡ If you need more time in the country, apply for a 60-day tourist visa prior to arrival at a Thai embassy or consulate abroad. For business or study purposes, you can obtain 90-day nonimmigrant visas but you'll need extra documentation. Officially, on arrival you must prove you have sufficient funds for your stay and proof of onward travel, but visitors are rarely asked about this.

➡ If you overstay your visa the penalty is 500B per day, with a 20,000B limit; fines can be paid at any official exit point or at the **Bangkok Immigration Office** (☑02 141 9889; www.bangkok.immigration.go.th; Bldg B, Government Centre, Soi 7, Th Chaeng Watthana, Bangkok; ☺8.30am-noon & 1-4.30pm Mon-Fri; Ⓜ Chatuchak Park exit 2 & taxi, ⓢMo Chit exit 3 & taxi). Dress in your Sunday best when doing official business in Thailand and

do all visa business yourself (don't hire a third party). For all types of visa extensions, bring along two passport-sized photos and one copy each of the photo and visa pages of your passport.

➡ You can extend your stay for the normal fee of 1900B at the Immigration Office. Those issued with a visa exemption can extend their stay for an additional 30 days if the extension is handled before the visa expires. The 60-day tourist visa can be extended by up to 30 days at the discretion of Thai immigration authorities.

Women Travellers

➡ Everyday incidents of sexual harassment are much less common in Thailand than in India, Indonesia or Malaysia, and this might lull women familiar with those countries into thinking that Thailand is safer than it is. If you're a woman travelling alone, it's worth pairing up with other travellers when moving around at night or, at the least, avoiding quiet areas.

➡ Whether it's tampons or any other products for women, you'll have no trouble finding them in Bangkok.

Language

Thailand's, and therefore Bangkok's, official language is effectively the dialect spoken and written in central Thailand, which has successfully become the lingua franca of all Thai and non-Thai ethnic groups in the kingdom.

In Thai the meaning of a single syllable may be altered by means of different tones. In standard Thai there are five: low tone, mid tone, falling tone, high tone and rising tone. The range of all five tones is relative to each speaker's vocal range, so there is no fixed 'pitch' intrinsic to the language.

➡ **low tone** – 'Flat' like the mid tone, but pronounced at the relative bottom of one's vocal range. It is low, level and has no inflection, eg bàht (baht – the Thai currency).

➡ **mid tone** – Pronounced 'flat', at the relative middle of the speaker's vocal range, eg dee (good). No tone mark is used.

➡ **falling tone** – Starting high and falling sharply, this tone is similar to the change in pitch in English when you are emphasising a word, or calling someone's name from afar, eg mâi (no/not).

➡ **high tone** – Usually the most difficult for non-Thai speakers. It's pronounced near the relative top of the vocal range, as level as possible, eg máh (horse).

➡ **rising tone** – Starting low and gradually rising, sounds like the inflection used by English speakers to imply a question – 'Yes?', eg săhm (three).

WANT MORE?

For in-depth language information and handy phrases, check out Lonely Planet's *Thai phrasebook*. You'll find it at **shop.lonelyplanet.com**, or you can buy Lonely Planet's iPhone phrasebooks at the Apple App Store.

The Thai government has instituted the Royal Thai General Transcription System (RTGS) as a standard method of writing Thai using the Roman alphabet. It's used in official documents, road signs and on maps. However, local variations crop up on signs, menus etc. Generally, names in this book follow the most common practice.

In our coloured pronunciation guides, the hyphens indicate syllable breaks within words, and some syllables are further divided with a dot to help you pronounce compound vowels, eg mêu·a·rai (when).

The vowel a is pronounced as in 'about', aa as the 'a' in 'bad', ah as the 'a' in 'father', ai as in 'aisle', air as in 'flair' (without the 'r'), eu as the 'er' in 'her' (without the 'r'), ew as in 'new' (with rounded lips), oh as the 'o' in 'toe', or as in 'torn' (without the 'r') and ow as in 'now'.

Most consonants correspond to their English counterparts. The exceptions are b (a hard 'p' sound, almost like a 'b', eg in 'hip-bag'); d (a hard 't' sound, like a sharp 'd', eg in 'mid-tone'); ng (as in 'singing'; in Thai it can occur at the start of a word) and r (as in 'run' but flapped; in everyday speech it's often pronounced like 'l'). If you read our coloured pronunciation guides as if they were English, you shouldn't have problems being understood.

BASICS

The social structure of Thai society demands different registers of speech depending on who you're talking to. To make things simple we've chosen the correct form of speech appropriate to the context of each phrase.

When being polite, the speaker ends his or her sentence with kráp (for men) or kâ (for women). It is the gender of the speaker that is being expressed here; it is also the common way to answer 'yes' to a question or show agreement.

In this chapter the masculine and feminine forms of phrases are indicated where relevant with 'm/f'.

Hello.	สวัสดี	sà-wàt-dee
Goodbye.	ลาก่อน	lah gòrn
Yes.	ใช่	châi
No.	ไม่	mâi
Please.	ขอ	kŏr
Thank you.	ขอบคุณ	kòrp kun
You're welcome.	ยินดี	yin dee
Excuse me.	ขออภัย	kŏr à-pai
Sorry.	ขอโทษ	kŏr tôht

How are you?
สบายดีไหม   sà-bai dee măi

Fine. And you?
สบายดีครับ/ค่ะ   sà-bai dee kráp/
แล้วคุณล่ะ   kâ láa·ou kun lâ (m/f)

What's your name?
คุณชื่ออะไร   kun chêu à-rai

My name is ...
ผม/ดิฉันชื่อ...   pŏm/di-chăn chêu ... (m/f)

Do you speak English?
คุณพูดภาษา   kun pôot pah-săh
อังกฤษได้ไหม   ang-grìt dâi măi

I don't understand.
ผม/ดิฉันไม่เข้าใจ   pŏm/di-chăn mâi kôw jai (m/f)

ACCOMMODATION

Where's a ...?	...อยู่ที่ไหน	...yòo têe năi
campsite	ค่ายพักแรม	kâi pák raam
guesthouse	บ้านพัก	bâhn pák
hotel	โรงแรม	rohng raam
youth hostel	บ้าน	bâhn
	เยาวชน	yow-wá-chon
Do you have	มีห้อง ...	mee hôrng ...
a ... room?	ไหม	măi
single	เดี่ยว	dèe·o
double	เตียงคู่	đee·ang kôo
twin	สองเตียง	sŏrng đee·ang
air-con	แอร์	aa
bathroom	ห้องน้ำ	hôrng nám
laundry	ห้องซักผ้า	hôrng sák pâh
mosquito net	มุ้ง	múng
window	หน้าต่าง	nâh đàhng

DIRECTIONS

Where's ...?
... อยู่ที่ไหน   ... yòo têe năi

What's the address?
ที่อยู่คืออะไร   têe yòo keu à-rai

Could you please write it down?
เขียนลงให้ได้ไหม   kĕe·an long hâi dâi măi

Can you show me (on the map)?
ให้ดู (ในแผนที่)   hâi doo (nai păen têe)
ได้ไหม   dâi măi

Turn left/right.
เลี้ยวซ้าย/ขวา   lée·o sái/kwăh

It's ...	อยู่ ...	yòo ...
behind	ที่หลัง	têe lăng
in front of	ตรงหน้า	đrong nâh
near	ใกล้ๆ	glâi glâi
next to	ข้างๆ	kâhng kâhng
straight ahead	ตรงไป	đrong bai

EATING & DRINKING

I'd like (the menu), please.
ขอ (รายการ   kŏr (rai gahn
อาหาร) หน่อย   ah-hăhn) nòy

What would you recommend?
คุณแนะนำอะไรบ้าง   kun náa-nam à-rai bâhng

That was delicious!
อร่อยมาก   à-ròy mâhk

Cheers!
ไชโย   chai-yoh

Please bring the bill.
ขอบิลหน่อย   kŏr bin nòy

I don't eat ...	ผม/ดิฉัน	pŏm/dì-chăn
	ไม่กิน ...	mâi gin ... (m/f)
eggs	ไข่	kài
fish	ปลา	ƀlah
red meat	เนื้อแดง	néu·a daang
nuts	ถั่ว	tòo·a

Key Words

bottle	ขวด	kòo·at
bowl	ชาม	chahm
breakfast	อาหารเช้า	ah-hăhn chów
cafe	ร้านกาแฟ	ráhn gah-faa
chopsticks	ไม้ตะเกียบ	mái đà-gèe·ap
cold	เย็น	yen
cup	ถ้วย	tôo·ay
dessert	ของหวาน	kŏrng wăhn
dinner	อาหารเย็น	ah-hăhn yen
drink list	รายการ	rai gahn
	เครื่องดื่ม	krêu·ang dèum
fork	ส้อม	sôrm
glass	แก้ว	gâa·ou
hot	ร้อน	rórn
knife	มีด	mêet
lunch	อาหาร	ah-hăhn
	กลางวัน	glahng wan
market	ตลาด	đà-làht
plate	จาน	jahn
restaurant	ร้านอาหาร	ráhn ah-hăhn
spicy	เผ็ด	pèt
spoon	ช้อน	chórn
vegetarian	เจ	jair
with/without	มี/ไม่มี	mee/mâi mee

Meat & Fish

beef	เนื้อ	néu·a
chicken	ไก่	gài
crab	ปู	ƀoo
duck	เป็ด	ƀèt
fish	ปลา	ƀlah
meat	เนื้อ	néu·a

pork	หมู	mŏo
seafood	อาหารทะเล	ah-hăhn tá-lair
squid	ปลาหมึก	ƀlah mèuk

Fruit & Vegetables

banana	กล้วย	glôo·ay
beans	ถั่ว	tòo·a
coconut	มะพร้าว	má-prów
eggplant	มะเขือ	má-kĕu·a
fruit	ผลไม้	pŏn-lá-mái
guava	ฝรั่ง	fa-ràng
lime	มะนาว	má-now
mango	มะม่วง	má-môo·ang
mangosteen	มังคุด	mang-kút
mushrooms	เห็ด	hèt
nuts	ถั่ว	tòo·a
papaya	มะละกอ	má-lá-gor
potatoes	มันฝรั่ง	man fa-ràng
rambutan	เงาะ	ngó
tamarind	มะขาม	má-kăhm
tomatoes	มะเขือเทศ	má-kĕu·a têt
vegetables	ผัก	pàk
watermelon	แตงโม	đaang moh

Other

chilli	พริก	prík
egg	ไข่	kài
fish sauce	น้ำปลา	nám ƀlah
noodles	เส้น	sên
oil	น้ำมัน	nám man
pepper	พริกไทย	prík tai
rice	ข้าว	kôw
salad	ผักสด	pàk sòt
salt	เกลือ	gleu·a

QUESTION WORDS

What?	อะไร	à-rai
When?	เมื่อไร	mêu·a-rai
Where?	ที่ไหน	têe năi
Who?	ใคร	krai

soup	น้ำซุป	nám súp
soy sauce	น้ำซีอิ๊ว	nám see-éw
sugar	น้ำตาล	nám đahn
tofu	เต้าหู้	đôw hôo

Drinks

beer	เบียร์	bee·a
coffee	กาแฟ	gah-faa
milk	นมจืด	nom jèut
orange juice	น้ำส้ม	nám sôm
soy milk	น้ำเต้าหู้	nám đôw hôo
sugar-cane juice	น้ำอ้อย	nám ôy
tea	ชา	chah
water	น้ำดื่ม	nám dèum

EMERGENCIES

| Help! | ช่วยด้วย | chôo·ay dôo·ay |
| Go away! | ไปให้พ้น | bai hâi pón |

Call a doctor!
เรียกหมอหน่อย rêe·ak mŏr nòy
Call the police!
เรียกตำรวจหน่อย rêe·ak đam·ròo·at nòy
I'm ill.
ผม/ดิฉันป่วย pŏm/dì-chăn bòo·ay (m/f)
I'm lost.
ผม/ดิฉัน pŏm/dì-chăn
หลงทาง lŏng tahng (m/f)
Where are the toilets?
ห้องน้ำอยู่ที่ไหน hôrng nám yòo têe năi

SHOPPING & SERVICES
I'd like to buy ...
อยากจะซื้อ ... yàhk jà séu ...

How much is it?
เท่าไร tôw-rai

That's too expensive.
แพงไป paang bai

Can you lower the price?
ลดราคาได้ไหม lót rah-kah dâi măi

There's a mistake in the bill.
บิลใบนี้ผิด bin bai née pìt ná
นะครับ/ค่ะ kráp/kâ (m/f)

TIME & DATES
What time is it?
กี่โมงแล้ว gèe mohng láa·ou

morning	เช้า	chów
afternoon	บ่าย	bài
evening	เย็น	yen
yesterday	เมื่อวาน	mêu·a wahn
today	วันนี้	wan née
tomorrow	พรุ่งนี้	prûng née
Monday	วันจันทร์	wan jan
Tuesday	วันอังคาร	wan ang-kahn
Wednesday	วันพุธ	wan pút
Thursday	วันพฤหัสฯ	wan pá-réu-hàt
Friday	วันศุกร	wan sùk
Saturday	วันเสาร์	wan sŏw
Sunday	วันอาทิตย์	wan ah-tít

TRANSPORT

Public Transport

bicycle rickshaw	สามล้อ	săhm lór
boat	เรือ	reu·a
bus	รถเมล์	rót mair
car	รถเก๋ง	rót gěng
motorcycle	มอร์เตอร์ไซค์	mor-đeu-sai
taxi	รับจ้าง	ráp jâhng
plane	เครื่องบิน	krêu·ang bin
train	รถไฟ	rót fai
túk-túk	ตุ๊ก ๆ	đúk đúk

When's รถเมล์คัน ... rót mair kan ...
the ... bus? มาเมื่อไร mah mêu·a rai
first แรก râak
last สุดท้าย sùt tái

A ... ticket, ขอตั๋ว ... kŏr đŏo·a ...
please.
one-way เที่ยวเดียว têe·o dee·o
return ไปกลับ bai glàp

NUMBERS

1	หนึ่ง	nèung
2	สอง	sŏrng
3	สาม	săhm
4	สี่	sèe
5	ห้า	hâh
6	หก	hòk
7	เจ็ด	jèt
8	แปด	bàat
9	เก้า	gôw
10	สิบ	sìp
11	สิบเอ็ด	sìp-èt
20	ยี่สิบ	yêe-sìp
21	ยี่สิบเอ็ด	yêe-sìp-èt
30	สามสิบ	săhm-sìp
40	สี่สิบ	sèe-sìp
50	ห้าสิบ	hâh-sìp
60	หกสิบ	hòk-sìp
70	เจ็ดสิบ	jèt-sìp
80	แปดสิบ	bàat-sìp
90	เก้าสิบ	gôw-sìp
100	หนึ่งร้อย	nèung róy
1000	หนึ่งพัน	nèung pan
1,000,000	หนึ่งล้าน	nèung láhn

I'd like	ต้องการ	dôrng gahn
a/an ... seat.	ที่นั่ง ...	têe nâng ...
aisle	ติดทางเดิน	dìt tahng deun
window	ติดหน้าต่าง	dìt nâh dàhng
ticket window	ช่องขายตั๋ว	chôrng kăi dŏo·a
timetable	ตารางเวลา	dah-rahng wair-lah

What time does it get to (Chiang Mai)?

ถึง (เชียงใหม่)	tĕung (chee·ang mài)
กี่โมง	gèe mohng

Does it stop at (Saraburi)?

รถจอดที่ (สระบุรี)	rót jòrt têe (sà-rà-bù-ree)
ไหม	măi

I'd like to get off at (Saraburi).

ขอลงที่(สระบุรี)	kŏr long têe (sà-rà-bù-ree)

Driving & Cycling

I'd like to	อยากจะ	yàhk jà
hire a/an ...	เช่า ...	chôw ...
4WD	รถโฟร์วีล	rót foh ween
car	รถเก๋ง	rót gĕng
motorbike	รถ มอร์เตอร์ไซค์	rót mor-đeu-sai
I'd like ...	ต้องการ ...	dôrng gahn ...
my bicycle repaired	ซ่อมรถ จักรยาน	sôrm rót jàk-gà-yahn
to hire a bicycle	เช่ารถ จักรยาน	chôw rót jàk-gà-yahn

Is this the road to (Ban Bung Wai)?

ทางนี้ไป (บ้านบุ่งหวาย) ไหม	tahng née bai (bâhn bùng wăi) măi

Where's a petrol station?

ปั๊มน้ำมันอยู่ที่ไหน	bâm nám man yòo têe năi

How long can I park here?

จอดที่นี่ได้นานเท่าไร	jòrt têe née dâi nahn tôw-rai

I need a mechanic.

ต้องการช่างรถ	dôrng gahn châhng rót

I have a flat tyre.

ยางแบน	yahng baan

I've run out of petrol.

หมดน้ำมัน	mòt nám man

GLOSSARY

This glossary includes Thai, Pali (P) and Sanskrit (S) words and terms frequently used in this guidebook. For definitions of food and drink terms, see p28, p32 and p249.

baht – *(bàat)* the Thai unit of currency

bòht – central sanctuary in a Thai temple used for the monastic order's official business, such as ordinations; see also *wí·hǎhn*

Brahman – pertaining to Brahmanism, an ancient religious tradition in India and the predecessor of Hinduism; not to be confused with 'Brahmin', the priestly class in India's caste system

BTS – Bangkok Transit System (Skytrain); Thai: *rót fai fáh*

chedi – see *stupa*

fa·ràng –a Westerner (person of European origin); also guava

gà·teu·i – *(kàthoey)* Thailand's 'third gender', usually cross-dressers and/or transgender people

gǒo·ay đěe·o – *generic term for a noodle soup dish*

Isan – *(ee·sǎhn)* general term used for northeastern Thailand

jataka (P) – *(chah·dòk)* stories of the Buddha's previous lives

kàthoey – see *gà·teu·i*

klorng – canal; spelt 'Khlong' in proper nouns

kǒhn – masked dance-drama

lék – little, small (in size); see also *noi*

mâa nám – river; spelt Mae Nam in proper names

mahathat – *(má·hǎh tâht)* common name for temples containing Buddha relics; from the Sanskrit–Pali term *mahadhatu*

mâi ben rai – Thai expression meaning 'No problem' or 'It's OK'

MRT – Metropolitan Rapid Transit, or Metro.

nám – water

nibbana (P/S) – nirvana; in Buddhist teachings, the state of enlightenment; escape from the realm of rebirth; Thai: *níp·pahn*

noi – *(nóy)* little, small (amount); see also *lék*

nôrk – outside, outer; spelt 'Nok' in proper names

ow – bay or gulf; spelt 'Ao' in proper nouns

prá – an honorific term used for monks, nobility and Buddha images; spelt 'Phra' in proper names

prang – *(brahng)* Khmer-style tower on temples

sangha – (P) the Buddhist community

satang – *(sà·đahng)* a Thai unit of currency; 100 satang equals 1 baht

soi – lane or small street

Songkran – Thai New Year, held in mid-April

sǒrng·tǎa·ou – (literally 'two rows') common name for small pick-up trucks with two benches in the back, used as buses/taxis; also spelt 'sǎwngthǎew'

stupa – conical-shaped Buddhist monument used to inter sacred Buddhist objects

tâh – pier, boat landing; spelt 'Tha' in proper nouns

TAT – Tourism Authority of Thailand

Thammayut – one of the two sects of Theravada Buddhism in Thailand; founded by King Rama IV while he was still a monk

thanǒn – *(tà·nǒn)* street; spelt 'Thanon' in proper nouns and shortened to 'Th'

T-pop – popular teen-music

túk·túk – *(đúk–đúk)* motorised, three-wheeled rickshaw

wâi – palms–together Thai greeting

wang – palace

wát – temple–monastery; spelt 'Wat' in proper nouns

wí·hǎhn – *(wihan, viharn)* any large hall in a Thai temple, usually open to laity

Behind the Scenes

SEND US YOUR FEEDBACK

We love to hear from travellers – your comments keep us on our toes and help make our books better. Our well-travelled team reads every word on what you loved or loathed about this book. Although we cannot reply individually to your submissions, we always guarantee that your feedback goes straight to the appropriate authors, in time for the next edition. Each person who sends us information is thanked in the next edition – the most useful submissions are rewarded with a selection of digital PDF chapters.

Visit **lonelyplanet.com/contact** to submit your updates and suggestions or to ask for help. Our award-winning website also features inspirational travel stories, news and discussions.

Note: We may edit, reproduce and incorporate your comments in Lonely Planet products such as guidebooks, websites and digital products, so let us know if you don't want your comments reproduced or your name acknowledged. For a copy of our privacy policy visit lonelyplanet.com/privacy.

WRITER THANKS

Austin Bush

A big thanks to Destination Editors Dora Ball and Clifton Wilkinson, as well as to all the people on the ground in Bangkok and northern Thailand.

Tim Bewer

A hearty *kòrp jai lǎi lǎi dêu* to the perpetually friendly people of Isan who rarely failed to live up to their reputation for friendliness and hospitality when faced with my incessant questions, in particular Prapaporn Sompakdee (especially for her crispy pork expertise) and Julian Wright. Special thanks to my wife Suttawan.

Anita Isalska

Big thanks to everyone who helped me on my travels in Thailand. Gratitude to Sai and Anna for the warm welcome and insights into the wild west, to the Tourism Authority of Thailand team in Kanchanaburi, and to Tim Bewer for helpful suggestions. I'd also like to thank the kids in Lopburi who helped this perplexed travel writer wriggle free from a prematurely locked temple ground. Thanks always to Normal Matt for crackly Skype calls and support.

Andy Symington

A great number of people, from taxi drivers to information officers, gave me excellent advice and help along the way; I'm very grateful to all of them. Specific thanks go to Siriporn Chiangpoon, Ian on Ko Chang, Maitri in Si Racha, Chayanan in Chanthaburi and the friendly Ang Sila volunteers.

ACKNOWLEDGMENTS

Climate map data adapted from Peel MC, Finlayson BL & McMahon TA (2007) 'Updated World Map of the Köppen-Geiger Climate Classification', Hydrology and Earth System Sciences, 11, 163344.

Illustrations pp62–3 and pp66–7 by Michael Weldon.

Cover photograph: Murals depicting scenes from the life of Buddha, Wat Pho, Jason Langley/AWL ©

THIS BOOK

This 13th edition of Lonely Planet's *Bangkok* guidebook was researched and written by Austin Bush, Tim Bewer, Anita Isalska and Andy Symington. Austin Bush wrote the previous two editions.

Destination Editors
Tanya Parker, Dora Ball, Clifton Wilkinson

Product Editors
Rachel Rawling, Kate Chapman

Senior Cartographers
Diana Von Holdt, Mark Griffiths

Book Designer
Virginia Moreno

Assisting Editors
Judith Bamber, Imogen Bannister, Michelle Coxall, Melanie Dankel, Andrea Dobbin, Bruce Evans, Jennifer Hattam, Gabrielle Innes, Rosie Nicholson, Lou McGregor, Lauren O'Connell, Tamara Sheward

Cover Researcher
Naomi Parker

Thanks to
Hannah Cartmel, Robin Daus, Grace Dobell, Keith A Liker, Charlotte Orr, Kathryn Rowan, Wibowo Rusli, Vicky Smith

Index

See also separate subindexes for:

 EATING P258

 DRINKING & NIGHTLIFE P259

 ENTERTAINMENT P260

 SHOPPING P260

 SPORTS & ACTIVITIES P261

 SLEEPING P261

Bangkok Maps

Sights

- Beach
- Bird Sanctuary
- Buddhist
- Castle/Palace
- Christian
- Confucian
- Hindu
- Islamic
- Jain
- Jewish
- Monument
- Museum/Gallery/Historic Building
- Ruin
- Shinto
- Sikh
- Taoist
- Winery/Vineyard
- Zoo/Wildlife Sanctuary
- Other Sight

Activities, Courses & Tours

- Bodysurfing
- Diving
- Canoeing/Kayaking
- Course/Tour
- Sento Hot Baths/Onsen
- Skiing
- Snorkelling
- Surfing
- Swimming/Pool
- Walking
- Windsurfing
- Other Activity

Sleeping

- Sleeping
- Camping
- Hut/Shelter

Eating

- Eating

Drinking & Nightlife

- Drinking & Nightlife
- Cafe

Entertainment

- Entertainment

Shopping

- Shopping

Information

- Bank
- Embassy/Consulate
- Hospital/Medical
- Internet
- Police
- Post Office
- Telephone
- Toilet
- Tourist Information
- Other Information

Geographic

- Beach
- Gate
- Hut/Shelter
- Lighthouse
- Lookout
- Mountain/Volcano
- Oasis
- Park
- Pass
- Picnic Area
- Waterfall

Population

- Capital (National)
- Capital (State/Province)
- City/Large Town
- Town/Village

Transport

- Airport
- Border crossing
- Bus
- Cable car/Funicular
- Cycling
- Ferry
- Metro/MTR/MRT station
- Monorail
- Parking
- Petrol station
- Skytrain/Subway station
- Taxi
- Train station/Railway
- Tram
- Underground station
- Other Transport

Routes

- Tollway
- Freeway
- Primary
- Secondary
- Tertiary
- Lane
- Unsealed road
- Road under construction
- Plaza/Mall
- Steps
- Tunnel
- Pedestrian overpass
- Walking Tour
- Walking Tour detour
- Path/Walking Trail

Boundaries

- International
- State/Province
- Disputed
- Regional/Suburb
- Marine Park
- Cliff
- Wall

Hydrography

- River, Creek
- Intermittent River
- Canal
- Water
- Dry/Salt/Intermittent Lake
- Reef

Areas

- Airport/Runway
- Beach/Desert
- Cemetery (Christian)
- Cemetery (Other)
- Glacier
- Mudflat
- Park/Forest
- Sight (Building)
- Sportsground
- Swamp/Mangrove

Note: Not all symbols displayed above appear on the maps in this book

MAP INDEX

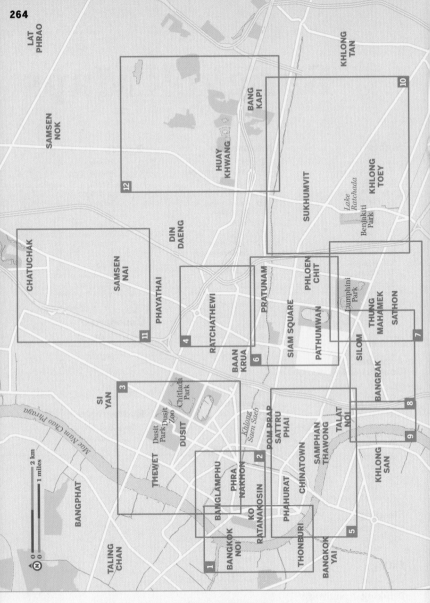

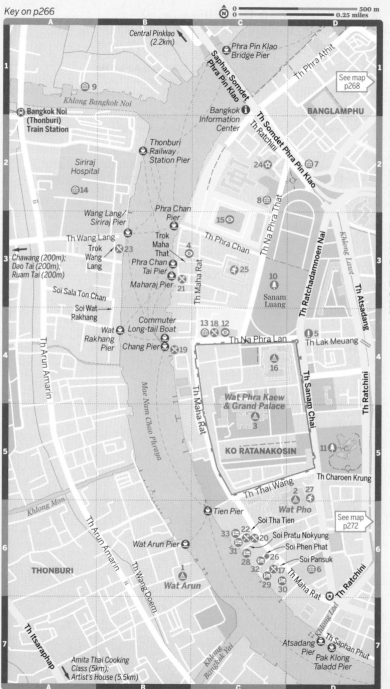

0   500 m
0   0.25 miles

Central Pinklao
(2.2km)

Phra Pin Klao
Bridge Pier

Saphan Somdet
Phra Pin Klao

Th Phra Athit

See map
p268

BANGLAMPHU

Bangkok
Information
Center

Th Somdet Phra Pin Klao

Th Ratchini

9

Khlong Bangkok Noi

Bangkok Noi
(Thonburi)
Train Station

Thonburi
Railway
Station Pier

Siriraj
Hospital

24

7

Th Na Phra That

8

14

Phra Chan
Pier

15

Khlong Lawt

Wang Lang/
Siriraj Pier

Th Phra Chan

Th Wang Lang

Trok
Maha
That

Th Ratchadamnoen Nai

Th Atsadang

Chawang (200m);
Dao Tai (200m);
Ruam Tai (200m)

23

Trok
Wang
Lang

4

25

10

Phra Chan
Tai Pier

Sanam
Luang

Soi Sala Ton Chan

Maharaj Pier

21

Soi Wat
Rakhang

Th Maha Rat

Commuter
Long-tail Boat

13 18 12

Th Na Phra Lan

5

Wat
Rakhang
Pier

Th Lak Meuang

Chang Pier

19

16

Th Sanam Chai

Th Ratchini

Mae Nam Chao Phraya

Wat Phra Kaew
& Grand Palace

3

KO RATANAKOSIN

11

Th Charoen Krung

Th Arun Amarin

Th Thai Wang

Khlong Mon

See map
p272

Tien Pier

2 27

Wat Pho

Soi Tha Tien

Wat Arun Pier

33

22

Soi Pratu Nokyung

31

20

Soi Phen Phat

THONBURI

1

28

26

Soi Pansuk

Th Wang Doem

32

17

6

Wat Arun

29

30

Th Maha Rat

Th Itsaraphap

Th Saphan Phut

Khlong Lad

Th Ratchini

Atsadang
Pier

Amita Thai Cooking
Class (5km);
Artist's House (5.5km)

Khlong
Bangkok Yai

Pak Klong
Taladd Pier

KO RATANAKOSIN & THONBURI *Map on p265*

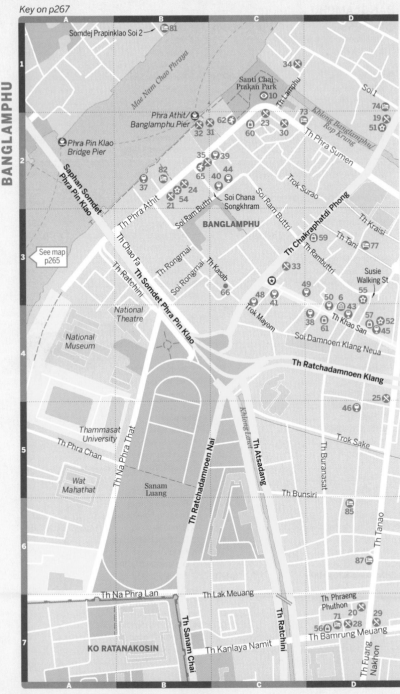

BANGLAMPHU

Somdej Prapinklao Soi 2 — 81

Mae Nam Chao Phraya

Santi Chai Prakan Park 10

Phra Athit/ Banglamphu Pier

Phra Pin Klao Bridge Pier

Th Lamphu

Soi 1

Khlong Banglamphu/ Rop Krung

73
74
19
51

34

62
32 31
60 23 30

Th Phra Sumen

Saphan Somdet Phra Pin Klao

Th Phra Athit

37 82
35 39
65 40 44
54 24
21

Trok Surao

Soi Ram Buttri

Soi Chana Songkhram

BANGLAMPHU

Soi Ram Buttri

Trok Surao

Th Chakraphatdi Phong

Th Kraisi

Th Tani 77

Th Chao Fa

Th Somdet Phra Pin Klao

Th Ratchini

Th Rongmai

Soi Rongmai

Th Kasab

66

59

33

Th Rambuttri

Susie Walking St

55

See map p265

National Theatre

National Museum

Trok Mayom

48
41

49

50 6
38 43
61 57
Th Khao San
45 52

Soi Damnoen Klang Neua

Th Ratchadamnoen Klang

25
46

Thammasat University

Th Phra Chan

Th Na Phra That

Th Ratchadamnoen Nai

Th Atsadang

Khlong Lawt

Trok Sake

Th Buranasat

Wat Mahathat

Sanam Luang

Th Bunsiri

85

Th Tanao

87

KO RATANAKOSIN

Th Na Phra Lan

Th Sanam Chai

Th Lak Meuang

Th Ratchini

Th Kanlaya Namit

Th Phraeng Phuthon
71 20
56 28 29
Th Bamrung Meuang

Th Fuang Nakhon

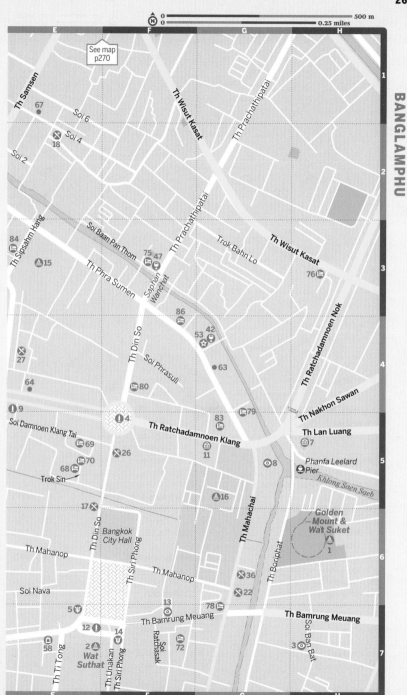

0 — 500 m
0 — 0.25 miles

See map
p270

Th Samsen
67
Soi 6
18 Soi 4
Soi 2

Th Sipsahm Hang
84
15
Th Phra Sumen

Soi Baan Pan Thom
75 47
Th Prachathipatai
Th Wisut Kasat
Th Prachathipatai
Trok Bahn Lo
76
Saphan Wanchat
86
53 42
Th Din So
Soi Phrasuli
27
64
80
63
Th Ratchadamnoen Nok
Th Nakhon Sawan
9
4
Th Ratchadamnoen Klang
83
79
Th Lan Luang
Soi Damnoen Klang Tai
69
26
11
7
68 70
Trok Sin
8
Phanfa Leelard
Pier
Khlong Saen Saeb
17
16
Golden
Mount &
Wat Suket
Th Mahanop
Bangkok
City Hall
Th Din So
Th Siri Phong
Th Mahanop
Th Mahachai
Th Boriphat
1
Soi Nava
5
13
36
Th Bamrung Meuang
22
78
Th Bamrung Meuang
Soi Ban Bat
58
12
14
Th Ti Tong
2
Wat
Suthat
Th Unakan
Th Siri Phong
Th Bamrung Meuang
Soi
Ratchasak
72
3

THEWET & DUSIT

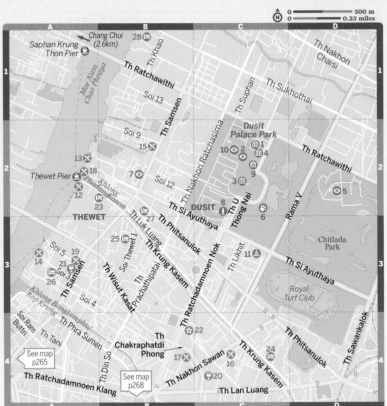

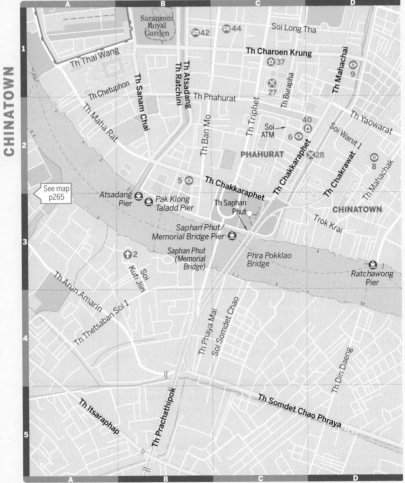

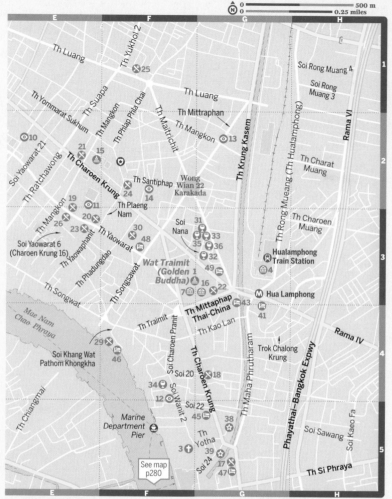

Key on p276

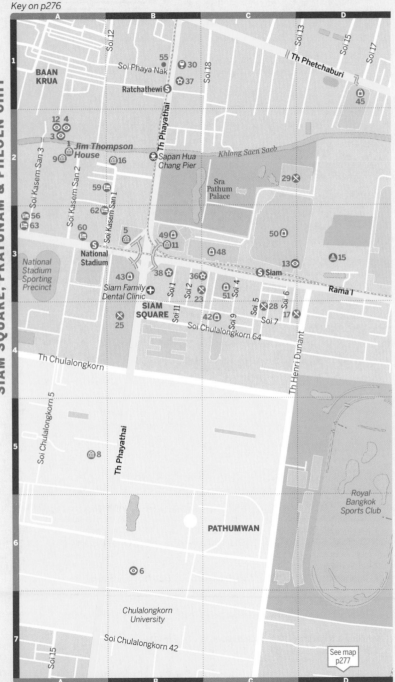

SIAM SQUARE, PRATUNAM & PHLOEN CHIT

BAAN KRUA

Soi 12

Soi Phaya Nak

55

30

37

Ratchathewi

Soi 18

Th Phayathai

Th Phetchaburi

Soi 13

Soi 15

Soi 17

45

12 4
3
1
Jim Thompson House
9
16

Soi Kasem San 3

Soi Kasem San 2

Soi Kasem San 1

Sapan Hua Chang Pier

Khlong Saen Saeb

Sra Pathum Palace

29

59

62

56
63

60

5

National Stadium

49
11

48

50

13

15

National Stadium Sporting Precinct

43

38

36

Siam

Rama I

Siam Family Dental Clinic

25

SIAM SQUARE

Soi 11

Soi 1

Soi 2

23

51

Soi 4

Soi 6

28

17

Soi 5

Soi 7

42

Soi 9

Soi Chulalongkorn 64

Th Henri Dunant

Th Chulalongkorn

Soi Chulalongkorn 5

Th Phayathai

8

Royal Bangkok Sports Club

PATHUMWAN

6

Chulalongkorn University

Soi Chulalongkorn 42

Soi 15

See map p277

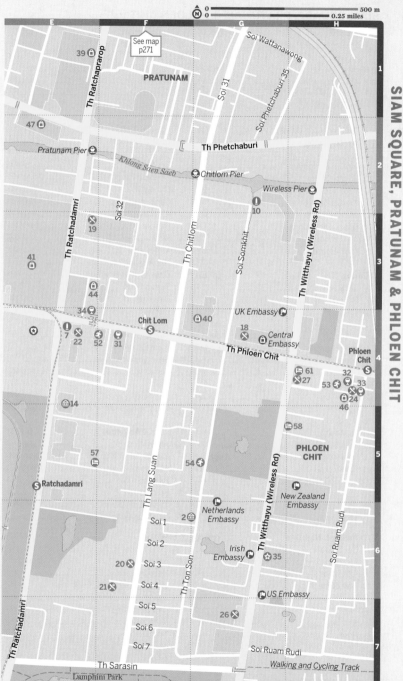

0 500 m
0 0.25 miles

E F G H

Soi Wattanawong

39

Th Ratchaprarop

PRATUNAM

Soi 31

Soi Phetchaburi 35

47

See map
p271

Th Phetchaburi

Pratunam Pier

Khlong Saen Saeb

Chitlom Pier

Wireless Pier

10

19

Soi 32

Th Ratchadamri

Th Chitlom

Soi Somkhit

Th Witthayu (Wireless Rd)

41

44

34

35

UK Embassy

Chit Lom

40

7 22 52 31

18

Central
Embassy

Phloen
Chit

Th Phloen Chit

61

32

27

53

33

24

14

46

58

57

PHLOEN
CHIT

Ratchadamri

54

Th Lang Suan

New Zealand
Embassy

Netherlands
Embassy

2

Soi 1

Soi 2

Irish
Embassy

35

Soi 3

20

Th Ton Son

Th Witthayu (Wireless Rd)

Soi Ruam Rudi

Soi 4

21

US Embassy

Soi 5

26

Soi 6

Soi 7

Th Ratchadamri

Soi Ruam Rudi

Walking and Cycling Track

Th Sarasin

Lumphini Park

SIAM SQUARE, PRATNAM & PHLOEN CHIT Map on p274

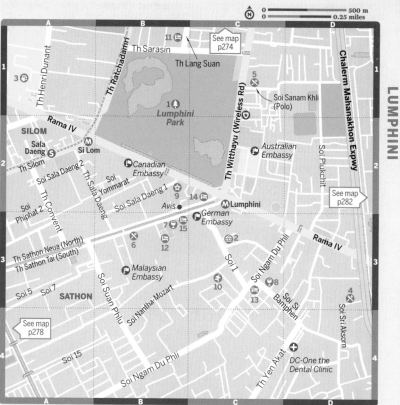

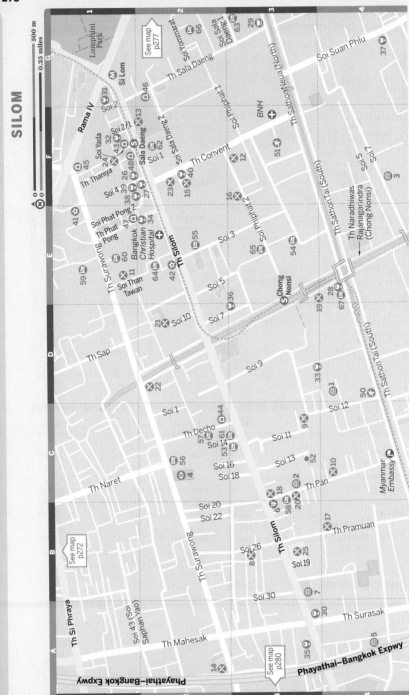

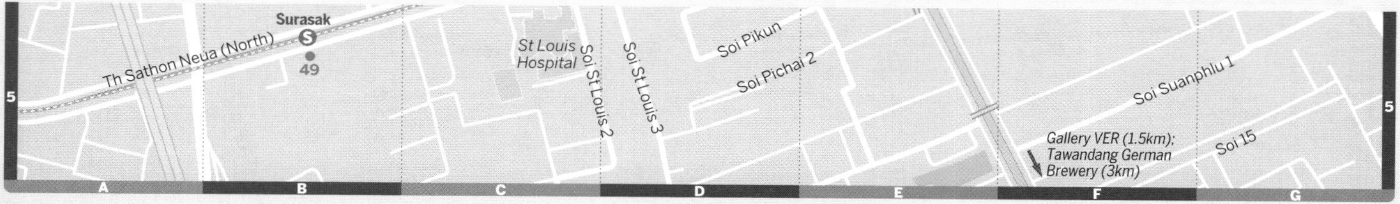

Gallery VER (1.5km);
Tawandang German
Brewery (3km)

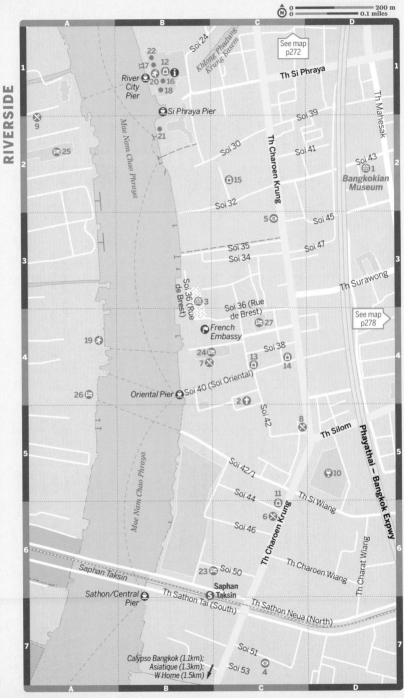

RIVERSIDE

See map p272

See map p278

A **B** **C** **D**

0   200 m
0   0.1 miles

Th Si Phraya

Soi 24

Khlong Phadung Krung Kasem

Th Maheसak

22
17   12
River   20 16
City   18
Pier

Si Phraya Pier

21

Soi 39

Soi 41

Soi 43
Bangkokian
Museum   1

9

Mae Nam Chao Phraya

25

Th Charoen Krung

Soi 30

15

Soi 32

Soi 45

Soi 47

5

Th Surawong

Soi 35
Soi 34

Soi 36 (Rue de Brest)

3

Soi 36 (Rue de Brest)

27

19

French
Embassy

Soi 38

24
7   13   14

26

Oriental Pier   Soi 40 (Soi Oriental)

Phayathai – Bangkok Expwy

2

Soi 42

8

Th Silom

10

Soi 42/1

11

Soi 44   Th Si Wiang

6

Soi 46

Th Charoen Krung

Mae Nam Chao Phraya

Saphan Taksin

23   Soi 50

Th Charoen Wiang

Th Charat Wiang

Sathon/Central
Pier

Saphan
Taksin

Th Sathon Tai (South)

Th Sathon Neua (North)

Soi 51

Calypso Bangkok (1.1km);
Asiatique (1.3km);
W Home (1.5km)

Soi 53   4

RIVERSIDE

SUKHUMVIT

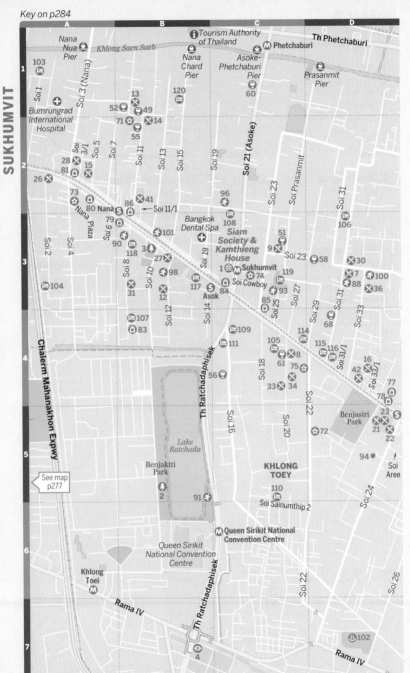

Nana Nua Pier

103

Soi 1

Bumrungrad International Hospital

Khlong Saen Saeb

Soi 3 (Nana)

Nana Chard Pier

Tourism Authority of Thailand

Phetchaburi

Th Phetchaburi

Asoke-Phetchaburi Pier

Prasanmit Pier

60

13
52
71
49
14
55
120

Soi 5
Soi 3/1
Soi 7
Soi 11
Soi 13
Soi 15
Soi 19

Soi 21 (Asoke)

Soi Prasanmit

Soi 23

Soi 31

28
81
26
73
80 Nana
Nana
79
90
118
31
3
27
12
98
101
86
41
Soi 11/1
96
108
Bangkok Dental Spa
Siam Society & Kamthieng House
51
9
74
Soi 23
58
106
30
7
88
100
36

15

Soi 9

Nana Plaza

Soi 2
Soi 4
Soi 6
Soi 8
Soi 10
Soi 12
Soi 14
Soi 19

104

117
Asok

Sukhumvit
Soi Cowboy
84
119
93
85
Soi 25
Soi 27
Soi 29
Soi 31
Soi 33
68

107
83
109
111
56

Th Ratchadaphisek

114
105
61
8
75
33
34
115
116
16
42
77
78
23
21
22
94
Soi 31/1
Soi 35/1
Benjasiri Park
Soi 18
Soi 20
Soi 22
72

Chalerm Mahanakhon Expwy

See map p277

Lake Ratchada

Benjakiti Park
2
91

Soi 16

KHLONG TOEY

110
Soi Sainumthip 2

Soi 24

Soi Aree

Queen Sirikit National Convention Centre

Queen Sirikit National Convention Centre

Khlong Toey

Rama IV

Th Ratchadaphisek

Soi 22

Soi 26

102

4

Rama IV

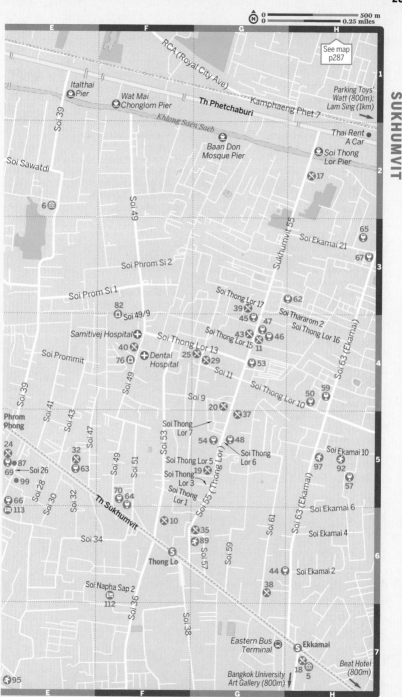

SUKHUMVIT *Map on p282*

SUKHUMVIT

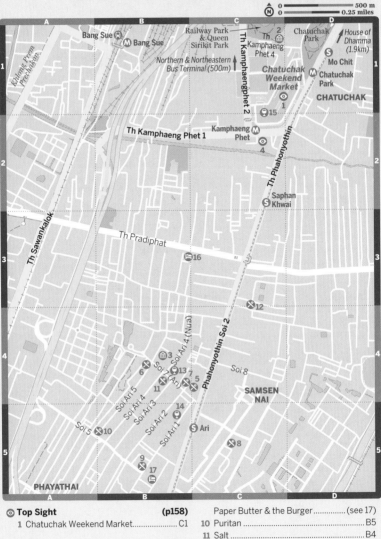

and a sense of
Wheeler needed
Asia overland to
end – broke but
inspired – they sat at their kitchen table writing and stapling together their first travel guide, *Across Asia on the Cheap*. Within a week they'd sold 1500 copies. Lonely Planet was born.

Today, Lonely Planet has offices in Franklin, London, Melbourne, Oakland, Dublin, Beijing and Delhi, with more than 600 staff and writers. We share Tony's belief that 'a great guidebook should do three things: inform, educate and amuse'.

Our Writers

Austin Bush

Bangkok, Amphawa Austin Bush came to Thailand in 1999 as part of a language study programme hosted by Chiang Mai University. The lure of city life, employment and spicy food eventually led Austin to Bangkok. City life, employment and spicy food have managed to keep him there ever since. These days, Austin works as a writer and photographer, and in addition to having contributed to numerous books, magazines and websites, has contributed text and photos to more than 20 Lonely Planet titles including *Bangkok*; *The Food Book*; *Food Lover's Guide to the World*; *Laos*; *Malaysia, Singapore & Brunei*; *Myanmar (Burma)*; *Pocket Bangkok*; *Thailand*; *Thailand's Islands & Beaches*; *Vietnam, Cambodia, Laos & Northern Thailand*; and *The World's Best Street Food*.

Tim Bewer

Phetchaburi, Khao Yai After brie... ...a-
sistant, Tim decided he didn't have ... ...he
stomach to work around those wh... ...k
around West Africa, during which t... ...
was to write a travel guide to parks... ...te
of Wisconsin. He's been a freelance t... ...ver

Anita Isalska

Ayuthaya Historical Park, Kancha... ...d
copywriter whose work for Lonely P... ...s
to Malaysian jungles, and plenty of p... ...rs
as an in-house editor and writer – wi... ...f-
fice – Anita now works freelance b... ...st-
house with a good wi-fi connection... ...or
a host of websites and magazines. R... ...

Andy Symington

Ko Samet Andy has written or wor... ...than a hundred book
other updates for Lonely Planet (e... ...ly in Europe and Latin Ame...
other publishing companies, and h... ...lished articles on numerou...
for a variety of newspapers, maga... ...nd websites. He part-owns...
ates a rock bar, has written a nove... ...currently working on sever...
and non-fiction writing projects. O... ...y from Australia, Andy mov...
northern Spain many years ago. When he's not off...
the world, he can probably be found watching the t...
local wines after a long walk in the nearby mountai...

Published by Lonely Planet Global Limited
CRN 554153
13th edition – Jul 2018
ISBN 978 1 78657 081 9
© Lonely Planet 2018   Photographs © as indicated 2018
10 9 8 7 6 5 4 3 2 1
Printed in China